THE IMPOSITION OF FORM

THE IMPOSITION OF FORM

STUDIES IN NARRATIVE REPRESENTATION AND KNOWLEDGE

CLAUDIA

J. BRODSKY

PRINCETON

UNIVERSITY

PRESS

Copyright © 1987 by Princeton University Press

Published by Princeton University Press, 41 William Street,
Princeton, New Jersey 08540
In the United Kingdom: Princeton University Press, Guildford, Surrey

ISBN 0-691-06717-1

This book has been composed in Linotron Sabon and Optima

Clothbound editions of Princeton University Press books
are printed on acid-free paper, and binding materials are
chosen for strength and durability. Paperbacks, although satisfactory
for personal collections, are not usually suitable for library rebinding

Printed in the United States of America by Princeton University Press,
Princeton, New Jersey

Designed by Laury A. Egan

CONTENTS

To my mother and father,
for all they have given to me

ACKNOWLEDGMENTS

I wish to thank the Mrs. Giles Whiting Foundation and the German Academic Exchange Service (Deutscher Akademischer Austauschdienst) for their assistance during different stages of the researching and writing of this book.

An earlier version of Chapter 2, section one appeared in *Philosophy as Literature/Literature as Philosophy*, edited by Donald Marshall (Iowa City: University of Iowa Press, 1987), pp. 185–204 (reprinted by permission). Earlier versions of Chapter 3 and Chapter 7 have appeared in *MLN* 97 (1982) and *MLN* 102 (1987), respectively.

I am grateful to Paul de Man and Peter Demetz, two extraordinary critics of literature, for their teaching, their analytical precision, their good-humored and helpful advice, and, most of all, for the example of their intellectual integrity. To Peter Demetz in particular I am most thankful for his early understanding and continuous encouragement of the interests reflected in this study. Discussions of narrative theory with Peter Brooks and Frederic Jameson have also greatly contributed to my own work in the field. I thank Robert Fagles and Ralph Freedman for their warm and generous support, and Mrs. Arthur Sherwood, Robert Brown, and Sherry Wert for their assistance at Princeton University Press.

Special thanks go to Edward Schiffer, Emily Jayne, Anne Janowitz, Richard Goodkin, Barbara Guetti, Peter Ponsa, Laura Agoston, Joshua Scodel, and Lise Davis for ensuring that in writing this book I did not also entirely write myself off. The wit, loyalty, and intelligence of these friends and colleagues were largely responsible for keeping a sometimes too, too frail mind alive. I also thank Richard Masotta and Jeff Amthor at the Yale University Computer Center for kindly guiding this stumbling pilgrim through the purgatory of word processing. Nancy Stone courageously undertook the organization of my bibliography and provided, with Joshua Stein, some welcome moments of respite from the plot of cognition.

Some indispensable final proofreading was unflinchingly provided by my mother.

Finally, I wish to thank both my parents for their unfailing faith and encouragement at each step taken toward the completion of this book. They may with good reason feel more relieved than I that at least this particular project is at an end.

PART 1

THE IMPOSITION
OF FORM

CHAPTER 1

INTRODUCTION

This work investigates narrative as a literary form composed of and presenting a particular paradox. That paradox, which the following chapters attempt to describe through analyses of specific eighteenth-, nineteenth-, and twentieth-century texts,[1] can perhaps be best introduced by a brief summation of the basic directions I perceive the study of narrative to take.

As the term "narratology," used currently to signify a broad variety of analytic methods, succinctly conveys, narrative is the literary form most generally understood to foster its own logical understanding. Defined as the means by which a story is told,[2] narrative is seen to combine all the elements necessary to a coherent presentation of experience by way of a governing, sequential development of thought. The elements of knowl-

[1] Since aspects of narrative are discernible in almost every use of language, I should first explain how I mean to use the term and how I see that meaning represented in the works I discuss. Rather than merely implement narrative form, the novels analyzed in this study reveal a preoccupation with the part played by narrative in understanding in general. What relates authors of such obvious historical, cultural, and stylistic diversity as Goethe, Austen, Balzac, Stendhal, Melville, and Proust is a common concern demonstrated in their narratives with the necessity, as well as necessary limitations, of narrative itself. Similarly, what relates the individual literary works analyzed to the investigation, in Chapter Two, of the epistemological philosophy of Immanuel Kant is the way in which Kant's critical limitation of knowledge to a formal knowledge of representations seems to describe a general theory of representational narration.

[2] Cf. Robert Kellogg and Robert Scholes, *The Nature of Narrative* (New York: Oxford University Press, 1966), p. 4: "By narrative we mean all those literary works which are distinguished by two characteristics: the presence of a story and a story-teller."

edge a narrative omits, whether or not such omissions are deemed intentional, are themselves first perceived and thus simultaneously, at least in part, explained, as salient absences within a logical sequence. The "picaresque" classification of such early narratives of experience as *La Vida de Lazarillo de Tormes* and Grimmelshausen's *Simplicissimus*, the later dominant motif of the *Bildungsroman*, as well as the popular genre of the detective story may all be seen to offer progressive variations upon this conception of knowledge as the goal to which narrative, by infinite, individual roads, tends. Experiments in narrative technique, relying on complexities of narrative voice or structure, such as those of Faulkner, Broch, and their contemporary successors, Cortazar, Vargas Llosa, and Marqués, or on more fundamental disruptions of the syntactic ordering of understanding, as attempted, a century after the innovations of Flaubert, by the French New Novelists, all rely first on the supposition that understanding itself is primarily narrative in nature: that similar to the "performance" of syntax in language, narrative provides the form by which any transformations of or deviations from the norm can be understood. Thus, "narratologists," whose theoretical models range in origin from Aristotle to A. J. Greimas, are commonly inclined, by a shared perception of narrative logic, to formulate a definitive "science" of narrative. Whether by way of reference to the *Poetics'* founding principle of an underlying unity of action in dramatic plot; the Russian formalists' distinction between plot itself (*sjužet*), and the sequential story (*fabula*) from which it is shaped; the semiotic conception of an internally coherent, self-contained network of signs; the structuralist identification of binary oppositions developed in Lévi-Strauss' study of myth; or Greimas's related notion of a "semiotic rectangle," or *combinatoire*, analysts of narrative form calculate their own knowledge of the object they study according to the density of internal logic their particular methods can display. The presupposition that knowledge itself coincides with an identification of form, and that such form can be recognized and reconstructed by way of a generative narrative "grammar"—much as a skillful detective would piece together the parts and uncover the motive of a criminal plot—is as implicit to narratology as its working analytic assumption that the words—or linguistic "parts"—composing a narrative "plot" can only mean what their formal grammatical function prescribes they must say.

This latter assumption links formal analyses of narrative to an opposed and equally prevalent approach: the study of narrative as a primarily representational medium. Seen as a means of representing material reality, narrative seems especially dependent upon the extratextual referents which narratological analyses, in concentrating upon structural factors, necessarily discount. Extending from Plato and Aristotle to the essays of Erich Auerbach, the roots of mimetic criticism, as of narratology, underlie the history of literary criticism and can only be indicated cursorily here. But the selection of narrative as the literary form which best serves an interest in "realism," and in which the referential rather than formal function of language is seen in turn to hold sway, bears directly upon the conflicting concerns of narratology. For just as the diachronic and causal dimensions of a story lend themselves most readily to logical delineation, so the fact that a story *is* being told depends, at a minimum, upon some referential perception of its subject. Thus questions of biography, history, political ideology, personal psychology, and countless others to which the proposition of mimetic narrative gives way focus upon the power of narrative not to order but to illustrate. Analogously, whereas formal analyses reflect a methodological predilection for texts already conceived to be "pure fictions"—myths, folk and fairy tales, and scientific and utopian fantasies, whose so-called "referents" are always understood to remain between quotation marks—mimetic critics often equate the rise of narrative as a literary form with that of the referentially laden "realist" novel.[3] As narratologists strive toward a more fully formalized knowledge of their object of study, mimetic critics seek, as if reflected in that object, a fuller understanding, or practical knowledge, of a nonnarrative world. The division between these two approaches is, of course, not as clean (nor are the ap-

[3] Cf. Ian Watt, *The Rise of the Novel* (Berkeley: University of California Press, 1957).

proaches themselves as all-inclusive) as these summary comments may at first suggest. It is helpful to recall, for example, that the description of "a novel" as "a mirror one walks along the length of a road," was first formulated as an epigraph to *Le Rouge et le noir*. That description is all the less easy to dismiss when one considers that its author (who attributes it to another source, with which it shares only the word "mirror") is generally recognized as one of the least mimetically inclined "realist" novelists of his century. Just as Stendhal presents the principle of mimesis as the definition of his literary form, proceeding to invoke that definition later in the novel as its narrator's defense against moral attacks, and yet offers almost no evidence in his own narratives of its validity, so the critical problem of the relation between the logical and referential dimensions of narrative may be more readily obscured than solved by their severing.

For it must be significant of narrative as a literary form that while logical causation most determines its shape, the fact that it has a shape, that it is a carefully plotted fiction, appears at once incidental to the perceived life of its referents. Conversely, the fact that the medium of narrative is discourse, i.e., signs whose meaning can be either referentially or figurally (formally) understood, appears eradicated at the moment their formal function is hypostatized. Thus, as opposed to the identification of a dialectic between content and form which has continued to orient the interpretation of poetry (before, during, and after the New Criticism), the critical route departing from narrative seems to have taken the stranger contour of a single direction doubling upon itself. That doubleness, in distinction from the dialogical, differential structure ascribed *to* narrative by the late Russian formalist Mikhail Bakhtin,[4] appears more like an internal repetition of the same. Narratological analysis seems condemned by the vigor of its commitment to a "science" of literature to mirror or subdivide form by form. Thus Greimas's recent hypothesis of "levels of gram-

---

[4] See, in particular, Bakhtin, *Problems of Dostoevsky's Poetics* (Ann Arbor, Mich.: Ardis, 1973), and *The Dialogic Imagination*, ed. Michael Holquist (Austin: University of Texas Press, 1981).

mar" not only doubles a "conceptual" or "fundamental" grammar with that of its "anthropomorphic" or "narrative surface," but proposes the doubling of accompanying semantic levels as well.[5] Meaning, rather than being made manifest through the transformations of a semiotic model, would reside at the formal level of the model itself. If the distinction between semiotics and semantics appears all but nominally lost in the process, it is because the elaboration of a narrative grammar can only account for narrative meaning as constitutive of the very model of that grammar. According to the logic of narratological analysis, semantics and semiotics must be reduced to formal reflections of each other. Similarly, mimetic approaches to narrative which appeal directly to formal considerations tend to redefine form as the expressive medium of a referential-historical context. The most formally sensitive and methodologically sophisticated of these approaches today is thus, significantly, and I think not accidentally, Marxist in orientation. Extraordinarily detailed historical and psycho-biographical studies, such as those by Barbéris of Balzac and Sartre of Flaubert, locate the conditions of narrative "production" in those of "le mal du siècle" or "de la Famille."[6] Outstanding contributions to a Marxist understanding of literary form, prepared for in the Hegelian analysis of Lukács's seminal—and in significant ways still unsurpassed—*Theory of the Novel* (first published in 1916), afforded technical methods of analysis in the early narratological work of the Russian formalists, reanalyzed in relation to social forms by Adorno and

[5] See "Eléments d'une grammaire narrative," in *Du sens* (Paris: Editions du Seuil, 1970), pp. 157–83. In this, as in his previous formulation (*Sémantique structurale* [Paris: Larousse, 1966]), Greimas follows the major shift in Chomsky's theory of transformational grammar from the proposition of an unlimited generational power deriving from the syntactic "base" to an imposition of constraints upon possible transformations and incorporation, into the base, of semantically dependent, lexical features. See, in particular, Chomsky's "Remarks on Nominalization," in *Readings in English Transformational Grammar*, ed. Roderick A. Jacobs and Peter S. Rosenbaum (Waltham, Mass.: Ginn and Co., 1970).

[6] See Jean Paul Sartre, *L'Idiot de la famille* (Paris: Gallimard, 1971), 3 vols.; Pierre Barbéris, *Balzac et le mal du siècle: contribution à une physiologie du monde moderne* (Paris: Gallimard, 1970), 2 vols.

Horkheimer, and presently being advanced by way of psychoanalytic and semiotic categories in the work of such contemporary American critics as Frederic Jameson, astutely replace
the notion of a narrative mirror upon the world with a perception of form as a plotting of social opacity, or ideology. As described by Jameson in the hybrid terminology required by a
"textual" analysis of historical ideology, the "referential sub-
text," rather than objective content, of narrative is "reconstructed" by Marxist methods.[7] Those methods may differ
among themselves—as Jameson's use of Freud, Greimas, La-
can, and Althusser indicates—but not in the purpose toward
which they are employed: the reproduction of a historical moment which representation itself can only deform.[8] Yet while
representation, mimetically or referentially conceived, is dis-

[7] See, for example, Jameson's statement in, "Of Islands and Trenches: Neutralization and the Production of Utopian Discourse," *Diacritics* Summer
1977: "it is useful to stress the process of reconstruction itself, as a corrective
to the naive idea that the analyst or the historian can gaze into some 'objective'
realm of social or national political ideology and there empirically discover the
solution to his structural problem. Ideology does exist objectively, but not in
the form of a text: like the unconscious it is therefore not directly accessible to
us, but only insofar as we have reconstructed it in what has today come to be
called 'textual' form, with which the literary text can then be placed in an active relationship of reaction, transformation, reflection, repression or whatever. To omit the description of this stage—the reconstruction of the referential sub-text, the hypothetical textualization of ideology—is to perpetuate the
illusion that 'sociological' analysis is something one can add on to a structural
analysis of texts or not, as one's own temperment dictates" (p. 12).

[8] The relationship between Marxist criticism and the methods of analysis it
seeks to integrate is thus described as the fulfillment of the latter by the former.
As Jameson, again combining methodologies, has argued for the ultimacy of
their "completion" in Marxism: "There is not only the evident fact that most
of us have been formed in one or the other of those older 'methods'; there is
the far more basic presupposition that the Marxist point of view is secretly
present in all these methods—if only as that reality which is repressed . . . that
consciousness which is threatening and which the *mauvaise foi* of critical formalism then projects out of itself as its converse or its nightmare. So we do not
have to be defensive about a Marxist literary criticism; that is more properly
the stance of those who want to flee from history. Nor do we need to suggest
that Marxism is an *alternative* to those methods: rather, it is to be seen as their
completion, and as the only method which can really finish what it is they all
in their various ways set out to do" (Frederic Jameson, "Criticism in History,"
in *Weapons of Criticism* [Palo Alto, Calif.: Ramparts Press, 1976], p. 32).

counted as a means of practical knowledge by Marxist theorists, the twin principles of ideology and history, each conceived as univocally significant, are posed instead as referents in its place. Narrative, understood as an inherently distortive form, is analyzed as the ideological counterpart of the unrepresentable, historical, real. Thus narrative, as a literary form, ultimately serves the ends of its contents, as much for the aspects it deletes as for those it includes from a social context.[9] In order for a formal investigation to be significant of historical "praxis," it must signify knowledge of a referent: knowledge which is itself practical.[10] Whether that referent is seen to be embodied in a particular historical moment which the narrative, as literary "history," documents, or in "History" as such, unrealized at any particular moment but ideologically represented in narrative form, the recognition of narrative *as* form is used finally to underscore the practical relevance of narrative content.

The tendency within the study of narrative to convert form into referential meaning, and meaning into logical form, leads to the point of departure of the present study. The division in narrative theory which narrative by its own nature seems to effect is proposed to structure the nature of all cognition by Kant: the radical theoretical premise of Kant's epistemology is that the very possibility of knowledge must be divided between "pure" and "practical" reason. Similar to the narratological understanding of narrative, Kant's *Critique* of knowledge, and proposed "science" of metaphysics, understands "pure reason" as an inherently formal and causally ordered faculty. While "practical reason" should provide "positive" access to the "thinking" of "things-in-themselves," the objective claims

---

[9] See *ibid.*, pp. 32f.: "Our hypothesis is, then, that all apparently formal statements about a work bear within them a concealed historical dimension of which the author is not often aware. . . ."

[10] Cf. Julia Kristeva's description of literature as the "practical" link between "history" and "knowledge": "As the borderline between a signifier where the subject is lost and a history that imposes its laws on him, literature appears as a specific mode of *practical knowledge*" (*Desire in Language: A Semiotic Approach to Literature and Art*, ed. Leon S. Roudiez [Oxford: Basil Blackwell, 1980], p. 96 *et passim*; emphasis in text).

of "pure reason" are limited to a "negative" knowledge of "phenomena": mere "appearances" of objects as "represented" by the mind according to the *a priori* mental "forms" of time and space. Thus, viewed from a literary, rather than epistemological, critical standpoint, the world we refer to according to Kant is always prefigured in its meaning. Kant's epistemological system, most remarkably, makes almost no reference to its own cognitive means, language, because more than any other cognitive system, it presupposes an equation of linguistic forms with those of cognition. Kant's theory of knowledge is specifically *critical* in that it replaces the possibility of pure, or unmediated, experience with experience necessarily mediated formally as representation. Our empirical perceptions, Kant hypothesizes, are themselves *a posteriori* to the *a priori* forms of the mind. In the metalanguage of properly linguistic forms, it could be said that perception, for Kant, occurs at the moment when the formalization of "natural" language as literature, of referential as figural meaning, appears as a conceptual activity already at its end. In grounding all empirical knowledge upon its *a priori* formalization, Kant proposes that all referents already take the form of representations: the given of all empirical reason is to "represent" experience, thus perceiving reality in the figural condition which "literary" or representational language first effects. In accordance with formal *or* mimetic theories of narrative, Kant's system of knowledge can therefore be seen to describe a system of narrative—and to describe experience as *the* narrative—par excellence. For it ensures both the referential and formal functions of the mind by excluding the occurrence, for the mind, of that which is not already "known": the formless, the ambiguous, the unrepresented, or unnamed.

The use of an analysis of Kant in relating narrative to knowledge should be seen in opposition both to the New Kantianism (often called "historical materialism") of current philosophies of knowledge, such as Althusser's distinction between "real objects" and "objects of knowledge" in his theory of "theoretical practice,"[11] as well as uncritical, aesthetic idealisms (called

[11] Cf. Louis Althusser and Étienne Balibar, *Reading Capital* (London: NLB, 1970 [*Lire le Capital*, Paris: Maspero, 1968]), p. 54 *et passim*.

"Kantianism"), like that of Cassirer's *Philosophy of Symbolic Form*, which replaces the limited mediating power of aesthetic judgment formulated by Kant with the notion of a "spiritual" synthesis between art form and object.[12] As Althusser uses the Kantian distinction between epistemological and real objects—in Kant, phenomena and things-in-themselves—in order to propose their (entirely non-Kantian) synthesis in "theoretical practice," Cassirer turns Kant's famous dictum concerning the purposelessness of aesthetic objects into grounds for praising the highly intentional forms of symbol and myth. While their debts to Kant are obviously dissimilar—in Althusser's case, apparently not even conscious—the two philosophers present examples of purely speculative and aesthetic derivations from Kant from which the present concern with his distinctly literary relevance should be strongly distinguished. That is, the reading of Kant vis-à-vis a literary form has as little in common with his adaption to exclusively epistemological or aesthetic ends as narrative itself shares either with Althusser's proposed "field of knowledge" or Cassirer's concept of "myth." The emphasis on Kant's grounding of cognition in representations of experience clearly relates to Hermann Cohen's early *Kant's Theory of Experience* (1871),[13] which later initiated the Kantian Marburg School in German philosophical thought.[14] Among contemporary readers of Kant, however, it is the Marxist philosopher Lucio Colletti whose interest in the theory of knowledge of the *Critique*

[12] *The Philosophy of Symbolic Forms*, 3 vols. (New Haven: Yale University Press, 1953 [Berlin: Bruno Cassirer, 1923–29]). See, in particular, I:85–90, "The Problem of Meaning," for a discussion of the ability of myth, as a prefigural mode, to think "the thing-in-itself" (p. 89), and I:187–97, "Mimetic, Analogical, and Symbolic Expression," in which the formal "limits" of the "sign" are said to be "surpassed" by the "deeper spiritual content" of the "symbol" (p. 197).

[13] Hermann Cohen, *Kants Theorie der Erfahrung* (Berlin: Dümmler, 1871 [reedited by the author in 1886]).

[14] Cohen's reading of Kant was most prominently rejected by his successor, Martin Heidegger. For Heidegger's own interpretation, or conceptual assimilation, of Kant as a wholly *non*cognitive thinker, see his *Kant und das Problem der Metaphysik* (Frankfurt: Klostermann, 1951 [first pub., 1929]). The Marburg School itself, however, was to be terminated, at least symbolically, after Heidegger with the departure of Cassirer from Germany in 1933.

comes closest to the approach to Kant presented here. Colletti's unpopular preference for Kant, as epistemological thinker, over Hegel, strictly distinguishes the premises of metaphysical epistemology from those of metaphysical ontology. His recognition of the purely logical-hypothetical status of the Kantian thing-in-itself also directly opposes the uncritical Kantianism of Althusser, who regresses from Kant in claiming that speculative philosophy, as a science, can combine theoretical with practical epistemology. Colletti's important understanding of the essential *epistemological* distinction between real and phenomenal knowledge for Kant leads him, however, to delete the *Second Critique* entirely from his consideration of Kant's epistemology. Kant's key deduction of the possibility of practical knowledge—the counterweight with which the present analysis of Kant as epistemological "narratologist" concludes—is viewed by Colletti to belong exclusively to the field of ethics, which, unlike Kant, he dismisses from the field of cognition. Colletti, in other words, coherently reads Kant's speculative theory as the most successful epistemology of science because he knowingly isolates it from the same problem which Althusser fails to regard as a problem at all: the issue of the necessity of real, practical knowledge within Kant's system, a necessity addressed by the explicitly epistemological as well as moral function of the concept of "freedom" in the *Second Critique*.[15]

[15] "From a strictly epistemological point of view, there is only one great modern thinker who can be of assistance to us in constructing a materialist theory of knowledge—Immanuel Kant ... whereas in Hegel's philosophy there is no separation between the domain of ethics and politics and the domain of logic, because the two are integrally united in a single system, in Kant there is a radical distinction between the domain of knowledge and the domain of morality ... the concept [of the thing-in-itself] has a meaning in Kant's work that Marxists have never wanted to see ... the thing-in-itself is not a true object of cognition at all, but a fictitious object, that is nothing more than a substantification or hypostatization of logical functions, transformed into real essences ... and when Hegel announces that the thing-in-itself can be known, what he is in fact doing is to restore the old pre-kantian metaphysics" (Lucio Colletti, "A Political and Philosophical Interview," in *Western Marxism*, ed. New Left Review [London: Verso, 1978], pp. 315–50 [pp. 324–27]). Again, the single "thing-in-itself" Kant stipulates must indeed, in Colletti's terms, be "a true object of cognition" and no theoretical fiction is no "thing" but the *concept* of "freedom," which Colletti, in rightly combatting "the utterly ab-

In direct contrast to Colletti's focus upon Kant's speculative system as the basis for founding a truly scientific epistemology within Marxism is Jean-François Lyotard's assimilation of certain Kantian principles to a description of socially "legitimized" or "pragmatic knowledge." Pragmatic knowledge, as conceived by Lyotard, admits of no epistemology: it is a historically relative, institutionalized rendering of truth whose central form, Lyotard argues most strikingly, is that of "narrative" itself.[16] Yet by virtue of focusing on narrative as a means to the end of legitimation—as an entirely pragmatically determined, social form—Lyotard ignores the relation of narrative to its own means and content, representation, thereby reducing the form itself to its legitimizing function. Narrative, as a result, takes on the ritualized status of a myth or folk tale for Lyotard, and his two "grand narratives" of legitimization, the "political" and the "philosophical," said to account for the very development of epistemology—"the history of knowledge and its institutions"—are merely conceivable in turn as the myths of entire cultural histories, folk tales told on a global or macrosocial scale.[17]

Consistent with Lyotard's view of narrative as the fablelike

---

surd reading of Kant that has prevailed among Marxists," incorrectly relegates, with the entire *Second Critique*, to a "moral" and thus nonespistemological "domain" (p. 326).

[16] See Jean-François Lyotard, *The Postmodern Condition: A Report on Knowledge* (Minneapolis: University of Minnesota Press, 1984 [Paris: Editions de Minuit, 1979]); the sections, "The Pragmatics of Narrative Knowledge" (pp. 18–23), "The Narrative Function and the Legitimation of Knowledge" (pp. 27–31), and "Narratives of the Legitimation of Knowledge" (pp. 31–37), in particular. ["Narrative is the quintessential form of customary knowledge, in more ways than one" (p. 19); "Narrative knowledge makes a resurgence in the West as a way of solving the problem of legitimizing new authorities . . . the mode of legitimation we are discussing . . . reintroduces narrative as the validity of knowledge" (pp. 30–31).]

A specifically *non*narrative use of Kant has since been made by Lyotard in his formulation of the concept of "le différend"—"that which is not presentable within the rules of knowledge" (*Le Différend* [Paris: Editions de Minuit, 1983], p. 92). Most recently Lyotard has appealed directly to Kant's mediating concept of aesthetic judgment as the form for adjudicating (rather than legitimizing) the "heterogeneity" of cognitive "phrases" (rather than narratives) constitutive of the *différend* ("Judicieux dans le différend," in *La faculté de juger*, J. Derrida et al. [Paris: Editions de Minuit, 1985], p. 222).

[17] *The Postmodern Condition*, p. 31.

form of cognition is the cognitive approach to narratives already formalized as fables. Rather than identifying the role played by narrative in the institutionalization of knowledge as science, the "grammatical" analysis of narrative attempts to account for the form itself scientifically. Tzvetan Todorov's *Grammaire du Décaméron* is prefaced by the classically Kantian, epistemological proposition that its cognitive project "arises from a science which does not yet exist"—that science being in this case "Narratology, the science of narrative."[18] Todorov describes his formalizing study of the narratives of the *Decameron* as following directly in the classical European tradition of the grammatical formalization of language in general.[19] Yet his grammatical hypothesis is most indebted to contemporary developments in the theory of transformational grammar formulated by Noam Chomsky, who, like Kant, enjoys the dubious honor of remaining for the most part unmentioned in the literature of narratology. Chomsky, in turn, has noted his own omission of Kant from his discussion of the "philosophical" background of transformational grammar.[20] Yet his interest in seventeenth-century grammatical theory, and emphasis upon the "representational" level of linguistic performance, are easily identified as Kantian in scope.[21] In a

---

[18] Tzvetan Todorov, *Grammaire du Décaméron* (The Hague: Mouton, 1969), p. 10.

[19] *Ibid.*, p. 16.

[20] *Cartesian Linguistics* (New York: Harper & Row, 1966), p. 73.

[21] See in particular, *ibid.*, pp. 31–51: "Deep and Surface Structure" ("The deep structure is . . . represented in the mind as physical utterance [surface structure] is produced . . ." [p. 40f.]). On the distinction between "philosophical" (deep-structure generated) grammar and the descriptive "structuralist" grammar departing from Saussure, see *Language and Mind* (New York: Harcourt Brace Jovanovich, 1958), pp. 19–23, including Chomsky's suggestion that "the time has arrived to unite these two major currents and to develop a synthesis that will draw from their respective achievements" (p. 23). While Chomsky contends that "the clear intention of philosophical grammar was to develop a psychological theory, not a technique of textual interpretation" (p. 18), the "synthesis" he envisions is in fact more closely fulfilled by the conception of "textual interpretation" as combined grammatical and semiotic analysis advanced by narratology, just as it may be argued that that conception itself borders more closely on "psychological" (in the eighteenth-century sense of logical mental procedures) than on literary "theory."

recent work, Chomsky takes specific issue with Kant on the question of our "consciousness" of the mental rules by which we form representations, claiming that his own conclusion, that this cognitive dimension of language "may be unconscious," diverges from Kant's thesis that " 'All representations have a necessary relation to a *possible* empirical consciousness.' "[22] Such an observation, however, effectively underscores the similarity between the hypothesis of a deep structure governing all linguistic utterance and Kant's hypothesis that all perception is shaped by *a priori* mental forms. Rather than refuting Kant, Chomsky underestimates the stress placed upon the word "possible" by Kant, whenever that word modifies a condition of the epistemological system he proposes. Finally, Chomsky even recalls the noumenal dimension of Kant's epistemology in his references to the nongrammatical problem of "rule-governed acts that are freely undertaken." In the context of a universal theory of grammar, those acts are purely linguistic, and the freedom referred to is that of language in its "creative use." Yet few epistemologists or moral philosophers have come closer to Kant in his description of the noumenal status of "free" actions governed by the moral "law," and of which we can have no theoretical knowledge, than Chomsky in his discussion of the "mystery" of the "freedom" involved in "normal" or (grammatically) "legal" linguistic acts.[23] The lim-

---

In the *Logic*, Kant employs the linguistic analogy of a "purely formal," "general grammar" to describe logic as a possible "science of the pure form of thinking": "Und wir können uns eine Idee von der Möglichkeit einer solchen Wissenschaft machen, so wie von einer *allgemeinen Grammatik*, die nichts weiter als die blosse Form der Sprache überhaupt enthält, ohne Wörter, die zur Materie der Sprache gehören." [We can give ourselves an idea of the possibility of such a science as of a *general grammar*, which contains nothing other than the mere form of language as such, without words, which belong to the matter of language.] (Immanuel Kant, *Logik* [A 4], in *Werkausgabe*, 12 vols., ed. Wilhelm Weischedel [Frankfurt: Suhrkamp, 1977], VI:433–34; my emphasis).

[22] *Rules and Representations* (New York: Columbia University Press, 1980), p. 128.

[23] *Ibid.*, p. 222: "We have some understanding of the principles of grammar, but there is no promising approach to the normal creative use of language, or to other rule-governed acts that are freely undertaken. The study of grammar raises problems that we have some hope of solving; the creative use of language is a mystery that eludes our intellectual grasp."

itations of transformational grammar recognized by Chomsky with respect to linguistic experience can already be recognized as the very basis of epistemology for Kant. As Chomsky must formally limit linguistic theory in order to arrive at any universal understanding of language, Kant's *Critique* can be said to preserve the possibility of universal cognition by limiting our knowledge of empirical experience to a "deep structure grammar" of cognition: the *a priori* "rules" relating "representations" of experience in the mind.

The discussion of Kant in Chapter Two begins with the well-known description of his philosophy by Kleist. An investigation of the mistaken basis of Kleist's early summation of the "kantische Philosophie" leads into an analysis of the basic discursive principles of the *Critique* deduced specifically in the *Logic*. Kant's treatment, in the *Logic*, of the traditional distinction between "real" and "nominal definitions" results in a classification of all empirical, representational knowledge as nominal. The status of our only knowledge of experience, according to the *Logic*, is that of the representations composing narrative understood narratologically. The remaining problem of real knowledge is taken up in an investigation of that "experience" which threatens to disrupt our formal and nominal means of cognition: the mental perception of the sublime as described in the *Critique of Judgment*. Finally, Kant's deduction, in the *Critique of Practical Reason*, of the single concept of which we must have real rather than nominal, or narrative knowledge—"freedom"—is investigated for its own subversion of the critical principles deduced in the *Logic*. The imposition of "freedom" upon the *Critique* itself is shown to break with the "narratological" bases of Kant's theory of knowledge, for it results in Kant's own attempt to represent in narrative form real rather than nominal knowledge of experience.

Chapter Three discusses another theory of knowledge, Goethe's *Farbenlehre*, which takes "colors," rather than representations, to be the primary means of cognition. The "colors" of nature studied empirically by Goethe are, however, also described discursively in the "Color Theory" to compose the "language" of nature. Goethe's "natural science," while carried out by practical experiment, yields a theory of nature resembling a poetics: his "colors," once represented theoretically in discursive form, resemble the "colors" of language, discursive "images" or figures. Furthermore, Goethe's central interest in the "phenomenon" of color relates directly to this dual register of his object of study. Along with his revealing Postscript to the "Color Theory," Goethe wrote a novel which *represents* his theory: *Die Wahlverwandtschaften*. While no reading of the novel to my knowledge has viewed it in significant relation to the *Farbenlehre*, the "theory of elective affinities" referred to within and represented by its narrative is most specifically, it can be demonstrated, an objectified version of the theory of figuration outlined in the "Color Theory." The "novel" (so called by Goethe) *Die Wahlverwandtschaften* tells the figural bases of cognition described in the *Farbenlehre as* a story: it represents human passion for an external object as deriving from a moving passion for configuration, or form. The "coloring of relations" in *Die Wahlverwandtschaften* implies that empirical experience, as was concluded in the *Farbenlehre*, is inherently "colored" or figured in its very vision of external nature. Only a representational narrative, it is also implied, could provide us with "knowledge" of that fact. Yet any such narrative, considering the mistaken status of the "fact" in question, would have to proceed with unremitting "irony" (the term ascribed by Goethe to the undertaking of empirical science in the *Farbenlehre*) in the enterprise of discursively enlightening its readers.

The question of whether irony is a dimension inherent in all narration is directed to the narratives of Jane Austen in Chapter Four. The three novels discussed primarily, *Mansfield Park, Sense and Sensibility*, and *Persuasion*, are linked by their treatment of the two fundamental elements of narrative stories—character and action—in relation to the experience of cognition. That experience is represented in Austen to take part of both sense and sensibility, or reason and sensation, and thus Austen's narratives closely resemble the theory of the dual nature of knowledge hypothesized by Kant. Yet Austen's novels also represent the influence upon sense and sensibility of persuasion: a noncognitive experience which can appeal equally, in the shape of conviction, to reason or sense, or, in the sensory effect of pleasure, to the senses. What has widely been viewed as Austen's comic "irony" may result from her own knowledge that neither sense nor sensibility can "know" completely, and that narrative itself, in necessarily taking the logical form of "sense," must attempt falsely to "persuade" its readers—as the forced resolution of *Sense and Sensibility* makes most apparent—that it also offers an adequate representation of the senses.

Chapter Five considers two traditionally "realist" novels, *Illusions perdues* and *Le Rouge et le noir*. The disparity between conceptual and sensory knowledge conventionally represented through character is effectively replaced in these novels by their subordination of character, as well as knowledge, to narrative action. In Lucien de Rubempré and Julien Sorel, Balzac and Stendhal represent "characters" who do not experience cognition but rather embody its means. Lucien, the "poet," motivates the narrative in which he takes part not because of any particular cognitive sense or aesthetic sensibility he possesses but because of the persuasive effect of his own external beauty. The plot of *Le Rouge et le noir* develops in accordance with the gradual advancement of Julien; yet Julien, rather than logically plotting his own course of action, moves forward in the novel thanks to the pure appearance of logical thinking conveyed by his memory. The two characters, their narratives imply, are granted narrative mobility—in the one case, in the mode of erratic, nonprogressive movement, in the other, in the more traditional form of a coherent, diachronic development—because narrative itself excludes any impediment to action in knowledge. Balzac's review of Stendhal, repeated in part within the text of *Illusions perdues*, hypothesizes that narrative literature can be classified according to its employment of either "images" or "ideas." Yet both these novels demonstrate that images and ideas, poetry and thinking, can only take the form of appearances within narration: in being *represented* they effect action rather than represent perception.

Chapter Six discusses Herman Melville's *Pierre, Or the Ambiguities*, a novel that questions the validity of novels, of narrative representations in the first place. The novel presents a representation which takes no part in narration: a picture which, although a portrait, i.e., a straightforward mimetic representation, seems to *say* in being seen that it means something other than what it represents. As long as the significance of this representation remains immediately unknown, it generates no causal narrative sequence. As soon as its meaning appears certain, the ensuing narrative appears wildly overdetermined: an allegory of the narrative principle of plotted causality. Yet whether novels can be identified with the mechanism of plot, whether narrative representations, as forms of cognition, are either verbal *or* visual and thus unambiguous in their medium, are questions which remain undetermined by the overdetermination of *Pierre* . . . , in as much as *Pierre* . . . itself remains a novel in ambiguous relation to *the Ambiguities*.

Finally, Chapter Seven analyzes Proust's *A la recherche du temps perdu*, the narrative which appears to elide the entire problem of the status of representational cognition by deriving from the direct effect of sensory experience upon the mind. The story the narrator tells of his alternation between voluntary and involuntary memory represents narrative form as a direct function, whether willed or spontaneous, of the senses. Perhaps more than any other modern narrative, the *Recherche* is, as it was for Proust, the narrative to end all narratives, not only because its circular structure ends by stating its own beginning, but because that beginning claims to start not with narration at all but with sensation. Yet this narrative of a personal history regained directly through the senses is internally complicated by another story it tells, "Un amour de Swann," in which memory functions as a form-producing and self-deluding fiction, and time is not only not rewritten but put to waste. The story of Swann represents memory *as* the capacity for forming representations, and rather than remaining confined within its attribution to a third person, the counterrepresentation of memory in "Un amour de Swann" reveals an encompassing conflict within the delineation of the narrator's own story. Thus, in seeming ignorance of the contradictory conceptions of narrative it provides, the *Recherche* presents a logical model of narration as elusive and evocative of knowledge of experience as the narrator's own part-referential, part-representational object of knowledge, Albertine. In representing all knowledge of experience in the form of narration, the *Recherche* most resembles the comprehensive theory of knowledge of Kant's *Critique*. In remembering Swann, whose own form of memory it cannot, in its own terms, remember, it represents the "freedom" it does not "know" of narration itself.

CHAPTER 2

KANT AND
NARRATIVE THEORY

At that time of year, when one invited the Duchesse de Guermantes to dinner, making haste so that she wouldn't already be engaged, she would refuse for the only reason a *mondain* would never have thought of: she was going to depart on a cruise to visit the fjords of Norway which interested her. The *gens du monde* were stupified by it and, without concerning themselves with imitating the Duchesse, they experienced, nevertheless, the kind of alleviation at her action which one has in Kant when, after the most vigorous demonstration of determinism, one discovers that above the world of necessity there is that of freedom. All invention of which one had never been advised in advance excites the spirit, even of those who don't know how to profit from it.
—MARCEL PROUST, *Le Côté de Guermantes*

When Heinrich von Kleist wrote precipitously to Wilhelmine von Zenge in 1801, "Mein einziges, mein höchstes Ziel ist gesunken, und ich habe keines mehr" [My only, my highest goal has sunken, and I have none left],[1] it was not to some reversal imposed upon their formal engagement that he referred, nor to any disillusionment on his part with the romantic attachment between them. The reason Kleist gave Wilhelmine for the sense

---

[1] Heinrich von Kleist, *Sämtliche Werke und Briefe*, 2 vols., ed. Helmut Sembdner (München: Carl Hanser Verlag, 1961), II:634. (All English translations are my own.)

of purposelessness he had come to suffer was his reading of the critical philosophy of Imannuel Kant. "Wenn alle Menschen statt der Augen grüne Gläser hätten." [If all men had green glasses instead of eyes],[2] is Kleist's famous attempt to formulate, for the benefit of his fiancée's understanding, the radical equation of all cognition with the formation of mental representations set forth in Kant's deduction of the only possible knowledge reason may claim. The image Kleist employs of vision conceived in colored glass may seem, in its reference to distinctly physical circumstances, a particularly inadequate or inappropriate analogy for the founding of a philosophical system concerned with a reconception of reason itself. The purely intellectual nature and purpose of Kant's *Critique* may in fact be seen to be conveyed most accurately by Kant's own chosen metaphor for his endeavor: that of a "revolution" in metaphysics most closely resembling the Copernican revolution in physical sciences for its power to change not the objects but the very *Denkart*, the "way of thought," of philosophy.[3] For the particular status quo to be affected by Kant's revolution were the mental procedures which we ourselves conceive of as governing speculative thought. Yet, any further acquaintance with Kleist's life should serve to remind us that the experience his image compares to the consequences of "Kantian philosophy"[4] is no more physically concrete than the specific course of action, attributed to reading Kant, that image is used to explain. For Kleist's letter announces his impending departure on a needed diversionary excursion through Germany to France from which as writer, and as Wilhelmine's intended, he will to all intents and purposes never return.[5]

<hr />

[2] *Ibid.*, II:634.

[3] Immanuel Kant, *Werkausgabe*, 12 vols., ed. Wilhelm Weischedel (Frankfurt: Suhrkamp, 1977): *Kritik der reinen Vernunft* B XXIII, III:28. (All quotations from Kant are from this edition.)

[4] Kleist, II:634.

[5] *Ibid.*, II:635: "Ach, es ist der schmerzlichste Zustand ganz ohne ein Ziel zu sein. . . . In dieser Angst fiel mir ein Gedanke ein. Liebe Wilhelmine, lass mich reisen. . . . Denn ich kehre um, *so bald ich weiss, was ich tun soll*" [Oh, to be without a purpose is the most painful condition. . . . In this fear a thought occurred to me. Dear Wilhelmine, let me travel away. . . . For I will turn around *as soon as I know what I should do . . .*].

In employing Kleist as a means of introducing Kant within the context of a critical investigation of narrative, this discussion leaves aside the question, certainly of interest in itself, of whether Kleist's reference to Kant at this pivotal instance of communication did not provide him with an effective intellectual fiction serving to take the place of a less convenient, more immediate, truth. Few writers have succeeded, in life no less than in fiction, in confusing the mental and physical realms of experience as thoroughly as Kleist, or in thus provoking more perpetual and indefinite speculation as to the "reality" of events presented in either. Whatever its particular motivation for articulation, the "Kantian crisis" in Kleist's life, since designated as such by literary history and isolated to have been initiated at this moment in his life, finds its most direct expression in the central dilemma outlined in the same letter. Kleist writes, "Wir können nicht entscheiden, ob das, was wir Wahrheit nennen, wahrhaft Wahrheit ist, oder ob es uns nur so scheint. Ist das letzte, so *ist* die Wahrheit, die wir hier sammeln, nach dem Tode nicht mehr—und alles Bestreben, ein Eigentum sich zu erwerben, das uns auch in das Grabe folgt, ist vergeblich—" [We cannot decide if that which we name truth is truly truth, or if it only appears to us as such. If the latter, then the truth which we gather here *is*, after death, no longer—and all striving to acquire possessions which would follow us into the grave is in vain—].[6] Apparently speaking out of a desire for artistic immortality already frustrated in its own anticipation, Kleist represents, and seriously misrepresents, the major problem implied by Kant's critical theory as one of cognitive undecidability. If "what we name truth only appears to us as such," then it may also lack all objective validity and be "gathered" to outlive us, as the permanent "possession" after which we have striven, "in vain." (The peculiarity of Kleist's formulation should, however, be especially noted here. For since he indicates that the desired end of all striving is specifically for our possessions to "follow us into the grave," the particular immortality despaired of by Kleist appears in its conception already in contradiction, or crisis, with itself.) "What we name

[6] *Ibid.*, II:634.

truth" will be named for the purposes of this discussion "representational narrative" or "narrative fiction," and the special relevance of Kant to an examination of narrative can be read in the very terms of the brief and mistaken summary Kleist offers. For in ascribing the situation of an inability to "decide" upon truth to a distinction between, on the one hand, what we perceive as and "name truth," and, on the other, that which would be "truly truth," Kleist demonstrates, far more successfully than if he had intended to, the more correctly Kantian and troubling notion that between "what we name truth" and the "truly true" no distinction can within reason be made.

The best exposition of Kant's *Critique of Pure Reason* (1781) is given by Kant himself in his *Prolegomena to Any Future Metaphysics* (1783), the concise, explanatory sequel to the extensively schematic *First Critique*, written to render its major hypothesis more accessible to the public as well as to inhibit the popularization of its misconception by scholars of philosophy. A "Kantian" analysis of narrative, were such a derivation from Kant—even in purely mechanical, methodological terms—at all feasible, is in any case neither the aim nor the recommendation of the present study. Instead, Kant's indication of the critical necessities and difficulties involved in composing any understanding of knowledge will be considered in relation to the particular problems inherent in the composition and understanding of narrative. As the following analysis should begin to indicate, the formal suppositions underlying all current epistemic systems of "narratology" can be recognized to owe no more fundamentally, if also no less consciously, to any other single philosophical work than Kant's *Critique*. At the same time, however, and for reasons which, as will be developed later, the structures of reason "criticized" and of narrative fiction share, a science of narrative based on Kant's *Critique* seems as ill-advised as Kant's own expectation of a systematic "science" of knowledge to follow his philosophical project. Thus, rather than a straightforward delineation of the principles deduced in the *First Critique*, the return to their misrepresentation by the author whose own narratives most clearly and disquietingly represent them in practice, seems a more promising approach to their distinctly literary scope. The dilemma of cognitive uncertainty described by Kleist, while adding to the persuasive tension of his own plea for understanding, in fact reduces, as it divides, the full force and purport of Kant's hypothesis. For the central premise of Kant's critical deduction is that any demonstration of the possibility of knowledge must necessarily and simultaneously be the limitation of knowledge to the apprehension, or in Kleist's words, the "gathering," of what "appears to us" alone. In order for any object to be understood or even objectified—those mental operations, in strict conformity with Kant's hypothesis, being essentially the same—that object must be made present to us by the formal intuitions and relational mechanisms which compose our perceptions independent of and prior to any material sensation of the object itself. Since those forms and connectives are not inferred from but are instead constitutive of experience, we can never claim to "know," without their mediation, what we may only "think" as "things-in-themselves": "things" not already represented, and *as* representations, sequentially connected by perception in the mind.[7]

"Representation" (*Vorstellung*), the central term in Kant for the "appearance" (*Erscheinung*) of things our minds construct, thus signifies the antithesis of its aesthetic meaning of *mimesis*, as well as its significance, in political practice, of a part standing ethically—formally by synecdoche—for a

---

[7] Kant, *KrV*:B XXV–XXVII, pp. 30–31: "Dass Raum und Zeit nur Formen der sinnlichen Anschauung, also nur Bedingungen der Existenz der Dinge als Erscheinungen sind, dass wir ferner keine Verstandesbegriffe, mithin auch gar keine Elemente zur Erkenntnis der Dinge haben, als so fern diesen Begriffen korrespondierende Anschauung gegenben werden kann, folglich wir von keinem Gegenstande als Dinge an sich selbst, sondern nur so fern es Objekt der sinnlichen Anschauung ist, d.i. als Erscheinung, Erkenntnis haben können . . . , dass wir eben dieselben Gegenstände auch als Dinge an sich selbst, wenn gleich nicht *erkennen*, doch wenigstens müssen *denken* können." [That space and time are only forms of sensory intuition, thus only conditions of the existence of things as appearances, that we have no further concepts of understanding, as well as no elements for the cognition of things, than in so far as an intuition corresponding to these concepts can be given, following which we can have no knowledge of an object as thing-in-itself, but only in as far as it is the object of sensory intuition, that is, an appearance . . . , that we must at least be able, when not exactly to *cognize*, to *think* these very objects also as things-in-themselves.]

whole. For we do not "know" reality by a copy we make of it, nor know from one selected member a larger constituency to which it pertains. What we "know" and all that we know *is* representation: the appearances which identify the reality we experience just as discourse, in articulating our understanding of experience, should logically constitute the identity of those appearances by name. Thus to distinguish what "we name truth" from that which would be "truly truth" is to remain, tautologically and squarely, within the limitations of knowledge deduced by Kant rather than depart from or transcend them to a knowledge whose "truth" would take no name. In brief, if less than satisfactory response to Kleist's complaint: the "truth" as it "appears to us" is one to which we have no alternative in Kant, most especially that of forgetting that all alternatives imagined must be false. The unashamed repetitiveness, the apparent tediousness of Kant's own discursive style—as compared negatively by Kant himself to the writings he credits with having awakened him from his "dogmatic slumbers": the "subtlety" and "charm" of the "attack" upon metaphysics carried out by his "acute" predecessor, David Hume[8]—the "dry," "exacting" quality which Kant trusted would preserve his work from wide and rapid "popularity,"[9] owes in no small measure to his *Critique*'s constant recollection and reminder that the only "truth" separating critical thought from the illusions of all forms of idealism[10] remains a thought to which we may only refer by name.

---

[8] Kant, *Prolegomena zu einer jeden künftigen Metaphysik die als Wissenschaft wird auftreten können*, A 18, V:121: "Es ist zwar nicht jedermann gegeben, so subtil und doch zugleich so anlockend zu schreiben, als *David Hume* . . ." [It does not fall to every man to write as subtly and still at the same time as charmingly as *David Hume* . . .].

Ironically, Kant's style of writing has recently come under critical scrutiny for the very qualities openly criticized by Kant himself; see Jean-Luc Nancy, "*Logodaedalus* (Kant écrivain)," *Poétique* 21 (1975).

[9] *Ibid.*, A 17, V:120: "Popularität [darf] folgen, aber niemals den Anfang machen" [Popularity may follow but never constitute the beginning"].

[10] See Kant's description of the "empirical idealism of Descartes": "wirkliche Sachen (nicht Erscheinungen) in blosse Vorstellungen zu verwandeln" [the transformation of real things (not appearances) into mere representations], versus the "mystical idealism of Berkeley," "der umgekehrt blosse Vor-

Thinking in language is in fact the activity defined *as* philosophy by Kant, in contradistinction to the form of reason carried out by intuition, mathematics. The deduction of the specifically modal difference between mathematics and philosophy is presented by Kant in the *Methodenlehre* terminating the *First Critique* as well as in Section III, "On the Concept of Philosophy in General," of the Introduction to the *Logic*. As modes of knowledge, Kant reasons, both philosophy and mathematics (under which Kant primarily understands Euclidian geometry) propose to understand their objects of investigation through a coordination of concepts or representations. What distinguishes them is not any integral distinction between the objects they study—the separate categories of quantity and quality described instead by Kant to overlap[11]— but, as Kant argues for the first time, the ways in which those objects are formally conceived. The concepts of mathematics, according to the understanding of representation afforded by the *Critique*, are representations of intuitions "constructed *a priori*," or without the aid of experience, whereas the concepts of philosophy are themselves the representations of experience, and thus necessarily *a posteriori*, or dependent upon empirical perception to be thought.[12] Mathematics, in other

---

stellungen zu Sachen macht" [who, by reverse order, makes mere representations into things], *Prolegomena*, A70–71, V:157–58, and his "Widerlegung des Idealismus," *KrV* B 274–75, III:254.

[11] Kant, *KrV* B 743, IV:614; *Logik* A 22–23, VI:445–46.

[12] Kant, *KrV* B 740–54, IV:612–22; *Logik* A 22–23, VI:446. See, in particular, Kant's example of the intuition of a triangle: "So konstruiere ich einen Triangel, indem ich den diesem Begriffe entsprechenden Gegenstand, entweder durch blosse Einbildung, in der reinen, oder nach derselben auch auf dem Papier, in der empirischen Anschauung, beidemal aber völlig a priori, ohne das Muster dazu aus irgend einer Erfahrung geborgt zu haben, darstelle . . ." [This is how I construct a triangle, in that I represent the object corresponding to the concept either through mere imagination, in pure intuition, or according to the latter on paper, in empirical intuition, in both cases however, fully *a priori*, without having borrowed the pattern for it from any experience at all . . .] (*KrV* B 741, IV:613).

On the distinction between an "empirical concept" (a representation "derived from external experience") and the representation of an intuition *a priori*, see also the initial discussion of the "fundamental," "intuitional" "representation" of space in the *First Critique*, "On Space" ["Space is no empirical

words, intuits the forms it investigates "*in concreto*"—the "concrete" here, however, signifying the negative of precisely that condition with which it is most commonly identified, namely, the empirical.[13] For the forms which *are* the concepts of mathematical reason are in Kant's terms "concrete," are fully synthetic, complete, and particular, and thus yield no occasion for discursive speculation, to the extent that unlike "things" empirically experienced, they are, exclusively, all that they appear to be—should the term "appearance" still be considered a serviceable designation for the manifestation to the mind of forms which the mind itself constructs. Neither construed mentally from physical sensation, nor conceived "conceptually," that is, by way of discursive relations, the cognitions of mathematical reason might best be described instead as "natural," were nature itself "constructed *a priori*" of purely formal objects reason could "know."

Philosophical knowledge, or knowledge derived "*from* concepts,"[14] is also composed by *a priori* intuitions, the mental forms of time and space. But those intuitions, rather than being self-sufficient, or mentally capable of representing themselves, are only formally constructive in as far as they are practically applied. They represent what they are not—the sensation of matter—to the mind as phenomenon. The concepts of philosophy, according to the *Critique*, are thus grounded no less in sensory experience than in the mental representation of that experience. Consequently, and most decisively, the knowledge derived from those representations, for the reason that the latter are *not* purely or "concretely" intuitional, must

---

concept that is drawn from external experience . . . ," and following] (*KrV* B 38, III:72ff.).

[13] Kant, *Logik* A 23, VI:446: "In der Mathematik braucht man die Vernunft in concreto, die Anschauung ist aber nicht empirisch, sondern man macht sich hier etwas a priori zum Gegenstande der Anschauung." [In mathematics one uses reason *in concreto*, the intuition however is not empirical, rather, one makes oneself something into the object of intuition *a priori*.]

[14] Kant, *KrV* B 741, IV:613: "Die *philosophische* Erkenntnis ist die *Vernunfterkenntnis* aus *Begriffen*, die mathematische aus der *Konstruktion* der Begriffe . . ." [*Philosophical* knowledge is the *knowledge of reason from concepts*, mathematical knowledge, from the *construction* of concepts . . .].

in turn be understood to *refer*, as well as to confer form.[15]
Since the sources of its cognitions are unavoidably twofold—
"springing," as Kant writes, from "zwei Grundquellen," "two
fundamental sources"[16]—philosophical reasoning must understand its own referents to refer with certainty solely to representations, rather than things in their essence, while recognizing the essentiality of referentiality, of an object given by
experience, to its mode. "The great fortune" met with by nonempirical reasoning in mathematics "naturally brings about
the supposition," Kant cautions in the *First Critique*, that "all
concepts" can be considered purely intuitional, and thus reason itself, capable of "becoming master over nature."[17] Such a
"pure philosophy," however, only "bungles about in nature,"
Kant continues, without rendering the "reality" of its concepts
intuitable, or those concepts themselves thereby more credible.[18] The difficulties consciously encountered by a *critical* philosophy, by contrast, lie precisely in its recognition of the heterogeneity of its concepts. For the very motive for "criticizing"

---

[15] The necessary inclusion of both empirical sensation (*Sinnlichkeit*) and
representational understanding (*Verstand*) within an understanding of cognition is explained by Kant as deriving from their codetermining relation. Both
faculties must however be viewed in strict separation if the understanding of
cognition aimed at, as opposed to the *experience* of cognition that understanding describes, is itself not to depend upon the sensory. Thus Kant further specifies that this fundamental relation can only function as a closed structure:
both sensation and understanding would cease to take part in knowledge if
they chiastically "exchanged functions." "Ohne Sinnlichkeit würde uns kein
Gegenstand gegeben, und ohne Verstand keiner gedacht werden. Gedanken
ohne Inhalt sind leer, Anschauungen ohne Begriffe sind blind. . . . Beide Vermögen, oder Fähigkeiten, können auch ihre Funktionen nicht vertauschen.
Der Verstand vermag nichts anzuschauen, und die Sinne nichts zu denken. Nur
daraus, dass sie sich vereinigen, kann Erkenntnis entspringen." [Without sensory experience no object would be given to us, and without understanding
none would be thought. Thoughts without content are empty, intuitions without concepts are blind. . . . Also, both faculties, or capabilities, cannot exchange their functions. Understanding can intuit nothing, and the senses cannot think. Only in that they unite with each other can knowledge spring from
them.] (*KrV* B 76, III:98.)

[16] *Ibid.*, B 74, III:97 ("unsere Erkenntnis entspringt aus zwei Grundquellen
des Gemüts").

[17] *Ibid.*, B 752–53, IV:621.

[18] *Ibid.*, B 753, IV:621.

philosophical reason is that its "representations" are conceived both "*a priori* in intuition," and "*a posteriori*" according to the "matter of phenomena" given only "by means of experience."[19] The name Kant gives in the *Logic* to this condition of epistemological "heterogeneity," inherent in and definitive of philosophy, is specifically that of its linguistic modality, "discourse": "herein . . . mathematics has an advantage over philosophy, in that the cognitions of the former are intuitive, those of the latter, on the contrary, only *discursive*."[20]

Knowledge which is "only discursive" is limited by its dependence upon nonformal, sensory perception. Thus the discourses of philosophy and of experience, rather than held in distinction by the desire for an ideal knowledge, must be recognized as a single discourse subject to critical judgment with as much regard to its referential veracity as to its formal ability to convey logically. The mistaken perception of his own epistemology as ideal or "transcendental," instead of "critical," is forcefully disputed by Kant in the *Prolegomena*. Kant is forced in turn, however, by the power and pervasiveness of that misperception, to announce in the *Prolegomena* a de facto rewriting of the *First Critique*. He states his wish to replace the term "transcendental"—even as that modifier had been limited in the *First Critique* to describing the mental "faculty" (*Vermögen*), rather than objective exercise, of cognition—entirely by the single word, "critical," hoping thereby to impede future developments of the same mistake.[21] The confusion, which has

[19] *Ibid.*, B 749, IV:618. It should be noted here that this dual temporal register accorded the single term "representation" in English, is signaled in German by Kant's use of *two* terms to mean "representation": *darstellen*, to represent "a priori in der Anschauung," and *vorstellen*, to represent "a posteriori." *Vorstellung*, in that it means the representation of experience, is thus used most frequently throughout the *Critique*.

[20] Kant, *Logik* A 23, VI:446: "herein hat also . . . die Mathematik einen Vorzug vor der Philosophie, dass die Erkenntnisse der erstern intuitive, die der letztern hingegen nur *diskursive* Erkenntnisse sind." See *KrV* B 176-77, III:187, for Kant's discussion of the "heterogeneous" (*heterogen*) nature of representational cognition.

[21] Kant, *Prolegomena* A 71, V:157–58: "Das Wort transzendental aber, welches bei mir niemals eine Beziehung unserer Erkenntnis auf Dinge, sondern nur aufs *Erkenntnisvermögen* bedeutet, sollte diese Missdeutung verhüten. Ehe sie aber denselben doch noch fernerhin veranlasse, nehme ich diese Benen-

nonetheless grown to blur all lines of lexical distinction over time, of the negative premise of Kant's *Critique* with a historical apex in the affirmation of idealism, can be seen, however, to have been more thoroughly refuted before this attempted retraction[22] on Kant's part. For Kant's initial determination of the necessarily *discursive* mode of philosophical reasoning is itself the necessary logical condition for an implicitly *critical* theory of knowledge. Departing from formal idealists and empirical skeptics alike, Kant maintains the ultimacy of a structural and thus indismissable bond between philosophy and that matter which is all but philosophy, material sensation. Discourse, the mental intermediary between philosophy and the senses, is also the grounds for the limitations to be recognized, the fallibilities to be criticized, in both. The inherently self-critical dimension of all philosophical reasoning for Kant is its own constitution of discursive representation: its constitutional and indispensable link, in other words, to the representational discourse conventionally taken as the object of criticism, literature.

Kant suggested that understanding conceptualized sensation by *writing* it in linguistic form: "the concepts of understanding," he writes, "serve only, so to speak, to spell out appearances, in order to make them legible as experience."[23] He further compared the rules by which we comprehend and connect experience cognitively to the rules of "grammar" in a lan-

---

nung lieber zurück und will ihn den kritischen genannt wissen" [But the word transcendental, which in my use of it never signifies the relationship of our knowledge to things, but only to the *faculty of knowledge*, should guard against this mistaken meaning. Before it, however, goes on to give rise to the very same, I prefer to retract this designation and want (my so-called idealism) to be known to be named critical].

See also the Introduction to the *Logik*, sec. IV, "A Short Sketch of the History of Philosophy," A 39–40, VI:457: "Unser Zeitalter ist das Zeitalter der *Kritik*, und man muss sehen, was aus den kritischen Versuchen unsrer Zeit, in Absicht auf Philosophie und Metaphysik insbesondre, werden wird." [Our age is the age of *criticism*, and one must see what becomes of the critical experiments of our time, with regard to philosophy and metaphysics in particular.]

[22] Kant, *Prolegomena* A 71, V:158.

[23] *Ibid.*, A 101, V:180–81: "die reine Verstandesbegriffe . . . dienen gleichsam nur, Erscheinungen zu buchstabieren, um sie als Erfahrung lesen zu können."

guage, adding that the constitution of both "are in fact very much related," as no amount of "particular experience" in the one case, or "real use of words" in the other, could fully account for the universality of either.[24] Similar to the intelligibility of meaning afforded by a regulative grammar, the understanding of "how truth is possible" is declared in the *Logic* to be itself unproblematic, "since here [in the judgment of truth] understanding acts according to its essential laws."[25] For the same reason, however, the one cognitive possibility which understanding must fail to comprehend is its own apparent and autonomous abuse: the mistaking, as if against its laws, of falsity for truth. Kant continues in the *Logic* to explain why such errors cannot actually pertain to understanding itself:

> *Wie . . . Irrtum in formaler Bedeutung des Worts*, d.h. wie die *verstandeswidrige Form des Denkens* möglich sei: das ist schwer zu begreifen, so wie es überhaupt nicht zu begreifen ist, wie irgend eine Kraft von ihren eigenen wesentlichen Gesetzen abweichen solle. . . . Hätten wir nun keine andre Erkenntniskraft als den Verstand: so würden wir nie irren. Allein es liegt, ausser dem Verstande, noch eine andre unentbehrliche Erkenntnisquelle in uns. Das ist die *Sinnlichkeit*, die uns den Stoff zum Denken gibt und dabei nach andern Gesetzen wirkt, als der Verstand.— Aus der Sinnlichkeit, an und für sich selbst betrachtet, kann aber der Irrtum auch nicht entspringen, weil die Sinne gar nicht urteilen.
>
> Der Entstehungsgrund alles Irrtums wird daher einzig und allein in dem *unvermerkten Einflusse der Sinnlichkeit auf den Verstand*, oder, genauer zu reden, auf das Urteil, gesucht werden müssen. Dieser Einfluss nämlich macht, dass wir im Urteilen bloss *subjektive* Gründe für *objektive* halten und folglich den *blossen Schein der Wahrheit* mit *der Wahrheit selbst verwechseln*. Denn darin besteht eben

---

[24] *Ibid.*, A 118, V:192.
[25] Kant, *Logik* A 76, VI:480. The epistemological function accorded "judgment" in the *Third Critique* is made clear at this moment, when "truth" rather than "taste" is at issue, in the *Logic*: "denn Irrtum sowohl als Wahrheit ist nur im Urteile" [Then error as well as truth are only in judgment].

das Wesen des Scheins, der um deswillen als ein Grund anzusehen ist, eine falsche Erkenntnis für wahr zu halten.[26]

How . . . error, in the formal meaning of the word, that
is, how the *form of thinking which is contrary to understanding* is possible: that is difficult to grasp, just as it is
impossible to grasp how any power should shy from its
own essential laws. . . . Now, if we had no power of cognition other than understanding: so we would never err.
However, there lies outside understanding yet another indispensable source of cognition in us. That is sensory perception, which gives us the material of thought and
thereby acts according to other laws than those of understanding.—From sensory perception, considered in and of
itself, error can, however, also not arise, because the
senses do not judge at all.

The basis for the arisal of all error therefore must be
sought, solely and alone, in the *unnoticed influence of sensory perception upon understanding,* or, to speak more
precisely, upon judgment. This influence, namely, brings
us to hold merely *subjective* reasons for *objective* ones in
judging, and consequently, to mistakenly exchange the
mere seeming appearance of truth for *the truth itself.* For
therein consists the very essence of the seeming appearance, which on that account is to be seen as a basis for
holding a false cognition to be true.[27]

Just as its prerequisite, sensory experience, forces even formal knowledge, that of appearances, to be represented by discourse rather than made present in intuition, the involvement
of sensory perception in cognition entails our susceptibility to

---

[26] *Ibid.,* A 76-77, VI:480-81.

[27] The tenuous status of the concept of error in Kant is well conveyed by the
figure just cited of a "power shying from its own essential laws." For such a
power (*Kraft*) we most readily understand a purely physical force—such as
gravity (*Schwerkraft*) or atomic power (*Atomkraft*), whose "laws" can be as-
certained through calculation, equation, and empirical experiment—rather
than the power of judgment (*Urteilskraft*) meant by Kant here. Yet at the same
time questions of truth value could not apply to the purely dynamic function
of a physical force; considerations of truth arise solely with regard to that
"power" whose function is necessarily *referential*: the power of judging phenomena.

mistakes. Neither understanding alone, whose rules, like the
conventional laws of a language, can no more be broken without notice than misjudged, nor the senses themselves, which
are not governed formally, and thus as Kant observes, "do not
judge at all," is attributed with the "mistaken exchange" of
"false cognitions for true." Instead, the convergence, void of
reflection, between material sensation and conceptualization—"the unnoticed influence of sensory perception upon understanding"—is given to be the "basis for the arisal of all error"; the same basis, that is to say, given in the *Logic* for
knowledge itself.[28] Furthermore, like "true" knowledge, "false
cognitions" necessarily take a discursive form. Kant proceeds
to suggest that once the manifestation of error in a *Schein*, or
"*seeming* appearance," is recognized, the error may be recognized as confined to the form of its appearance alone: "Denn
man kann doch vielleicht recht haben in der Sache und nur un-
recht in der Manier, d.i. dem Vortrage" [Then one can perhaps
be right in substance and only wrong in manner, i.e., in elocu-
tionary form].[29] Language may fail to represent knowledge
correctly; yet knowledge "in substance," "in der Sache," can
never be conceived independently of its "elocution," whether
the latter be viewed as a particular "manner," or the universal
regularity of cognition itself. Philosophy which limits itself
critically to the representation of experience must commit its
representations to valid statements, or definitions; its errors,
consequently, are also committed in the course of its own discursive exposition. For once knowledge is recognized *as* discursive, there is nothing "in substance," which is to say, outside of discourse, which can be known either to correct error
or distinguish it formally from true statements. It is thus without any promise of probable improvement in the future that
Kant may (and must) admit openly, and with remarkable
equanimity, in the *First Critique*, that "philosophy swarms
with faulty definitions."[30]

Indeed, the near indifference with which Kant indicates the
inevitable preponderance of errors in philosophy can itself be

[28] See footnote 15.
[29] Kant, *Logik*, A 83, VI:484.
[30] Kant, *KrV* B 759, IV:625n: "Die Philosophie wimmelt von fehlerhaften
Definitionen. . . ."

seen to indicate the singular nature of his *Critique*. For Kant's candid treatment of discursive errors, rather than obliquely concealing a problem of cognition by its admission, points directly to the more redoubtable fact that errors in themselves are in no way centrally disruptive of his conception of knowledge. Deceptions stemming from the senses of perception and their representation gain so little and such detached attention in Kant—in comparison not only with the empirical as well as Cartesian tendencies in philosophy which Kant succeeded but with the limitations of reason relentlessly exposed throughout the *Critique* itself—because within the context of those same limitations, cognitive error is a concept of effective inconsequence. The deemphasis upon the essential epistemological opposition between truth and falsity, within a philosophical project concerned foremost with exposing the foundations of knowledge, is the logical and highly heterodoxical result of Kant's understanding of the means by which cognition proceeds. As discussed above, those means are deduced by Kant to belong specifically to discourse. But what we may understand by discourse, employed by necessity, as it is daily, with respect to experience, can only partially correspond to the critical understanding of discourse by which that necessity is deduced independently, or *a priori*. For the epistemological criticism of pure, or idealized, reason, whose point of departure is the unconditionally discursive nature of knowledge, must also identify the articulations of reason with discourse independent of any single given experience. Thus, according to the logic of "representational" language informing the *Critique*, the significance of statements in their extension and of the very words they employ to designate sense is severed from any direct equation with their only known subject matter, particular experience. Stated in more familiar theoretical terms, the meaning of the language used in the service of reason submitted to criticism is rather precisely that of the *language* employed, according to the criticism of literature, by concepts of fiction. "Fiction" itself, for the very same reason, while later substituted by neo-Kantians for the concept of criticism,[31] is a concept largely

---

[31] I refer primarily, of course, to Vaihinger's reception of Kant's epistemology as "die Fiktion des Als Ob," or fiction of mental analogy, from which the

alien to the explicit considerations of the *Critique*. The identification of representational narrative, understood as fiction,
with reason functioning within the limits of criticism, is based
instead upon the relationship both share with knowledge.
Structured internally upon principles of sequential logic and
causality, the individual discourses of narrative fiction and of
reason cross at the question of the representational nature, *and*
referential reality, of the knowledge they afford. Thus the issue
of fictionality is raised in Kant not in terms of fiction itself, or
of error, but, on the contrary, under the category of reliable
statements of knowledge, "definitions." While the abstract
clarity of Kant's analysis of definitions may seem immediately
to cloud its significance for literary thought, a closer inspection
of his examination of this most fundamental form of discursive
knowledge shows it to describe, with disorienting precision,
the unsuspected premises upon which both the concept and
interpretation of "fiction" are built.

Narrative and Knowledge in Kant's *Logic*

Kant's deduction of the status of definitions begins, in sec. 100
of the *Methodenlehre* of the *Logic*, with the distinction between definitions of "analytic" and "synthetic" composition.
Analytic definitions are specified to correspond to a "given
concept"; synthetic definitions, to a "made concept"; and

present consideration of real as *opposed* to representational knowledge must
diverge. See Hans Vaihinger, *Die Philosophie des Als Ob* (Leipzig: Felix Meiner Verlag, 1911).

Perhaps departing from Vaihinger, Ralph Freedman has compared the dual-
istic nature of narrative in the novel—its "seeming to be about real objects in
the external world . . . while being actually about fictional objects in an imaginary world"—with "Kantian" criticism. (Freedman, "The Possibility of a
Theory of the Novel," *The Disciplines of Criticism*, ed. Peter Demetz et al.
[New Haven: Yale University Press, 1968], pp. 57–77 [p. 72].) Yet Freedman
goes on to offer what is perhaps the only critical observation available on the
relation of the novel, and the "theory of the novel," specifically to an implicitly
Kantian theory of "representational" "*knowledge*": "one may consider the
novel as a particularly philosophical genre, not because it states philosophical
propositions (though it may also do that), but because even its most conventional forms constantly illustrate, dramatize, portray the interplay of minds
and objects as representations of the act of knowledge" (p. 74).

both are further subdivided as either *a posteriori* or *a priori* in cognitive origin.[32] The first two of these preliminary oppositions (between analytic and synthetic definitions, and their objects, given and made concepts) prove rapidly to be purely formal distinctions. For the sequential mode of investigation carried out in analysis determines that its results, unlike those of synthesis, can never be known to be conclusive; similar to an exclusively metonymic narration, a definition by analysis would be, by definition, necessarily incomplete. Thus sec. 104, the only moment in the *Logic* dealing solely with analytic definitions, also disqualifies them from further epistemological consideration: "Da man durch keine Probe gewiss werden kann, ob man alle Merkmale eines gegebenen Begriffs durch vollständige Analyse erschöpft habe: so sind alle analytische Definitionen für unsicher zu halten" [Since there is no test through which one can become certain of whether or not one has exhausted all the characteristics of a given concept through complete analysis: so all analytic definitions are to be considered uncertain].[33]

The distinction between concepts made *a priori* and *a posteriori* is, however, fundamental, and relates directly to the modal distinction between mathematics and philosophy discussed earlier. A definition which is an *a priori* synthesis of a concept is again called a "construction" by Kant, since it "makes" the object it simultaneously defines. By contrast, a synthetic *a posteriori* definition would be an "exposition [of appearances]": a definition based upon an "empirical" rather than an "arbitrary synthesis," as Kant calls the wholly nonexperiential modality of mathematical conceptualization.[34] Kant insists at first that all definitions, whether of "arbitrarily made," "mathematical concepts," or of "empirically made," "experiential concepts," must be composed synthetically rather than anaytically: "Denn auch bei den Begriffen der letztern Art, z.B. den empirischen Begriffen Wasser, Feuer, Luft u. dgl. soll ich nicht zergliedern, was *in ihnen* liegt, sondern durch

[32] Kant, *Logik* A 217, VI:572.
[33] *Ibid.*, A 220, VI:574.
[34] *Ibid.*, A 218, VI:573.

Erfahrung kennen lernen, was *zu ihnen* gehört" [Then also with respect to . . . the empirical concepts, water, fire, air, and the like, I should not itemize what lies *within them*, but learn through experience what belongs to *them*].[35] In the deductive moment proceeding from that premise, however, the very possibility of defining an empirical concept is denied. For experience, like its discursive representation in the mind, can never be fully and simultaneously made present. As no word can be considered final in the course of representing experience, no discursive knowledge of experience can be considered sufficient and no definition of experiential concepts thus truly definitive. Since discourse, in other words, is an inexhaustible mode of conveying, its empirical definitions can never be exhaustive of the object they are intended, rather than "arbitrarily" "constructed," to convey. As Kant concludes in sec. 103: "Da die Synthesis der empirischen Begriffe nicht willkürlich, sondern empirisch ist und, als solche, niemals vollständig sein kann (weil man in der Erfahrung immer noch mehr Merkmale des Begriffs entdecken kann): so können empirische Begriffe auch nicht definiert werden" [Since the synthesis of an empirical concept is not arbitrary but empirical and, as such, can never be complete (because one can always discover more attributes of the concept by experience); so empirical concepts also cannot be defined].[36]

A definition of any concept relating to experience is thus more accurately called an "exposition" or "description" (sec. 105), whereas a mathematical definition, the only truly synthetic, because nonexperiential, definition is renamed by Kant a "declaration" of "what one understands under a word": "was man unter einem Worte versteht."[37] The concept of a cognitive definition itself—of the identification of any object for the purposes of knowledge, performed linguistically by the form of equation stored within the grammar of language, verbal predication—is maintained as a working concept by Kant, which upon logical analysis is divided and replaced. Like the

[35] *Ibid.*
[36] *Ibid.*, A 219, VI:573.
[37] *Ibid.*, A 219, VI:574.

unrestricted conceptions of reason and of experience which Kant maintains it is the task of philosophy to oppose, the articulation of reason by means of definitions is critically determined by Kant to involve *two* activities, each unidentifiable with definitions understood ideally or empirically, and each distinct from the other both in object and in mode. Returning to the striking marginalization of the problem of error in Kant, it can now be seen that reason—due to the same discursive nature which relates it to experience in the first place—must be recognized to merely approximate experience through a series of predications rather than identify its reality with a single definition in the mind. Reason, once criticized, could thus only be held accountable for error insofar as it forgets its limitations as representational discourse and "declares" to be essentially true statements which can only "describe."

Sequential, expository "description" whose conceptual basis represents experience may seem in itself a concisely adequate description of narrative fiction. Definitions which cannot rigorously be considered definitions, which are logically "incomplete," only "a part of a definition," and yet offer "a true and useful representation of a concept,"[38] are comparable with the statements we understand to compose narrative when viewed from the perspective of its representational realism. The fundamental act of understanding the *story* of a narrative requires that we comprehend and keep in mind its representations. To view narrative with regard to its "realism," however, is to view realism itself as the style or orientation of a work regarded, without apparent paradox, as "fiction." Thus, like the definitions Kant determines to be more precisely mere "approaches" or "approximations" *Annäherungen*,[39] no epistemological claims, or only self-consciously weak ones, are found to be made by a representational discourse assumed at its outset to be fiction. Finally, the modesty of cognitive purpose ascribed to narrative fiction is in turn attributed twofold to the discourse of narrative analysis, literary criticism.

[38] *Ibid.*, A 221, VI:575: "so ist auch eine unvollständige Exposition, als Teil einer Definition, eine wahre and brauchbare Darstellung eines Begriffs."
[39] *Ibid.*, A 220, VI:574.

But what has been called fictionality here is not the fact of faulty definition in Kant, or the result of the uncertainty of discursive cognition. The radicality of the fiction involved in the critical composition of cognition lies instead in those definitions Kant finds to be necessarily true. For the articulations of knowledge which alone are capable of presenting syntheses, in that they are independent of, or "arbitrary" with regard to, experience, are deduced by Kant to be entirely, and immodestly, identical with discourse. Fully synthetic definitions may be called "declarations," Kant stated, "insofar as through them one declares one's thoughts," not as to the understanding of experience, but specifically, as cited above, as to "what one understands under a word."[40] "Was man unter einem Worte versteht" is the only possible object of definitons which "are not only always possible but also necessary."[41] We must always know, and thus be able to define by declaration, what we understand to be represented by a word: a word *as a word*, rather than as a referential marker of experience. For Kant specifies that such knowledge is only "the case with mathematicians":[42] with knowledge composed of "concrete *Anschauungen*," that term of vision best translated into English as "intuitions," since it means to conceive or have a view of that for which no particular empirical experience accounts.[43] Thus the sole object of a definition which must be accurate, by critical definition, is that manifestation we know as a word. The "matter" of knowledge, in terms of Kant's epistemology, is, in other words, a dictionary: discursive declarations of the concepts constructed by discourse; words stating thoughts of what is understood under words. The fictionality Kant's criticism of reason proposes can perhaps be most effectively distinguished from that concept of fiction allowing for its description as "realism" (or for that matter as truly "fictional" fiction, or

[40] *Ibid.*, A 219, VI:574.

[41] *Ibid.*, A 219, VI:574: "Solche Definitionen willkürlicher Begriffe, die nicht nur immer möglich, sondern auch notwendig sind. . . ."

[42] *Ibid.*, A 219, VI:574 ("Dies ist der Fall bei den *Mathematikern*").

[43] Kant, *KrV* B 741, IV:613: "Zur Konstruktion eines Begriffs wird also eine *nicht empirische* Anschauung erfordert" [For the construction of a concept a nonempirical intuition is required].

"fantasy") by the thought of a dictionary read without access to memory or imagination: a dictionary cut off from all sensory visualization, related only within itself and, of course, "concretely," to other books.

The image of such a dictionary and the hypothesis of such a reading—both, incidentally, *a posteriori*, or referring to experience, and thus no accurate definitions of knowledge in Kant—are merely offered here as antidotes to the confusion of verbal and nonverbal representation most commonly underlying discussions of verisimilitude in fiction: the equation of words with plastic or pictorial renderings which, for the purposes of critical thinking, should seem a far greater conceptual shock. But Kant's own understanding of cognitive definitions exceeds the mode of antidotal oppositions, just as his critical project, meant to contribute medicinally to the well-being of philosophical procedure, extended further than the disproof of skepticism at which it initially aimed. For the discussion of definitions in the *Logic* proceeds to distinguish the reality from the facticity of the modes it deduces. Section 106 divides definitions into those whose meaning must be understood to be "nominal" and those whose meaning must be known to be "real."

> Unter blossen *Namen-Erklärungen* oder *Nominal-Definitionen* sind diejenigen zu verstehen, welche die Bedeutung enthalten, die man willkürlich einem gewissen Namen hat geben wollen, und die daher nur das logische Wesen ihres Gegenstandes bezeichnen, oder bloss zur Unterscheidung desselben von andern Objekten dienen. *Sach-Erklärungen* oder *Real-Definitionen* hingegen sind solche, die zur Erkenntnis des Objekts, seinen innern Bestimmungen nach, zureichen, indem sie die Möglichkeit des Gegenstandes aus innern Merkmalen darlegen.
> *Anmerk. 1.* Wenn ein Begriff innerlich zureichend ist, die Sache zu unterscheiden, so ist er es auch gewiss äusserlich; wenn er aber innerlich nicht zureichend ist: so kann er doch bloss in *gewisser Beziehung* äusserlich zureichend sein, nämich in der Vergleichung des Definitums

mit andern. Allein die *unumschränkte* äussere Zuläng-
lichkeit ist ohne die innere nicht möglich.[44]

Under mere *name-explanations* or *nominal definitions*
are those to be understood which contain the meaning
which one wished to give arbitrarily to a certain name,
and which thus denote only the logical essence of their object, or merely serve to differentiate the same from other
objects. *Thing-explanations* or *real definitions*, on the
other hand, are those which suffice for the cognition of an
object according to its internal determinations, in that
they display the possibility of the object from internal
characteristics.

Note 1. When a concept is internally sufficient for dif-
ferentiating a thing, it is also externally so; but when it is
not internally sufficient, it can merely be externally so
when in a certain relationship, namely, in the comparison
of the definitum with other definitums. Unlimited external sufficiency is, however, impossible without the internal.

In keeping with the spare economy characterizing the composition of the *Logic*, this particular deductive moment appears untroublingly straightforward and precise. "Nominal
definitions" are said to define, as designated, knowledge which
is effective in name alone. A "name" here is the "arbitrarily
given" designation of the "meaning" a definition "contains";
that is, by way of a specifically nominal definition a certain
meaning is made known to correspond to a certain name, but
no knowledge of any measure is afforded of a nonnominal object. Whether viewed with regard to the individual name defined or with respect to that object's further relations, the
meaning of a nominal definition is thus limited to the performance of a purely logical signifying function: it articulates
the "logical essence" of its object, "or merely differentiates"
that object from other objects or names of meaning. Its own
adequacy, like that of any denotation, could only be known
based on evidence external to itself. But as a statement of

[44] Kant, *Logik* A 221–22 VI:575.

meaning known to have been attributed "arbitrarily," in the absence of any qualitative correlation with its object, the demonstration of the sufficiency of a nominal definition can never lead from logic to a knowledge of the empirical. What is meant by a nominal definition, or "name explanation," arises "merely" in the "relationship" composed by its own "comparison . . . with other definitums." Thus Kant's understanding of the distinction of meaning effected by nominal definitions alone fundamentally anticipates the modern semiological analysis of language in its entirety: that of a differential, rule or grammar-generated, and in itself only arbitrarily referential, signifying system.[45]

Yet "real definitions," or "explanations of things," are defined by Kant to depart from a semiological model in extending to "the cognition of an object." "Real definitions" do not describe an object empirically but display, according to its "internal determination," its very "possibility." "Explanations of things" define their reality, and the reality of which they provide knowledge is defined in turn by "things" irrespective of names and comparative relations. The identification of the objects of definitions as being either "things" or "names" is itself a conventional distinction made for the purpose of securing a noncontradictory method for epistemology, i.e., one which

---

[45] Among the now classic texts in the traditions of semiotics, structuralism, and their mutual offspring, narratology, see Ferdinand de Saussure, *Cours de linguistique générale* (Paris: Payot, 1978 [Geneva, 1915]); Vladamir Propp, *The Morphology of the Folktale* (Austin: University of Texas Press, 1977 [orig. pub. 1928]); Claude Lévi-Strauss, *Structural Anthropology* (New York: Basic Books, 1963 [Paris, 1958]), including the source study for all structural analyses of narrative, "The Structural Study of Myth," pp. 206–31 (see also *The Savage Mind* [Chicago: University of Chicago Press, 1973 (Paris, 1962)] and *Introduction to a Science of Mythology*, 4 vols. [New York: Harper Torchbooks, 1973 (Paris, 1966)]); Roland Barthes, *Eléments de sémiologie* (Paris: Editions de Seuil, 1964); "Introduction à l'analyse structurale des récits," *Communications* 8 (1966); A. J. Greimas, *Sémantique structurale* (Paris: Larousse, 1966); *Du sens* (Paris: Editions de Seuil, 1970), including "Eléments d'une grammaire narrative," pp. 157–83; *Maupassant* (Paris: Editions de Seuil, 1976); Umberto Eco, *A Theory of Semiotics* (Bloomington: Indiana University Press, 1970); Gérard Genette, "Le discours du récit," in *Figures III* (Paris: Editions de Seuil, 1972); and Claude Bremond, *La logique du récit* (Paris: Editions de Seuil, 1973).

would prescribe, on purely logical grounds, the functions of its discourse, or means.[46] Its earliest formulation by Aristotle in the *Posterior Analytics* relates to the particular emphasis placed upon the epistemological role of definition in his *Metaphysics*. In his refutation—especially relevant to the epistemologies preceding Kant—of what he terms "one-sided theories," those that hold that nothing, or everything, is true,[47] Aristotle introduces the concept of definition, or statements of "meaning," as a way of substituting semantic "truth" for questions of true being: "we must postulate . . . not that something is or is not, but that something has a meaning, so that we must argue from a definition, viz. by assuming what falsity or truth means" (*Metaphysics* IV.8.1012a29–1012b8).[48] While Aristotle's definition of definitions in the *Metaphysics* presents a precise description of a purely nominal semantics—"the definition rests on the necessity of . . . meaning something; for the form of words of which the word is a sign will be its definition"[49]—the *Posterior Analytics* stipulates two kinds of definition:

> Since definition is said to be the statement of a thing's nature, obviously one kind of definition will be a statement

[46] Kant, *Logik* A 216, VI:571: "Die Methodenlehre soll die Art vortragen, wie wir zur Vollkommenheit des Erkenntnisses gelangen.—Nun besteht eine der wesentlichsten logischen Vollkommenheiten des Erkenntnisses in der Deutlichkeit, der Gründlichkeit und systematischen Anordnung derselben zum Ganzen einer Wissenschaft. Die Methodenlehre wird demnach hauptsächlich die Mittel anzugeben haben, durch welche diese Vollkommenheiten des Erkenntnisses befördert werden" [The Theory of Method should present the way in which we arrive at the perfection of knowledge. Now one of the most essential logical perfections of knowledge consists in the clarity, the thoroughness, and systematic ordering of the same into the whole of a science. The Theory of Method will thus be principally charged with presenting the means through which these perfections of knowledge are furthered].

[47] The references here are to Heraclitus' "doctrine . . . that all things are and are not" that "seems to make everything true," including "contradictories which cannot be at the same time true," and "that of Anaxagoras, that there is an intermediate between the terms of a contradiction" that "seems to make everything false," while one side of the contradiction must be true" (*The Basic Works of Aristotle*, ed. Richard McKeon [New York: Random House, 1941], pp. 750–51).

[48] *Ibid.*, p. 751.

[49] *Ibid.*, p. 750.

of the meaning of the name, or of an equivalent nominal formula. . . . But it is difficult thus to learn the definition of things the existence of which we do not genuinely know. . . . Another kind of definition is a formula exhibiting the cause of a thing's existence. Thus the former signfies without proving, but the latter will clearly be a quasi-demonstration of essential nature. . . . On the other hand, the definition of immediates is an indemonstrable positing of essential nature. (*Posterior Analytics* II.10.93b28–94a10).[50]

The range of real definitions, from the "quasi-demonstration" to "indemonstrable positing," is stated to differ from demonstrations of essential nature merely in "grammatical form"— the linguistic "arrangement of [the definition's] terms"[51]— while the examples given for nominal definitions are mathematical concepts.[52] Thus the bases of both kinds of definition remain discursive and the exclusively logical grounds for the categorical distinction between them, undeduced.

Leibniz, preceding Kant, in his *Schriften zur Logik und Methodenlehre* (1684), founds the distinction between "nominal" and "real definitions" upon the sequential analysis ("Aufzählung der Merkmale") carried out in the former as opposed to the exposition, as in a geometrical proof, of the "possibility" of an object given in the latter.[53] He also concedes, however, that once formulated and "accepted," the "truths" of nominal definitions may be substituted for real definitions,[54]

---

[50] *Ibid.*, pp. 169–70.

[51] *Ibid.*, p. 170.

[52] *Ibid.*, p. 166 ("for the geôméter assumes the meaning of the word triangle, tion of something supersensory]; and the major definition of the sublime as shall prove in defining essential nature? Triangle? . . . if we consider the methods of defining actually in use . . . *why* should the thing named in the definition exist? Why, in other words, should this be the formula defining circle? One might equally well call it the definition of mountain copper . . .").

[53] G. W. Leibniz, *Hauptschriften zur Grundlegung der Philosophie*, Hrsg. Ernst Cassirer (Hamburg: Felix Meiner Verlag, 1966), I:41, 43.

[54] *Ibid.*, I:44: "Hieraus erhellt, dass jede Realdefinition zum mindesten die positive Behauptung einer Möglichkeit in sich schliesst. Ferner sind zwar die Benennungen willkürlich, dennoch aber folgen, wenn sie einmal gesetzt sind, aus ihnen notwendige Konsequenzen und Wahrheiten, die zwar von dem einmal angenommenen Charakteren abhängen, trotzdem aber real sind" [From

and describes real definitions themselves as arising from an "analysis carried out to its end"[55]—the possibility of which, as discussed earlier, is disproven and replaced by the concept of *a priori* synthetic definitions in Kant.[56] The distinction between real and nominal definitions is also drawn upon by Pascal in an essay devoted unusually to methodology, "Réflexions sur la géometrie en général; De l'esprit géométrique et de l'art de persuader" (1658–59?).[57] As the conjunctive title of the essay suggests, Pascal's understanding of cognition departs from a discursive model of logic linking mathematics to rhetoric as well as semiotics.[58] In opposition to both Leibniz and Kant, he in

---

this it becomes clear, that every real definition contains within itself at least the positive contention of a possibility. Furthermore, while designations are indeed arbitrary, once they are posited, necessary consequences and truths follow from them, which while dependent upon the accepted (denominating) characters, are nevertheless real].

[55] *Ibid.*, II:169 ("Schriften zur Metaphysik II" [1692]): "Überdies besteht noch ein grosser Unterschied zwischen den verschiedenen Arten der Realdefinitionen. . . . Führt [die Definition] . . . die Analyse bis ans Ende und bis zu den ursprünglichen Begriffen durch, ohne nur das Geringste vorauszusetzen, das eines *a priorischen* Beweises seiner Möglichkeit bedürfte, dann ist die Definition vollkommen oder eine *wesentliche*" [Beyond this there exists yet a greater difference between the different kinds of real definitions. . . . If (the definition) carries the analysis out till its end and through to the original concepts, without having presupposed even the slightest that would have required an *a priori* proof of its possibility, then is such a definition complete, or an essential one].

[56] Kant, *Logik* A 220, VI:574.

[57] Pascal, *Oeuvres*, ed. L. Brunschvicg, P. Boutroux and Félix Gazier (Paris: Librairie Hachette, 1914), IX:240–90. The two parts of the essay, previously published separately, are considered in the Brunschvicg edition to belong to "a single writing of which they probably form two successive drafts" (see "Introduction," IX:231).

[58] Pascal's departure from the Aristotelian model of definitions resulting from his exclusive emphasis upon the *linguistic* articulation of cognition is well noted in Brunschvicg's commentary on the *Pensées et opuscules* (Paris: Librairie Hachette, 1909): "Pascal conforms here to the Aristotelian distinction between the definition of words and definition of things. Aristotle expressed in an inexact manner which falsified the notion a real difference between two kinds of definition which it is important to note here. In the latter case, an object being proposed to me, a horse, for instance, I search for its distinctive characteristics; the determination of these characteristics constitutes the definition of the thing. In the former case I possess a certain number of characteristics, for example: 'a figure delineated in one spatial place and

fact allies "définitions de noms" with the "freely" made definitions of geometry, indicating, moreover, their tendency to overlap with "définitions de choses" when attempting to define concepts of mathematical discourse which are not purely mathematical in origin: the *choses* of discourse, as they are called by Pascal, or, as they are also called by Leibniz after him, "mots primitifs."[59] Kant, following Leibniz, goes on in sec. 106 to identify mathematical definitions as "real." But the consequences of that identification, once made within the context of the *Critique*, entail a rupture no less between Kant's and Leibniz's own epistemologies than between the two categories of definition themselves. In terms of the literary, rather than explicitly epistemological, ordering of the forms of meaning, the separation between kinds of cognitive statements Kant's *Logic* proposes signifies a break between the semantic possibilities of poetry and representational prose. For Kant's analysis of definitions further specifies that the "names" attributed "arbitrarily," because only nominally, with definitive meaning

---

formed by two right angles which cut each other two by two,' and I seek whether there exists an object, at least an ideal one, to which these characteristics pertain, the determination of the object with the aid of these characteristics constitutes the mathematical definition. Now it is remarkable that Pascal does not indicate here one or the other of these kinds of definition: it is in truth a denomination, and all denomination, being conventional, is arbitrary" (p. 166).

[59] Pascal, *Oeuvres*, IX:253; Leibniz, *Hauptschriften* . . . , I:41: "Die Nominaldefinition besteht in der Aufzählung der Merkmale oder der Konstituentien, die hinreichen, das Objekt von allen anderen zu unterscheiden. Wenn man hierin fortfährt und diese Konstituentien wiederum in ihre Bestimmungen auflöst, so gelangt man schliesslich zu den primitiven Begriffen, die entweder, absolut genommen, keine Bestimmungen oder doch keine solche haben, die von uns weiter erklärt werden können" [The nominal definition lies in the enumeration of the characteristics or constituents that suffice to distinguish the object from all other objects. When one proceeds therein and further breaks down these constituents into their determinations, so one arrives finally at primitive concepts that, seen absolutely, have either no determinations or none that can be further explained by us].

The necessary hypothesis of the concept of a "mot primitif," arising whenever philosophy considers the epistemological status of its own constitutive discourse, has been most significantly treated in contemporary philosophy under the designations "white" or "erased" metaphors in Jacques Derrida's "La mythologie blanche," *Poétique* 5 (1971).

are themselves the only objects which may be made known to us through "experience." The second moment of sec. 106 begins: "Erfahrungsgegenstände erlauben bloss Nominalerklärungen"—"Experiential objects allow for merely nominal explanations." All that we know on the basis of experience—which, it is the founding premise of the *Critique* to remind us, *is all that we know*—is restricted to an exclusively nominal significance. The passage in full prohibits any confusion of nominal knowledge with real:

2. Erfahrungsgegenstände erlauben bloss Nominalerklärungen.—Logische Nominal-Definitionen gegebener Verstandesbegriffe sind von einem Attribut hergenommen; Real-Definitionen hingegen aus dem Wesen der Sache, dem ersten Grunde der Möglichkeit. Die letztern enthalten also das, was jederzeit der Sache zukommt—das Realwesen derselben.—Bloss verneinende Definitionen können keine Real-Definitionen heissen, weil verneinende Merkmale wohl zur Unterscheidung einer Sache von andern eben so gut dienen können, als bejahende, aber nicht zur Erkenntnis der Sache ihrer innern Möglichkeit nach.

In Sachen der Moral müssen immer Real-Definitionen gesucht werden;—dahin muss alles unser Bestreben gerichtet sein.—Real-Definitionen gibt es in der Mathematik; denn die Definition eines willkürlichen Begriffs ist immer *real*.[60]

2. Experiential objects allow for merely nominal explanations.—Logical nominal definitions of given concepts of understanding are taken from an attribute; real definitions, by contrast, from the essence of the thing, the first ground of its possibility. The latter thus contain that which always pertains to the thing—the real being of the same.—Definitions based on mere negation cannot be called real definitions, because negating attributes can serve to distinguish one thing from another just as well as

---

[60] Kant, *Logik* A 222, IV:576.

positing ones, but cannot serve toward the recognition of the thing according to its internal possibility.

In moral matters real definitions must always be searched for—all our striving must be directed in that direction. There are real definitions in mathematics; then the definition of an arbitrary concept is always *real*.

The distinction between "name explanations" and "cognitions of things" brought forward in Kant's deduction of the only possible epistemology bears with it the formal relation of epistemology itself—lexically, the "discourse of knowledge"—to the discourse known as narrative fiction. For the only certain knowledge discourse affords of all objects of experience, the "logical, nominal definition" of phenomenal perception, reduces those objects to their identification with a single, defining "attribute." The formulation of empirical perceptions proposed in the *Logic* thus resembles that of literary figurations already recognized for their "intended meaning": that gained at the loss of their reference to a "real being." In other words, knowledge—necessarily of experience—in Kant, reads like a poetry purified of all ambiguities: not a "poésie pure," but one whose "meaning" *must* be recognized as well as realized to be merely logically and nominally significant. The understanding, as well as the critical bracketing, of that "meaning" is assured by its limitation to single tokens of significance distinguished only in their relation to each other and replacing any relation between the naming and the "being of a thing." Just as every known experience in Kant's epistemology is the representation of an "appearance," the definitions of experience articulate appearances of meaning rather than articulating meaning itself. They use language as language is always used in the course of narrating a "fiction": as a relational medium for the representation of experience to which it (language) bears relationship only in name.

For the narration of a fiction departs from the premise of a *full* substitution of representation for experience. Whatever the credibility of its "content," the sense of sufficiency afforded by a representational fiction arises first from the coherence of its form: narration appears to exhaust, or to comprehend, experience by subordinating its representations to its causal structure, or "story." Thus fiction, as opposed to poetry, can only "tell" a story by designating a single, identifiable level of meaning; by speaking as if in names rather than words. That is, the language of the discourse we "know" to be fiction may, *as* fiction, do just about anything: it may compose and coordinate complex plots, exploiting the very notion of causality it appears to put into question; it may structure narrative action to imitate the scenes and suspense of drama; it may articulate physical settings as well as personal subjectivities, historical events as well as peculiarities of character, describe, develop, speculate, transform, and in so doing instruct and intrigue us, move, confuse, or simply amuse us. But in order to compose itself as a fiction of any fashion, the language of fiction must first function like a language of names, i.e., it must indicate the referents *meant* by the experience it defines in text. At the same time, the relationship of fiction to its referents, like that of names, is understood to be no less "arbitrary" and artificial in reality than binding in function. Thus, by definition, one never asks of a narrative called a "fiction," as of a poem, if its representations, even when most "realistic" or "historically" accurate, are true, nor for that matter considers a poem, even when narrative in form and overtly "fictive" or mythological in content, to be precisely an intentionally *nominal* rendering of reality, a fiction.

What we know of all we experience, of all those occurrences defined as they are narrated by the essential form of narrative *and* of grammar, predication, is, according to the logic of reason submitted to criticism, the nominal or prefigured knowledge afforded by a narrative fiction. Experience *is* narration in Kant, already envisioned or formally structured by the "intuitions" of time and space, connected sequentially by the central mental category of causality,[61] and known by no other means than those it names. Mathematical objects, of which we have

---

[61] See especially, Kant's deduction of the categories as "*a priori* cognitions" in "The Transcendental Deduction of Pure Concepts of Understanding," sec. 4, in the *First Critique*: "the categories are nothing other than the conditions of thinking internal to a possible experience, just as space and time contain the conditions for the intuition of the same" (*KrV* A 111, III:170).

no "experience," in the Kantian sense of a necessarily *a posteriori*, phenomenal experience, are thus, strictly speaking, not objects of knowledge at all but reality. The *Realwesen* of a thing, that which is "always pertinent to it" and "the first ground of its possibility,"[62] is defined in mathematical definitions, it should be recalled, as "what one understands by a word." The cognitive reality of a "thing" is, according to the *Critique*, not a "thing itself" (of which we can have no knowledge), nor its arbitrary designation as an object of experience, but the *word* for the thing itself: the word not as a "referent" or the representation of a referent (i.e., in Kant, of another representation),[63] since it is unrelated to experience and not in itself an intuition, nor as a figure standing arbitrarily for a referent and integrating it into a system of nominal meanings. The word "word" here instead articulates *and* designates the reality we neither "experience" nor narrate, which pure reason, separated from experience by criticism—in Kant's terms—"constructs."

Knowledge of reality, rather than of phenomena, in Kant, thus disrupts all logical and nominal narration. Discourse, or words, are the critical means of translating between philosophical reason and empirical experience. Yet real knowledge, Kant proposes, is as such neither philosophical nor experiential. It is not a narrative story told through causally connected representations, not the understanding of a narrative at all but of "a word": the means of representation which itself tells no story. Real knowledge, according to the *Critique*, would be to know not what words "mean" but why words *are*—the necessary and necessarily literary medium between cognition and experience. The *Logic* of Kant's *Critique*, like that of any discursive criticism, demonstrates that the real knowledge to-

---

[62] Kant, *Logik* A 222 IV:576. Cf. Aristotle's founding description of a real definition as linking the knowledge of a thing's internal causality to that of its existential reality: the words composing a real definition would be "a formula exhibiting the cause of a thing's existence" (*Posterior Analytics* II.10.93b39–40 [*The Basic Works of Aristotle*, p. 170]).

[63] Cf. *KrV* A 109, III:169: "Alle Vorstellungen haben, als Vorstellungen, ihren Gegenstand, und können selbst wiederum Gegenstände anderer Vorstellungen sein." [All representations, as representations, have their object, and can themselves in turn be the objects of other representations].

ward which discursive knowledge inevitably "strives," but which, at the same time (recalling Kleist), it can never claim to "possess," is precisely what one understands under "discourse" itself: "was man unter einem Worte versteht."

The Appearance of the Sublime
in the *Third Critique*

If our knowledge of experience shares the discursive characteristics of a representational fiction, the fundamental problem posed by Kant's critical epistemology is that of defining what "real," or nonrepresentational, nonnominal cognition would be like before it itself is figured as an object of experience. It remains to be "known" how we *can* know in a way which does not represent anything else but is itself, arbitrarily and nonreferentially, "constructive." The *Critique* must demonstrate how our necessarily discursive understanding of a definition understood *as* discourse would operate. Or, in more "concrete" terms, the terms of "reality" offered here, Kant's epistemology must afford us knowledge of what it would be like to read a definition and thereby read *only* "what one understands under a word": to read what always pertains to words themselves rather than their significance in pertaining to a narrative relating phenomena as "experience."

The question of "what it would be like" already indicates that in order to pursue the logical consequences of a *critical* theory of knowledge, we continue to need a representation of some kind.[64] The areas specified by Kant to be those articu-

---

[64] The same problem is articulated by Kant in his extension of the formal mental "categories" to the context of empirical phenomena, "in order to show how it is at all possible that *pure concepts* of the understanding can be applied to phenomena." (*KrV* B 177, III:187: "um nämlich die Möglichkeit zu zeigen, wie *reine Vertstandesbegriffe* auf Erscheinungen überhaupt angewandt werden können.") The fact, Kant explains, that the concepts of philosophy, unlike those of "all other sciences," "are heterogeneous," signifies that there "must be a third something . . . an intermediary representation" that "enables" that "application" ["In all other sciences, where the concepts through which the object is generally thought are not so different and heterogeneous from those which represent it *in concreto* as it is given, it is unnecessary, because of the application of the former to the latter, to give a special exposition. Now it is

lated by "Real-Definitionen"—"(die) Mathemmatik" and "Sachen der Moral"[65]—suggest that the field of representation to which we should look is that in which mathematics and moral matters are seen to meet: Kant's "Analytic," in the *Critique of Judgment*, "of the Sublime." For reasons which should become clear, Kant's deduction of an *a priori* faculty of judgment is itself not central to the analysis of Kant carried out in this investigation. The tendency of literary criticism to focus exclusively upon this particular branch of Kant's tripartite critical project speaks most forcefully for the misapprehension with which Kant's *Critique* has continued to be received since its early adoption for pedagogical purposes by such major figures in the theory of aesthetics as Schiller and Coleridge.[66] For

---

clear that there must be a third something which must stand in similitude with categories on the one hand and with appearances on the other . . ." (III:187)].

This "third," or "intermediary representation," Kant explains, "would have to be pure (fully nonempirical) and yet *intellectual* on the one hand, and *sensual* on the other" (III:188). In this particular case, the "mediating representation" described is the *Schema* (III:189). As the intermediary representations necessitated by the logical development of the *Critique* itself, the schemata may be seen to represent the necessity of the entire "Third" (intermediary and heterogeneous) Critique.

See also Andrew Gelley's excellent consideration of the Kantian schemata as representing an "interplay between the phenomenal and the linguistic" (or "sensible and conceptual") comparable to Roman Jakobson's well-known hypothesis of the movement between the paradigmatic (metaphoric) and syntagmatic (metonymic) poles constituting poetic language, in "Metonymy, Schematism and the Space of Literature," *New Literary History* 3 (1980), pp. 469–87 (p. 484).

[65] See footnote 60.

[66] I refer of course primarily to Coleridge's *Biographia Literaria* and Schiller's *Ästhetische Briefe*, works that translate the epistemological systematization of aesthetic concepts offered in the *Third Critique* into principles of "aesthetic instruction." An important exception to this ultimately neo-Kantian, while chronologically post-Kantian, tendency is Walter Benjamin's analysis of the concept of "criticism," rather than of aesthetics, in the thought of the early romantics: his *Magister* dissertation, "Der Begriff der Kunstkritik in der deutschen Romantik" *Gesammelte Schriften* [Frankfurt: Suhrkamp, 1974], I.1:7–122). Benjamin's own concept of the criticism of art can be identified, in that work, to develop most directly from Kant's concept of epistemological criticism.

The most recent critical philosophical treatment—concentrating on Kant's discussion of the beautiful—of the distinctively aesthetic relation between the

no volume of Kant's investigations is in a critical sense less literary, less conscious of the problems posed by the intervention of discourse in reason, than the *Critique of Judgment*, which, itself intended to intervene as mediator between the *Critiques of Pure*, and *of Practical Reason*, was placed after them in the analytically sequential, but logically *post factum* position of the *Third Critique*. Indeed, perhaps its own *a posteriori* placement has contributed to the fact that, rather than viewed, as Kant proposes,[67] as the mental intermediary between the possibility of empirical understanding deduced in the *First Critique*, and that of nonempirical reason deduced in the *Second*, the *Third Critique* has been overwhelmingly identified with its relation to the former alone: with the "feeling of pleasure" experienced when the empirical perception of a "purposeful" or "beautiful" "form" brings "understanding and imagination" into the "free play" of "reciprocal harmony."[68] The widely held and less frequently examined notions of aesthetic "pleasure" and "free play"—post-Enlightenment conventions of the criticism of all artistic media—are directly traceable to Kant's deduction of the role of *understanding*, rather than individual vision or flight of fancy, in the judgment of the beautiful. At the same time, any singular adherence to those conceptions must fall short of the full breadth of aesthetic mediation as Kant conceived it. For while the judgment of beauty, or aesthetic "taste," is most closely related in the *Third Critique* to phenomenal understanding, the judgment of the sublime is related

(pictorial) "presentation" and (discursive) "representation" of "truth" in the *Third Critique*, is Jacques Derrida's *La verité en peinture* (Paris: Flammarion, 1978, p. 10, *et passim*).

[67] See Kant's "Vorrede" to the *Kritik der Urteilskraft*, in particular: "Ob nun die *Urteilskraft*, die in der Ordnung unserer Erkenntnisvermögen zwischen dem Verstande und der Vernunft ein Mittelglied ausmacht" (Kant, *KUk* BV, X:74) [Now whether the *power of judgment*, which constitutes a middle link, in the order of our faculties of cognition, between understanding and reason], and sec. III of the "Einleitung": "Von der Kritik der Urteilskraft, als einem Verbindumgsmittel der zwei Teile der Philosophie zu einem Ganzen" (B XX–XXVI, X:84–87) ["On the Critique of Judgment as a means of joining the two parts of the philosophy into a whole"].

[68] For the initial deductions and coordination of these key concepts, see, in particular, in the "Analytik des Schönen," B 27–35, X:131–36.

to *reason*,[69] deduced at the outset of the *First Critique* by Kant, and reiterated in the Introduction to the *Critique of Judgment*, to be separated from understanding by the "chasm" dividing the "suprasensory" from sensory "appearances": "die grosse Kluft, welche das Übersinnliche von den Erscheinungen trennt."[70] While the universal recognition of beauty depends upon the formal power of understanding, the sublime is recognized to be "found" in a "formless object" perceived "at cross-purposes with the power of judgment" itself.[71] The su blime is

[69] See, in the "Analytik des Erhabenen," B 94, X:178–79: "Also, gleichwie die ästhetische Urteilskraft in Beurteilung des Schönen die Einbildungskraft in ihrem freien Spiele auf den *Verstand* bezieht, um mit dessen *Begriffen* überhaupt (ohne Bestimmung derselben) zusammenzustimmen: so bezieht *sich* dasselbe Vermögen in Beurteilung eines Dinges als erhabenen auf die *Vernunft*, um zu deren *Ideen* (unbestimmt welchen) subjektiv übereinzustimmen . . ." [Thus, just as aesthetic judgment in the judgment of the beautiful relates imagination, in its free play, to *understanding*, in order to concord with the latter's concepts (without any determination of them), so the same faculty, in the judgment of a thing as sublime, relates itself to *reason*, in order to agree subjectively with the latter's *ideas* (undetermined which ideas) . . ."].

[70] *Ibid.*, B LIII, X:106; see also B XIX–XX, X:83–84, on the bridging of the "unoverseeable chasm" [*unübersehbare Kluft*] by way of a "concept" (that of aesthetic judgment) that can itself yield "neither theoretical nor practical knowledge."

[71] "Analytik des Erhabenen," B 74–76, X:165–66: "das Erhabene . . . an einem formlosen Gegenstande zu finden . . . [welcher] der Form nach *zwar* zweckwidrig für unsere Urteilskraft . . . und gleichsam gewalttätig für die Einbildungskraft erscheinen mag, *aber* dennoch nur um desto erhabener zu sein geurteilt wird" [to find the sublime in a formless object, which, while it works at cross-purposes with our judgment in its form, . . . and simultaneously may appear to do violence to our imagination, is only for all that judged to be that much more sublime].

Kant's articulation of the antiformal premise of the sublime is—from the *a priori* formal standpoint of his critical undertaking—scrupulously hesitant thoughout the *Third Critique*. In the "Einleitung" he states that the *Critique of Judgment* must "collapse" or "decompose" (*zerfallen*) into two main parts: "the judgment of taste . . . related to the beautiful," and that judgment "sprung from a feeling of the spirit and related to the sublime." In order for the "pleasure" taken in judgement to stem from the judging "subject," as well as the "object" judged, "the view of objects according to their form, even their nonform" [ihrer Form, ja selbst ihrer Unform nach], must be included in the critical investigation of judgment (B XLVIII; X:103).

Within the "Analytik des Erhabenen" itself, the sublime is opposed to the beautiful as being located "also' in formless objects [The beautiful in nature

in fact described by Kant to border upon disabling understanding by setting its link to the beautiful, the power of imagination to bring together sensory intuitions,[72] in contradiction with the imageless, or suprasensory, power of pure reason, thus denying us any access to objective, "positive" pleasure as it prohibits imagination's free play.[73]

Part of the reason for the tendency of readers of the *Third Critique* to collapse its analyses of the beautiful and the sublime may lie in the natural difficulty involved in maintaining

---

touches upon the form of the object, which exists in limitation; the sublime, by opposition, is also to be found in a formless object . . ." (B 75, X:165)], and a sense of "pleasure" (*Wohlfallen*) is said to be found in the consideration of an object "even when it is considered as formless" (B 83, X:170–71). [See also B 79, X:168, for Kant's further attempt to distinguish between form and formlessness even while integrating the latter into his formal system: "aesthetic judgments which touch upon the form of the object" are conceptualized as "qualitative"; those which judge the "formlessness" "we call sublime" are considered to be "quantitative," thus leading into Kant's discussion, immediately following this observation, of the "mathematical sublime" (sec. 25, X:169–84).] These cautious formulations on Kant's part should not be construed as a retreat from the necessarily radical nature of the sublime which he deduces critically. It is rather precisely the problem of indicating a radical formlessness within the context of a critical project that founds itself, and its opposition to idealism, upon the strict limitations of formal knowledge, which is articulated each time Kant falls short of directly constating that which, in the terms of his *Critique*, he cannot "know": *Unform*.

[72] See, in the "Analytik des Schönen," B 28, X:132: "Nun gehören zu einer Vorstellung, wodurch ein Gegenstand gegeben wird, damit überhaupt daraus Erkenntnis werde, *Einbildungskraft* für die Zusammensetzung des Mannigfaltigen der Anschauung und *Verstand* für die Einheit des Begriffs . . ." [Now to a representation through which an object is given, so that a cognition can come of it at all, belong imagination, for the bringing together of the manifold of the intuition and *understanding* for the unity of the concept . . ."].

[73] Cf. the "Allgemeine Anmerkung" [zur] "Analytik des Erhabenen," B 117, X:195: "Das Wohlgefallen am Erhabenen der Natur ist daher auch nur *negativ* (statt dessen das am Schönen *positiv* ist), nämlich ein Gefühl der Beraubung der Freiheit der Einbildungskraft durch sie selbst, indem sie nach einem andern Gesetze, als dem des empirischen Gebrauchs, zweckmässig bestimmt wird" [Pleasure taken in the sublime of nature is thus also only *negative* (instead of, as in the beautiful, *positive*), namely, a feeling of the robbing of the freedom of the imagination through itself, in that it is purposefully determined according to a law other than that of empirical use]; and the description of the "feeling of the sublime" as "an act of violence against our imagination" [gewalttätig für unsere Einbildungskraft], already cited (footnote 71).

the separations between the individual mental "faculties" (*Vermögen*) of understanding, imagination and reason, adduced by Kant to the two different modalities of aesthetic judgment. The reason, however, that the confusion of the sublime and the beautiful usually accrues to the conception of the beautiful lies in the larger, rational difficulty structuring the entire *Critique*. For "reason" is not only not to be mistaken for "understanding" in Kant: it is most importantly deduced in the *Second Critique* to pertain not to speculation at all but to *practice*. That is, the *Critique of Pure Reason* yields as its consequence the *a priori* laws of understanding, or of reason limited practically to conceiving empirical phenomena, whereas the *Critique of Practical Reason*, paradoxically, but in conformity with its title, aims at deducing a reason whose "practice" would itself be pure, i.e., independent of its application to any phenomenal field. Just as we traditionally associate reason with purely theoretical speculation and understanding with an applied or practical context, the concept of the sublime is most readily assimilated to that of the freedom of imagination which has been equated with our perception of beauty since Kant. The sublime, however, in invoking reason, is included by Kant in the realm of practice: what distinguishes the occurrence of the sublime for us is "the use" it makes of the sensory objects of imagination, rather than any disinterested contemplation of the "purposeless purposefulness" of their form.[74] What identifies the sublime is the impossibility of ob-

[74] The idea of the "use," rather than cognitive role, of imagination is first introduced by Kant as grounds for the appendixlike status of the "theory" of the sublime in the "aesthetic judgment of the purposefulness of nature" [(was) aus der Theorie (des Erhabenen) einen blossen Anhang zur ästhetischen Beurteilung der Zweckmässigkeit der Natur macht]: "weil dadurch keine besondere Form in dieser [der Natur] vorgestellt, sondern nur ein zweckmässiger Gebrauch, den die Einbildungskraft von ihrer Vorstellung macht, entwickelt wird" (B 78, X:167) [because through (the theory of the sublime) no particular form in nature is represented, but only a purposeful use by the imagination of its representations is developed]. In the description of the mathematical sublime, that of the "absolutely large" (*schlechthin gross*), however, it is the "use" which "judgment makes . . . of certain objects," rather than the size of "the sensory objects" themselves, which is considered "schlechthin gross," that is, the very source of the sublime (B 81, 85, X:169, 172). Finally, the "feeling" of

jectively experiencing that which reason, at the practical expense of the senses, can think. Thus, while judgment of the beautiful depends upon understanding, as delimited by the relations and concepts of phenomenal cognition, judgment of the sublime is bound by the pure power of the practice of reason to think "ideas" without limitation:[75] to think the non-phenomenal, nonperceptual realm of practice removed irrevocably from the sphere of cognitive reason by the *First Critique*.

While organized as an analysis proceeding by logical steps or "moments" and taking part in the larger tripartite scheme organizing each volume of the *Critique* (i.e., the sequence: "Analytic," "Dialectic," and "Theory of Method"),[76] Kant's

---

the sublime, that of an "unattainability" which "obligates us . . . to *think*" that which we cannot "objectively represent," is attributed to "the use of imagination" by reason (B 115–16, X:193–94).

[75] The "ideas" thought in the sublime continue to be thought in Kant *non*-ideally, that is, "*as* representation," yet it is the unlimited "totality" of "Nature" which is at once named as the subject of that representation. See B 115–16, X:194: "die Natur selbst in ihrer Totalität, als Darstellung von etwas ubersinnlichem, zu denken" [to think nature itself in its totality as the representation of something supersensory]; and the major definition of the sublime as analogous to a representation of nature: "Man kann das Erhabene so beschreiben: es ist ein Gegenstand [der Natur], *dessen Vorstellung das Gemüt bestimmt, sich die Unerreichbarkeit der Natur als Darstellung von Ideen zu denken*" [One can describe the sublime the following way: it is an object (of nature) *whose (a posteriori) representation determines our mental state to think the unattainability of nature as a(n) (a priori) representation of ideas*] (B 115, X:193).

[76] Due to the distinctive nature attributed by Kant to judgments of beauty, i.e., their relationship to subjective pleasure and independence from conceptualization, the last of these three basic branches, the *Methodenlehre*, is included under another group of judgments concluding the *Third Critique*: the "teleological," or "intellectual" and "objective" judgments, which, unlike those of beauty, refer to a "purpose" inhering in nature rather than in a "Produkt der Kunst" (B 286, X:318). Kant's differentiation, in the "Analytik der teologischen Urteilskraft," between the kind of formal purposiveness which appeals to our sense of pleasure and which we call "beautiful," and that which is conceptually, rather than sensuously, given and called "objective" or "intellectual," includes an explanatory aside on the inappropriateness of nominally combining the two into the popular designation, "intellectual beauty." Perhaps no better gloss than this concise observation can be found for the mysterious spirit addressed in Shelley's famous poem: "Man ist gewohnt, die er-

exposition of the sublime is in fact not absent of moments displaying the logical difficulties which any description, not to speak of deduction, of the sublime must raise. The complexity of an analytic process, whose "deductive moments" necessarily contain textual moments in which analysis and description appear at odds, cannot be simply accounted for by an identification of its systematic and critical functions as has been summarily offered here. Furthermore, any excursus, however brief, on the sublime itself may seem particularly irrelevant to an investigation of that form of literature—narrative fiction—least given by its own sequential nature to what we conceive to be moments of sublimity. But in light of the restrictions placed upon the discourse of experience in the *Logic*, the proximity of the sublime to pure, or nonexperiential, reason and accom-

---

wähnten Eigenschaften, sowohl der geometrischen Gestalten, als auch wohl der Zahlen, *wegen* einer gewissen, aus der Einfachheit ihrer Konstruktion nicht erwarteten, Zweckmässigkeit derselben a priori zu allerlei Erkenntnisgebrauch, *Schönheit* zu nennen; und spricht z. B. von dieser oder jener *schönen* Eigenschaft des Zirkels, welche auf diese oder jene Art entdeckt wäre. Allein es ist keine ästhetische Beurteilung, durch die wir sie zweckmässig finden; keine Beurteilung ohne Begriff, die eine blosse *subjektive* Zweckmässigkeit im freien Spiele unserer Erkenntnisvermögen bermerklich macht: sondern eine intellektuelle nach Begriffen, welche eine objektive Zweckmässigkeit, d. i. Tauglichkeit zu allerlei (ins Unendliche mannigfaltigen) Zwecken deutlich zu erkennen gibt. Man müsste sie eher eine *relative* Vollkommenheit, als eine Schönheit der mathematischen Figur nennen. Die Benennung einer *intellektuellen Schönheit* kann auch überhaupt nicht füglich erlaubt werden; weil sonst das Wort Schönheit alle bestimmte Bedeutung, oder das intellektuelle Wohlgefallen allen Vorzug vor dem sinnlichen verlieren müsste."

[One is accustomed to name the already mentioned properties of geometrical figures as well as numbers, *beauty*, because of a certain, and, from the simplicity of their construction, unexpected a priori purposiveness of (such figures) for various cognitive uses; and one speaks, for example, of this or that *beautiful* property of the circle, which in this or that way was discovered. It is however not through an aesthetic judgment that we find them purposive; no judgment without concepts which makes a merely *subjective* purposiveness in free play noticeable to our faculties of cognition: but an intellectual judgment according to concepts, which makes an objective purposiveness, i.e., a usefulness for infinitely varied purposes, clearly recognizable. One should have named it the *relative perfection* rather than the beauty of the mathematical figure. The designation of *intellectual beauty* is thus also not at all permissable; because if it were the word beauty would lose all determined meaning, or intellectual pleasure, all priority over the sensory] (B 277–78, X:312).

panying distance from sensory representation, imply a relation of the sublime to the articulations of "real definitions." And "real definitions," it should be recalled, are defined by Kant to "*construct*" "concrete" knowledge discursively, thus departing from the model of knowledge by which all experience, once defined, is turned into a merely nominal, narrative fiction.

As the concept of a definition is effectively replaced in the *Logic* by those of "description" and "declaration," the term "judgment" is itself fully appropriate to the analysis of neither the beautiful nor the sublime in the *Third Critique*. Since every experience of phenomena, according to Kant, is in the first place a formally coherent, mental representation, *all* phenomenal perception may as well be called aesthetic "judgment," whether or not every experience, eventually recognized to have been "purposeless," may also be considered, at that moment, to have been "beautiful." Similarly, the "ability to think" in excess of any "measure" or "form" of sensory experience[77] brings the sublime closer to the "declarations of thoughts" identified with real definitions than to an empirical act of understanding, or judgment. The specific modalities of the sublime identified by Kant, the "mathematical" and the "dynamic" (sec. 25–28), both bring the "suprasensory" "demands" of reason[78] in conflict with the sensory determinations of imagination.[79] The two modalities are in fact effec-

---

[77] "*Erhaben ist, was auch nur denken zu können ein Vermögen des Gemüts beweiset, das jeden Massstab der Sinne übertrifft*" [*Sublime is that which proves, even only in the ability to think it, a faculty of the mental state which exceeds every sensory measure*] (B 86, X:172).

[78] "die Stimme der Vernunft, welche zu allen gegebenen Grössen, selbst denen, die zwar niemals ganz aufgefasst werden können . . . Totalität fordert" (B 91, X:176–77) [the voice of reason which, of all given dimensions, even those that can never be fully conceived, . . . demands totality].

[79] "Denn so wie Einbildungskraft und *Verstand* in der Beurteilung des Schönen durch ihre Einhelligkeit, so bringen Einbildungskraft und *Vernunft* hier durch ihren Widerstreit, subjektive Zweckmässigkeit der Gemütskräfte hervor: nämlich, ein Gefühl, dass wir reine selbständige Vernunft haben, oder ein Vermögen der Grössenschätzung, dessen Vorzüglichkeit durch nichts anschaulich gemacht werden kann, als durch die Unzulänglichkeit desjenigen Vermögens, welches in Darstellung der Grössen (sinnlicher Gegenstände) selbst unbegrenzt ist" (B 99, X:182) [Then just as imagination and *understanding* through their harmony, so imagination and *reason* bring forth the

tive deductive means because they serve to demonstrate, as the immediacy of the sublime requires, the very necessity of their own negation as mediation. Stated in brief, the mathematical sublime arises in the attempt of reason to think as a synchronically "given whole," that which the comparative measurement and incremental number systems of mathematics must fail to represent: "the absolutely large," or "the infinite . . . in its totality."[80] The dynamic sublime, occasioned by our confrontation with the "unmitigable power of nature," leads to the "discovery" ("as long as we find ourselves" in a position of personal "safety") of the power of "our faculty of reason": a power "which is not nature," and which is "called forth" by the recognition of our natural "physical powerlessness."[81] The dynamic sublime thus apprehends nature as an active subject of power to which no means of mental representation, in being static, can correspond. The mathematical sublime, by contrast, involves means of abstract or symbolic figuration which, always capable of surpassing any given object in nature, can never represent nature, or its own progressive movement, as a synchronic, static totality. Both modalities therefore offer particularly useful categories for a formal analysis seeking to maintain the sublime—if the sublime itself is to remain an *aesthetic* concept—on the margins of representation. For the fundamental instance of "formlessness" these subordinating categories serve to "represent" is an imbalance, irresolvable through any transformation, between the very relations of representation.

Yet *as* categories the mathematical and dynamic sublime must also be recognized to run counter to the occurrence they are employed as logical means to describe. For just as any remaining trace of formal representation, attributed on the basis of the critical limitation of reason to the sublime, remains in

subjective purposefulness of the mental powers through their conflict: namely, a feeling that we have pure, self-sufficient reason, or a faculty for assessing dimensions whose superiority can be made visible through nothing other than the insufficiency of the former faculty (imagination), which in the representation of the dimensions (of sensory objects) is itself unlimited].

[80] See in particular, *ibid.*, B 81, X:169; B 91–92, X:176–77; and B 99, X:181.

[81] *Ibid.*, B 104–105, X:185–86.

conflict with the unlimited, and thus unrepresentable, "ideas" the sublime brings to mind, so the "mathematical" and the "dynamic," once conceptualized as modalities, must themselves be seen as critical concepts serving the analysis of an essentially noncritical occurrence, i.e., one brought about by specifically nonconceptual, directly perceptual means. In short, insofar as it does succeed in its task of analysis—and indeed it would be difficult to name the philosopher before or since Kant whose *analysis* of the sublime significantly surpasses his—Kant's investigation of the sublime removes us further, in Kant's own terms, from its "real definition." Thus, it is without any sense of the pejorative that it can and should be said, that there is nothing itself inductive of the sublime in Kant's "Analytic of the Sublime."

There is, however, a description of the sublime which occurs twice in the *Third Critique* and is itself neither subjected to analysis nor ascribed conceptually to any modality. That description, to return to the *Logic*, may be read instead as an "arbitrary" construction: a logically undifferentiated, or "real," "definition." The difficulty it raises is that just as the possibility of such a definition is denied to all phenomenal or representational cognition, the sublime it presents seems to trespass upon the knowledge we *must* have of experience: the critically prefigured knowledge afforded by a representational fiction.

The first time this description arises is in fact not directly within the "Analytic," and the occurrence referred to is not specifically named the sublime. At the close of the "General Remarks" to the "Analytic of the Beautiful," Kant ostensibly introduces a further distinction between two modalities of beauty. The paragraph is, however, the very last in the *Third Critique* before the "Analytic of the Sublime" begins, and may be seen as a transitional moment in which the category of the beautiful is made, by the very course of its analysis, to give way to the sublime. The particular syntactic difficulty of the passage calls for a translation as closely parallel to it as possible within English word order:

> Noch sind schöne Gegenstände von schönen Aussichten auf Gegenstände . . . zu unterscheiden. In den letztern

scheint der Geschmack nicht sowohl an dem, was die Einbildungskraft in diesem Felde *auffasst*, als vielmehr an
dem, was sie hierbei zu *dichten* Anlass bekommt, d.i. an
den eigentlichen Phantasien, womit sich das Gemüt unter-
hält, indessen dass es durch die Mannigfaltigkeit, auf die
das Auge stösst, kontinuierlich erweckt wird, zu haften;
so wie etwa bei dem Anblick der veränderlichen Gestalten
eines Kaminfeuers, oder eines rieselnden Baches, welche
beide keine Schönheiten sind, aber doch für die Einbildungskraft einen Reiz bei sich führen, weil sie ihr freies
Spiel unterhalten.[82]

Beautiful objects still remain to be differentiated from
beautiful views of objects. . . . In the case of the latter,
taste appears not to adhere so much to that which imagination, in this field, *comprehends*, as to the occasion it receives hereby *to compose poetry*, i.e., to adhere to the fantasies of its own with which our mental disposition
converses while it is continuously awakened by way of the
variousness the eye stumbles upon; so, approximately, as
by the view of the changeable forms of a fire in a hearth,
or of a rippling brook, neither of which in themselves constitute beauty, but which yet both bring with them an attraction for imagination because they support [or main-
tain] its free play.

The beautiful view of an object is distinguished here from an
object judged to be "beautiful" in and of itself. The difficulty
in Kant's proposition of the distinction lies precisely in its own
traditionalism. For the difference between what "is," and what
we "view" as, "beautiful"—indeed the very conception of
such a difference—has been eliminated not only by the critical
limitation of beauty, like that of knowledge, to phenomenality, but by the premise that all judgments of phenomena are
universalities. While aesthetic judgments, as opposed to cognitions, rest upon no concept of their object and thus invoke
(at least in the case of the beautiful) subjective or mental "free
play," such "play" is itself recognized by the mind *as* aesthetic

---

[82] *Ibid.*, B 73, X:164; emphasis in text.

experience. It is not some ultimate decision about that experience which is considered by Kant to constitute an aesthetic
judgment: "play" in the *Third Critique is* "free" precisely in
the sense that it is *not* a game in which one side (is it or is it not
beautiful) will win. Thus aesthetic judgment in Kant is not
"subjective" in any of the private, nonanalytical or alogical, or
even self-reflexively phenomenological senses we now give the
term. It is instead termed "transcendentally subjective" because it names a formally universal experience. Thus, to state
of an object that it is beautiful is to state all that pertains to
one's "view of an object," as well as that of every reasoning
"subject" who can see. Yet Kant proposes a distinction his
own *Critique* has already made obsolete in order to introduce
a second modality of, or verb for, vision. To the mental act of
judging by the very virtue of seeing, designated *auffassen* (to
comprehend or conceive), he juxtaposes the action he names
dichten (to compose or write poetry). Both actions relate to the
"play" of "imagination," but the latter represents the possibility, at odds with the formal "comprehension" or "conception"
of objects of beauty, that *das Gemüt*, a fluid presence of mind,
mental state or disposition, will fix instead upon its own *Phantasien*. Whereas "auffassen," the act of understanding at sight,
is a visual modality whose definition might best be considered
the *Critique*'s entire deduction of phenomenally limited cognition, "dichten" can barely be considered a modality at all.
While attributed to imagination, it is described as an immediate occurrence rather than a mental operation: the event of the
eye's unforeseen meeting with nonconformity, its "happening
to come across . . . changeable forms" which themselves can
never be seen to crystallize into a "beauty" of form. "Dichten," the verbal infinitive of poetry, is a verb of vision so di-
vested of the modal qualities of formal comprehension that it
seems to happen *to* the eye, and to that sensory organ alone,
rather than serving to relate and subordinate sight to representation. Thus "dichten," like "[die] Mathematik" and "Sachen
der Moral," seems congruent with the requirements of a "real
definition" in that rather than discursively conceptualizing
empirical experience, it "arbitrarily" composes its own objects
of experience, the imagination's "Phantasien." Furthermore,

the function of the term "Phantasien" in Kant's critical thought should in no way be confused with the roles currently ascribed to it in our almost thoughtlessly post-Freudian discourse. For the mental "fantasies" referred to here do not derive imagined significance from displaced causal relations, recurrent substitutions for repressed images, or any other figural mechanism of hiding and revealing: the *fort/da* game of making meaning. Nor could "desire" ever be identified as their motivating force. A "fantasy" is instead Kant's word *for* poetry minus all considerations of poetic or imaged meaning. The "fantasies" of "dichten" are what the mind "converses with" when not representing sensory experience but discoursing with itself: when the "eye," the sensory link of the mind to formal representation, finds itself mentally immobilized by a continuous movement of forms, an unbroken and nonprogressive motion which, even while it is being perceived, affords the mind no single point or moment of empirical reference. The central pertinence of "dichten" to the sublime and strict divergence from the beautiful is decisively rendered in its second textual version. For reasons of economy, I cite and translate this page-long passage from the "General Remarks" to the "Analytic of the Sublime" with some abbreviation, including statements directly comprising the description in question and deleting Kant's extensive enumeration of the elements of knowledge that description means to exclude:

> Wenn man also den Anblick des bestirnten Himmels *erhaben* nennt, so muss man der Beurteilung desselben nicht Begriffe von Welten, von vernünftigen Wesen bewohnt . . . zum Grunde legen, sondern bloss, wie man ihn sieht, als ein weites Gewölbe, was alles befasst. . . . Eben so den Anblick des Ozeans nicht so, wie wir, mit allerlei Kenntnissen (die aber nicht in der unmittelbaren Anschauung enthalten sind) bereichert, ihn *denken* . . . sondern man muss den Ozean bloss, wie die Dichter es tun, nach dem, was der Augenschein zeigt, etwa, wenn er in Ruhe betrachtet wird, als einen klaren Wasserspiegel, der bloss vom Himmel begrenzt ist, aber ist er unruhig, wie einen

alles zu verschlingen drohenden Abgrund, dennoch erhaben finden können.[83]

Thus when one names the sight of the starred sky *sublime*,
so one must not lay concepts of worlds inhabited by rational beings . . . at the foundation of this judgment, but
rather simply the way one sees it, as an extensive vault
that touches all. . . . Just so must the sight of the ocean
[not be judged sublime] according to the way that we, en-
riched with miscellaneous bits of knowledge (which are,
however, not contained within immediate vision [or in-
tuition]), *think* it . . . but rather, merely as the poets do it,
according to that which the appearance in [or appearance
on the surface of] the eye shows—approximately, when it
is regarded while quiet, as a clear mirror of water which is
merely bounded by the sky, but when it is unquiet, as an
abyss threatening to devour all—must one still be able to
find [the ocean] sublime.

What "die Dichter" are stated here "to do," or what the verb
"dichten" in the previous passage does, stands in direct opposition to the description of poetry as "the beautiful art" of
Dichtkunst—a pleasurable form of linguistic play constructed
artificially of given concepts and appealing to our understanding—to which the literary in general is reduced throughout the *Third Critique*.[84] Moreover, the critical, and itself

[83] *Ibid.*, B 118–19, X:196; emphasis in text.

[84] See, in particular, in the section following the "Analytik des Erhabenen,"
the "Deduktion der reinen ästhetischen Urteile," B 137, X:211: "Daher lässt
sich ein junger Dichter von der Überredung, dass sein Gedicht schön sei, nicht
durch das Urteil des Publikums, noch seiner Freunde abbringen . . . ," and following [Thus it is that a young poet will not let himself be swayed from the
persuasion that his poem is beautiful by the judgment of his audience nor that
of his friends . . .]; the definition of *Dichtkunst* as "die Kunst," "ein freies Spiel
der Einbildungskraft als ein Geschäft des Verstandes anzuführen" [the art of
presenting the free play of imagination as the business of understanding] in the
paragraph on "redende Künste" under the "schöne Künste" (sec. 51), B 205,
X:258; and Kant's most lengthy description of *Dichtkunst* in the "Verglei-
chung des ästhetischen Werts der schönen Künste untereinander" (sec. 53), beginning with B 214, X:265, and ending with the statement which most clearly
presents *Dichtkunst* as the reversal of *dichten*: "[Die Dichtkunst] spielt mit
dem Schein, den sie nach Belieben bewirkt, ohne doch dadurch zu betrügen;

"merely" "approximately" translatable term for what poets see, *Augenschein*, introduces an intrusion of lexical *and* referential status upon the central cognitive concept of the entire *Critique*: the phenomenal form of the "Erscheinung" to which all possible knowledge is systematically limited and which every sensory *Anblick* has been posited, *a priori*, to take. "Augenschein," a new and never fully repeated lexical construction in Kant,[85] is adequately defined neither by the given concepts which compose it, "eye" and "[mere, or seeming] appearance," nor by its external, logical relations to other nominal referents in the description. Since the modality joining "Auge" to "Schein" cannot be objectively known with certainty, the construction of this word appears instead "arbitrary," "concrete," or fully "intuitive." Yet "Augenschein" *is* a word consisting *of* words with referential meanings, rather than a purely spatial form or nondiscursively delimited, geometrical figure. As a word we cannot understand *nominally*, or within the limits prescribed to discourse, its clarification would seem to come closest to demanding a "real definition."

For what the poets are "shown" in the "Augenschein" of the

---

denn sie erklärt ihre Beschäftigung selbst für blosses Spiel, welches gleichwohl vom Verstande und zu dessen Geschäfte zweckmässig gebraucht werden kann" (B:215, X:265–66) [(The art of poetry) plays with the seeming appearance which it effects at will, without, however, deceiving thereby; for it explains its occupation itself as mere play, which can nevertheless be used by understanding for its purposive occupations].

In accordance with the mental premises of the *Critique*, Kant proves less reductive in his consideration of the subjective conditions of "beautiful art"— "Genie," "Talent," and "Natur"— than in his discussions of the necessarily limited objects of art themselves (see B 183–84, X:243–44).

[85] The only other instance, to my knowledge, of a related construction in the *Critique* is remarkable in that, while almost compositionally identical, it connotes a radically contrary meaning. Its reference is neither to the discursive nor the sublime but to the beautiful in the plastic arts, in particular, painting. The "beautiful depiction," rather than abysslike vision, "of nature" is described here by Kant to be based upon an "artificial representation" combining *Sinnenschein* (seeming sensory appearance) with *Ideen*: "*die Malerkunst* als die zweite Art bildender Künste, welche den *Sinnenschein* künstlich mit Ideen darstellt, würde ich in die der schönen *Schilderung* der Natur . . . einteilen" (B:208–209, X:261) [The art of painting, as the second of plastic arts, which artificially represents the seeming appearance of the senses with ideas, I would categorize under (the art) of the beautiful depiction of nature].

ocean is anything but the cognitive "Erscheinung" of the ocean. In place of the finite particulars understood to be arbitrarily denoted by the word "ocean," what the poets see, is, "ocean": the infinitely flat (a "mirror of water" itself additionally "clear" of deceiving reflections) or the infinitely deep ("an abyss" destroying our own ground of perspective in "threatening to devour all"), and thus dimensionless *Realwesen* which appears to us in the form of the word. Rather than what we "know" to be named by "ocean," the nonconceptual sight of the poets sees "was man unter einem Worte versteht," when a word is not the logical and nominal means of designating meaning: of identifying an object, initiating a predicative statement, or even figurally creating meaning. The "Augenschein" of "ocean" is instead precisely what it appears to be: the static surface or unresting groundlessness "shown" by the word for the thing itself.

"Freedom" in the *Second Critique*

In using Kant's description of the "ocean" as seen by poets, to suggest the discourse of a "real definition," this analysis of course remains within the realm of sensory perception, and thus of representation, just as Kant's use of "the poets" and of the term, "Augenschein," maintains we still must be able to "find" what we "merely" see "sublime," and as his definition of the sublime, earlier in the "Analytic," insisted upon our ability to at least "think" nonsensory "ideas" in the form of representation.[86] The "ocean," even its "Augenschein," can be comprehended within a narrative *as long as it can be described*, and thus become an object of nominal signification. In attempting to indicate, from the sensory middle ground of the aesthetic, the potential scope of fully unmediated reason, Kant's descriptions of the sublime in the *Third Critique* proceed to represent instances of unmediated sensation. But in the *Second Critique*, the final focus of this analysis, Kant can be seen to face the problem of demonstrating the possibility of a "real definition" without any access to representation. For the defining aim of the *Critique of Practical Reason*, described in

[86] See footnote 75.

advance in the Preface to the *First Critique* as the singularly "important" and "positive use" against which the purpose-fully "negative" thrust of the *Critique* as a whole is to be weighed,[87] is the indication of the complete independence of reason from the senses. As should be recognized with regard to each part of the whole of Kant's critical project, the interest presented by the moment, to be considered next, in the *Second Critique* lies not in an inevitably relative, since ultimately tex-tual, assessment of its "success" or "failure," but in the con-sequences it poses for the *Critique*'s own major "representa-tion": that of the cognition of all experience as a coherent and nominal discourse, or narration.

The name for the independence from all sensory conditions in Kant is "freedom." "The concept of freedom," our *knowl-edge* of that independence as it is, rather than "appears," is designated by Kant in the Preface to the *Second Critique* as the *Schlussstein*, or architectonic "keystone," of "the entire build-ing of a system of pure, and even of speculative, reason."[88] The only object of knowledge in the *Critique* deriving in no meas-ure from sensory perception or formal intuition, and thus nec-essarily divorced from all mechanisms of phenomenal cogni-tion, the "freedom" of reason in its moral use[89] is the

---

[87] Kant, *KrV* B XXIV–XXV, III:29–30.

[88] Kant, *KprV*, A 4, VII:107–108: "Der Begriff der Freiheit, so fern dessen Realität durch ein apodiktisches Gesetz der praktischen Vernunft bewiesen ist, macht nun den *Schlussstein* von dem ganzen Gebäude eines Systems der reinen, selbst der spekulativen, Vernunft aus, und alle andere Begriffe (die von Gott und Unsterblichkeit), welche, als blosse Ideen, in dieser ohne Haltung bleiben, schliessen sich an ihn an, und bekommen mit ihm und durch ihn Bestand und objektive Realität, d.i. die *Möglichkeit* derselben wird dadurch *bewiesen*, dass Freiheit wirklich ist; denn diese Idee offenbaret sich durchs moralische Gesetz" [The concept of freedom, in as far as its reality is proven through an apodictic law of practical reason, constitutes the keystone of the entire building of a system of pure, even of speculative, reason, and all other concepts (those of God and immortality), which, as mere ideas, remain with-out support within speculative reason, now join themselves to (the concept of freedom) and receive with and through it existence and objective reality, that is, the possibility of the latter is proven by the fact that freedom really is; for this idea reveals itself through the moral law].

[89] See the Preface to the second edition of the *First Critique* (B XXV, 11:30), for Kant's grounding of the "positive" "use" value of the *Critique* in the de-duction of a "practical use of pure (or moral) reason": "Daher ist eine Kritik,

fulfillment of the negative use of sensory limitations for the expansion of the power of reason in the sublime. The connection between the suprasensory concept of freedom and the violence done to the senses by the sublime is formulated with considerable theoretical emphasis at various moments throughout the *Third Critique*.[90] It is returned to directly after the description of the sublime as "Augenschein" with what must be viewed, even for Kant, as unusually categorical vigor. The proposition that the sublime is an instance of "aesthetic purposefulness"—though its nearest sensory likeness, as just suggested, may be at moments a bottomless abyss—is declared true by its purely conceptual, rather than analytical, subsumption to the unqualified equation of all "aesthetic purposefulness" with the "lawful" "freedom" of "judgment" itself. Kant writes—with considerable violence to our own senses—as if merely reflecting a known identity of fact: "Die ästhetische Zweckmässigkeit ist die Gesetzmässigkeit der Urteilskraft in ihrer *Freiheit*" [Aesthetic purposefulness is the lawfulness of the power of judgment in its *freedom*].[91]

---

welche die erstere [die spekulative Vernunft] einschränkt, so fern zwar *negativ*, aber, indem sie dadurch zugleich ein Hindernis, welches den letztern Gebrauch einschränkt, oder gar zu vernichten droht, aufhebt, in der Tat *positivem* und sehr wichtigem Nutzen, so bald man überzeugt wird, dass es einen schlechterdings notwendigen praktischen Gebrauch der reinen Vernunft (den moralischen) gebe . . ." [Thus a Critique, which limits (speculative reason), is to that extent, negative, but in that it eliminates an obstacle which threatens to limit, or even to destroy, the use (of speculative reason), it is in fact of positive and very important use, as soon as one is persuaded that there is an absolutely necessary practical use of pure reason (the moral use) . . .].

[90] In the "Allgemeine Anmerkung" to the "Analytik des Erhabenen," the sublime is described to exist "merely in the *relation* in which the sensory in the representation of nature is judged as appropriate for its possible suprasensory use" (B 113–14, X:192); the "violence" of reason is described to be "represented" as "exercised" through "imagination itself, as through a tool of reason," and also as "a feeling of the theft of the freedom of imagination through itself," its "sacrifice" (B 116–17, X:194–95). The connection between the concept of "freedom" and the "aesthetic" "sacrifice" of the senses to reason is made most clear when Kant states that "the power of the moral law" (or freedom), which "supersedes all other powers," "is only able to make itself aesthetically knowable through sacrifices" of (sensory rather than moral) "freedom" (B 120-1, X:197–98).

[91] *Ibid.*, B 120, X:197; emphasis in text.

That the "power of judgment," or any other power, should "in its *freedom*," be "lawful"—this direct contradiction of the common understanding of "lawfulness" and "freedom" as at least nonidentical, if not directly contradictory—is the central principle derived in function of pure reason which the *Critique of Practical Reason* sets out to prove. For the *Critique of Practical Reason* "should merely demonstrate," Kant writes in its Preface, "*that there is pure practical reason*,"[92] i.e., that unlike theoretical or speculative reason, the reason of practice need not be related to any objects of experience. The "power" which brings about pure practice, rather than phenomenal cognition or aesthetic contemplation, is the "will," and thus the proof of a pure, practical reason must first distinguish the power to will from any of the particular objects toward which it might be directed. In order to be fully determined as a power in itself, the will must be conceived instead as "legislative" (*gesetzgebend*): as a mode *of* determining. Its exercise is thus opposed, most importantly, to our "faculty of desire" in that it remains independent of the changing empirical conditions upon which our "happiness" at different moments seems contingent.[93] A will which, unlike "desire," could not be affected by feelings of "pleasure or displeasure" since it functions irrespective of all sensory experience, would finally be nothing more than "the mere form" of willing. Independent of all sensory "appearances," as it takes no appearance of its own, that "form" of the will as lawgiver could only be conceived in turn by reason.[94]

[92] *KprV*, A 3, VII:107: "Warum diese Kritik nicht eine Kritik der *reinen* praktischen, sondern schlechthin der praktischen Vernunft überhaupt betitelt wird, obgleich der Parallelism derselben mit der spekulativen das erstere zu erfordern schient, darüber gibt diese Abhandlung hinreichenden Aufschluss. Sie soll bloss dartun, *dass es reine praktische Vernunft gebe*, und kritisiert in dieser Absicht ihr ganzes *praktisches* Vermögen" [Why this Critique is called simply a Critique of Practical Reason rather than of *pure* practical reason, although the parallelism between it and (the Critique of Speculative Reason) seems to demand the latter, will be indicated extensively in this treatise. (The treatise) should merely demonstrate *that there is pure practical reason*, and for that reason it criticizes reason's entire practical faculty].

[93] This important distinction can only be briefly referred to here. See *ibid.*, A 44–48, VII:132–35; and A 51, VII:137, in particular.

[94] *Ibid.*, A 51–52, VII:138; emphasis in text: "Since the mere form of a law

"The will [which] . . . is a free will" is one whose "determination" as "law" is the legislative "form" of determination itself. As such it "must be thought" as "independent" of the "causal law" which determines, insofar as we know them, the "relations of appearances," or empirical phenomena, "to each other." The *form* of a "free will," as opposed to that of appearances, must thus itself be the condition determining the possibility of a "positive," "practical use of reason": the single "broadening" of the power of reason (beyond the limits of its speculative application to phenomena) hypothesized as the "use" of all philosophical criticism at the outset of the *First Critique*.[95] For the "concept of a free will," Kant specifies further on in the *Second Critique*, provides us with our only "view to noumena," i.e., it fulfills the all important critical stipulation articulated in the Second Preface to the *First Critique*, that "we must be able at least to think, if not actually know, things-in-themselves. For were that not the case the 'unrhymed proposition' would result that phenomenal appearance was without something which there appears."[96] Maintaining his critical prescriptions for all empirical knowledge,

---

can only be represented by reason, and thus is no object of the senses, and consequently also does not belong among appearances: so the representation of [this form] as the ground of determination of the will differs from all other grounds of determination of occurrences in nature according to the law of causality, for these determining grounds must themselves be appearances. If, however, no other determining ground of the will can serve as its law except this general lawgiving form: so must such a will be thought in complete independence from the natural law of appearances in relation to each other; namely, the law of causality. Such an independence, however, is called *freedom*, in the strictest, that is transcendental, understanding. Thus a will, which the mere lawgiving form of a maxim can alone serve as law, is a free will."

[95] *KrV*, BXXXV, III:30.

[96] The term Kant uses here to describe a pure appearance without substance is an *ungereimte[r] Satz*: "Denn sonst würde der ungereimte Satz daraus folgen, dass Erscheinung ohne etwas wäre, was da erscheint" (*KrV*, B XXVI–XXVII, III:31). The phrase is particularly apt in that such an epistemology of pure appearances would indeed approach the "pure poetry" Kant's critical epistemology denies. For it would provide knowledge, not "without rhyme or reason," but knowledge whose reason would include no nonconceptual component—such as that provided poetry by the sensory, material hinges of "rhyme."

Kant refers the nonempirical, noumenal status of a "free will" to the wholly nonsensory modes of its own derivation and presentation, underscoring that, while its conception must remain "theoretically empty," its practical "application," for the same reason, must be considered "real":

> Nun ist der Begriff eines Wesens, das freien Willen hat, der Begriff einer causa noumenon und, dass sich dieser Begriff nicht selbst widerspreche, dafür ist man schon dadurch gesichert, dass der Begriff einer Ursache, als gänzlich vom reinen Verstande entsprungen, zugleich auch seiner objektiven Realität in Ansehung der Gegenstände überhaupt durch die Deduktion gesichert, dabei seinem Ursprunge nach von allen sinnlichen Bedingungen unabhängig, . . . auf Dinge als reine Verstandeswesen allerdings angewandt werden könne. Weil aber dieser Anwendung keine Anschauung, als die jederzeit nur sinnlich sein kann, untergelegt werden kann, so ist causa noumenon, in Ansehung des theoretischen Gebrauchs der Vernunft, obgleich ein möglicher, denkbarer, dennoch leerer Begriff. . . . Nun aber der Begriff einer empirisch unbedingten Kausalität theoretisch zwar leer . . . ist . . . so habe ich zwar keine Anschauung, die ihm seine objektive theoretische Realität bestimmte, aber er hat nichts desto weniger wirkliche Anwendung, *die sich in concreto* in Gesinnungen oder Maximen *darstellen lässt*, d.i. praktische Realität, die angegeben werden kann; welches denn zu seiner Berechtigung selbst in Absicht auf Noumenen hinreichend ist.[97]

Now the concept of a being that has free will is this concept of a *causa noumenon*, and one is assured that the concept does not contradict itself in that the concept of a cause, as entirely sprung from pure reason, is at the same time assured of its objective reality in view of objects in general through deduction, and thereby, [being] in its origin, independent of all sensory conditions, . . . [such a concept] can certainly be applied to things as pure beings

[97] Kant, *KpV*, A 97–99, VII:171–73; my emphasis.

of understanding. But because no intuition, which can always only be sensory, can be brought in support of this application [of the concept of a being with free will to things themselves], so a *causa noumenon* is, in view of the theoretical use of reason, an empty, if still possible and thinkable, concept. . . . Now however the concept of an empirically unconditioned causality may be empty . . . as I have no intuition which could determine its objective theoretical reality, but it has no less real application, *which lets itself be represented "in concreto"* in intentions or maxims, i.e., practical reality which can be indicated; this is then sufficient to justify it even with a view to noumena.

"The concept of a *causa noumenon*," of "an empirically unconditioned causality," is saved from "contradicting itself" by the general, deductive nature of its origin. Causality as a concept "sprang completely from pure understanding," "independent of all sensory conditions," and thus the concept of noumenal causality, or "freedom," remains "possible" for practical as well as speculative reasons while devoid of all "objective" or cognitive content. The "reality" of unconditional "freedom," rather than made known in name alone by theoretical reason, is "represented *in concreto*" when applied in practice. "*In concreto*," the adverbial phrase used in the *Logic* to distinguish the intuitions of pure forms comprising mathematical knowledge from the formal intuitions of sensory matter discursively represented in philosophy, is used by Kant to describe the self-representation, in practice, of "freedom." "Freedom," like the purely spatial forms of mathematics, presents its own reality *concretely* in that it *is* the independence from all so-called "concrete," or empirically given forms of experience. The concept of "freedom" offers "a view to noumena" because it is itself a form represented "*in concreto*," rather than a formal means of speculatively representing specific phenomena. "Freedom," in other words, emerges as the one discursive object or concept in Kant's critical epistemology which, like the objects of mathematical intuitions, can and must be adequately defined by a "real definition." For "what one understands under [the] word," "freedom," throughout the *Critique*, is precisely an absolute absence of relation to, and the equally absolute insignificance of, all logically constituted, nominal meanings. Sharing none of the premises of "knowledge" in Kant, i.e., those of a representational *and* logical, because strictly nominal, narrative fiction, and stemming from neither sensory and formal, nor form-constructing and mathematical, intuition, the concept of "freedom," critical for the entire *Critique*, must be shown by Kant to derive from no other cognitive source than the *Critique*. If it is to maintain itself as a *critical* system, rather than resort to either philosophical dogmatism or idealism, the *Critique* must include within itself the "real definition" of "freedom." "Freedom" cannot simply be made the name of another critical hypothesis, an *a priori* form or category fulfilling an articulated function in Kant's architectonic system, but must instead be defined as to its own self-determining possibility.[98] Thus, while Kant's theory of knowledge yields the form of narrative as its *a priori* necessity, it must also formulate the question, for the sake of its own critical "thinking," which the purely analytic, "narratological" view of narrative necessarily fails to raise: how does any concept come to signify constructively? How, within the *Critique*, does the nonnominal concept of "freedom" arise?

Under the category of real definitions, Kant specified in the *Logic*: "A definition is *genetic* when it produces a concept through which the object can be presented *a priori in concreto*; such are all mathematical definitions."[99] The arisal or "genesis" of "freedom" in the *Second Critique*, the "real definition" which produces it *in concreto* as a concept, begins in the *Anmerkung* to the initial naming of "freedom" cited above (see footnote 94) with the question of whether our knowledge of a pure, practical reason derives first from "freedom" itself or from its form as legislative, "the moral law":

[98] See footnote 60 on the requirements of "real definitions."

[99] Kant, *Logik* A 222, VI:576: "Eine Definition ist *genetisch*, wenn sie einen Begriff gibt, durch welchen der Gegenstand a priori in concreto kann dargestellt werden; dergleichen sind alle mathematische Definitionen" [A definition is *genetic* when it can produce a concept, through which the object can be represented *a priori in concreto*. Such are all mathematical definitions].

Freiheit und unbedingtes praktisches Gesetz weisen also wechselsweise auf einander zurück. Ich frage hier nun nicht: ob sie auch in der Tat verschieden seien, und nicht vielmehr ein unbedingtes Gesetz bloss das Selbstbewusstsein einer reinen praktischen Vernunft, diese aber ganz einerlei mit dem positiven Begriffe der Freiheit sei; sondern wovon unsere *Erkenntnis* des unbedingt-Praktischen *anhebe*, ob von der Freiheit, oder dem praktischen Gesetze. Von der Freiheit kann es nicht anheben; denn deren können wir uns weder unmittelbar bewusst werden, weil sein erster Begriff negativ ist, noch darauf aus der Erfahrung schliessen, denn Erfahrung gibt uns nur das Gesetz der Erscheinungen, mithin den Mechanism der Natur, das gerade Widerspiel der Freiheit, zu erkennen. Also ist es das *moralische Gesetz*, dessen wir uns unmittelbar bewusst werden (so bald wir uns Maximen des Willens entwerfen), welches sich uns *zuerst* darbietet, und, indem die Vernunft jenes als einen durch keine sinnliche Bedingungen zu überwiegenden, ja davon gänzlich unabhängigen Bestimmungsgrund darstellt, gerade auf den Begriff der Freiheit führt. Wie ist aber auch das Bewusstsein jenes moralischen Gesetzes möglich?[100]

Freedom and unconditional practical law thus refer reciprocally to each other. I do not ask here if they are also in fact different, rather than the unconditional law being the mere self-consciousness of a pure practical reason, the latter however being identical with the positive concept of freedom. But instead [I ask] where our *knowledge* of the unconditional practical arises from, whether from freedom or from the practical law. It cannot arise from freedom; for we can neither become immediately conscious of the latter, because our first concept of it is negative, nor infer it from experience, for experience only gives us to recognize the law of appearances and with it the mechanism of nature, which is precisely the counterplay to freedom. Thus it is the *moral law* of which we become immediately conscious (as soon as we model maxims of the

[100] Kant, *KpV*, A 52–53, VII:139; emphasis in text.

will), which offers itself to us *first*, and, in that reason represents it as a ground of determination not to be outweighed by and completely independent from sensory conditions, leads directly to the concept of freedom. How, however, is the consciousness of this moral law possible?

In stating that he will "not ask" if "freedom" and its formal articulation, "the unconditional practical," or "moral" "law," "are in fact different," Kant raises, and drops as critically irrelevant, the central concern of approaches to literary criticism no more contemporary than Aristotle's *Poetics* nor less Aristotelian than the New Criticism: the distinction, made even as it is refuted, between textual content and textual form. What concerns Kant is not the questionable reality of that distinction, itself "demonstrable" only by means of access to the "disproven," i.e., the involuntary identity between content and form relied upon by each communicative utterance, but with which, form or content, "the moral law" or "freedom," our *knowledge* of their single meaning—here "the unconditional practical," or "pure practical reason"—begins: "wovon unsere *Erkenntnis* des unbedingt-Praktischen *anhebe*." At this moment Kant critically denies that we can derive knowledge of a pure reason of practice from its content, "freedom" itself, since "freedom" is "in the first place a negative concept"; it means, as discussed above, the absence of all speculative meaning and the radical irrelevance of the cognitive conditions set down in the *First Critique*. The obvious consideration that such knowledge cannot be derived from "experience," whose "law of appearances," the causal "mechanism of nature," is precisely the opposing force, or "counterplay" (*Widerspiel*), to "freedom," is offered next by Kant so as to lend a deductive appearance to the conclusion he in fact reaches here by default, namely, that the "moral law" is known "first" and "leads" secondly to the concept of "freedom": "Also ist es da *moralische Gesetz* . . . welches sich uns *zuerst* darbietet, und . . . gerade auf den Begriff der Freiheit führt."

Yet to specify the *order* in which our cognition of practical reason takes place is in no way to determine *how* it takes place. The question of modality is never exhausted by the subdivision of means into a sequence, and the integrity of Kant's own critical purpose is perhaps best proven by the final question ending this passage: "How, however, is the consciousness of this moral law possible?" Twice within the passage cited, Kant describes the means of arriving at that consciousness as "immediate" (*unmittelbar*). We could not "become immediately" aware of "freedom," because "the concept of freedom" can only be conceived of *by means of* the negation of all cognitive concepts, and thus it is the "moral law" alone "of which we become immediately conscious" (dessen wir unmittelbar bewusst werden). The "moral law" is said to "present itself," and to be represented by "reason," "to us" (das moralische Gesetz . . . sich uns . . . darbietet . . . die Vernunft jenes darstellt) without any access to the means of presentation. For all means of cognition *represent*, rather than make present, in Kant, and thus the indication of any form of mediation here would change the "moral law" into a mere phenomenal appearance *lacking* "something which there appears":[101] its "concrete," or "practical reality," "freedom." Finally, the problem Kant poses of "how" we can know the form of practical reason is as much in contradiction with the necessary premise of "immediate" presentation as it reflects the epistemological necessity of "thinking" "real definitions" themselves.

Barred from all means of representation, as well as the immediacy of intuition, Kant's investigation of how the "keystone" of his own critical thinking can become an object of knowledge (*Erkenntnis*), or, for that matter, of mere consciousness (*Bewusstsein*), reverts directly to the purely structural means by which the division of reason into theoretical and practical realms was first hypothesized: the relational, rather than representational, form of analogy. With direct relevance to this moment in the *Second Critique*, Jacques Derrida has suggested that the recurrence of the form of analogy in the *Third Critique* itself marks and stands for the "abyss" between the sensory and suprasensory cited above.[102] For Kant re-

[101] See footnote 96.

[102] See footnote 70, and Derrida, *La vérité en peinture*, p. 43. Derrida's observation, that if analogy is the "abyss" and "active recourse of the entire *Critique*," the "symbol" would, by analogy, be its (static, noncritical) "bridge"

sponds to the question of cognitive origins he has posed by comparing the strictly incomparable ways we "become conscious" of "pure practical laws" and "pure theoretical principles": "Wir können uns reiner praktischer Gesetze bewusst werden, eben so, wie wir uns reiner theoretischer Grundsätze bewusst sind, indem wir auf die Notwendigkeit, womit sie uns die Vernunft vorschreibt, und auf Absonderung aller empirischen Bedingungen, dazu uns jene hinweiset, Acht haben. Der Begriff eines reinen Willens entspringt aus den ersteren, wie das Bewusstsein eines reines Verstandes aus dem letzteren"[103] [We can become conscious of pure practical laws just as we are conscious of pure theoretical principles, in that we attend to the necessity with which reason prescribes them to us, and to the removal of all empirical conditions to which reason directs us. The concept of a pure will springs from the first, as the consciousness of a pure understanding springs from the second]. The use of the analogical ("eben so, wie . . . wie . . .") is, however, unavoidably improper here since not the functions of reason, schematically delineable as parallel (theoretical reason is to phenomena as practical reason is to freedom), but the very cognitive bases, including noncongruent temporalities ("bewusst werden" vs. "bewusst sind"), of those functions are being compared. That is, while theoretical reason may be compared theoretically with practical, phenomena, most importantly, may *not* be compared—above all not theoretically— with "freedom," for there is specifically no basis proper to *theoretical* reason upon which the concept of freedom in practical reason can be compared (phenomena are not to freedom as theoretical is to practical reason). Indeed, in the "concept of freedom," Kant concludes next as he abandons the position of analogy, practical reason poses the theoretical with its "most

["L'analogie de l'abîme et du pont par-dessus l'abîme, c'est une analogie pour dire qu'il doit bien y avoir une analogie entre deux mondes absolument hètèrogènes, un tiers pour passer l'abîme, cicatriser la bèance et penser l'ècart. Bref un *symbole*" (p. 43)] can itself be seen to offer a concise critique of Cassirer's reification of Kant's formally *analogical* aesthetic theory into a theory of the expressive content of "symbolic forms" (see Ernst Cassirer, *The Philosophy of Symbolic Forms*, 3 vols. (New Haven: Yale University Press, 1955).
[103] Kant, *KpV*, A 53, VII:139.

insoluble problem." The "problem" of conceiving of "freedom," that of generating, by way of discourse, a nonrepresentational, "real definition," is in fact formulated by Kant as the means by which reason itself overrules the possibility of a comfortably structural, hypostatized analogical "solution." Rather than allowing for its easy theoretical assimilation by a purely formal gesture of logical disposition, the "concept of freedom," Kant writes, is raised by reason "so as" to place theory in "the greatest embarrassment," "predicament," or more literally, "mispositionment" (*Verlegenheit*).

Yet in the course of recapitulating—*so as* to explain that predicament—the fundamental theoretical principle that "freedom" "explains nothing in appearances," this passage on the cognitive genesis of "freedom" suddenly turns from the speculative to the "concrete": it enacts, or "immediately" presents its own object of explanation, the "freedom" which *is* "predicament." Rather than predicating the "concept of freedom" by its "real definition," it calls "freedom" a "piece of daring" whose "introduction into science" owes not to reason at all but to force. "Freedom," the only critical basis for our linking logic to any form of knowledge, is said to be made known to us solely by the "imposition" of the "moral law" "upon us." I quote this recapitulative movement in full as it yields, by a kind of discursive inadvertence, the central "definition" of "freedom," and "practical" criticism of reason, presented in the *Critique*. Kant proceeds from the premise of analogy as follows:

> Dass dieses die wahre Unterordnung unserer Begriffe sei, und Sittlichkeit uns zuerst den Begriff der Freiheit entdecke, mithin *praktische Vernunft* zuerst der spekulativen das unauflöslichste Problem mit diesem Begriffe aufstelle, um sie durch denselben in die grösste Verlegenheit zu setzen, erhellet schon daraus: dass, da aus dem Begriffe der Freiheit in den Erscheinungen nichts erklärt werden kann, sondern hier immer Naturmechanism den Leitfaden ausmachen muss, überdem auch die Antinomie der reinen Vernunft, wenn sie zum Unbedingten in der Reihe der Ursachen aufsteigen will, sich, bei einem so sehr wie

bei den andern, in Unbegreiflichkeiten verwickelt, indessen dass doch der letztere (Mechanism) wenigstens Brauchbarkeit in Erklärung der Erscheinungen hat, *man niemals zu dem Wagestücke gekommen sein würde, Freiheit in die Wissenschaft einzuführen, wäre nicht das Sittengesetz und mit ihm praktische Vernunft dazu gekommen, und hätte uns diesen Begriff nicht aufgedrungen.*[104]

That this is the true organization of our concepts, and that morality first reveals to us the concept of freedom, while *practical reason* first raises this most insoluble problem for speculative reason in order to place it through [this concept] in the greatest predicament, is made clear by the following: that—because nothing in appearances can be explained from the concept of freedom, but rather [in the case of appearances] the mechanism of nature must always constitute the guiding thread; and because the antinomy of pure reason involves itself on both sides in inconceivabilities when it attempts to rise to the unconditional along a series of causes, while at least the former (the mechanism of nature) has usefulness in the explanation of appearances—*one would have never arrived at the piece of daring of introducing freedom into science, if the moral law, and with it practical reason, had not come and imposed that concept upon us.*

In a sense, the necessary attempt to articulate a "real definition" of "freedom" has been interrupted by the very nature of the "imposition" it declares. "Freedom," in other words, has imposed itself upon the *Critique*: discourse and reality have coincided *in discourse* to produce what may as well be called, if referred to at all, a "real definition." Yet what "imposes" "the concept of freedom" "upon us" is not "freedom" itself, but its *form* ("das Sittengesetz") or "moral law" ("[hätte] das Sittengesetz . . . uns diesen Begriff nicht aufgedrungen"). Furthermore, the "content" of the "moral law," what we "know" through its "practical application" at this empirically uncon-

---

[104] *Ibid.*, A 53–54, VII:139–40; final emphasis added.

ditioned moment, is not "freedom" but the "immediate" means of *aufdringen*, or "imposition": force. What we "know" from its "real definition" is thus both the near semantic opposite of "freedom" and a textually "concrete" "presentation" implying the full disruption, rather than a "keystone" or foundation, of any formal understanding of knowledge. For force, whether viewed as an externally imposed violation of deductive logic, or as the exposed product of logic in *logical* contradiction with itself, is not an object of formal, cognitive proof. It is not, in Kant's terms, even the concept of such an object. Thus "what one understands under [the] word," "freedom," the "real definition" of its internal "possibility," is the real impossibility of understanding "words" when "free": of knowing nominatively when discourse, the vehicle of knowledge, is itself "real," i.e., absolved equally of empirical reference and logical constraint. For what "there appears" to us, when "there" is the necessarily nonrepresentational "form" of "freedom," is not "something" referrable to any cognitive and logically integrable phenomenon,[105] nor for that matter to a cognitively suspendable, or "aesthetic" moment of phenomenal "free play," but the noncognitive and fully playless force—henceforth designated in the *Second Critique* the "fact" (*Faktum*)[106]—of formal appearance.

---

[105] See footnote 96.

[106] See the *Anmerkung* to sec. 7 which follows the "deduction" just cited: "Man kann das Bewusstsein dieses Grundgesetzes ein *Faktum der Vernunft nennen*, weil man es nicht aus vorhergehenden Datis der Vernunft, z.B. dem Bewusstsein der Freiheit (denn dieses ist uns nicht vorher gegeben), herausvernünfteln kann, sondern weil *es sich für sich selbst uns aufdringt* als synthetischer Satz a priori, der auf keiner, weder reinen noch empirischen Anschauung gegründet ist. ... Doch muss man, um dieses Gesetz ohne Missdeutung als *gegeben* anzusehen, wohl bemerken: dass es kein empirisches, sondern das einzige *Faktum* der reinen Vernunft sei ..." [One can *name* the consciousness of this basic law a *fact of reason*, because one cannot pretend to reason it out of foregoing data of reason, such as the consciousness of freedom (for the latter is not pregiven to us), but rather, because *it imposes itself, for itself, upon us*, as a synthetic proposition a priori, which is based upon neither pure nor empirical intuition. ... Yet, in order to regard this law without any misinterpretation as *given*, one must well note: that it is no empirical fact but rather the sole fact of pure reason ..."] (A 55–56, VI:141–42; my emphasis).

The "introduction" of "freedom" "into science," that "piece of daring" named by and imposed upon the *Critique* itself, does not occur, finally, without momentarily "freeing" the *Critique*'s own theory of cognition. Before being absorbed as an *"a priori* given fact," the emergence of "freedom," the necessary *"causa noumenon,"* causes the *Critique* to break its most fundamental laws regarding the *a priori* composition and cognition of phenomena. The nonnarrative moment demanded by the equation of all *knowledge* with narration "presents itself" most clearly as an epistemological "predicament" in the return made immediately within the text to phenomenality. For Kant is further forced by the imposition of the form of "freedom" to refer directly, or *non*critically, to a world of "real" or nonphenomenal experience for its proof. The *Anmerkung* concludes by replacing hypothetical epistemological criticism with purely empirical hypotheses of cognition: the concept of knowledge understood as a logical and representational narrative, with the fiction of immediately referential narratives which could "confirm" the "ordering of concepts," such as "freedom," "in us." Immediately subse-

---

This *a posteriori* translation of the "real definition" of "freedom" arising in [A 53] into an *"a priori* given fact" is later repeated without any reference to the force of its "imposition" *(aufdringen)* at all. See in particular [A 96] preceding the equation of free will with a "causa noumenon": "Die objektive Realität eines reines Willens, oder, welches einerlei ist, einer reinen praktischen Vernunft ist im moralischen Gesetze *a priori gleichsam durch ein Faktum gegeben"* [The objective reality of a pure will, or, of that which is identical to it, a pure practical reason, *is given, so to speak, a priori through a fact*] (VII:171; my emphasis).

Singular reference to the facticity of the "fact" of "freedom" in the *Second Critique* has been made in passing by Theodor Adorno. See "Juliette, or Enlightenment and Morality," in *The Dialectic of Enlightenment* (New York: The Seabury Press, 1972 [New York: Social Studies Assoc., 1944], p. 85. Observing that Kant has "recourse to ethical force as fact" because his "attempt . . . to derive the duty of mutual respect from a law of reason finds no support in the *Critique*," Adorno describes that attempt as "conventional . . . of bourgeois thought." Ignoring Kant's own recognition of the unavoidable problem "freedom" posed the *Critique*, he dismisses the concept of a "mere form of law," like the concept of the *Critique* itself, as an historicized ideological form, mistranslating it into immediately instrumental terms of practical gain: "The citizen who would forego profit only in the Kantian motive of respect for the mere form of law would not be enlightened, but superstitious—a fool."

quent to the word *aufgedrungen*, the *Critique* "experiences"
briefly, and in the form of a narration, its own peripety:

> Aber auch die Erfahrung bestätigt diese Ordnung der Be-
> griffe in uns. Setzet, dass jemand von seiner wollüstigen
> Neigung vorgibt, sie sei, wenn ihm der beliebte Gegen-
> stand und die Gelegenheit dazu vorkämen, für ihn ganz
> unwiderstehlich: ob, wenn ein Galgen vor dem Hause, da
> er diese Gelegenheit trifft, aufgerichtet wäre, um ihn so-
> gleich nach genossener Wollust daran zu knüpfen, er als-
> denn nicht seine Neigung bezwingen würde. Fragt ihn
> aber, ob, wenn sein Fürst ihm, unter Androhung dersel-
> ben unverzögerten Todesstrafe, zumute, ein falsches
> Zeugnis wider einen ehrlichen Mann, den er gerne unter
> scheinbaren Vorwänden verderben möchte, abzulegen,
> ob er da, so gross auch seine Liebe zum Leben sein mag,
> sie wohl zu überwinden für möglich halte. Ob er es tun
> würde oder nicht, wird er vielleicht sich nicht getrauen zu
> versichern; dass es ihm aber möglich sei, muss er ohne Be-
> denken einräumen. Er urteilet also, dass er etwas kann,
> darum, weil er sich bewusst ist, dass er es soll, und *erkennt
> in sich die Freiheit*, die ihm sonst ohne das moralische
> Gesetz *unbekannt* geblieben wäre.[107]

> But experience also confirms this ordering of concepts in
> us. Suppose that someone pretended that his lust were ir-
> resistible to him when the desired object and the oppor-
> tunity concurred: ask him whether, if a gallows were
> erected before the house where he faced this opportunity,
> so that he would be hung on it immediately afer gratifying
> his lust, if he then would not control his passion. One
> should not guess very long what he would answer. Ask
> him, however, whether, if his sovereign demanded of him,
> under the threat of the same immediate penalty of death,
> that he bear false witness against an honest man whom he
> wished to ruin under seeming pretexts, whether in that
> case he considered it possible that he would overcome his
> love of life, no matter how great that love was. Whether

[107] Kant, *KpV*, A 54, VII:140; my emphasis.

he would do so or not he would probably not trust himself to say for sure; that it might be possible for him to do so he must admit without further deliberation. Thus he judges that he can do something because he is conscious that he should, and *recognizes in himself the freedom* which without the moral law would have remained *unknown* to him.

In the story Kant tells of the man before the gallows, experience is presented as a contingent set of circumstances: *"when the desired object and the opportunity concurred . . . if* a gallows . . . were erected [where] he faced this opportunity . . . *if* his sovereign demanded of him . . . *whether* he would do so or not. . . ."* Yet contingency here, rather than providing the "matter" we perceive formally as phenomena, is introduced as the immediately referential means by which we "recognize in ourselves" "freedom," or the "real." In referring to experience not as phenomena but as a form of proof, Kant not only breaks the laws of his own speculative philosophy but turns back the methods of moral philosophy to a preconceptual mode of empirical observation. Like the imaginary subject of Kant's story, *Kant's story* tells us that we can only become cognizant of "freedom" through a series of experiences stipulated to be contingent, to be *un*determined narratively, and thus not constitutive of cognition at all. If it is to "confirm" the "keystone" concept of "freedom," Kant's narrative must indicate that its content is "real"; insofar as it does, it is in Kant's terms an absolute fiction. For the hypothesis of a man who *might* refuse, upon pain of death, to give false witness pretends to present the truth of experience without representing it, and thus is the "false witness" to the "honest" epistemological project of the *Critique.* Kant's narrative is the fiction of a nonnominal narrative his own critical epistemology exposes. Unlike the hypothetical choice it grants a nameless "someone" (*jemand*), thereby generating a classic plot of equivocal experience, its necessity for its author, "Kant," is unequivocal, nonexperiential, "real." It arises to prove, to fill, to *narrate* a form which is itself known only to be without logical shape or referential extension. The form of what Kant calls "freedom," and whose content the *Critique* shows to be force, can neither be intuited as an "*a priori* given form" nor identified with a representation of experience. Excluded by Kant's criticism from the only possible knowledge confirmed by his theory, it is the one form in the *Critique* whose occurrence may indeed be "recognized"— while in a singularly non-epistemological sense—as its "keystone." For it is the one form which, rather than take part in, must, as it does, produce narrative.

Kant's critical theory of cognition, it has been argued, describes cognition in the form of narration. As stipulated in the *Logic*, the single object of real, rather than nominal, narrative knowledge would be the means of narration, words themselves. Finally, our knowledge of reality in coherent, narrative form rests upon the necessity of our knowing the single individual word deduced in the *Second Critique* to mean the absence of all causal and nominal narrative relations: "freedom." In Goethe's *Wahlverwandtschaften* and *Farbenlehre*, we encounter, by contrast, a narrative that describes a theory of cognition. Unlike Kant's speculative and purposefully systematic critical theory, Goethe's *Farbenlehre* derives from a series of discrete empirical experiments: it claims that "color," the "material" aspect of aesthetic objects specifically subordinated by Kant, in its "purest" state, to form,[108] is in fact constitutive of our very knowledge of empirical experience. Goethe substi-

---

[108] See, in the "Analytik des Schönen," *Kritik der Urteilskraft*, X:139–40: "Eine blosse Farbe . . . ein blosser Ton . . . ob zwar beide bloss die Materie der Vorstellungen, nämlich lediglich Empfindung, zum Grunde zu haben scheinen, und darum nur angenehm genannt zu werden *verdienten* . . . sich nur insofern für schön zu *gelten* berechtigt halten, als beide *rein* sind; welches eine Bestimmung ist, die schon die Form betrifft. . . . Das Reine aber einer einfachen Empfindungsart bedeutet: dass die Gleichförmigkeit derselben durch keine fremdartige Empfindung gestört und unterbrochen wird, und gehört bloss zur Form . . ." [A mere color . . . , a mere sound, although both appear to have at their basis merely the matter of representations, that is, solely sensation, and thus only *deserve* to be called pleasant . . . can only be held justifiably *to pass* for beautiful when they are both *pure*, which is a determination which has to do with form. . . . The pureness of a simple manner of sensation means, however, that the uniformity of the latter is not disturbed or interrupted by any foreign sensation and pertains merely to form . . .].

tutes the concept of the *a priori* fact of phenomenal "color" for the Kantian *a priori* of form. Similarly, "freedom," rather than recognized as the basis for theoretical speculation which the *Color Theory* will be required to deduce, is openly referred to by Goethe as the enabling condition of empirical observation employed by the natural scientist at will. Such "freedom" of cognition is represented in *Die Wahlverwandtschaften* as human passion. Like the concept of "freedom" in Kant, that passion is not formally narrative in and of itself. It is narrated, instead, in the literary form of a "novel." While the formal representations of phenomena compose an *a priori* cognitive narrative in Kant, the phenomenon of "color" studied empirically in the *Farbenlehre* is represented *in* narrative form in *Die Wahlverwandtschaften*.

CHAPTER 3

THE COLORING OF RELATIONS:
DIE WAHLVERWANDTSCHAFTEN
AS *FARBENLEHRE*

After this the orchestra seats began, the residence of mortals
forever separated from the somber and transparent realm to
which the limpid and reflecting eyes of the water goddesses,
in their flat and liquid surface, served here and there as
boundaries. For the folding-seats on the shore, the forms of the
monsters in the orchestra were painted in these eyes following
the single laws of optics and according to their angle of
incidence, as happens with those two parts of external reality
to which, knowing that they do not possess even the most
rudimentary soul analogous to our own, we would judge
ourselves mad if we addressed a smile or a look: minerals and
persons with whom we are not in relation.
—MARCEL PROUST, *Le Côté de Guermantes*

The technical translation of *Die Wahlverwandtschaften* as
"Elective Affinities" may be seen to be related to the larger interpretative problems complicating any understanding of the
novel as a whole. The individual parts of the compound German noun are, of course, *Wahl* (choice) and *Verwandtschaften* (kin, or [family or blood] relations), their literal or lexical
translation as a unit yelding "chosen kin" (or "blood relations
of choice") as the novel's more immediately paradoxical title.
An unexpected discrepancy arises here upon inspection between the "technical" and "literal" significations of a single

term. Thus the attempt to identify the equivalent of "Wahl-verwandtschaften" in another language makes evident a semantic difficulty already present in its "original" form. The dilemma faced by any reader, as much as translator, of the novel is that "technical" and "literal"—modifiers customarily used interchangeably in referring to the faithful, rather than figural, rendering of meaning—are in this case indicative of dissimilar meanings. In spite of the overwhelming conformity in the history of the novel's translation,[1] in order to understand the significance of its title, the word serving ostensibly to represent the work, we must choose between two equally and therefore inadequate "proper" meanings while recognizing the *form* they appear in to be one.

The root of the problem appears to lie most clearly in the past, and its solution, in a brief etymological exercise. To discover how we are meant to understand the meaning of "Wahlverwandtschaften," we may need only verify the usage of the term contemporary to the novel's composition. Conveniently, and perhaps not coincidentally, Goethe has us look no further in that direction than early in the novel itself. He includes, in the well-known fourth chapter of Part One, a didactic lesson in the meaning accorded his title throughout Europe at the turn of the century.[2] During a recitation given by Ed-

---

[1] One noteworthy exception to the use of the technical term as the novel's title is the first French translation of *Die Wahlverwandtschaften: Ottilie, ou le pouvoir de la sympathie* (trans. Breton [Paris: Veuve le Petit, 1819]).

[2] *The Grimm Deutsches Wörterbuch* offers the following definitions of the word: "(1) in der Chemie die eigenschaft zweier Körper, von denen der eine oder beide anderweit verbunden sind, sich zu vereinigen, affinitas electiva . . . (2) das Wort ist, insofern den Körpern eine wahl zugeschrieben wird, von menschlichen Verhältnissen hergenommen und erregte als solche Goethes Aufmerksamkeit . . ." [(1) in chemistry the characteristic of two bodies, of which one or both are in another way bound, of uniting themselves, affinitas electiva . . . (2) the word, in as far as it ascribes a choice to these bodies, is taken from human circumstances and as such called Goethe's attention . . .].

In connection with the first definition, Grimm's cites Albertus Magnus as the first to use the term, followed by Galileo, Geoffrey (1718), and Torbern Bergman (*De Attractionibus Electivis*, 1775 [trans. 1782]). Following the second definition a series of remarks by Goethe on the meaning of the term is cited, including the following observations in conversation with Riemer: "hier ist eine Trennung, eine neue Zusammensetzung entstanden und man glaubt sich nunmehr berechtigt, sogar das Wort Wahlverwandtschaft anzuwenden,

uard, consisting of "technical" rather than "poetic" or "discursive" content,[3] Charlotte admits to having misconceived the referent of his speech. She claims that upon hearing the term read aloud she had thought immediately of a pair of her own relations[4] and that she was surprised, upon turning her at-

---

weil es wirklich aussieht als wenn ein Verhältnis dem andern vorgezogen, eins vor dem andern erwählt würde . . . in diesem fahrenlassen und ergreifen, in diesem fliehen und suchen, glaubt man wirklich eine höhere Bestimmung zu sehen; man traut solchen Wesen eine Art von wollen and wählen zu, und hält das Kunstwort verwandtschaften für vollkommen gerechtfertigt . . . so halte ich es doch für ein Glück . . . dass diese Natur- und Wahlverwandtschaften unter uns eine vertrauliche Mittheilung beschleunigen . . ." [here a separation, a new combination is arisen, and one now believes oneself justified in applying even the word *Wahlverwandtschaft* because it really appears as if one relation were preferred, were chosen over the other . . . in this letting go and grasping, in this fleeing and searching, one really believes that one sees a higher determination; one trusts to such beings a kind of willing and choosing, and holds the technical term *Verwandtschaften* to be fully justifiable . . . so I hold it for a piece of good fortune . . . that these nature- and *Wahlverwandtschaften* accelerate a familiar communication among us . . .].

While describing the justice of applying the term's significance in natural science to human relations, Goethe carefully qualifies his observations ("one now believes oneself justified"; "because it really appears as if"; "one really believes"; "one trusts . . . and holds . . . to be fully justifiable"; "so I hold it for a piece of good fortune"; "accelerate a familiar communication"), thereby maintaining the question of the propriety of the term's usage in *either* realm in an unresolved state of suspension.

[3] Johann Wolfgang von Goethe, *Die Wahlverwandtschaften, Goethes Werke* Bd. 6, ed. Benno von Wiese (Hamburg: Christian Wegner Verlag, 1955), p. 269. All quotations from Goethe, unless otherwise noted, are from this edition of his works; all translations are my own.

[4] I state "claims" because it is not clear at this moment, like so many others of structural significance in the novel, whether what is reported actually did occur. Charlotte's statement directly follows the narrator's description of Eduard's extreme discomfort at having his recitations accompanied by an on-reader: "Eine seiner besonderen Eigenheiten, die er jedoch vielleicht mit mehrern Menschen teilt, war die, dass es ihm unerträglich fiel, wenn jemand ihm beim Lesen in das Buch sah" (*Ibid.*, VI:269) [One of his particular characteristics, which he however shared perhaps with a great number of men, was that it became unbearable for him when someone looked on in his book as he read]. On this particular occasion, the narrator continues, since there were "three" present (he, Charlotte, and the Captain), and his reading did not "have a view toward" the "excitement of feeling" or the "imaginative power," Eduard's customary "precaution" against such an occurrence was "unnecessary." Nevertheless, or because he cannot be cautious enough, "als er sich nachlässig gesetzt hatte, . . . Charlotte ihm in das Buch sah" (VI:269) [as he carelessly sat

tention back to the subject under discussion, to discover it referred to "wholly inanimate things."[5] The error Charlotte raises is promptly righted by Eduard, who soundly attributes his wife's confusion to the metaphorical nature of the term he has read: "Es ist eine Gleichnisrede, die dich verführt und verwirrt hat" [It is a figure of speech that misled and confused you]. Emphasizing the exclusive reference of the metaphor, in its present context, to elements found objectively in nature ("Hier wird freilich nur von Erden und Mineralien gehandelt" [Here obviously only earth and minerals are being treated]), Eduard goes on to offer a striking axiom as explanation of his wife's misapprehension: "aber der Mensch ist ein wahrer Narziss; er bespiegelt sich überall gern selbst, er legt sich als Folie der ganzen Welt unter"[6] [But man is a true Narcissus; he gladly mirrors himself everywhere, he lays himself out as a foil (or the French *folie*, "madness") under the entire world].

---

down, . . . Charlotte looked into his book] Eduard's highly charged rebuke, notably constituted of metaphors which substitute inanimate objects for parts and the whole of his own person—"Das Geschriebene, das Gedruckte tritt an die Stelle meines eigenen Sinnes, meines eigenen Herzens . . . ein Fensterchen vor meiner Stirn, vor meiner Brust angebracht . . . Wenn mir jemand ins Buch sieht, so ist mir immer, als wenn ich in zwei Stücke gerissen würde" (VI:269) [The written, the printed takes the place of my own mind, my own heart . . . a small window is brought before my forehead, before my breast. . . . When someone looks into my book as I read, it is always to me as if I were ripped into two pieces.]—is followed by the narrator's description of Charlotte's talent for neutralizing "lively" discussion (VI:270). It is in the context of attempting to change the tone and direction of Eduard's speech, introduced by a petition for sure pardon (" 'Du wirst mir meinen Fehler gewiss verzeihen' ") (VI:270) ["Surely you will forgive me my mistake"], that she refers to a mistaken reference on her part. While the actual validity of the latter error cannot be constated, it serves sequentially to replace a former error (that of on-reading) as its excuse.

[5] " 'Ich hörte von Verwandschaften lesen, und da dacht ich ebengleich an meine Verwandten, an ein paar Vettern, die mir gerade in diesem Augenblick zu schaffen machen. Meine Aufmerksamkeit kehrt zu deiner Vorlesung zurück; ich höre, dass von ganz leblosen Dingen die Rede ist, und blickte dir ins Buch, um mich wieder zurechtzufinden' " *ibid.*, VI:270) ["I heard read of relations and there I thought immediately of my relatives, a pair of cousins, with whom just at this moment I have to do. My attention turned back to your reading; I hear that the talk is of wholly inanimate things, and I glanced in your book in order to find my way again"].

[6] *Ibid.*

The modern reader of *Die Wahlverwandtschaften* will be quick to identify the ironic import of this interchange between husband and wife. For the validity of Eduard's observation is most obviously applicable to the theory of "elective affinities" itself. Whether commenting upon the fallacy of an accepted scientific mode of perception, or correcting a momentary mistake in perception on Charlotte's part, Eduard proceeds to answer the question, directly posed here by Charlotte, of "what, by *Verwandtschaften*, is actually meant,"[7] by describing the technical meaning accorded the word by science. In cooperation with the Captain, he upholds the empirical referentiality of a term which figures chemical interactions upon the patterning of interpersonal attractions. Such an anthropomorphism of nature, a common if unconscious tendency in the scientific theory of the later eighteenth and early nineteenth centuries, was already gaining prominence as a basis of historical speculation in the works of such contemporary philosophers as Herder, and would later be made into an exclusive epistemological mode, as rendered most explicit in the theoretical anthropology of Feuerbach. Viewed historically, the problem of understanding posed by different "literal" and "technical" translations of "Wahlverwandtschaften" would then date from the inception, and philosophical contextualization, of a specifically technical usage which was itself translated from subjective experience. This theoretical means of describing and conceptualizing empirical data, and therein of transcribing empirical observation as scientific truth, appears in retrospect to have always been figural in premise.

The theory of "elective affinities" having been refuted and replaced by atomic chemistry, the impropriety of its founding assumption—the application of a human attribute to natural phenomena—seems, from the vantage point afforded by intervening theories, all too plain. Mere temporal distance would enlighten any reader enough to ascribe that outdated conception to the very *human* nature Eduard describes. Indeed, Eduard's axiom could even be extended further: man, the mortal Narcissus, can be seen to outdo the demigod of Ovidian mythology in needing no mirror as the medium of his reflection.

---

[7] *Ibid.*

"*He* mirrors *himself* everywhere" in the very content of his misconceptions. Perhaps more difficult to assimilate, however, is that the justice of that appraisal was formulated by the most clearly Narcissus-like of all the novel's characters, on behalf of a theory that had itself been misconceived.

While the technical meaning of "Wahlverwandtschaften" can thus be recognized in the present as an essentially misplaced figuration, its literal meaning, in escaping the issue of historical determination, cannot be similarly assumed to escape the confusion of which history is conceived. In accounting for the term's transposed technical meaning as a stage in the development of science, its literal or lexical significance inevitably acts as a constant of comparison. Yet it is not immediately apparent that the semantic correction of a past anthropomorphism will supply a proper referent in its place. It would still remain for us to identify the object of the unchanging meaning to which a provisional and improper meaning is then to be compared. The problem, initially and generally posed, remains whether "Wahlverwandtschaften," in its most literal meaning, means what it says. If "elective affinities" between elements in nature referred figuratively to attractions between persons, does it necessarily follow that the "relations" signified by the term's lexical translation are definable as interpersonal? Furthermore, spanning both objective references of the term, there remains the question of whether the "relations" indicated signify, as they are designated, the consequences, whether intimate or elemental, of "choice."

The issue of whether "Wahlverwandtschaften" refers to relations between people or in nature refers *Die Wahlverwandtschaften* to the major corpus of Goethe's own "natural science" writings, *Zur Farbenlehre.*[8] While the novel tells a story

---

[8] A relation between the two works has been suggested by Hans Reiss in his introduction to the Blackwell edition of *Die Wahlverwandtschaften* (Oxford, 1971). In discussing the technical meaning of the novel's title, Reiss notes "the impact of Goethe's scientific studies and the affinity of the novel to *Zur Farbenlehre* (the theory of Colours), Goethe's principal scientific treatise" (p. xv). Whether by intention or coincidence, Reiss's use of the word "affinity" here both repeats the problem posed by Goethe's "chosen" title and expands it, interestingly, to include its "relation" with the "color theory."

A connection between the works has been indicated by Thomas Fries (*Die*

of relationships of love, the *Farbenlehre* speculates upon observations of color relations. In it an analysis of color founded in essential transparency is rejected and "nature," in its most phenomenal aspect, is observed to enact the occurrence of its appearances.[9] "Color," however, is a term that may also signify more than one possible meaning; its commonly understood figural signification is that of a figure of speech or rhetorical trope. According to the latter meaning, Goethe's "color theory" is suggestive of other theories of "color" whose usage of the term is figural from the start, and whose object of investigation is therefore discursive rather than "natural" by definition. While the production of linguistic "color" is generally viewed as the distinguishing, synthesizing capacity of poetry, its technical and theoretical analysis is assigned to the fields of applied rhetoric and aesthetic philosophy respectively. Thus the formation, in language, of figures or "colors," of denominating elements that cannot be identified with their referents, is responded to by a division of the labor of language into interlocking poetic and analytic functions. The presumption that these functions plot the curve of an intended (or chosen) meaning displaces the problem of the purely discursive points at

---

Wirklichkeit der Literatur [Tübingen: Max Niemeyer Verlag, 1975]), but remains undeveloped in his study. Criticizing Goethe's natural science theory along loosely drawn ideological and rhetorical lines, Fries concludes that Goethe's somewhat mystified "goal" in the *Farbenlehre* was the founding of an "organic of speech" (p. 84). In discussing the novel, however, Fries demonstrates a critic's mystification before the figure of Ottilie, who represents for him, simultaneouly and unproblematically, both " 'ein natürliches Leben' " (in Hegel's words [p. 129]) and an "Allegorie der Kunst" (p. 128).

[9] Cf., in this regard, Wittgenstein's posthumously published *Remarks on Colour* (Ludwig Wittgenstein, *Remarks on Colour*, ed. G.E.M. Anscombe, trans. Linda L. McAlister and Margarete Schättle [Berkeley: University of California Press, 1978], p. 34e): "A *natural history* of colours would have to report on their occurrence in nature, not on their *essence*. Its propositions would have to be temporal ones." Wittgenstein's late occupation with color takes Goethe's *Farbenlehre* as its direct predecessor. Of particular interest is his suggestion of the latter's relevance to cognitive theory in another observation elucidating the term "nature" used above: "Someone who agrees with Goethe finds that Goethe correctly recognized the nature of colour. And here 'nature' does not mean a sum of experiences with respect to colours, but it is to be found in the concept of colour" (p. 32e).

which they intersect. The problems posed by the appearance of "colors" of discourse—problems paradoxically preserved by the same divisive treatment meant to solve them—are well represented by the *Farbenlehre* and *Wahlverwandtschaften*. For the dissimilarity between the two works extends beyond divisions of discursive purpose into the more fundamental distinction upon which the ascription of purpose to discourse depends: the distinction between the composition of truth and its illusion, between writing formulated as science and the writing of fiction. The *Farbenlehre* regards the manifestation of color as both the primary object and constitutive subject of the natural scientist's investigations. It describes those investigations, however, in singularly discursive terms. Once "noted and named," Goethe proposes in the "Vorwort" to the *Farbenlehre*, such phenomenal "appearances" form a "language of nature" whose theory in turn "enriches" it and "eases its communication."[10] The tenuous scientific status of a theory derived from a "language of nature" is reflected in the uneven recognition which Goethe's "color theory" has received. Considered as a systematic scientific treatise, the *Farbenlehre* has been criticized for its methodological and empirical errors, while practicing artists, aestheticians, and language philosophers have commended and attempted to reproduce its individual experiments and insights.[11] The critical reception of *Die Wahlverwandtschaften*, by contrast, has focused less upon the poetic than upon the ethical character of Goethe's characters,

---

[10] Goethe, "Vorwort," *Zur Farbenlehre*, XIII:315–16.

[11] See Rilke Wankmüller, "Die Aufnahme von Goethes Farbenlehre," *Naturwissenschaftliche Schriften*, XIII:610–15, including Helmholtz's objection, "dass Goethe der Natur wie einem Kunstwerk entgegengetreten sei und die Gesetze der Natur in sinnlicher Form gesehen habe, das Gesetz selber jedoch nicht gesucht habe" [Goethe faced nature like a work of art and saw the laws of nature in sensory form without however searching for the law of nature], and Du Bois-Reymond's condemnation of the *Farbenlehre* as " 'totgeborene Spielerei eines autodidaktischen Dilettanten,' der vor allem 'der Begriff der Kausalität fehle' " ["the stillborn playing of an autodidactic dilettante," which "lacked," above all, "the concept of causality"] (XIII:614, 615). Cf. also the internally contradictory, but no less interesting, defense of "Goethe's science" from the standpoint of its consideration *as* science, in Heinrich Henel's "Type and Proto-Phenomenon in Goethe's Science," *PMLA* 71 (1956).

interpreting their actions and emotions as objective evidence of a classical, romantic, or even materialist, text, by way of an unusually dense admixture of aesthetic and moral judgment.[12] A second and rarer critical response has attended to the difficulties involved in identifying any specific aesthetic or moral stance to which the novel adheres, difficulties abetted by its evasive but ever-present third-person narrator, as well as the provocatively inconclusive commentary offered by its author.[13]

If *Die Wahlverwandtschaften* is read, however, not for what

---

[12] For the novel's reception by its contemporaries, see *Die Wahlverwandtschaften*, VI:621–45. The negative response it received in America is described by F. Wahr in *Emerson and Goethe* (Ann Arbor, Mich.: George Wahr, 1915) ("Of all Goethe's works that which was most misunderstood and subjected to the most abusive criticism was doubtless the 'Elective Affinities . . .'" [pp. 111–12]). The study summarizes the rejection by the American Transcendentalists of the "morally harmful import" of Goethe's "realism"—its representation of "the true" in distinction from that of "the good"—while attempting to gloss that perception by stressing the particular cultural biases and linguistic difficulties which might have accounted for their failure to recognize Goethe's "moral heroism."

The interpretation of the novel by contemporary Goethe scholars, concerned primarily with the identification of its affiliations within the Goethe canon, is reviewed by Barnes in *Goethe's Die Wahlverwandtschaften* (London: Oxford, 1967), pp. 14–26.

[13] See, in particular: Paul Stöcklein, "Stil und Sinn der *Wahlverwandtschaften*" in *Wege zum späten Goethe* (Hamburg: Schröder, 1960), pp. 9–80, and "Einführung in die *Wahlverwandtschaften*" in *Goethes Werke, Gedenk-Ausgabe* (Zürich: Artemis Verlag, 1949), IX:681–719; Walter Benjamin, "Goethes *Wahlverwandtschaften*" in *Walter Benjamin, Gesammelte Schriften*, ed. Tiedemann and Schweppenhäuser (Frankfurt: Suhrkamp, 1974), I:1:123–201; Eric A. Blackhall, *Goethe and the Novel* (Ithaca, N.Y.: Cornell University Press, 1976); and Barnes, *Goethe's Die Wahlverwandtschaften*.

For Goethe's own remarks on the novel, see *Werke*, VI:621–26, and *Conversations with Eckermann* (New York: Dunne, 1901), pp. 63, 166–67, 295–96, and 212 (May 6, 1829) especially, beginning with a comparison to *Faust*: "The only production of greater extent, in which I am conscious of having labored to set forth a pervading idea, is probably my *Wahlverwandtschaften*. This novel has thus become comprehensible to the understanding; but I will not say that it is therefore better. I am rather of the opinion, that the more incommensurable, and the more incomprehensible to the understanding, a poetic production is, so much the better it is."

its story tells us about itself (as kind of text) or its subjects (as types of characters), but for how it tells that story—the way in which its narrative unfolds—it may be seen to transpose the problem of the appearance of figuration into a literary form with neither theoretical nor poetic status proper: the novel.[14]

[14] Indeed, the fact that *Die Wahlverwandtschaften* was written as a novel (explicitly entitled, when first announced for publication in 1808, *Die Wahlverwandtschaften, ein Roman* [*Werke*, VI:621]), rather than as a "kleine Erzählung" or "Novelle," as Goethe is reputed to have originally planned, has itself proved problematic for its critics. Unlike the necessarily economic constructions of the latter genres, the indefinite relation between form and content implied in the designation, "ein Roman," has prompted critics to restrict or modify the application of the term to *Die Wahlverwandtschaften* by specifying, with notable variety, what kind of "Roman" it is. Barnes lists some critical typifications of the novel and suggests the problems inherent in each, but then goes full-circle to classify it as "Novelle-like": "It is not easy to fit *Die Wahlverwandtschaften* into any one of the usual German categories of the novel, if we wish to refine on Goethe's own description of it: 'ein Roman.' It is generally accepted that Ottilie is the heroine, but the reader is denied insight into her state of mind in Part I, and in Part II is confronted with her sudden intuitions and the mysterious pictorial style of the conclusion; a state of affairs which scarcely favours the use of the term 'Entwicklungsroman.' Borcherdt's employment of the word 'Ereignisroman' is difficult to match with the great importance of the Journal. The use of the term 'Gesellschaftsroman,' which Solger's interpretation might seem to justify, is invalidated by the restriction of the main characters to Edward's estate; although Goethe's remark to Riemer: 'Er äusserte seine Idee bei dem neuen Roman, "Die Wahlverwandtschaften" sei: Soziale Verhältnisse und die Conflikte derselben symbolisch gefasst darzustellen" [He expressed his idea with regard to the new novel, "The *Wahlverwandtschaften*": to represent social relations and their conflicts grasped symbolically], would seem to support Solger, providing 'symbolisch gefasst' is disregarded. It is not a confessional work: although Goethe appears to treat it as such, the use of a narrator precludes the term 'Erkenntnisroman.' It has often been regarded as an 'Eheroman' and marriage, not love, mistakenly conceived to be the main theme of the novel. The German description which takes account of most of its features seems to be 'ein novellistischer Roman' " (pp. 5, 13–14).

In qualifying the status of Goethe's novel in terms of its form (*novellistischer*) and without regard to its content, however, Barnes moves further away from the problem, presented by *Die Wahlverwandtschaften*, of the novel *as* form. More importantly, the question of why we should "wish to refine on Goethe's own description," "ein Roman," is not even recognized as such, but merely assumed as a probability. To pose that question is to suggest that this particular novel impels its own external mediation, and that each attempt at its typification will be to some extent in error; in other words, that the under-

Rather than effecting meaning through the patterning of concepts or of images, novels can perhaps be most simply conceived as the development, through mimetic narrative, of a dominant, discursive theme. In accordance with such a description, Goethe's novel could be said to explore the thematics of misplaced affections, drawing their necessary consequences from a fictive set of circumstances. Yet necessarily included within the novel's development is the narrative of how that development is understood, from its most "realistic" or descriptive details to its prescriptive or "poetic" speculations. The part played by understanding or cognizance within the fiction implies that the problem of meaning opened to discussion by its theme must first be accounted for on the level of its form. For while the significance of representations must be predicated upon understanding, understanding is discursively, rather than mimetically, composed. Consequently, the question of discursive figuration—of how representations in the narrative are made to relate—must be addressed in turn. If, like the immediate significance of its title, the final meaning of Goethe's narrative is as compelling as it is obscure, it is because the events of errant passion composing the novel's story also compose the way in which that story is understood, by the novel's characters, the subjects and objects of its action, and its narrator, their discursive source. Structured like their understanding, those events are available to discursive analysis as narrative moments representing differing discourses upon (and of) errant passion: figural representations making the movement of Eros appear meaningful. For in order for "errant" relations of meaning, for "color," to appear, language as a mode of reference must substitute for its referents, make them into its medium. The figural relation of representations involves a break with their conventional correlations, a movement within language from what is properly, while arbitrarily, meant by a word to a meaning which, while improper, seems significantly to fit. If the fit can then be called "figural mean-

---

standing of the novel's events outside the novel—by its critics—are also represented by those events: as described in this study, by errant passions made legible as figurations.

ing," the movement itself, like that of Eros, may well be called "Wahlverwandtschaften": "relations" whose meaning is made indeterminable as truth or as fiction in that their structure of meaning can never be determined to arise by "choice."

Yet an understanding of meaning as it appears in discursive objects need not structure our understanding of any other objective phenomena. Linguistic relations are no more equatable with relations within nature than the word "color," used as a discursive artifice to mean the formal medium of meaning, a "figure of speech," is identical to the immediate, surface quality of objects its literal meaning denotes. We may conceive discursive meaning to be governed by a dialectic with our perception of nature, each responding to, even transforming, the other. But discourse, in the very terms of that relation, cannot be considered "natural." It appears instead, as noted above, to be the identifying attribute of a distinctly "human nature": man as part of nature plus the power of articulation. Our perceptions of objects in nature, ourselves and others included, are carried out by an additional, artificial means. Hence human relations, such as those represented in *Die Wahlverwandtschaften*, depend most clearly upon mediation to appear. The fact that the relations depicted in the novel are unstable, their passions irresolvably out of place, suggests not only the saying that "to err is human," but the possibility that errors may inhere in our most meaningful mediations. Relations which seem most natural may, by their appearance, perpetuate our mistakes. In order to understand the story of "Wahlverwandtschaften," errant passions which seem to occur by nature, the investigation of the appearance of linguistic meaning should be turned upon nature's own phenomenality and the question asked: how does "color" proper appear?

By his own account, Goethe spent approximately half his life in the vigorous study of natural color. Although the two major publications of his experiments, *Beiträge zur Optik* (1791) and *Zur Farbenlehre* (1810), were shunned by intellectual and scientific establishments alike, Goethe defended his "natural science" writings as resolutely as he defended the crucial role played in nature by color. In a letter to Zelter (1832) he describes their rejection as one "of the most important experiences" of his advanced age, and claims to "praise" not the comprehension of his work but its perception as inevitably "destructive" of institutionalized miscomprehension.[15] Writing in a constructive rather than destructive vein to Joseph Carl Stieler (1829), Goethe described the lack of interest in his studies as indeed appropriate to certain scientific circles, and declared his distance from them. Of the "forty years" and "two octavo volumes" dedicated to the investigation of color, he writes, "it is perhaps little enough time and attention to give this subject," and continues:

> Den Mathematiko-Optikern verzeih ich gern, dass sie nichts davon wissen wollen; ihr Geschäft ist in diesem Fache bloss negativ. Wenn sie die Farbe aus ihren schätzbaren Objektivgläsern los sind, so fragen sie weiter nicht danach, ob es einen Maler, Färber, einen die Atmosphäre und die bunte Welt mit Freiheit betrachtenden Physiker, ein hübsches Mädchen, das sich ihrem Teint gemäss putzen will, obs diese in der Welt gibt, darum bekümmern sie sich nicht. . . .
> Dagegen lassen wir uns das Recht nicht nehmen, die Farbe in allen Vorkommnissen und Bedeutungen zu bewundern, zu lieben und womöglich zu erforschen.[16]

I gladly forgive the mathematical opticians for not wanting to know anything about it; their occupation with this area is merely negative. When they have gotten color out of their precious object lenses they do not ask further if there is a painter, a dyer, a physicist who considers the atmosphere and the multicolored world with freedom, a beautiful girl who wants to adorn herself according to her complexion; they do not concern themselves with whether there are any of these in the world. . . .
We, on the other hand, will not be deprived of the right to admire color in all its occurrences and meanings, to love it and, whenever possible, to research it.

[15] Letter of Feb. 4, 1832. *Goethes Briefe*, IV Bde. (Hamburg: Christian Wegner Verlag, 1967), IV:469–70.
[16] Letter of Jan. 26, 1829. *Ibid.*, IV:319–18.

The conjunction of a physicist and a pretty girl adorning herself according to her complexion may make the "freedom" of observation appealed to by Goethe appear immediately suspect as a means of experimentation. The opening of the "Vorwort" to the *Farbenlehre* in fact includes a statement of Goethe's skepticism toward the scientist's endeavor to "express" any empirical object in its essence. Yet Goethe proceeds to reclaim the right to experimentation *and* expression by rejecting the fundamental empirical assumption of a static essence-appearance relation and positing colors, phenomenal aspects of objects in nature, to be the actions or deeds (*Taten* [the former meaning connoting processes; the latter, their completion]), and sufferings or passions (*Leiden* [the latter meaning taken from the text of the New Testament: "Die Leiden Christi"]) of an essential aspect of nature, light:

> Denn eigentlich unternehmen wir umsonst, das Wesen eines Dinges auszudrücken. Wirkungen werden wir gewahr, und eine vollständige Geschichte dieser Wirkungen umfasste wohl allenfalls das Wesen jenes Dinges. Vergebens bemühen wir uns, den Charakter eines Menschen zu schildern; man stelle dagegen seine Handlungen, seine Taten zusammen, und ein Bild des Charakters wird uns entgegentreten.
>
> Die Farben sind Taten des Lichts, Taten und Leiden. In diesem Sinne können wir von denselben Aufschlüsse über das Licht erwarten. Farben und Licht stehen zwar untereinander in dem genausten Verhältnis, aber wir müssen uns beide als der ganzen Natur angehörig denken, denn sie ist es ganz, die sich dadurch dem Sinne des Auges besonders offenbaren will.[17]

> For, actually, we attempt in vain to express the essence of a thing. We become aware of [phenomenal] effects, and a complete story of these effects would well take the essence of the thing into account. We make the effort to depict the character of a human being in vain; if, on the

---

[17] Goethe, *Zur Farbenlehre*, XIII:315.

other hand, we set his actions and deeds together, a picture of that character will confront us.

Colors are the actions of light, actions and passions. In this sense we can expect the same conclusions with regard to light. Colors and light stand to each other in the most exact relation, but we must think of them both as belonging to all of nature, for it is nature entirely which thus wants to reveal itself particularly to the sense of the eye.

An analogy is set up here between the structures of appearance ("ein Bild . . . wird uns entgegentreten") in man and in nature. "Light" in the second paragraph substitutes for "the character of a human being" in the first, and "colors," for human "actions and deeds." A reversal of those substitutions would transform the "complete story of [phenomenal] effects" to follow this introduction into an allegorical narrative of phenomena effected by man. Goethe's designations of the object of his study—"color's occurrences and meaning," the "actions and passions" of light—seem equally, if not more appropriate to the objects of discursive analysis: "colors" as nonmimetic conveyors of meaning, or figures. The extension of the analogy between human and natural essences into analogous phenomenal modes is indeed made explicit by Goethe slightly later on, as he states that nature "speaks with itself," and "to us," as we do, in language.[18] While we, however, may assume knowledge of whom we speak to and what we say, the specific intentionality of the speech here ascribed to nature must remain uncertain. What we may interpret as messages meant for our understanding could instead be parts of a dialogue between nature and itself. Similarly, the issues of the cause and origin of the "language" nature seems to speak—whether they lie with us or in itself; whether its analysis should therefore be speculative or empirical—are made undeterminable by Goethe's description. Linguistic and symbolic relations which seem to arise as the consequence of human perceptions and designations are identified with and replaced by a reference to *Natursprache*. The validity of a "color theory" based upon a study of nature is un-

[18] *Ibid.*, XII:315–16.

derscored within this equation; at the same time, neither side of the equation remains stable long enough to exist without it:

> Man hat ein Mehr und Weniger, ein Wirken, ein Wider-streben, ein Tun, ein Leiden, ein Vordringendes, ein Zu-rückhaltendes, ein Heftiges, ein Mässigendes, ein Männ-liches, ein Weibliches überall bemerkt und genannt, und so entsteht eine Sprache, eine Symbolik, die man auf ähn-liche Fälle als Gleichnis, als nahverwandten Ausdruck, als unmittelbar passendes Wort anwenden and benutzen mag.
>
> Diese universallen [Bezeichnungen], diese Natur-sprache auch auf die Farbenlehre anzuwenden, diese Sprache durch die Farbenlehre, durch die Mannigfaltig-keit ihrer Erscheinungen zu bereichern, zu erweitern und so die Mitteilung höherer Anschauungen unter den Freunden der Natur zu erleichtern, war die Hauptabsicht des gegenwärtigen Werkes.[19]

All over one noticed and named a more and a less, a work-ing, a striving against, a doing, a suffering, a pushing for-ward, a holding back, a vehemence, a moderation, a mas-culine and a feminine, and so arises a language, a symbolic, which one can apply and use in similar cases as metaphor, as closely related expression, as immediately fitting word.

To apply these universal [designations], and also this language of nature, to the theory of colors, to enrich this language through the theory of colors, through the var-iousness of its appearances, to broaden and thus to ease the communication of higher intuitions among the friends of nature, this was the major intention of the present work.

The substitution of a *Symbolik* named by man with a natu-ral language of "universal designations" turns back upon and further specifies itself ("*eine* Sprache . . . *diese* Natursprache . . . *diese Sprache*") as do the relations between both the lan-guage and its theory, and the language and the many forms in

[19] *Ibid.*, XIII:316.

which it appears ("diese Natursprache . . . *auf* die Farbenlehre anzuwenden . . . *durch* die Farbenlehre, *durch* die Mannigfaltigkeit ihrer Erscheinungen"). The distinctions of movement, mass and quality stated here to shape the colors of a language of nature studied by science can be renamed—as they are by Goethe—discursive "images" or rhetorical "colors": a language whose "use" in context indiscriminately spans a full range of improper, or nonreferential, effects, i.e., those of "metaphor," as well as "related expression," and "immediately fitting word." Yet introductory passages such as these, whose own continually moving reversals between discourse and nature refuse priority or even identity to either phenomenon in isolation, render such a clear (one could say close to colorless) denomination questionable, precisely by problematizing whatever we might believe "literal" or "natural" color to be. Goethe's insistence, throughout the *Natural Science Writings*, upon the revealing involvement of phenomenal appearances, such as color, in nature, and the practical use of scientific observation, implies that neither "science" nor "nature" are to be simply excluded from investigations which invoke them.[20]

Although the "method" of Goethe's scientific practice has been explicated,[21] and the props and "color cards" of his ex-

[20] See footnote 17 above: "wir müssen uns beide [Farbe und Licht] als der ganzen Natur angehörig denken," and the following fragments in the *Maximen und Reflexionen* (*ibid.*, XII:434, 449): "Die Phänomene sind nichts wert, als wenn sie eine tiefere Einsicht in die Natur gewähren oder wenn sie uns zum Nutzen anzuwenden sind" (503).

"Die Natur auffassen und sie unmittelbar benutzen ist wenig Menschen gegeben; zwischen Erkenntnis und Gebrauch erfinden sie sich gern ein Luftgespenst, das sie sorgfältig ausbilden und darüber den Gegenstand mit der Benutzung vergessen" (620).

[Phenomena only have worth when they provide a deeper insight into nature or when they are applicable to our use.]

[It is given to few to grasp nature and to use it without mediation; between cognition and use (most) gladly fabricate a phantom that they carefully cultivate and in so doing forget the object along with its use.]

[21] See "Goethes Methode," in "Anmerkungen zur *Farbenlehre*," *ibid.*, XIII:615–27. For Goethe on "method," see *Maximen* 436, 553, 631, and especially 551: "Cartesius schrieb sein Buch de Methodo einige Male um, und wie es jetzt liegt, kann es uns doch nichts helfen. Jeder der eine Zeitlang auf

periments schematically reproduced,[22] his conception of color as the "movements and designations . . . promoting any form of life"[23] prohibited any but an extemporaneous series of empirical approaches (*Versuche*) to its study. In an essay of April 1792, later entitled, "Der Versuch als Vermittler von Objekt und Subjekt" [The Experiment as Mediator of Object and Subject], Goethe specifies the "half arbitrary, half artificial" nature of the phenomena that the mediation "we call experimentation" must repeatedly reconstruct.[24] For this reason, the textual arrangement of the results of individual "Versuche[n]" must follow the sequential order of experimentation itself rather than a prefigured, "systematic form": "Diese Materiellen müssen in Reihen geordnet und niedergelegt sein, nicht auf eine hypothetische Weise zusammengestellt, nicht zu einer systematischen Form verwendet"[25] [These materials must be ordered and laid down in series, not put together in a hypothetical manner, not employed to fit a systematic form]. From their inception, both the empirical experiments, carried out in daylight, and discursive composition of the "color theory" were directed specifically against the restrictive manipulation and systematization of color which resulted in Newton's Optics:

Dass Newton bei seinen prismatischen Versuchen die Öffnung so klein als möglich nahm, um eine Linie zum Lichtstrahl bequem zu symbolisieren, hat eine unheilbare Verirrung über die Welt gebracht, an der vielleicht noch Jahrhunderte leiden.
Der Newtonische Irrtum steht so nett im Konversa-

---

dem redlichen Forschen verharrt, muss seine Methode umändern" (*ibid.*, XII:440) [Descartes rewrote his book *On Method* a few times, and as it is now, it still cannot help us. Anyone who persists at length at honest research has to change his method].

[22] See, Matthaei, *Goethes Farbenlehre, passim*, for full-color copies accompanying specific experiments.

[23] "Bewegungen und Bestimmungen . . . irgendeine Art von Leben befördend" (*Zur Farbenlehre*, XIII:316).

[24] *Ibid.*, XIII:14. A first draft of "Der Versuch als Vermittler von Objekt und Subjekt" was sent to Schiller in 1798; it was later published by Goethe in the journal, *Zur Naturwissenschaft überhaupt* (1823).

[25] *Ibid.*, XIII:20.

tions-lexikon, dass man die Oktavseite nur auswendig lernen darf, um die Farbe fürs ganze Leben los zu sein.[26]

That Newton, in his prismatic experiments, took the
smallest possible opening in order to comfortably sym-
bolize a line into a ray of light, brought an incurable ab-
erration upon the world, from which perhaps centuries to
come will still suffer.

The Newtonian error stands so neatly in the dictionary
of conversation that one may merely learn the page by
heart in order to be rid of color for one's entire life.

In opposition to Newton's "comfortable symboliz[ation]"
of light in the form of a "line," a severe limitation of that primary *Urphänomen* symbolized here, in turn, in transparently
sexual terms (the isolation, through "the smallest possible
opening," of a single ray into a dark room), Goethe posed the
volatile counterpremise that "certain colors are inherent to
certain forms of life."[27] Formal objects are thus claimed to be
animate in their structure, and nature, once revealed by light
"through eyesight" (see footnote 17), already invested with
color. This "scientific" understanding of nature is reminiscent
of the well-known discovery of resignation[28] at the opening of
Faust II: "Am farbigen Abglanz haben wir das Leben"
(I.4727) ["In colored reflection (or refraction) we have life]. Its
emphasis upon color as a living and constituent quality of
form, whose source of life (in light and in the eye) must be recognized as "ungraspable" and impractical,[29] irreducible to an

---

[26] *Maximen*, XII:462–63 (687, 689).

[27] "Gewisse Farben sind gewissen Geschöpfen eigen" (Matthaei, *Goethes
Farbenlehre*, p. 14).

[28] Goethe uses this term to designate our recognition of "original phenomena" whose occurrence empiricism cannot account for: "Wenn ich mich beim
Urphänomen zuletzt beruhige, so ist es doch auch nur Resignation; aber es
bleibt ein grosser Unterschied, ob ich mich an den Grenzen der Menschheit re-
signiere oder innerhalb einer hypothetischen Beschränkheit meines bornierten
Individuums" (*Maximen*, XII:367, no. 20) [When I finally come to rest at the
original phenomenon, that, too, is still only resignation; but a great difference
remains in whether I resign myself at the boundaries of humanity or within the
hypothetical limitedness of my narrow-minded individuality].

[29] "Je weiter man in der Erfahrung fortrückt, desto näher kommt man dem

ordered spectrum amounting to white light and the mechanical faculty of lexical "memorization" (see footnote 26), ensured the systematic failure of Goethe's "color theory," although in a manner which its correction by optics cannot fully comprehend.

For while Goethe carefully divides his study of colors into the three categories of their basic affiliations—the "physiological," "belonging to the eye"; the "physical," brought to appearance through a colorless medium; and the "chemical," "belonging to the object"[30]—the results of his investigations are found to have been contaminated by the very employment of empirical observation. In his 1820 *Nachwort zur Farbenlehre*, Goethe redefines the "physiological colors" as "those, that are . . . the beginning and end of all color theories . . . and rather than regarding them as fleeting mistakes in seeing, they are now held as norm and guideline for all residual evidence."[31] The status of colors whose appearance is produced by the eye characterizes, or could be called the "symbolic" of, the "language of nature" which the discursive scientist "first makes visible as text."[32] If our knowledge of nature, as Goethe argues, must include phenomenal appearances as well as form, it is because formal perceptions are always colored by the activity of cognition. For any "attentive observation" of objective phenomena invokes its own interpretative "transposition"

Unerforschlichen; je mehr man die Erfahrung zu nutzen weiss, desto mehr sieht man, dass das Unerforschliche keinen praktischen Nutzen hat" [The further one goes back into experience, the nearer one comes to the ungraspable (or unresearchable); the more one knows how to use experience, the more one sees that the ungraspable has no practical use].

"Das schönste Glück des denkenden Menschen ist, das Erforschliche erforscht zu haben und das Unerforschliche ruhig zu verehren" [The most beautiful piece of fortune of the thinking man is to have researched the researchable and to quietly honor the unresearchable] (*ibid.*, XII:406, 467, nos. 299, 718).

[30] *Zur Farbenlehre*, XII:325.

[31] "Diese sind es, die als Anfang und Ende aller Farbenlehre bei unserm Vortrag vorangestellt worden, die auch wohl nach und nach ihrem ganzem Wert und Würde anerkannt und anstatt dass man sie vorher als flüchtige Augenfehler betrachtete, nunmehr als Norm und Richtschnur alles übrigen Sichtbaren festgehalten werden" (Matthaei, *Goethes Farbenlehre*, p. 40).

[32] "Denn eigentlich sollte der Schreibende . . . die Phänomene . . . als Text erst anschaulich machen" (*Zur Farbenlehre*, XIII:321).

into "theory." The defense of a theory, in turn, transforms "fleeting mistakes" of perception into the norms and guidelines of knowledge. That recognition, circular and inevitable in its consequences, is Goethe's own. It is also, as he asserts, the "necessary" cognitive condition for achieving results that, like color itself, will be "living" and "useful" in effect. He states the centrality of theory to sight itself:

> Ist es doch eine höchst wunderliche Forderung, die wohl manchmal gemacht, aber auch selbst von denen, die sie machen, nicht erfüllt wird: Erfahrungen solle man ohne irgendein theoretisches Band vortragen und dem Leser, dem Schüler überlassen, sich selbst nach Belieben irgendeine Überzeugung zu bilden. Denn das blosse An-blicken einer Sache kann uns nichts fordern. Jedes Anse-hen *geht über* in ein Betrachten, jedes Betrachten in ein Sinnen, jedes Sinnen in ein Verknüpfen, und *so kann man sagen, dass wir schon bei jedem aufmerksamen Blick in die Welt theoretisieren.* Dieses aber mit Bewusstsein, mit Selbstkenntnis, mit *Freiheit* und, um uns eines gewagten Wortes zu bedienen, mit *Ironie* zu tun und vorzunehmen, eine solche Gewandtheit ist nötig, wenn die Abstraktion, vor der wir uns fürchten, unschädlich und das Erfah-rungsresultat, das wir hoffen, recht lebendig und nützlich werden soll.[33]

It is truly a demand to be wondered at which, while sometimes made, is not even fulfilled by those who make it: one should present experiences without their being bound together theoretically and leave it to the reader, or the student, to form any persuasion which appeals to him. For mere looking at a thing gets us nowhere. All looking is *transposed* into a considering, all considering into a thinking, all thinking into a joining together, and *so one can say that at every attentive glance in the world we are already theorizing.* To do and to undertake this, however, with consciousness, with self-knowledge, with *freedom*, and—to use a daring word—with *irony*, such dexterity is necessary if the abstraction, which we fear, is to be harm-

[33] *Ibid.*, XIII:317; (my emphasis).

less and the result for experience, for which we hope, truly
living and useful.

Carried out as strictly "natural science," Goethe's attack
upon the violent circumscription of nature—the break up of
the force of light into a static spectrum of colors and the dissolution of colors into complementary transparency—understands itself as an ironical discourse which must prove as
"theory" the fiction of objectified color, of color as the
natural appearance of form, in order to render any theory of
objectification, of formal conceptualization *without* color
(*Abstraktion*), a fiction. The movement of vision from an
objective referent (the "mere looking at a thing") to its own
"theoretization" is the coloring of all empirical perception
demonstrated in the "color theory." The discursive model implied here for the process of cognition holds equally for that of
experimentation, or concrete "mediation." As Goethe redefines the latter in "Der Versuch als Vermittler . . . ":

> das heisst ein Versuch, viele Gegenstände in ein gewisses
> fassliches Verhältnis zu bringen, das sie, streng genom-
> men, untereinander nicht haben, daher die Neigung zu
> Hypothesen, zu Theorien, Terminologien und Systemen,
> die wir nicht missbilligen können, weil sie aus der Orga-
> nisation unsers Wesen notwendig entspringen müssen.[34]

> this is called an experiment: the bringing of many objects
> into a certain graspable relation which, strictly speaking,
> they do not have among themselves; thus the proclivity
> for hypotheses, theories, terminologies, and systems, of
> which we cannot disapprove, because they must spring
> necessarily from the organization of our being.

The power to form relations ("Gegenstände in ein . . . Verhältnis zu bringen") lacks the power to prove their validity ("das
sie, streng genommen, untereinander nicht haben"). The "proclivity" for theory is a function of that paradox, and as such
one of which we are "unable to disapprove"; its source, since
denied any relation to objects themselves, is here "necessarily"

[34] *Ibid.*, XIII:16.

displaced onto the internal structure of the experimenter's own "being." In the context of prefacing an investigation which calls itself a "theory"—in the "Vorwort" to the *Farbenlehre*—the problems of authority and proof brought to light in "Der Versuch als Vermittler . . ." are replaced with assertions of self-conscious "freedom" and "irony," disclaimers all the more persuasive for their apparent candor.

For, ironically enough, "das Erfahrungsresultat," or experience in which the reception of that theoretical fiction results, may itself appear so "living" and "useful" as to give the fiction the appearance of truth. One wholly persuaded reader of the "color theory" views Goethe's "achievement" as a real counterproof to "idealistic philosophy," which would reduce color to a purely subjective phenomenon, "as well as to the technical science of physics,"[35] which must deny the role of subjectivity in objective perception. When the same reader goes on to state, "With so much greater right may we be glad that Goethe saves colors as real for our world,"[36] he replaces the fiction of a world without color with that of "real" color in a properly human world, disregarding his own recognition of the "error through which the material status of color is saved." The *Farbenlehre* enthusiast notes that Goethe attributed to pure "images" of color, in the shape of auras or borders, the mode of mutually effective "things." He focuses incisively upon the discursive problem of distinguishing image from object posed by Goethe's science, analyzing the "explanation" of the color experiments as follows:

> This explanation of the colored borders cannot be maintained. It is already doubtful to say that the image [*Bild*] is broadened or narrowed; an "image" ["*Bild*"] is not a thing to which the like can happen. A picture [*Bild*] on the wall is a thing, a body, an individual, to which change can happen; the appearance of color which Goethe treats is not. It is even more doubtful when Goethe says that the image apparently moves itself, that the colored column strives *out of the image* [Bild], etc.

[35] Fritz Seidel, *Goethe gegen Kant* (Berlin: Altberliner Verlag, 1949), p. 75.
[36] *Ibid.*, p. 75.

One has to oppose such thinking if one does not want to fall prey to the errors which follow from it: an insect can strive out of a circle, but not a colored column. . . . And if one wanted to let pass the material content, which is perhaps correct in itself, Goethe's deciding contention is still untenable: that through the displacement of the primary image [*Hauptbilde*] a secondary image [*Nebenbild*] arises. Here a doubtful mode of expression and of thinking leads into error.[37]

A "Bild" (a discursive image) is not a "Bild" (a concrete portrait); to regard it as such is "to fall prey to errors." The right to celebrate the restoration of a constitutively colored world must reject the theoretical figuration of colors *as* images which not only "effect and transform" each other, but appear to be "striving out of" their imaged form. Such claims for the independent animacy of color are attributed to a "doubtful mode" of cognitive expression on Goethe's part. Confusion sets in here between the "colors" under investigation and those of the investigative discourse. The latter, even if at first held in distinction from a hypothetically "correct material content," prove to lead to the "decisive" and "untenable" assertion of color, as image, compelling color into being: "that through the displacement of the primary image a secondary image arises." Expressive form and content may be conceded as mutually effective, but colors themselves may not be, if the world of color saved by theory is to be identified as ours. The fact that the "natural science" of such a world must be written "mit Ironie" if it is to be true to nature, makes the imaging of its experiments at once literally unacceptable and the necessary "mode" of their explanation, their being understood.

Colors in the *Farbenlehre* are figured as images which interact like objects. Unlike objects, however, they are also said to move in departure from their form. The "Bilder" of *Die Wahlverwandtschaften* are human lives moved by passion; its narrative tells a story in which their relations are transformed. Included in the above critique of Goethe's description of color

[37] *Ibid.*, pp. 79–80; my emphasis.

as a moving displacement of form was the contrary assertion, "an insect can strive out of a circle, but not a colored column." Returning to the problem of what its title, "Wahlverwandtschaften," means, we may examine whether the characters of the novel, its objectified "images," share the same freedom of choice in their movements as the color enthusiast's insect, or, for that matter, its mere capability ("*can* strive out of a circle"). In order to understand the specifically *narrative* character of *Die Wahlverwandtschaften*, we must know whether those characters enter into and break the circle[38] of their relations at will, and thus can be considered the cause of their own figurations, or whether the substitutions they carry out merely plot the path of a governing intention by name. The proper referent of "relations of choice" may be the "natural language" of "colors" the narrative produces, its "figural meaning," or it may imply a stable structure of meaning, a static spectrum of "colors" independent of the "living" motions from which it is formed.

These opposing views of the events narrated in the novel are mediated on one level, as already suggested, by the novel as *literary* form. For the discourse of a narrative fiction combines the appearance of meaning, "actions and passions" ("Taten und Leiden"), with the endeavor to explain them; each occurrence engages its "observation" or "glance" ("Blick") in the voice of narrator, character, or author. Everywhere within a novel, someone must be known to be envisioning and something must be said to be seen. The possibility of purely conceptual, generic, or sensory relations, played out in the composition of philosophy and verse, is never fully excluded from the discursive content of the novel. But its realization would most clearly betoken the failure of the novel: the impossibility of

---

[38] The term *Kreis* (circle) refers to and is used to reconstruct the relations of colors in the *Farbenlehre*. It is used throughout *Die Wahlverwandtschaften*, by characters and narrator alike, to name the shape taken by the interrelations of human lives. See, for example, VI:412: "Wie die Erscheinung von bedeutenden Menschen in irgendeinem Kreise niemals ohne Folge bleiben kann" [As the appearance of significant people in any circle can never remain without consequence], et passim.

composing a story.[39] Moreover, because appearances in the novel are always part of a continuing narrative, each becomes involved in the understanding of its relations to others. In other words, the novel *takes form as* a "transposition" into "theoretization": the narration of what it designates into the shape and appearance of a coherent, logically and causally connected, fiction.

While a theoretical science which refers to nature must be prefaced by an explicitly ironical stance in order to account for the objective "errors" of its explanations, the irony of the novel is invoked in its status as "fiction." That status is upheld, ironically, only to the extent that the referents of its discourse are understood as "real." Irony appears subsumed whenever we mistake that "literary" reality for truth, and strengthened by the very fact that we do so. The capability of the novel as form is to make narrative the measure and mode of understanding, to make "actions and passions" appear consequences of a cause,[40] for as a "fiction" rather than a "theory," it can refer to the "ungraspable" "original phenomena" of nature—the act of seeing and the light we see by—within its story by name.

Within *Die Wahlverwandtschaften* the images indicated by those referents indicate something in turn about the relation between articulation and understanding: the inevitable need to know intention by referent, meaning by word, a character by its name. They are designated, most directly, as the power of man to mediate vision in language, and of light to make objects visible: "Mittler" and "Luciane." Some maintain superstitiously, the narrator informs us, that Mittler was destined to his vocation by his name: "Diejenigen, die auf Namensbedeutungen abergläublisch sind, behaupten, der Name Mittler habe ihn genötigt, diese seltsamste aller Bestimmungen zu

---

[39] The brief life of the *nouveau roman* may serve to indicate as much, although the sense of a story was never fully excluded from that experiment in randomly sequential narrative.

[40] Other narratives, such as histories and biographies, often approach the novel in discursive effect; in as far as their function is to claim fidelity to their referent and that causality inheres not in narration but in the designated occurrences themselves, they fall short of the novel as history and biography.

ergreifen"[41] [Those who are superstitious about the meanings
of names contend that the name Mittler had made it necessary
for him to choose this strangest of all (occupational) determi-
nations]. The purpose by which Mittler determines his life may
have been determined by the accident, believed significant, of
his being called by a certain word, an otherwise abstract referent transformed into a proper noun. If the relevance of the
term, "Mittler," to the character and his vocation is viewed instead as purely fortuitous, the novel may be seen to parody its
own purpose, that of making its referents known through a sequence of narrated actions. Yet Mittler is referred to as a mediator *while* his activities are shown to signify anything but his
name: throughout the novel they entail polarities as their result. Whether called upon by others or by knowledge of his
craft, Mittler, who refuses to appear without acting, to waste
time where he is not needed (his first appearance in the narrative prefaced by his own question and condition, "ob es not
tue"[42] [is there need]), always acts at the wrong moment and
to powerfully divisive effect. Mittler's own recognition of the
temporal basis of effective mediation is referred to by the narrator in the final chapter of the novel, when his appearance is
to prove most poorly timed: "Der hartnäckige Mann wusste
nur zu wohl, dass es einen gewissen Moment gibt, wo allein
das Eisen zu schmieden ist"[43] [The obstinate man knew only
too well that there is a certain moment alone when the iron is
to be forged]. Ottilie has already entered and is to leave the
room in which he speaks transformed, seen by Charlotte before Mittler can be interrupted ("ehe sie ihn noch unterbrechen
konnte, sah sie schon Ottilien, deren Gestalt sich verwandelt
hatte, aus dem Zimmer gehen" [before she could interrupt him
she saw Ottilie, whose figure had transformed itself, go out of
the room]), as the mediator gives voice to the "good fortune"
of maintaining relations which are "indissolubly bound."[44]
His speech in praise of discursive mediation propels the invisible progress of Ottilie's death, destabilizing the circle of rela-

[41] Goethe, *Die Wahlverwandtschaften*, VI:255.
[42] *Ibid.*, VI:253.
[43] *Ibid.*, VI:481.
[44] *Ibid.*, VI:483.

tions which had settled for a second time. Indeed, the disturbing period preceding the formal return of those relations can only be properly referred to in "Mittler" 's name: "Jedes unerfreuliche, unbequeme Gefühl der mittlern Zeit war ausgelöscht"[45] [Every unhappy, uncomfortable feeling of the intervening time was dissolved].

Discursive mediation, as personified and understood by Mittler, depends upon proper timing to be enacted; once enacted, it produces further "actions and passions" rather than the formal stability it intends. Reflecting upon their own errors, characters compelled to transgress the form of their relations view Mittler and time itself as the necessary mediators of their mistakes. These mobile images of human nature understand their own movements in terms of temporal predication, conceiving of "der mittlern Zeit" as the time in which they take on meaning. Charlotte's belief in Eduard's eventual return only echoes Eduard's earlier insistence upon a belated marriage to Charlotte. Her interpretation, in retrospect, of their "imagination's" double adultery[46] as a "new binding of

[45] *Ibid.*, VI:479.

[46] The power of imagination to make the absent present, while only as an image or simulacrum of itself, is weirdly given "rule" *over* material reality here in the appearance of the infant Otto, offspring of Charlotte and Eduard, who unmistakably resembles the objects of their errant imaginings while making love, the Captain and Ottilie. The well-known narrative detail of Otto's bizarre facial resemblances is often viewed as a "supernatural" aspect of Goethe's story. In that it violates not only the moral bond of marriage between Charlotte and Eduard but the speculative division, based on the premise of the mutual exclusivity of "presence" and "absence," between imagination and matter, or images and objective vision, Otto's appearance may be viewed instead as the most *un*adulteratedly "natural" detail of the novel: the single representation most literally "native" to this particular narrative. For it unites the very act of relating with the power of imagination and thus the visible, empirical "reality" resulting from the formation of relations with the images (or *Bilder*) viewed mentally by imagination. Put in the more general terms provided by Kant, "Otto" is what would always "appear" if the "free play of imagination" described in the *Third Critique* were itself united with the "freedom" of the "moral law": a visibly incriminating "false witness" to either one form of "freedom" or the other, that of consequent, "concrete," and moral action or the inconsequent imaginings of the mind. The narrator acquaints us with the "rights" of "imagination" in a novel in which Kant's moral and imaginative "freedom" are made, through representation, to embrace: "In der

their relations"[47] is countered by Eduard's reading of the "many clear signs"[48] which prove his claim to Ottilie. Included in these signs, as he explains later to the Captain, is that of his own survival in battle. Eduard decides to substitute himself for a glass etched with his own initials which he has misconceived as standing for his union with Ottilie: "mich selbst will ich an die Stelle des Glases zum Zeichen machen, ob unsre Verbindung möglich sei oder nicht"[49] [in the place of this glass I will make myself into a sign of whether our bond is possible or not]. Its duration as a sign (of what it is not) transforms his life into a symbol. After "seeking death," Eduard comes to view his own appearance as an image of a single and unmediated significance: "Ottilie ist mein, und was noch zwischen diesem Gedanken und der Ausführung liegt, kann ich für nichts bedeutend ansehen"[50] [Ottilie is mine, and whatever still lies between this thought and its execution I cannot view as meaningful].

Like the "movements" of nature cited in the *Farbenlehre*, the motion of passion is first "colored" with meaning when substituted for by "language," "discourse" or "speech" ("diese Natursprache," Mittler's "Rede") whose own "phenomena," "signs," must be seen *as* mediations, requiring sequential time to be understood. Thus meaning, by the same token, is subject to the appearance of mediation, i.e., a phenomenality which as *mere* appearance may be false. Eduard's misinterpretation of the unchanged letters on a glass substitutes another meaning for one earlier intended. More disarming, because achronistic in effect, is the reverse situa-

---

Lampendämmerung sogleich behauptete die innre Neigung, behauptete die Einbildungskraft ihre Rechte über das Wirkliche: Eduard hielt nur Ottilien in seinen Armen, Charlotten schwebte der Hauptmann näher oder ferner vor der Seele, und so verwebten, wundersam genug, sich Abwesendes und Gegenwärtiges reizend und wonnevoll durcheinander" (*ibid.*, VI:321) [In the dusky light of the lamp, inner inclination, the power of imagination, at once claimed their rights over the real: Eduard held only Ottilie in his arms, the Captain floated, near or far, before Charlotte's soul, and so absent and present, wonderfully enough, wove enticingly and rapturously through each other].

[47] *Ibid.*, VI:358–59.
[48] *Ibid.*, VI:447.
[49] *Ibid.*
[50] *Ibid.*

tion. Appearances that seem identical to those of a former moment may impose upon relations a meaning no longer pertinent, thereby obliterating the significance they have garnered over time. The narrator explains such repetition as a common occurrence conditioned by the "nature" of man. That "nature," enumerated to encompass both internal and external circumstances which change "interminably," is observed by the narrator to be itself "unchangeable":

> Was einem jeden Menschen gewöhnlich begegnet, wiederholt sich mehr, als man glaubt, weil seine Natur hiezu die nächste Bestimmung gibt. Charakter, Individualität, Neigung, Richtung, Ortlichkeit, Umgebungen und Gewohnheiten bilden zusammen ein Ganzes, in welchem jeder Mensch wie in einem Elemente, in einer Atmosphäre schwimmt, worin es ihm allein bequem und behaglich ist. Und so finden wir die Menschen, über deren Veränderlichkeit so viele Klage geführt wird, nach vielen Jahren zu unserm Erstaunen unverändert und nach äussern und innern unendlichen Anregungen unveränderlich.[51]

> What every human being customarily encounters repeats itself more than one believes, because one's nature determines one most closely in that regard. Character, individuality, inclination, direction, location, surroundings, and habits form together a whole in which each human being, as if in an element, or in an atmosphere, swims, in which it is only snug and comfortable for him. And so to our astonishment we find humanity, about whose changeability there are so many complaints, after so many years, unchanged, and after unending external and internal disturbances, unchangeable.

This general observation of human nature can be seen to personify Goethe's enigmatic lyric title, "Dauer im Wechsel" [Duration in Change]. Yet within the context of a temporally continuous narrative, relations of images which appear immediately as they once appeared must be viewed as "seeming" images or illusions, and their mistaking, named and "par-

---

[51] *Ibid.*, VI:478.

doned" as deluded vision or "madness." The narrator continues:

> So bewegte sich auch in dem täglichen Zusammenleben unserer Freunde fast alles wieder in dem alten Gleise. Noch immer äusserte Ottilie stillschweigend durch manche Gefälligkeit ihr zuvorkommendes Wesen, und so jedes nach seiner Art. Auf diese Weise zeigte sich der häusliche Zirkel als ein *Scheinbild* des vorigen Lebens, und der Wahn, als ob noch alles beim alten sei, war verzeihlich.[52]

> So almost everything in the daily life together of our friends moved again in the old track. Ottilie still expressed her obliging being silently through many complaisances, and so [continued] everything in its way. In this manner, the domestic circle showed itself as a *seeming image* of its previous life, and the madness, that everything was still as it had been, was pardonable.

The signs of "madness," those that eradicate temporality through their purely spatial perception, are not misconstrued in this case from an inscription on a glass. Instead they are read, while never having been *written*, in nature:

> Die herbstlichen Tage, an Länge eben jenen Frühlingstagen gleich, riefen die Gesellschaft um eben die Stunde aus dem Freien ins Haus zurück. Der Schmuck an Früchten und Blumen, der dieser Zeit eigen ist, liess glauben, als wenn es der Herbst jenes ersten Frühlings wäre; die Zwischenzeit war ins Vergessen gefallen. Denn nun blühten die Blumen, dergleichen man in jenen ersten Tagen auch gesäet hatte; nun reiften Früchte an den Bäumen, die man damals blühen gesehen.[53]

> The autumn days, identical in length to those very days of spring, called the company [of friends] back into the house from outdoors at the very same hour. The ornament of fruits and flowers, which properly belongs to this time, let one believe that it was the fall of that first spring;

---

[52] *Ibid.*, VI:479; my emphasis.
[53] *Ibid.*

the time between had fallen into oblivion. For now bloomed the flowers which one had sown in those first days; now ripened the fruits on the trees which one had then seen blooming.

The external landscape of the narrative, the "element" or "atmosphere" to which its characters return, is directly described here as a deceptive field of artifice or "ornament." The "flowers" and "fruits" which are said to mislead, however, do so because the "nature" from which they spring is that of narration itself. For only in the course of a chronological narrative can the face of nature be said to substitute for itself: only when understood to interact as figures can "natural" phenomena in one place ("For now bloomed the flowers") be read to replace others in another place ("fruits on the trees which one had then seen blooming"), and thus to appear proper to a single period of time ("the ornament . . . which properly belongs to this time"). Moreover, temporal demarcations which are arbitrary and unavailable to vision in themselves—the length of days, a specified hour—take on in recurrence their own misconceived appearance of identity: "days, identical in length . . . at the very same hour." "The time between" the separation and rejoining[54] of "Wahlverwandtschaften," the duration which the novel itself has mediated through narration, falls "into oblivion." At such a moment the narrative can only continue by envisioning its own discourse as overcome. The return of relations which are unmediated and repeat their own history is ascribed, through rewriting in retrospect, to an "unbeschreibliche, fast magische Anziehungskraft" [an indescribable, almost magical force of attraction], as the narrator describes an "indescribable . . . force" by referring to the forms of meaning

[54] Parallel occurrences are said in the *Farbenlehre* to mark our awareness of the language of phenomenal relations in nature (see footnote 23): "Diese allgemeinen Bewegungen und Bestimmungen werden wir auf die verschiedenste Weise gewahr . . . jedoch immer als verbindend oder trennend, das Dasein bewegend und irgendeine Art von Leben befördernd" [We become aware of these general movements and determination in the most different ways . . . always, however, as binding or separating, moving Being and furthering life in any way].

of which it has no need: vision, discourse, intentionality of thought, distinctions:

> Nach wie vor übten sie eine unbeschreibliche, fast magische Anziehungskraft gegeneinander aus. Sie wohnten unter einem Dache; aber selbst ohne gerade aneinander zu denken, mit andern Dingen beschäftigt, von der Gesellschaft hin- und hergezogen, näherten sie sich einander. . . . Nur die nächste Nähe konnte sie beruhigen, aber auch völlig beruhigen, und diese Nähe war genug; nicht eines Blickes, nicht eines Wortes, keiner Gebärde, keiner Berührung bedurfte es, nur des reinen Zusammenseins. Dann waren es nicht zwei Menschen, es war nur Ein Mensch im bewusstlosen vollkommnen Behagen, mit sich selbst zufrieden und mit der Welt. . . . Das Leben war ihnen ein Rätsel, dessen Auflösung sie nur miteinander fanden.[55]

Now as before they exercised an indescribable, almost magical force of attraction upon each other. They lived under the same roof, but without even thinking exactly of one another, occupied with other things, drawn here and there by the company of friends, they approached each other. . . . Only the closest proximity could calm them, but could also fully calm them, and this proximity was enough; there was no need for a glance, a word, a gesture, a touch: only for pure being together. Then it wasn't two human beings, it was only One in unconscious, perfect comfort, content with himself and with the world. . . . Life was to them a riddle whose solution they found only with one another.

The activity of mediation endows vision with significance, sight with the color of what is seen, the movement of passion with the name and meaning of love. At the same time, and at the price of its own appearance, it strengthens the relations it fails to recognize and severs those it intends to secure as bonds. In the absence of mediation, in "reine[m] Zusammensein," errant passions and perceptions must be viewed, at the very

[55] *Ibid.*, VI:478.

least, as "pardonable," since, unrelated by discourse to understanding, they can never be conceived of, let alone as going
wrong. Like living color "Bilder" which are seen through experimentation and explained to bring each other into being,
the human images of the novel's story, brought together by a
practical *Versuch*,[56] are said to find with each other alone the
solution of the riddle posed by life. The ongoing narration of
those relations must refer to their arresting of discursive meaning as delusion. But within the event the narrative recounts *as*
figuration, within "Wahlverwandtschaften," as narrative duration is forgotten and neither choice of object nor designation
of meaning obtains, a *Scheinbild* (see footnote 52) *is* a "*Bild*,"
an image or metaphor (the name of a movement within language which both replaces and refers); *is* a *Bild*, a portrait or
picture (an object intended to imitate another, to objectify
movement at a moment in time). The experience in which such
an occurrence results is figured in turn as a consciousless, com-
modious unity. The very bases of the novel's unsettling story
appear suspended: "Dann waren es nicht zwei Menschen, es
war nur Ein Mensch im bewusstlosem Vollkommenen Be-
hagen, mit sich selbst zufrieden und mit der Welt" [Then it
wasn't two human beings, it was One in unconscious, perfect
comfort, content with himself and with the world]. Hence its
irony as fiction is never more far-reaching. For devoid of the
time and means with which to distinguish between appear-

---

[56] "Versuch" is used in a properly scientific context, although predicated in
distinctly discursive terms, by the Captain in explaining "Wahlverwandtschaften" to Charlotte: "Sobald unser chemisches Kabinett ankommt, wollen
wir Sie verschiedene Versuche sehen lassen, die sehr unterhaltend sind und einen besseren Begriff geben als Worte, Namen und Kunstausdrücke" (VI:273)
[As soon as our chemical cabinet arrives, we want to have you see different
experiments that are very entertaining and provide a better conception than
words, names, and technical expressions]. It was previously used by Charlotte,
however, in reference to the initiation of "Wahlverwandtschaften" as an experiment in human relations. Describing herself as no longer able to resist Eduard's desire to invite the Captain, she posits: "Lass uns den Versuch
machen!" [Let's perform the experiment!]—a command that she then qualifies
in terms of time: "Das einzige, was ich dich bitte: es sei nur auf kurze Zeit an-
gesehen" (VI:256) [The only thing which I ask of you is that it be planned (or
"viewed") for a short time].

ances, the "self," and the "world"—not to speak of an accompanying sense of contentment—cannot begin to be known.

The novel offers up its irony as self-evident in designating the condition upon which mediated meaning depends. Mittler, the character, may be viewed as misguided and verbose, and his relation to the narrator's own occupation easily overlooked by an interest in the story's outcome. The character called Luciane, however, is distinguished foremost by her desire to confuse. The one literally familial relation in the novel (aside from the infant Otto, who appears related to parents other than his own), she shares with her mother, Charlotte, no rapport to speak of. Luciane's chief activity is to clothe herself in false appearances; she brings *Scheinbilder* to vision by intention. The narrator explains why her arrival in the story is surrounded by "so much baggage":

> Nicht umsonst hatte sie so vieles Gepäcke mitgebracht, ja es war ihr noch manches gefolgt. Sie hatte sich auf eine unendliche Abwechselung in Kleidern vorgesehen . . . so erschien sie . . . auch . . . im wirklichen Maskenkleid, als Bäuerin und Fischerin, als Fee und Blumenmädchen. Sie verschmähte nicht, sich als alte Frau zu verkleiden, um desto frischer ihr junges Gesicht aus der Kutte hervorzuzeigen; und wirklich verwirrte sie dadurch das Gegenwärtige und das Eingebildete dergestalt, dass man sich mit der Saalnixe verwandt und verschwägert zu sein glaubte.
>
> Wozu sie aber diese Verkleidungen hauptsächlich benutzte, waren pantomimische Stellungen und Tänze, in denen sie verschiedene Charaktere auszudrücken gewandt war.[57]

> Not for nothing had she brought so much baggage along; indeed still more followed her. She had taken care to have an unending change of clothes . . . so she appeared . . . also . . . in real costume, as a farmwoman and a fisherwoman, as a fairy and a flowergirl. She did not disdain dressing herself as an old woman in order to be able to show, as all the more fresh, her young face from

[57] *Ibid.*, VI:379.

out of the cowl; and she really confused thereby the present and the imagined in such a manner that one believed oneself related and in-lawed with this nymph of the hall.

The purposes for which she mainly used these costumes, however, were pantomime presentations and dances, in which she was dexterous in expressing different characters.

Luciane impersonates figures as pictures. Onstage and off, her mode of reference is mimetic: a mimetics, however, which obviates reference to the purpose of displaying the identity of the imitator. She draws attention to herself by representing what she is not, focusing her own attentions upon those who "represent something of significance,"[58] while prohibiting at the same time that her actions and appearance be probed. Demanding to be seen, she keeps the spectators she attracts at a proper distance, in the dark:

> Sie wollte mit jedermann nach Belieben umspringen, jeder war in Gefahr, von ihr einmal angestossen, gezerrt, oder sonst geneckt zu werden; niemand aber durfte sich gegen sie ein Gleiches erlauben, niemand sie nach Willkür berühen, niemand auch nur im entferntesten Sinne, eine Freiheit, die sie sich nahm, erwidern; und so hielt sie die andern in den strengsten Grenzen der Sittlichkeit gegen sich, die sie gegen andere jeden Augenblick zu übertreten schien.[59]

> She wanted to jump around everyone at her pleasure, everyone was in danger of being at one time bumped into by her, tugged, or in some other way teased; no one, however, was allowed to permit himself to do the same to her, no one was allowed to touch her at will, no one, even in the most remote sense, to return the freedom that she took for herself; and so she held the others within the strictest

[58] *Ibid.*
[59] *Ibid.*, VI:387. Luciane's intentionally confusing play at *imitation*, her capriciously egotistical "freedom" of action and "strict" imposition of "moral" "boundaries" upon others can be easily read here as ironic narrative (per)versions of Kant's "freedom" of imagination and the universal moral law.

boundaries of morality with regard to herself, boundaries which she appeared at each moment to overstep with regard to others.

The relations Luciane provokes and controls by choice parody the literal meaning of "Wahlverwandtschaften," as the mention of her choice in pets, an ape whose absence requires his replacement with a portrait,[60] comments clearly upon her own representation within the novel. The fiction makes its irony *as* a representational fiction most apparent in its own representation of self-conscious fiction-making; indeed, what stranger and more fitting way for the fiction to make its irony visible than in the disguise(s) of a character named for light.[61]

For in her volubility, her mimicry, her artifice and its props, Luciane is most revealing of illumination in the novel. Her actions and words give voice to an opposition played out in the narrative between herself and her *Gegenbild* or counterimage, the character in whose mere presence relations are colored and come to life. The narrator describes the strenuous diversions imposed upon Ottilie's comings and goings by Luciane:

> Ottilie sollte mit auf die Lust- und Schlittenfahrten . . . sie sollte weder Schnee noch Kälte noch gewaltsame Nachtstürme scheuen, da ja soviel andre nicht davon stürben. Das zarte Kind litt nicht wenig darunter, aber Luciane gewann nichts dabei: denn obgleich Ottilie sehr einfach gekleidet ging, so war sie doch, oder so schien sie wenigstens immer den Männern die Schönste. Ein sanftes Anziehen versammelte alle Männer um sie her, sie mochte sich in den grossen Räumen am ersten oder am letzten Platze befinden. . . .[62]

> Ottilie was supposed to come along on pleasure and skating trips . . . she was supposed to shy from neither snow

---

[60] *Ibid.*, VI:382.

[61] The misnomer in the novel of "Luciane" is noted by Paul Stöcklein, yet accounted for, ironically, as a phenomenon of "nature," rather than the narrative's own, irony or "ambiguity": "Die Natur ist zweideutig. Es ist am Menschen, wozu sie in ihm wird" [Nature is ambiguous. What she becomes in man depends upon him]. (Stöcklein, "Einführung in die *Wahlverwandtschaften*," p. 711).

[62] Goethe, *Die Wahlverwandtschaften*, VI:388.

nor cold nor violent nightstorms, since so many others wouldn't die from them. The tender child suffered not a little, but Luciane won nothing thereby; for although Ottilie went very simply clothed, she was, or at least she always appeared to the men, the most beautiful. A soft attraction gathered all the men around her, whether she found herself in the first or the last place in the large rooms. . . .

Figured like the sun itself, Ottilie is said to undergo the same verbal modality attributed to light in the *Farbenlehre*: she "suffers" Luciane's extravagant activity as she does intemperate weather. Simple in her dress, yet most beautiful, "or at least . . . always appear[ing]" so, she attracts those around her independent of the temporal order or position in space in which she appears, outshining the character called light whose movements she is made to accompany. Most unlike Luciane, she arrives eclipsed in the narrative but for the reference to a single gesture whose intention is misunderstood.[63] Following directly thereafter, in time and in narration, is the novel's most concisely worded interchange, so brief as to go unnoticed, vertiginous in effect when seen, which marks Eduard's first mistaking of, and passion for, Ottilie. He falsely ascribes to her a part in discursive intercourse:

> Den andern Morgen sagte Eduard zu Charlotten: Es ist ein angenehmes unterhaltendes Mädchen.

[63] Ottilie physically reenacts an earlier time in her life as an unmediated, or fully nondiscursive, means of "remembering" it; the pure externality of her action is however falsely interpreted as a figural gesture intending a conventional significance: "das liebe Kind eilte, sich [Charlotten] zu nähern, warf sich ihr zu Füssen und umfasste ihre Kniee. 'Wozu die Demütigung!' sagte Charlotte, die einigermassen verlegen war und sie aufheben wollte. 'Es ist so demütig nicht gemeint,' versetzte Ottilie, die in ihrer vorigen Stellung blieb. 'Ich mag mich nur so gern jener Zeit erinnern, da ich noch nicht höher reichte bis an Ihre Kniee und Ihrer Liebe schon so gewiss war' " (*ibid.*, VI:281).

[The dear child hurried to approach (Charlotte), threw herself at her feet and grasped her knees around. "Why the show of humility!" said Charlotte, who was to some extent embarrassed and wanted to raise her up. "It isn't meant to be so humble," replied Ottilie, who remained in place. "I only like so much to remember that time when I didn't reach further than your knees and was already so certain of your love."]

Unterhaltend? versetzte Charlotte mit Lächeln: sie hat
ja den Mund noch nicht aufgetan.

So? erwiderte Eduard, indem er sich zu besinnen
schien: das wäre doch wunderbar![64]

The next morning Eduard said to Charlotte: She is a
pleasant, talkative [or entertaining] girl.

Talkative? replied Charlotte with a smile: she hasn't
even opened her mouth yet.

Is that so? responded Eduard, as he seemed to think it
over: that would of course be wonderful!

In the absence of any articulation on Ottilie's part, the "experiment" in "chosen relations" is already underway. Charlotte's
correction of Eduard, at this moment and others, and the narrative mediation of similar ascriptions into the form and appearance of a meaningful story, can neither compensate for
nor fully explain its effect. Moreover, the novel figures its own
knowledge of that fact in the very vocabulary of narration it
employs. From the setting in which it takes place, a landscape
arranged and rearranged to afford "einen vortrefflichen Anblick" (an excellent view) (Chapter 1, first page), to its own semantic and syntactic qualifications of vision—most notably
the ubiquitous appearances of the verb, "scheinen," almost
mistakable for an auxiliary upon which the meaning of main
verbs formally depends—the fiction refuses not to see outside
itself, nor to see itself *as such*, as fiction.

The involvement of Ottilie in the narrative promises to grant
to the mobile relations into which she is drawn a closed stability of form. The motivating interest of these relations is expressed by Eduard in his early proposal to invite the Captain
to help him on his estate. More attractive than "people of the
land" who "have the proper knowledge" but "communicate"
it in a "confused and dishonest" manner, and "the university
educated" who are schooled in communication but "lack immediate insight into the matter," is a middleman between discursive and cognitive reliability, a friend. Eduard explains to
Charlotte: "Vom Freunde kann ich mir beides versprechen;

[64] *Ibid.*, VI:281.

und dann entspringen noch hundert andere Verhältnisse daraus, die ich mir alle gern vorstellen mag, die auch auf dich Be-
zug haben und wovon ich viel Gutes voraussehe"[65] [I can
promise myself both from a friend; and then a hundred other
relations spring therefrom, all of which I enjoy imagining to
myself, which also relate to you, and from which I foresee alot
of good]. Like the child of an imagined act of adultery, the "relations" Eduard envisions, once visually imagined, must both
concretely appear in and "color" the narrative. Eduard's repeated and futile attempts to decline his friend at the insistence
of Charlotte, narrated at the opening of the next chapter
(VI:249–50), resemble the series of *Farbenlehre* "Versuche" in
their entirely sequential, logically unsubordinated, narrative
relation. Indeed, the only "explanation" offered for his unsys-
tematic behavior will prove to be the novel's greatest under-
statement, both of Eduard's character and its own inability to
demonstrate character as conclusive: "Sich etwas zu versagen,
war Eduard nicht gewohnt[66] [Eduard was not accustomed to
denying himself anything].

Charlotte proves no more capable of controlling the discussion of "foreseen" relations. She reopens her conversation
with Eduard "possibly in the persuasion," the narrator speculates, that "frequent discussion" is most certain to dull the
"purpose" of a particular desire.[67] Yet repetition, as narrated,
incurs instead the surfacing of several desires. Eduard appears
transformed in speech from a "married man" into a "lover,"
and the consideration of an additional relation, formerly denied by a "violence" directed against the self, is articulated.
Through the mediation of letters which describe her, Ottilie is
first mentioned to Eduard, seen as a "lover": "Ich befinde mich
in einer ähnlichen Lage wie du und habe mir schon eben die
Gewalt angetan, die ich dir nun über dich selbst zumute"[68] [I
find myself in a situation similar to yours and have already
done myself the violence which I believe you now inflict upon
yourself]. Following a further exchange of letters, the Captain,

[65] *Ibid.*, VI:245.
[66] *Ibid.*, VI:249.
[67] *Ibid.*, VI:250.
[68] *Ibid.*

and shortly thereafter, Ottilie arrive. The "beautiful girl," whose inability to "show" her own "abilities" draws "excuse after excuse" from her headmistress, is to function as the "fourth" term in an analogy whose characters are letters themselves, "A," "B," "C," and "D," drawn to illustrate the otherwise invisible principle of the "theory" of "Wahlverwandtschaften."[69]

Yet the analogical bases of the relations in which Ottilie is to participate in theory do not remain symmetrical once actualized in practice. Eduard's "use" of the "formula" of "Wahlverwandtschaften" as a "metaphor" for the relations between the four friends is soon complicated by his vision of himself, "B," *returning* to "A" (Charlotte) *and* "O": " 'Was sollte B denn anfangen, wenn ihm C [der Hauptmann] entrissen würde? . . . Freilich . . . er kehrte zu seinem A zurück, zu seinem A und O' "[70] [What should B then do when C is ripped from him. . . . Naturally (literally: "freely") . . . he would turn back to his A, to his A and O]. Ottilie does indeed provide "company" for Charlotte, whose proximity to Eduard has been displaced by the Captain.[71] On the other hand, she furthers the disruption and transformation of the relations she completes. Her actions offer the exclusively external conditions upon which Eduard's passion can be considered appropriate and an improper relation, named love. In the course of transcribing Eduard's writing, the characters of her script appear to change into those she copies and are interpreted by Eduard to evidence the uncontested and unconstated ("Ottilie schwieg" [Ottilie remained silent]) conclusion: " 'Du liebst mich!' "[72] The recurrence of a pure form on the part of a copyist for whom the very appearance of form at all, of the mere external shape of written characters, may be the only "con-

[69] *Ibid.*, VI:251, 275-76.

[70] *Ibid.*, VI:276, 281.

[71] *Ibid.*, VI:282. The displacement and generation of "personal" relations in *Die Wahlverwandtschaften* are perhaps best described by the objection, cited earlier, to the interaction between color "Bilder" noted by Goethe in the *Farbenlehre*: "that through the displacement of the primary image a secondary image arises" (see Seidel, *Goethe*, pp. 79–80).

[72] *Die Wahlverwandtschaften*, VI:323–34.

tent" to be transmitted, is seen as an intentional act of personal imitation. Shapes of notation devoid of reference are interpreted to embody, as mimetic vehicles, the most significant of meanings. Indeed, what relation could appear more significant than that of the figure of light to the man who believes she means to love him.

Ottilie's presence bodily represents light in a "tableau vivant" ("das ganze Bild war alles Licht"[73] [the whole picture was entirely light]); her face reappears in the images of angels painted where she sits; her eyes, around which the appearance of her beauty revolves, convey a sense to all who see them: a phenomenal occurrence like the colors which spot our vision when we attempt to look at the sun. As notable as the emphasis on her persuasive beauty is the absence, in the narrative, of a description of Ottilie's inner "character." The conjunction of these two conditions has been viewed by one of the novel's most suggestive readers, Walter Benjamin, as Goethe's transgression of the "boundaries" between narrative (Epik) and "painting." [74] For Benjamin, Ottilie personifies not the light of true meaning, the essence of the romantic topos, "die Schöne Seele," but its soulless appearance, *Schönheit* without significance. Her death is correctly noted to be equally empty of meaning since its mode—abstinence from eating—was already a way of life and offers no "discursive form" in which to be understood.[75] Benjamin's argument approaches an explicit

[73] *Ibid.*, VI:405.

[74] See Benjamin, "Goethe's *Wahlverwandtschaften*," pp. 178–79: "in [Ottiliens Dasein] bleibt wirklich Schönheit das Erste und Wesentlichste. . . . In der Tat sind in Ottiliens Gestalt die Grenzen der Epik gegen die Malerei überschritten. Denn die Erscheinung des Schönen als des wesentlichen Gehaltes in einem Lebendigen liegt jenseits des epischen Stoffkreises. Und doch steht sie im Zentrum des Romans. Denn es ist nicht zu viel gesagt, wenn man die Überzeugung von Ottiliens Schönheit als Grundbedingung für den Anteil am Roman bezeichnet" [in (Ottilie's being) beauty remains foremost and most essential. . . . In fact the boundaries of epic and painting are overstepped in Ottilie's figure. For the appearance of the beautiful as the essential content of a living being lies beyond epic subject matter. And yet it stands in the center of the novel. For it would be no overstatement to designate the persuasion of Ottilie's beauty as the fundamental condition for the interest in the novel].

[75] See *ibid.*, p. 176: "Kein sittlicher Entschluss kann ohne sprachliche Gestalt, und streng genommen ohne darin Gegenstand der Mitteilung geworden

warning against the acceptance of a free play of appearances, as deduced by Kant to inform the experience of beauty in plastic arts, in the properly meaningful aesthetics of discursive arts. In describing the form of Goethe's novel as "arabesque-like," rather than formally constructive ("Gestalt bauen" [figure building]), Benjamin also conforms to the Analytic of the Beautiful in the *Third Critique*.[76]

---

zu sein, ins Leben treten. Daher wird, in dem vollkommenen Schweigen der Ottilie, die Moralität des Todeswillens, welcher sie beseelt, fragwürdig. Ihm liegt in Wahrheit kein Entschluss zugrunde *sondern ein Trieb*. Daher ist nicht, wie sie es zweideutig auszusprechen scheint, ihr Sterben heilig. Wenn sie aus ihrer 'Bahn' geschritten sich erkennt, so kann dies Wort in Wahrheit einzig heissen, dass nur der Tod sie vor dem innern Untergange bewahren kann. Und so ist er wohl Sühne im Sinne des Schicksals, nicht jedoch die heilige Entsühnung, welche nie *der freie*, sondern nur der göttlich über ihn verhängte *Tod* dem Menschen werden kann" (my emphasis). [No moral decision can come into being without discursive form, and strictly stated, without therein becoming an object of communication. Thus the morality of the desire to die which animates Ottilie becomes, in her complete silence, questionable. At the base of that desire lies not a decision *but a drive*. Thus her dying is not, as she appears to express it ambiguously, holy. If she recognizes herself as having stepped from her "path," that can only mean that death alone can save her from her inner downfall. And thus that death is clearly atonement in the sense of fate, but not however holy expiation, which only the death hung over man by God and never a *free death* can become].

Most interesting in Benjamin's formulation here is his confusion of *Trieb* (drive or instinct) with "freedom": the "Trieb," which he states lies "at the basis" of Ottilie's death and for which reason it cannot be viewed as "holy," is followed and substituted by his reference to that death as "freely" chosen, "der freie Tod," and thus (equally) unholy. The "nondiscursive form" ("ohne sprachliche Gestalt") of Ottilie's dying seems to bring about contradiction in any discursive form that would attempt to give it content, including this most astute of critical formulations on Benjamin's part.

[76] "In dieser [Schönheit] darf die deutsche Dichtung keinen Schritt über Goethe hinaus wagen, ohne gnadenlos einer Scheinwelt anheimzufallen. . . . In dem Roman baut diese nicht sowohl Gestalten, welche oft genug aus eigener Machtvollkommenheit formlos als mythische sich einsetzen, auf, als dass sie zaghaft, gleichsam arabeskenhaft um jene spielend, vollendet und mit höchstem Recht sie auflöst" (*ibid.*, pp. 182, 180) [German poetry may dare take no step past Goethe in this (presentation of) beauty, without falling into a world of appearances without grace. . . . The (form of this) novel does not construct figures, which, out of their own fullness of power, often install themselves formlessly as mythical, but rather timidly, playing about them, as it were, arabesque-like, completely and with the highest right, dissolves them].

Yet the inconsequent "world of appearances" to which Benjamin refers *Die Wahlverwandtschaften*, seen to be centered upon Ottilie's silent visibility, fails to account for the novel *as a form* which mediates the sight of its own center—be it of beauty as an immediate, nondiscursive phenomenon, of eyes which seem to speak upon being seen, or of the cryptic and literally concealed content of a *Tagebuch*—into the fictional development of a story. Its story is an hypothesis of the visual *Bilder*, or images, the novel narrates. Vision of Ottilie is always transformed by narration, as it is by the narrative's characters, into an understanding of its consequences: the appearance of "actions and sufferings of light," "transposed" by the merest "glance" into a "theorizing" of their meaning. Moreover, the narrative includes its own explanatory, or "theoretical," fiction. The actions and passions Ottilie brings to light are themselves effects, it is revealed, of a narrative overheard. Ottilie's own "path of motion," or *Bahn*, that which has shaped the context of her relations with others, is explained to have been shaped by her own understanding of a story told of her life. Arising from apparent slumber after Otto is declared dead, Ottilie acknowledges the significance of a similar moment following her own mother's death when, aware of movement, especially of speech, but unable or unwilling to move or express herself, neither sleeping nor awake but lying "dormant," she "grasped" or "comprehended" Charlotte's narration of her "fate":

> "Damals sprachst du mit einer Freundin über mich; du bedauertest mein Schicksal, als eine arme Waise in der Welt geblieben zu sein; du schildertest meine abhängige Lage und wie misslich es um mich stehen könne, wenn nicht ein besonderer Glückstern über mich walte. Ich fasste alles wohl und genau, vielleicht zu streng, was du für mich zu wünschen, was du von mir zu fordern schienst. Ich machte mir nach meinen beschränkten Einsichten hierüber Gesetze; nach diesen habe ich lange gelebt, nach ihnen war mein Tun und Lassen eingerichtet. . . .
> Aber ich bin aus meiner Bahn geschritten, ich habe

meine Gesetze gebrochen, ich habe sogar das Gefühl derselben verloren, und nach einem schrecklichen Ereignis
klärst du mich wieder über meinen Zustand auf, der jam-
mervoller ist als der erste. . . ."[77]

"At that time you talked with a friend about me; you regretted my fate as a poor orphan left on earth; you depicted my dependent situation and how prone to misfortune I could be if a special lucky star did not rule over me.
I grasped everything that you seemed to wish for me and
to demand of me fully and exactly, perhaps too strictly.
Within the limits of my own insights I thus made laws for
myself; according to these laws I have lived for a long
time, my acting and suffering [to be done] were arranged
according to them. . . .

But I have stepped from my path, I have broken my
laws, I have even lost the feeling of them, and after a hor-
rible event you enlighten me again as to my condition,
which is more lamentable than the first. . . ."

The course taken by a character serving as a narrative personification of light is predicated upon a narrative personify-
ing her as "poor," and an "orphan left on earth"; portraying
her "situation" as "dependent," prone to general misfortune,
and in need of the rule of a "lucky star." Ottilie's appearance
within the novel could be said to carry out all of these representations, or just as "fully and exactly," none. The story
which names Ottilie as its object, and Ottilie's own comprehension of its speaker's apparent wishes and demands, are figurations of occurrences whose justice cannot be appraised.
Something of their sense, however, emerges in their enactment
for a second time. For Ottilie reveals to Charlotte the "laws"
of her "acting and suffering," the "secret of the movement of
her life,"[78] upon perceiving what appears to be a repetition of
"the same:"[79] Charlotte's explanation of how she is to live.
This second narrative of "enlightenment" informs Ottilie's de-

[77] Ibid., VI:462.
[78] Ibid., VI:464.
[79] Ibid., VI:462.

cision to withdraw from her relation with Eduard. In light of the intervening events, its fundamental misunderstanding of Ottilie's status is clear. Charlotte observes and hypothesizes:

> "Und betrachten Sie nur diese unglückliche Schlum-mernde! Ich zittere vor dem Augenblicke, wenn sie aus ihrem halben Totenschlaf zum Bewusstsein erwacht. Wie soll sie leben, wie soll sie sich trösten, wenn sie nicht hof-fen kann, durch ihre Liebe Eduarden das zu ersetzen, was sie als Werkzeug des wunderbarsten Zufalls geraubt hat?"[80]

> "And just look at this unhappy, dormant child! I tremble before the moment when she wakes out of her half-dead sleep into consciousness. How should she live, how should she comfort herself, when she cannot hope to re-place for Eduard through her love that of which, as a tool of the strangest accident, she has robbed him?"

The loss to be felt by Eduard of a son he wishes he never had is imagined by Charlotte by mistake. The intentionality of that misconception is again available to question. Charlotte's ref-erence to Ottilie's present state of unconsciousness (also mis-taken), and the sudden non sequitur ending her speech—"An mich darf in diesem Augenblick nicht gedacht werden" [At this moment one shouldn't even think of me]—may be viewed as indications of her own unconscious desire to be overheard and provoke the response she receives. The hand played by Ottilie in Otto's drowning is open, of course, to similar suspicions. But once an interpretation based on intentionality is assumed to explain the characters' actions, the actions are themselves limited to their understanding in terms of character. The her-meneutic circle here described is discredited by Goethe, as dis-cussed above, in the "Vorwort" to the *Farbenlehre*, in which investigations of "human character" are explained to be in vain, since character is only made perceivable in actions. The action resulting from Charlotte's false apprehension here is the positing of Ottilie as "replacement" for Otto: a substitution viewed, entirely incorrectly, to be both of necessity and im-

[80] *Ibid.*, VI:460–61.

probable adequacy. From the premise of that postulate, by which lives are figurally exchanged, a diachronic narrative of modality ensues: "*Wie* soll sie leben, wie" [*How* should she live, how"]. The fiction of an objectively necessary basis for Ottilie's relation to Eduard replaces the former narrative representation of her absolute "dependency," and gives rise to the formulation of new internal "laws." Thus the very movements of Ottilie, the novel's own "ungraspable" *Urphänomen*, are colored by their imaging into causal, narrative form.

In order for Ottilie, an "orphan" on earth, to be related, her presence must be purposefully contained within a "path," broken as unintended relations arise. Light is figured, and its surrounding phenomena illuminated, by a limiting of "understanding" or "insight"; its participation within a story is made possible by the "self-imposition" of limits as rule of law.[81] The *Farbenlehre*, a series of experiments in objective appearances, posits rules comprehending "all residual visible evidence." The "norm and guideline" for the vision of empirical color are, by ironical authority, the colors of vision (or "physiological colors"). A study of phenomenality models its own requirements upon the perception of false appearances: colors whose "objectivity" arises in the eye.

Like the "character" of light and the "theory" of colors we see, the "speech" or "language" in which we "see" them must abide by its own "laws" before being shaped into a story, or made to perform as mediation. Phenomenal objects may be identified as human or in nature, the relations which figure them, as chosen or given. Necessarily nonphenomenal, however, are the rules according to which they are identified at all. As the means of constructing *any* relations, these rules must also function exclusive of choice. They govern the making of

[81] Ottilie's speech suggests evident parallels between her own presence in this ironically representational "novel" and Kant's "introduction" of the "keystone" object of real cognition into the representational epistemology of the *Critique*. Like Kant's conception of the "*causa noumenon*" "freedom," Ottilie, the figure of light of Goethe's narration, understands that the possibility of her "relation" to narrative "phenomena" depends upon the necessity of her own self-legislation: "Ich machte mir . . . Gesetze" [I made myself . . . laws].

meaning without regard to making sense, operate universally, rather than by election, and irrespective of the content of their constituency. Their power can only be considered violent (or beneficent) by the abuse of being envisioned, i.e., attributed with a content, design, or purpose of its own. Effective like the force of motion itself, or the movement between the syntactic patterning of words, they are infinitely transformable, capable of conveyance, and unmindful of their semantic consequences. They are therefore all the more attractive to theoretical hypothesis and narrative fiction: "experiments" in language endeavoring to render the strictness of its conventions significant. Since their own modality, however, is the very one they investigate, these *Versuche* can never be objectively controlled.

The "natural science" of color finally defines itself as a system based on inherent, investigative error. The failure of those engaged in "Wahlverwandtschaften" to understand or mend their ways may be seen as the consequence of original errors of passion. Yet the occasion for the novel to end, for the movements of light on earth to cease, is given by the motion of discourse itself. Talking within the circle of friends, Mittler comes upon his favorite subject, or *Lieblingsmaterien*: the "barbaric" status of "prohibitive laws and institutions." Compelled to mediate the rules upon which human relations are founded, he cannot choose to begin or end his speech. At this moment, like many others—"always, whenever he found the opportunity"—he is "overpowered" or forced "to express the reasoning" of mediation, "acting," by speaking, to immediate and unintended effect:[82]

[82] *Ibid.*, VI:481. The capability inhering in speech to present a pertinence to its listeners (in this instance, an unseen listener, Ottilie) which, while not intended or even known, is nonetheless direct in effect was commented upon in the narrative after the relation of life lived in transit given by the visiting English lord: "Man müsste ganz in Gesellschaft schweigen, wenn man nicht manchmal in den Fall kommen sollte; denn nicht allein bedeutende Bemerkungen, sondern die trivialsten Äusserungen können auf eine so missklingende Weise mit dem Interesse der Gegenwärtigen zusammentreffen" (VI:433–34) [One would have to remain wholly silent in society in order to avoid such an encounter; for not only meaningful remarks but the most trivial expressions can, in a most dissonant way, coincide with the interest of those present]. The problem of regular articulation indicated here is the very possibility that it may

Brach nun einmal unter Freunden seine Rede los, wie wir
schon öfter gesehen haben, so rollte sie ohne Rücksicht
fort, verletzte oder heilte, nutzte oder schadete, wie es sich
gerade fügen mochte.[83]

Once his speech broke loose among friends, as we have already seen more than often, it rolled along without hindsight, injured or healed, was useful or hurt, just as it happened to happen.

Autonomous and "without hindsight," the activity of mediation is carried away by its means. The story is kept moving in
the same manner. Knowingly named "a novel" by its author,
Die Wahlverwandtschaften renders its narrative voice the unrelenting vehicle of its own enterprise—that of the "reasoning" of mediation as literary form. After death, the narrator
continues, Ottilie's inanimate body is imagined to move and
address; its beauty attracts seekers of meaning in droves. Eduard dies, is placed next to Ottilie, and the permanence of their
position foreseen by donations to the church on Charlotte's
part: *Stiftungen* of the very type which her previous clearing of
gravestones had caused to be withdrawn, and whose intentional purpose she had attempted to prove senseless (Part II,
Chapter 1 [VI:361–63]).

---

be encountered, unsoundly, as relevant ("auf eine so missklingende Weise mit
dem Interesse . . . zusammentreffen"). The perceivable disturbance caused
precisely by the "interest of those present" in the Englishman's self-description
is next to be offset by a story concerning others. It is told by his traveling companion and included within the novel under its own title and generic heading:
"Die Wunderlichen Nachbarskinder," "Novelle" (VI:434). Although appearing as a full-blown fiction, the story brings about greater agitation on Charlotte's part—"Der Erzählende . . . bermerken musste, dass Charlote höchst
bewegt sei" [The narrator had to notice . . . that Charlotte was highly moved]
(VI:442)—an occurrence understandably suggested by the similarity between
the passion of the narrated *Nachbarskinder* and that of Ottilie and Eduard or
Charlotte and Eduard, lovers present and past. The "narrator," we realize,
cannot have known what he was saying; but little do we realize our own ignorance. For the tale is in basis true ("wirklich zugetragen" [VI:442]) and
evokes uneasiness not by bringing others indirectly to mind but because it en-
forces a literal referent of which it has no knowledge: the Captain, known to
Charlotte as the actual subject of its narrated events.

[83] *Ibid.*, VI:481.

Finally, the narrative cannot rest without positing the moment, of no greater duration than the "glance of an eye" (*Augenblick*), when the lovers who "rest" or lie idle "near each other" are to "awake together again."[84] The story which began by naming a referent "Eduard" *and then saying that it is doing so*: "—so nennen wir einen reichen Baron" [Eduard—thus we name a rich baron], proceeds along its path *past* the replacement of a name with an hypothesis of meaning: "Und wie er in Gedanken an die Heilige eingeschlafen war, *so könnte man wohl ihn selig* nennen"[85] [And as he fell asleep in thinking of the holy (child), so can he well be named blessed]. The story the narrative tells of the "colors" it sees, the fiction Goethe properly referred to as "relations of choice," keeps the novel, like Mittler, talking for too long.

"Irony" is the stated condition of Goethe's cognitive theory of natural appearances: its conscious recognition is said to grant the natural scientist "the freedom" to record those appearances in a necessarily mediated, or figural, form. Thus any empirical cognitive theory, Goethe seems to propose, must, by the fact of its discursive medium, be a "color theory," or theory of figures. *Die Wahlverwandtschaften*, it has been argued, represents figuration itself in the diachronic form of a story and the irony inherent in mediation in the name and actions of one of its characters. "Mittler," the professional mediator, is no more objectively "realistic" a narrative character than the empirically characterless Ottilie: as the vehicle of unconscious irony in the novel, his misperceptions speak neither for himself nor for Goethe as mimetic author but for the speculation stated in the *Farbenlehre* that cognitive representation always misrepresents its objects merely by deriving from empirical observation. Goethe may openly admit and accept the mistaken basis of any discursive cognitive theory in the context of his color "experiments." But discursive mistakes such as Mittler's and Charlotte's, which are said to shape the life and speed the death of Ottilie, or that of Eduard and Charlotte in envisioning the "experiment" in "chosen relations" to begin with, repre-

---

[84] *Ibid.*, VI:490.
[85] *Ibid.*, VI:242 (opening sentence), 490; my emphasis.

sent the consequential involvement of "irony"—in itself a purely formal, cognitive term—in the realm of practical action. Goethe's statement in the *Farbenlehre* that the natural scientist must figure empirical relations "with irony" thus appears to hold doubly for the narrative of his novel. Just as the name of the novel, "Chosen Relations," does not mean what it says, in either its "properly" (i.e., *metaphorically*) scientific or "metaphorically" (i.e., *properly*) anthropomorphic context, the narrator who "relates" *Die Wahlverwandtschaften* as a story must proceed with an irony which is all too evident. For in representing human passion as the "natural" "colors" of "language," figuration, he *must* speak "ironically" if he is to speak at all.

In the narratives discussed in Part Two, the cognitive problem stated openly in the *Farbenlehre*, and which underlies the irony of narration in *Die Wahlverwandtschaften*, is articulated by way of the different modal categories of representational narrative itself. In the narratives by Austen discussed first, an understanding of the relation between knowledge and discursive representation must be derived from the representational scope of the novels alone.

PART 2

FORMS OF
NARRATION

CHAPTER 4

AUSTEN: THE PERSUASIONS OF
SENSIBILITY AND SENSE

"Theoretical and Practical Knowledge" in *Mansfield Park*

Of the authors treated in this study, Austen is most strictly an author of narrative. No other explicitly critical, poetic, or speculative writings offer us directly conceptual or theoretical access to her novels. Jane Austen is first and last a novelist, and if irony, as Goethe's *Wahlverwandtschaften* suggests, and as Lukács's *Theory of the Novel* argued critically a century later,[1]

---

[1] See, in particular, Lukács's conclusion to the chapter in *The Theory of the Novel*, "The Historico-philosophical Conditioning of the Novel and its Significance": "Irony, the self-surmounting of a subjectivity that has gone as far as it was possible to go, is the highest freedom that can be achieved in a world without God. That is why it is not only the sole possible *a priori* condition for a true, totality-creating objectivity but also why it makes that totality—the novel—the representational art-form of our age: because the structural categories of the novel constitutively coincide with the world as it is today" (*The Theory of the Novel*, trans. Anna Bostock [Cambridge: MIT Press, 1971; first published in book form by P. Cassirer, Berlin, 1920]). The continuing relevance of Lukács' early theoretical work has only been underscored by the pseudoscientific developments, involving a misplaced reliance upon taxonomy and other static descriptive methods, that have largely determined the course of narrative theory in the past few decades. In spite of the strain of utopianism for which Lukács himself renounces the book in his Preface of 1961 (see *ibid*., pp. 11–23), and which, as he critically recognizes, is indeed central to the thesis it develops, the work remains unequaled in its identification of the dynamic form of the novel with the tensions informing the speculative philosophical tradition. At the same time, however, if Lukács's understanding of the novel

is the condition of representation inherent in *all* novels, then Austen, in the view of recent Austen criticism, appears the critics' novelist par excellence. The mention of all the studies of Austen which incorporate the concept of "irony" into their interpretations would comprise a bibliography of the upsurge in Austen scholarship over the past thirty years.[2] Yet Austen is

---

were not also based on the premise of a direct correlation between literary form and material history, the utopianism he denounces would probably play no part in his theory: as long as history is perceived to determine form, the desire for utopianism, or freedom from determination *and* form, will shape the history of theory. It is perhaps for this reason that Lukács consistently treats Goethe's *Wilhelm Meister* (see his discussion of the *Lehrjahre*: "*Wilhelm Meister's Years of Apprenticeship* as an Attempted Synthesis," *ibid.*, pp. 132–43), the romantic prototype of the conception of the novel *as* developmental history, or *Bildungsroman*, rather than the purposefully circumscribed, nonprogressively ironic novel, *Die Wahlverwandtschaften*.

Similar in structure to Lukács' view of literary irony as the result of a historical alienation of the self from experience is Paul de Man's view of the inherently allegorical alienation, represented ironically in the novel as story, of experience from cognition. The diachronic dimension of literary forms located by Lukács, following Hegel, in historical progression is located instead by de Man *within* the literary, diachronic form of allegory. Thus de Man considers Stendhal's *Chartreuse de Parme* "one of the first novel of novels" in that, unlike the purpose of synthesis represented in the metahistorical Bildungsroman, it ends with a represented separation between knowledge and experience: the perpetuation, in the events of its own story, of the "unbreachable distance" formalized artificially in the structure of allegory. See Paul de Man, "The Rhetoric of Temporality," *Interpretation: Theory and Practice*, ed. Charles Singleton (Baltimore: The Johns Hopkins University Press, 1969), pp. 173–209 (p. 209).

[2] While Austen's irony with regard to her characters was suggested in A. C. Bradley's "Jane Austen," *Essays and Studies by Members of the English Association* II (1912), pp. 7–36, the more recent view of irony as a means of narrative design in the novels was initiated by Reuben Brower's excellent examination of blended ironic and dramatic structures in *Pride and Prejudice*: "Light, and Bright, and Sparkling: Irony and Fiction in *Pride and Prejudice*," in *The Fields of Light* (New York: Oxford University Press, 1951). Among those following Brower have been Marvin Mudrick, *Jane Austen: Irony as Defense and Discovery* (Princeton: Princeton University Press, 1952); Lionel Trilling, "*Mansfield Park*," in *The Opposing Self* (New York: Viking Press, 1955), pp. 206–30; Wayne C. Booth, *The Rhetoric of Fiction* (Chicago: Chicago University Press, 1961), pp. 243–66; Robert Liddell, *The Novels of Jane Austen* (London: Longmans, 1963); Henrietta Ten Harmsel, *Jane Austen: A Study in Fictional Conventions* (The Hague: Mouton & Co., 1963); A. Wal-

also the novel reader's novelist: probably no author of English language fiction has enjoyed a more sustained or more singular loyalty of readership. As anyone who has chanced to name Austen in public as a personal favorite has discovered, her six completed novels, while immediately consistent in their representational content and considerably repetitive in their design and scope,[3] command the devotion of an extraordinary diversity of readers. Modern readers, whose tastes in narrative form and theme have been shaped by both gradual and radical developments in the technique of novel-writing since Austen's time, seem to concur in the longstanding appraisal of Austen first put to print by Walter Scott in 1816. Before turning to analyses of Austen's least obviously ironic works—*Mansfield Park, Sense and Sensibility,* and *Persuasion*—to question whether Austen, like Goethe's narrator in *Die Wahlverwandtschaften,* necessarily writes representational narrative "with

---

ton Litz, *Jane Austen: A Study in Her Artistic Development* (New York: Oxford University Press, 1965); Tony Tanner, "Introduction" to *Mansfield Park* (London: Penguin Books, 1966); Kenneth L. Moler, *Jane Austen's Art of Illusion* (Lincoln: University of Nebraska Press, 1968); Karl Kroeber, *Styles in Fictional Structure* (Princeton: Princeton University Press, 1971); Lloyd W. Brown, *Bits of Ivory: Narrative Technique in Jane Austen's Fiction* (Baton Rouge: Louisiana State University Press, 1973); Darrel Mansell, *The Novels of Jane Austen* (Bristol: Macmillan, 1973); and John Odmark, *An Understanding of Jane Austen's Novels* (Oxford: Basil Blackwell, 1981).

The best general discussion of irony with respect to Austen is offered in Andrew Wright's *Jane Austen's Novels: A Study in Structure* (London: Chatto & Windus, 1964), pp. 24–35 esp., and a recent critique of the ironic view of Austen is given by Jan Fergus in *Jane Austen: The Didactic Novel* (Totowa, N.J.: Barnes & Noble Books, 1983). Notable exceptions to the discussion of irony in recent Austen criticism are: Marilyn Butler, *Jane Austen and the War of Ideas* (London: Oxford University Press, 1975), and David I. Miller, "The Danger of Narrative in Jane Austen," in *Narrative and Its Discontents* (Princeton: Princeton University Press, 1981). Miller effectively replaces the concept of controlling authorial "irony" with that of the author's "ideology," arguing, where others have noted an ironic nonidentity between word and meaning, for an "ideologically inspired passage" between "signifier and signified," the latter itself identified with "the univocal language of the ideological" (pp. 76, 82, *et passim*).

[3] On the repetitive patterning of the novels, see in particular the chapter on "Narrative Art" in Mary Lascelles' seminal study, *Jane Austen and Her Art* (London: Oxford University Press, 1939), pp. 124f. esp.

irony," it may prove useful to investigate the more popular view of the novels initially linked *with* their criticism by Austen's contemporary, Scott.

In his review of *Emma*, written soon after the novel was published,[4] Scott includes a prefatory discussion of Austen's other works to that date. Remarking upon the narrative limits drawn anew by each succeeding novel, he concludes that "in this class" of narrative—that which the novels themselves serve largely to define—Jane Austen, as novelist, "stands almost alone."[5] The term "class," intended here to indicate a particular genre of narration, is used in another context by Scott to indicate the specific social and economic strata the novels represent. "The author of *Emma*," he suggests, is indeed entirely alone among English novelists in that she "confines herself chiefly to the middling classes of society."[6] Yet Austen's representation of newly emergent societal "classes" is in fact effective, Scott notes further, in as far as it transforms not so much the content as the function of representation. Austen's "middling classes," Scott reasons, serve to provide narration with a new epistemological middle ground of representation: a kind of narrative mean from which the significant causes and moral effects of actions can be most widely recognized. The source of that recognition would be the realm of one's own experience, since, as Scott remarks, "the narrative of all her novels is composed of such common occurrences as may have fallen under the observation of most folks; and her dramatis personae conduct themselves upon the motives and principles which the readers may recognize as ruling their own and that of most of their acquaintances. The kind of moral, also which these novels inculcate, applies equally to the paths of common life."[7] The novels of Jane Austen, in limiting their objective "class" of representation, expand our understanding to include not only the static realm of the particular objects

[4] Walter Scott, Review of *Emma* (unsigned), *Quarterly Review* 1816. Reprinted in *Jane Austen: The Critical Heritage* (London: Routlege & Kegan Paul, 1968), pp. 58–69.

[5] *Ibid.*, p. 64.

[6] *Ibid.*

[7] *Ibid.*

represented but the mental composition of our own "ruling" "motives and principles," as well as the dynamic "occurrences" "observed," external to us, in life.[8] Thus, what Austen seems to gain by narrowing the scope of her narratives is a new kind of power of narrative universalization. In "confin[ing] herself" to representing the middle classes[9] Austen appears less, as Scott himself will be viewed,[10] to prefigure the future analysis by Marx of Hegel's philosophy of historical reality in terms of class,[11] than to follow the analysis of a hypothesized cognitive reality in terms of mental representations proposed by Kant. For if, as Scott argues, Austen narrows the scope of narrative representation in order to effect a new universality of narrative comprehension, the span of social classes represented by her own reading public can be seen to indicate the continuing profit of that exchange. In limiting their objective focus of representation to a new middle class, Austen's novels effectively represent a "new" encompassing "class," that of understanding, belonged to by all those whose comprehension of life as they live it and "observe" it lived by others is itself modeled on their reading of representational fiction.

Scott opposes the self-imposed limits of Austen's novels, those that ally them most closely to "common life," to fictions which "remained fettered" instead to the "style" of the "ex-

---

[8] See Martin Price, "Manners, Morals, and Jane Austen," in *Nineteenth Century Fiction* 30 (1975), for a comparable discussion of the concept of "recognition" as the experience in reading promoted by Austen's fiction.

[9] Scott, in *The Critical Heritage*, p. 64: "her most distinguished characters do not rise greatly above well-bred country gentlemen and ladies; and those which are sketched with most originality and precision, belong to a class rather below that standard."

[10] See, most prominently, Georg Lukács, "Walter Scott," in *The Historical Novel* (Atlantic Highlands, N.J.: Humanities Press, 1974), pp. 30–62; on the "parallel" between "Scott's manner of composition and Hegel's philosophy of history," see pp. 39f.; on Scott's own choice of a *politically* "middle" position in his novels, see Lukács's *Probleme des Realismus* (Berlin: Aufbau Verlag, 1955), pp. 131–32.

[11] For the view of Austen as outstanding analyst of class, see David Daiches, "Jane Austen, Karl Marx, and the Aristocratic Dance," *American Scholar* XVII (1942), and, in particular, Daiches's more recent "Literature and Social Mobility," in *Aspects of History and Class Consciousness*, ed. Istvan Mészaros (London: Routledge & Kegan Paul, 1971) pp. 162–66 esp.

traordinary," the origin of the novel in "romance": "In its first appearance, the novel was the legitimate child of romance; and though the manner and general tone of the composition were altered so as to suit modern times, the author remained fettered by many peculiarities derived from the original style of romantic fiction . . . the reader expected to pursue a course of adventures more interesting and extraordinary than those which occur in his own life, or that of his next-door neighbours."[12] In addition to that of its "conduct," or plot—"the studied involution and extrication of the story"—"the difference . . . of the sentiments," Scott continues, is the "second broad line of distinction . . . between the novel, as formerly composed, and real life." Formerly, "the novelist professed to give an imitation of nature, but it was, as the French say, *la belle nature*."[13] Austen, by contrast, Scott proposes, is an author of "real," if not necessarily "beautiful nature." As he states in his summary of *Emma*, but with broader reference to the earlier *Sense and Sensibility* (1811) and *Pride and Prejudice* (1813): "The subjects are not often elegant, and certainly never grand; but they are finished up to nature, and with a precision which delights the reader."[14] By the same token, the only "faults" found by Scott in Austen's "precision" are the moments when, due to its very integrity, it fails to "delight" by making our experience of reading "fiction" too closely resemble our experience of life. "Characters of folly or simplicity," for example, will be no less faithfully and precisely rendered, with the result that "if too often brought forward or too long dwelt upon, their prosing is apt to become as tiresome in fiction as in real society."[15]

[12] Scott, in *The Critical Heritage*, pp. 58–59. The issue of Austen's choice of representational limits over the expansive landscapes and sentiments of romance has remained a source of contention in her reception. Scott's praise is followed in 1848 by Charlotte Brontë's equally celebrated statements of impatience with the novels (see *ibid.*, pp. 126–28). Virginia Woolf's response to Brontë, in her "Jane Austen" (*The Common Reader* [New York: Harcourt Brace & World, 1925], pp. 137–49), reiterates the ongoing nature of that debate.

[13] Scott, in *The Critical Heritage*, p. 61.

[14] *Ibid.*, p. 67.

[15] *Ibid.*, p. 68.

In this earliest serious evaluation of Austen by the most prominent novelist of her time, the ability to make representational discourse—"prosing"—so coincide with representation in "real society" that fidelity may appear a lack of artistry by its excess is esteemed to be the same feature distinguishing her writings from those of any other living novelist: their representation of "real life." While the specific objects of Austen's representations, like the "middling classes" of her century, have long since been discarded, transformed, or replaced, Austen's narratives show no signs of sharing their fate. The steady popularity of Austen's novels seems to indicate that material, societal, and literary-historical change notwithstanding—as well as an intervening popularization of the concept of class-consciousness itself—her representationally limited narratives continue to bring about an experience in reading coincident with our experience, whatever its particulars, of "real life."

This comprehensive, "real life" dimension of Austen's representation has come, through its own critical transformation, as mentioned above, to be called "irony." The novel that proves most troubling to contemporary discussions of Austen's "irony"—also the least universally popular of her works—is *Mansfield Park* (1814), and the most widely noted attempt to meet the challenge of the novel has been Lionel Trilling's essay, "*Mansfield Park*." What makes Trilling's study stand out is his acceptance of the description of Austen as ironist combined with a defense of *Mansfield Park* as the novel to which that description least pertains. At the center of *Mansfield Park* is no ironic development of action but a single character whose only attribute seems to be that of having "character" in the most impersonal sense.[16] Fanny Price, rec-

---

[16] Trilling opposes the portrayal of "character" to that of "personality" in the novel (*The Opposing Self*, p. 224). In agreement with Trilling on the absence of an ironic plot in the novel but in essential disagreement with him on Austen's motive or her resulting effect, is Marvin Mudrick's *Jane Austen: Irony as Defense and Discovery*, the first full-length study of the topic of irony in Austen to which the argument of Trilling's essay seems most directly to respond. See Mudrick, p. 159: "*Mansfield Park* has nothing of the equivocal tone of *Sense and Sensibility* or the sustained shaping irony of *Pride and Prejudice*: its prevailing tone is grave, its issue unequivocal. Fanny—center of the

ognized without exception as the least attractive of Austen's heroines and the least successful structural focus of all her novels, is praised by Trilling for the very absence of the endearing qualities she lacks. Fanny is a character without any perceivable "style," without any claims on our attention at all,[17] and thus exempt from the web of misleading appearances into which all other Austen heroines, as well as all the other characters in *Mansfield Park* are, at least at one moment, drawn. In addition, Fanny's judgment of others is as ineffectually as it is infallibly correct. She is not only free of all deception caused by phenomenal appearances but makes no attempt to persuade others of their mistakes. The purity of Fanny's character, placed at the center of the novel, excludes even the possibility of the central signature of Austen's narratives: a scene of personal, perceptual enlightenment in which the so-called irony of the preceding action is at once revealed and relieved through a recognition of the morally right. For Fanny not only always sees right: she never ventures to say that others see wrong. Such is the moral depth of her "character," Trilling contends, that the "irony" of the narrative can only be that of "irony directed against irony itself,"[18] and such is our own dependence upon the play of surface appearances that we, ironically, fail to read in Fanny's failure to speak a profundity of character exceeding our own.

Yet as all readers of *Mansfield Park* rarely fail to remember, the one moment in which Fanny is in fact forced to speak is when she is directly asked, and thus must actively refuse, to "play." In the famous incident of the family theatricals, Fanny, in whom surface and depth of meaning are represented as one, refuses to perform a personality not her own: to speak words

---

action—is no heroine indulged, at an ironic distance, by the author; she demands our earnest sympathy, and on her own terms."

[17] "The idea of morality as achieved style, as grace of ease, is not likely ever to be relinquished, not merely because some writers will always assert it anew, but also because morality itself will always insist on it. . . . Yet the idea is one that may easily deteriorate or be perverted. Style, which expresses the innermost truth of any creation or action, can also hide the truth; it is in this sense of the word that we speak of 'mere style.' *Mansfield Park* proposes to us the possibility of this deception" (Trilling, *The Opposing Self*, pp. 223–34).

[18] *Ibid.*, p. 224.

she does not mean, and thus to appear to mean as actor what her "character" does not. Trilling refers her stance on this issue—shared at first by Edmund before he is persuaded to play against Mary Crawford, and later reflected in Sir Thomas's disapproval upon his return—to the moral prohibition, dating from Plato, against dramatic impersonation as a possible form of personal "character" contamination.[19] If there is an irony in the novel which the novel itself, however, cannot dispel it is that Fanny's objection to the suggestion that she "play," while most obviously a rejection of the false premise of personification, is also the most direct statement of her own lack of persona. Fanny summarizes the specifically negative character of her own characterization within the narrative by saying, " 'No, indeed, I cannot act,' " and the frustration felt by the company of acting enthusiasts at this self-acknowledged inability most closely resembles, with respect to her default from all *narrative* action, the reader's own. As usual, Fanny, the moral center of the novel, is seated at the periphery of its action when inducted against her will into the "service" of acting:

> "Fanny," cried Tom Bertram, from the other table, where the conference was eagerly carrying on, and the conversation incessant, "we want your services."
>
> Fanny was up in a moment, expecting some errand, for the habit of employing her in that way was not yet overcome, in spite of all that Edmund could do.
>
> "Oh! we do not want to disturb you from your seat. We do not want your *present* services. We shall only want you in our play. You must be Cottager's wife."
>
> "Me!" cried Fanny, sitting down again with a most frightened look. "Indeed you must excuse me. I could not act any thing if you were to give me the world. No, indeed, I cannot act."
>
> "Indeed but you must, for we cannot excuse you . . . it will not much signify if nobody hears a word you say, so

[19] *Ibid.*, p. 218: "the fear that the impersonation of a bad or inferior character will have a harmful effect upon the impersonator, that, indeed, the impersonation of any other self will diminish the integrity of the real self."

you may be as creepmouse as you like, but we must have you to look at. . . ."

"It is not that I am afraid of learning by heart," said Fanny, shocked to find herself at that moment the only speaker in the room, and to feel that almost every eye was upon her; "but I really cannot act. . . . No, indeed, Mr Bertram, you must excuse me. You cannot have an idea. It would be absolutely impossible for me. . . . You must excuse me, indeed you must excuse me," cried Fanny, growing more and more red from excessive agitation, and looking distressfully at Edmund, who was kindly observing her, but unwilling to exasperate his brother by interference, gave her only an encouraging smile. Her entreaty had no effect on Tom; he only said again what he had said before; and it was not merely Tom, for the requisition was now backed by Maria and Mr Crawford, and Mr Yates, with an urgency which differed from his, but in being more gentle or more ceremonious, and which altogether was quite overpowering to Fanny. . . .[20]

Told that she need in no way change her own character but merely make herself *visible* at the needed moment (" 'you may be as creepmouse as you like, but we must have you to look at' "), Fanny, in the very act of refusal, is "shocked to find herself" indeed doing just as proposed, i.e., "to find herself at that moment the only speaker in the room, and to feel that almost every eye was upon her. . . ." Stating with "excessive agitation," " 'I cannot act,' " Fanny is of course, ironically, "acting," and it is a poor underestimation of Austen's own sophistication which overlooks the direct situational irony enacted in the unintended homology of word and action articulated here. It is also, as should begin to become apparent, a highly limited understanding of "irony"—as a concept in itself and as a means of interpreting Austen's narratives—from which such

[20] *Mansfield Park*, in *The Novels of Jane Austen*, ed. R. W. Chapman, 5 vols. (London: Oxford University Press, 1966), III:145–46. All quotations following from Austen's novels are from this edition.

an oversight inevitably stems. Trilling, arguing for the direct moral claims of the novel, no less than Mudrick and others arguing against them,[21] judges this scene in the terms of an impasse of ethics.[22] Similarly, whether contending the success or failure of Austen's intentions in the novel as a whole, critics have agreed that its specifically ethical content is presented, in Mudrick terms, "unequivocally" (see footnote 10), or, as Trilling writes, with "a certain hard literalness; that for the sake of its moral life, it must violate its own beauty by incorporating some of the irreducible prosy actuality of the world."[23] The occasionally "tiresome" quality of Austen's "prosing" of reality faulted originally by Scott is here praised as a "literalness" subordinated to the demands of a sterner and higher morality.[24] Yet were Fanny's response to the proposition of her "act-

[21] Mudrick, *Jane Austen*, p. 158: "Edmund and Fanny rigidly disapprove of such entertainment (although Fanny, of course, dares offer her opinion to no one but Edmund). As plainly as they represent the rock-like Sir Thomas in his absence, they do not surprise us by transforming custom into absolute morality. Their opposition is the traditional moral one; plays themselves may or may not be innocent, but players, by the very requirements of illusion, must be vulgar and immoral counterfeits; in respectable society, to play someone else is to degrade onself."

[22] Trilling opposes dramatic personification to Edmund's choice of the clergy for his "profession," speaking, in terms perhaps more suitable to the inactive Fanny than to Austen, of a fully playless, total identification of profession with "the self": "The election of a profession is of course in a way the assumption of a role, but it is a permanent impersonation which makes virtually impossible the choice of another. It is a commitment which fixes the nature of the self" (Trilling, *The Opposing Self*, p. 219).

[23] *Ibid.*, p. 223.

[24] Suggesting a certain lack of literal-mindedness in his "*Mansfield Park*," Trilling, in concluding the essay, goes on to describe the rigor of that morality in an encomium of Austen, here transformed by the critic into a kind of British middle-class Robespierre: "She is the first to be aware of the Terror which rules our moral situation, the ubiquitous anonymous judgment to which we respond, the necessity we feel to demonstrate the purity of our secular spirituality, whose dark and dubious places are more numerous and obscure than those of religious spirituality. . . . She herself is an agent of the Terror—we learn from her what our lives should be and by what subtle and fierce criteria they will be judged, and how to pass upon the lives of our friends and fellows. Once we have comprehended her mode of judgment, the moral and spiritual lessons of contemporary literature are easy. . . . Lawrence and Joyce, Yeats and Eliot, Proust and Gide, have but little to add save in the way of contem-

ing" itself viewed literally rather than explicated morally, perhaps the critical issue of moral versus stylistic and "ironic"
concerns would seem more an "excuse"—of the very nature
begged for repeatedly in this passage by Fanny—from the narrative's own "gentle," "ceremonious," and thus all the more
"overpowering" insistence upon the representation in the
novel of what Scott termed "real life."

Austen wrote one novel, *Northanger Abbey*, in which the
conviction that novels were or were not like "real life" was al-
ternately disproven. The novels read by Catherine Morland
are of the first kind mentioned by Scott, sentimental, gothic romance. Thus the parallel drawn within the novel, between our
comprehension of reality and of narrative fiction, itself appears a mere device of the fiction and undisturbing to our discursive cognition.[25] In *Mansfield Park*, however, Austen seems

---

porary and abstruse examples. To what extremes the Terror can go she herself
has made all too clear in the notorious passage in *Persuasion* in which she
comments on Mrs. Musgrove's 'large, fat sighings' over her dead scapegrace
son" (*ibid.*, pp. 228–29).

It is hard not to imagine Austen herself, not to speak of the range of later
authors leveled in one stroke before her, either shuddering or shaking her head
at this bizarrely totalitarian view of morality as transmitted specifically
through "literature," and thus of herself as at once literary and terrorist
"agent." For Trilling had insisted earlier in his essay that not morality alone
but its necessary identification with literature is what makes the author (we
would amend perhaps the critic) a merciless and ironyless "agent of the Terror": "Jane Austen puts the question of literature at the moral center of her
novel" (p. 219).

[25] Mudrick, however, who seems ultimately to view every determinately *literary* act commited by the author as evidence of an artistically crippling
"irony," condemns the novel—as he will all Austen's later works, with the exception of *Persuasion*, entirely (as in the case of *Mansfield Park*) or in part—
for the inevitably dissatisfying effect in which its "irony" results. While he defined the irony of *Northanger Abbey* as that which "overtly juxtaposes the
Gothic and the bourgeois worlds, and allows them to comment on each
other," he concludes that "irony, here . . . hardens perceptibly into rejection:
in *Northanger Abbey*, into a rejection not only of the illusionary world, but of
the realistic characters who disprove it—indeed, of the whole realistic basis of
the novel" (pp. 38, 59). What seems to antagonize the critic unduly about this
most decidedly comic of Austen's novels is that if the gothic, as he states,
should be made to appear ridiculous in light of its ongoing commentary by
reality, reality, by the function of that same "juxtaposition," must suffer to
some degree a similar effect.

to submit the novel to a fully desentimentalized version of "real life." That is, the world in which virtue would triumph without the aid of the plotted involutions of romance is a world, she suggests, in which, rather than acting either within a plot or in itself as plot-inducive, virtue does virtually nothing at all. This undoing within the novel of the efficacy of its own dependence upon plot—a structural tension within narrative which, as discussed below, takes a particularly dynamic form in Melville's *Pierre, Or the Ambiguities*—can perhaps be read most fruitfully as counterpoint or complement to the classical conception of the central necessity of plot to narrative, argued for most recently by Peter Brooks.[26] For *Mansfield Park*, in focusing upon Fanny, seems as disinterested in questions of plot as *Northanger Abbey* is plotted upon them. The two novels Austen named for proper places are as different as the worlds of moral conviction and romantic comedy, of purposefully limited and excessive imagination, which those places themselves function within the novels to represent. What strains our imagination, without the corresponding release of comedy, in *Mansfield Park*, is that its heroine, far from seeking plots in secret passageways or the contents of locked chests, spends most of her time either sitting quietly or doing other characters' bidding. The moral judgments she forms from that singularly unimposing position are themselves committed to a silence broken only by the categorical statement of self-effacement cited above: " 'I could not act any thing if you were to give me the world.' " Indeed, Fanny seems more willing, by the natural attrition of inaction, to lose whatever part of the world she has been given. She makes no attempt to prevent her poor health from worsening when the active wishes of others work to its certain detriment: she can no more retain the riding privileges secured her by Edmund (Chapter 7) than keep a fire lit to warm her in her own rooms (Chapter 32). In both those instances, we are made to realize, the wrongs done Fanny threaten her very bodily existence, yet she "cannot act" even where the mere de-

---

[26] See Peter Brooks, *Reading for the Plot* (New York: Knopf, 1984); for Brooks's own examination of the reversibility of that necessity, or the two-sided, "palinodal" nature of plot itself, see in particular his analysis of *Great Expectations* (Chap. 5, pp. 113–42).

sire for physical survival would be concerned. Instead, it is perpetually left to Edmund and, later, to his father to act, by their own initiative, on her behalf. Indeed, the affection Fanny feels for Edmund seems no more than the cumulative effect of the many times he has acted for her, without any form of solicitation from her, just as that of Sir Thomas for Fanny herself seems to stem from the opportunity to promote in her, as his adopted dependent, an improvement which the health and prosperity born to by his own daughters naturally precludes. The same inability "to act" also causes Henry Crawford's most improbable desire to marry Fanny. Henry's inclusion within the novel in fact gives further credence to a literal reading of Fanny's stated refusal in that, represented as most dextrously active in gaining the attentions of both Bertram sisters offstage, he is esteemed, even by Fanny, the best dramatic "actor" in the theatricals. While Fanny's consistent passivity in his regard is first welcomed by Henry as a refreshing challenge to his "acting" abilities, he is dismayed to find her unmoved even by what is clearly for him the "act" supreme: a serious proposal of marriage. Rather than speak her mind to her suitor or to anyone else, Fanny merely continues to flee his advances, leading Henry and his many advocates—the trusted Edmund included—to assume falsely that in order to accept him she should only need additional time.

The condition of physical and verbal inaction placed at the center of the novel, most directly articulated verbally in Fanny's avowal that she "cannot act," is best represented physically in the memorable scene of the visit to the Rushworth estate (Chapters 9-10). Indeed, what is most memorable about this "scene" is that we see almost nothing of it, for as readers we remain with Fanny, who herself remains before the invisible boundary of a ha-ha, waiting for the wandering Edmund and Mary Crawford to return. As the incident begins, Mary Crawford's engaging presence has made Edmund "forgetful" of Fanny's health; when Fanny, for once, speaks for herself in suggesting they rest from their walking, Edmund leads them to a bench, "well shaded and sheltered, and looking over a ha-ha into the park."[27] Mary, however, objects that her own well-

[27] Austen, III:94–95.

being requires further motion and another, if not necessarily better, view of her surroundings: " 'I must move.' said she, 'resting fatigues me.—I have looked across the ha-ha till I am weary. I must go and look through that iron gate at the same view, without being able to see it so well.' "[28] Convincing Edmund to walk with her without ever supplying a convincing reason—"She would only smile and assert. The greatest degree of rational consistency could not have been more engaging"[29]—Mary leads him away from Fanny, whose further movement would not be "suffered," in the understanding that they would return in "a few minutes."[30] As those minutes multiply, Fanny's watchful solitude is interrupted by another group of potential lovers: Maria Bertram, her fiancé, Mr. Rushworth, and Henry, who, as persuasive as his sister, is presently occupied in gaining Maria's affection for himself. As if unconsciously performing in a drawing room comedy, Fanny recapitulates her situation to the new arrivals—the narrative states briefly: "she told her story"—before Maria sends Rushworth searching for the key to the locked gate and, "taking a circuitous, and as it appeared to her, very unreasonable direction," passes with Henry "beyond" the range of "[Fanny's] eye."[31] As the pair moves from Fanny's and the reader's view, Julia Bertram appears; jealous of Henry's attentions, she is soon off in his direction once Fanny has narrated her essentially unchanged situation again. Having now been left alone for a second time for essentially the same reason, Fanny need only repeat her story; the narrator does the same, again merely stating, "Fanny explained."[32] Eventually, Rushworth returns, and Fanny, forced to begin another narration, tries to make "the best of the story"; by indirect suggestion she convinces Rushworth to follow Maria, thus finding "herself more successful in sending away, than in retaining a companion."[33] Finally, Fanny, grown "quite impatient" of the initial and still in-

[28] *Ibid.*, III:96.
[29] *Ibid.*
[30] *Ibid.*
[31] *Ibid.*, III:97, 100.
[32] *Ibid.*, III:100.
[33] *Ibid.*, III:103.

visible variables in her story, Edmund and Mary, "resolve[s] to go in search of them" herself. Before actually seeing them, she hears, coming, appropriately, from the direction of the ha-ha, the sound of Mary's laugh: "They were just returned into the wilderness from the park, to which a side gate, not fastened, had tempted them very soon after their leaving her . . . into the very avenue which Fanny had been hoping the whole morning to reach at last; and had been sitting down under one of the trees. This was their history. It was evident that they had been spending their time pleasantly, and were not aware of the length of their absence."[34]

Fanny, the heroine of a novel who states her own inability "to act" as "dramatis persona,"[35] "acts" here within the narrative as a personification of inaction, lacking, in addition, any means of personal expression. This episode, more suggestive of a dramatic interlude staged with the assistance of multiple swinging doors than the representation in a moral narrative of a visit to a country estate, could perhaps be regarded in another novel as intended to amuse; in one of Austen's "comic" novels it would probably be considered yet another "ironic" display. But the novel, *Mansfield Park*, at one with the place, sanctions no amusement at the medium of representation. Instead we are made by the narrative to share Fanny's frustration while the "action" of the novel takes place out of our sight. Adding to our sense of action *occluded* rather than represented by narrative is the fact that what Fanny *does* do, in this lengthy episode, is solely what the narrative does: she narrates. Fanny tells those who arrive where others have gone. Rather than state what Fanny says, the narrative itself need only refer, with the barest simplicity, to the fact that she narrates at all, for, in effect, Fanny could only say what the narrative has said already. Fanny, as nonactor, becomes narrator by default, and like the narrative voice of *Mansfield Park*, she has no dramatic "story" to tell. In his review of *Emma*, Scott does not refer to *Mansfield Park*: whether by choice or by oversight can only be

[34] *Ibid.*

[35] Austen uses the term in reference to the roles played in the theatricals; see *ibid.*, III:132.

conjectured.[36] But it can be said with the measure of conviction provided by the text of the novel itself that none of the "dramatis personae" praised in Scott's review were meant to figure in *Mansfield Park*. Whatever "drama" does take place in the novel happens, specifically, "beyond [Fanny's] eye," whether past a ha-ha, in the active world of London, or even out riding at Mansfield Park. And we, as readers made to see with Fanny, read the same narrative strangely devoid of narrative action which Fanny herself is forced to relate.

Narration without, and in the place of, action—words whose meaning can be spoken without threat of moral transgression in that they are merely "narrative," i.e., severed from any directly active relation to their speaker—also provides Fanny's ultimate role in the aborted theatricals. Fanny has already served "sometimes as prompter, sometimes as spectator" to the actors[37] when Mary Crawford comes to her alone for assistance. She assents to help but stipulates, " 'I must *read* the part, for I can *say* very little of it.' "[38] Edmund arrives shortly after Mary to the same purpose, and Fanny, thus relieved of the task of "reading," is wanted "only to prompt and observe them," although with the spectacle of Edmund and Mary "acting" as lovers before her—notably the only scene approaching "real" action in the novel—"she could not always pay attention to her book."[39] Yet when one of the actors fails to attend a group rehearsal, the mechanical function of "reading," rather than of "saying" with meaning, is thrust upon Fanny again: "some eyes began to be turned towards Fanny, and a voice or two, to say, 'If Miss Price would be so good as to *read* the part?' "[40] Fanny's reaction, unexpressed to the others, but again at one with the narrative which articulates it, is to question the grounds of her own presence at the rehearsals in the first place: "why had not she rather gone to her own room, as she had felt to be safest, instead of attend-

[36] Cf. the discussion of this omission on Scott's part in *Jane Austen: The Critical Heritage*, pp. 10–11.
[37] *Austen*, III:165.
[38] *Ibid.*, III:169; emphasis in text.
[39] *Ibid.*, III:170.
[40] *Ibid.*, III:171.

ing the rehearsal at all? She had known it would irritate and distress her—she had known it her duty to keep away. She was properly punished. 'You have only to *read* the part,' said Henry Crawford with renewed entreaty."[41] At precisely that moment the narrative is itself diverted, however, by an overtly "dramatic" turn: "the door of the room was thrown open, and Julia appearing at it, with a face all aghast, exclaimed, 'My father is come! He is in the hall at this moment.' "[42] But still, we are with Fanny, which is to say *not* "in the hall," where the dramatic confrontation narrated has already taken place. Fanny is rescued from "reading" by her uncle's unforeseen return; but the question she herself raised, before being saved by a theatrical moment stated *within* the narrative, remains important for her representation within the narrative as a whole. Why did she, as the character whose every perception is at once a moral judgment, not do what "she had felt to be safest" as well as "known to be her duty": "keep away" from the "acting" of which she immediately disapproved? The answer may lie with her own prompter to participation, Henry Crawford, for Fanny, while she assiduously avoids him as a suitor, cannot help admiring Henry as an actor. "As far as she could judge," the narrator states for Fanny during the rehearsals, "Mr. Crawford was considerably the best actor of all; he had more confidence than Edmund, more judgment than Tom, more talent and taste than Mr. Yates.—She did not like him as a man, but she must admit him to be the best actor, and on this point there were not many who differed from her."[43] The theme is taken up later in the novel when Fanny, even while attempting to discourage Henry's personal attentions, finds herself attending to his performative "reading" of a "speech" which she had been merely sight-"reading" to Lady Bertram:

> Crawford took the volume. "Let me have the pleasure of finishing that speech to your ladyship," said he. "I shall find it immediately." . . . Not a look, or an offer of help had Fanny given; not a syllable for or against. All her at-

[41] *Ibid.*, III:172.
[42] *Ibid.*
[43] *Ibid.*, III:165.

tention was for her work. She seemed determined to be interested by nothing else. But taste was too strong in her.
She could not abstract her mind five minutes; she was
forced to listen; his reading was capital, and her pleasure
in good reading was extreme. To *good* reading, however
she had been long used; her uncle read well—her cousins
all—Edmund very well; but in Mr. Crawford's reading
there was a variety of excellence beyond what she had
ever met with. The King, the Queen, Buckingham, Wol-
sey, Cromwell, all were given in turn; for with the happiest knack, the happiest power of jumping and guessing, he
could always light, at will, on the best scene, or the best
speeches of each; and whether it were dignity or pride, or
tenderness or remorse, or whatever were to be expressed,
he could do it with equal beauty.—It was truly dramatic.—His acting had first taught Fanny what pleasure a
play might give, and his reading brought all his acting before her again; Nay, perhaps with greater enjoyment, for
it came unexpectedly, and with no such drawback as she
had been used to suffer in seeing him on the stage with
Miss Bertram.[44]

Henry's "reading" is "*good* reading" because it combines
words with action; that is to say, with Fanny and the narrator,
"It was truly dramatic." At the same time, in bringing the
physical presence of "all his acting before her," his reading *represents* action, and as such can also be judged to be truly novelistic. The term "representation," indicating the specifically
artificial nature of a dramatic performance, had been used by
Austen earlier in the novel in reference to the amateur theatricals,[45] and what Henry's dramatic reading, like his dramatic
acting, shares most specifically with novels, although pointedly not with the novel *Mansfield Park*, is the ability to bring
about pleasure, the primary effect of representation. The word
"pleasure," repeated three times in the single paragraph just
cited, seems to relate most obviously to Henry Crawford's particularly seductive charms; it is due to Henry's "acting" that

[44] *Ibid.*, III:336–37.
[45] See: III:21: "the play . . . was within two days of representation."

even Fanny had learned "what pleasure a play might give." Yet perhaps one of the best kept secrets of *Mansfield Park*—a secret kept, that is, by the plot and tenor of the novel itself—is that the word "pleasure," in its many lexical and grammatical variants—"pleasant," "pleasing," "mispleased," "displeasure," "pleasurable," etc.—appears more frequently in the novel than any other abstract expression of sensory experience. There are few pages in succession in which a form of "pleasure" is not mentioned in the narrative, and many in which it is repeated two times or more.[46] Along with Austen's other alliterative abstract noun titles, *Pride and Prejudice* and *Persuasion*, *Mansfield Park*, by its own verbal insistence, could well have been entitled, *Pleasure*, although the *reading* of the word as title of this particular novel would in no way represent what the novel, in Fanny's terms, has to *say*. We "read" "pleasure" throughout *Mansfield Park*, but it is in Fanny's, and the narrative's, sense, not a "*good* reading." The word "pleasure" is not ultimately represented in action in the novel, neither in the "bad" end met by Maria Bertram with Henry, in which love causes the loss of family and society, nor in the "good" ending shared by Fanny and Edmund, in which love finally grants Fanny membership in both.[47] Love itself is not repre-

---

[46] For example, the incidence of forms of the term in the first half of the novel (through Vol. II, Chap. 6, pp. 3–237), runs roughly like this: pp. 22, 23, 36 (two times), 37, 42, 43, 45 (two times), 47, 48, 49, 52, 57, 59, 62, 63, 64, 65, 66, 68, 69, 70 (two times), 74, 75, 76, 78 (three times), 80, 84, 86, 88, 90, 96, 98, 100, 101, 103 (two times), 105 (two times), 106 (three times), 107, 112 (two times), 114, 116, 119, 127, 128, 132, 133, 134, 138, 143, 151, 156, 169, 171, 179, 183, 186 (three times), 190, 194, 198 (two times), 204, 208 (three times), 210 (two times), 215, 216, 219, 223, 226 (three times, including two uses in dialogue of the French *plaisirs*), 231 (two times), 233, and 234.

[47] Sir Thomas' original "objection" to taking Fanny into his household was the possibility of her presence ending in "cousins in love" (III:6). The narrator gives this account in closing of the reversal in his feelings when the novel, chiefly by attrition, takes the precise ending he had earlier feared, and Fanny, in the absence of the "disappoint[ing]" Crawfords, is to become "the daughter"—related in an unavoidably ambiguous past tense of narration—"that he wanted": "Sick of ambitious and mercenary connections, prizing more and more the sterling good of principle and temper, and chiefly anxious to bind by the strongest securities all that remained to him of domestic felicity, he had pondered with genuine satisfaction on the more than possibility of the two

sented to effect "pleasure" in *Mansfield Park*, which is why it seems most unlikely—as the cool reaction of the majority of its readers may well indicate—that it would be viewed, in Walter Scott's terms, as representing "real life."

But, for the very same reason, *Mansfield Park* cannot be said to follow the conventions of the genre Scott opposed to the novel: above all *Mansfield Park* is *not* a romance. This particular novel relies neither upon "irony," seen as the primary plot device of Austen's novels, nor upon any of the literary formulas which would identify it as a nonrealistic romance. How does it then, in positive terms, represent reality? By "reality," a set of given objects referred to discursively is not meant: certainly, no one can point to a "Fanny Price" in their acquaintanceship. Rather, the way in which reality becomes "real life" for us, the way in which we know and experience objects, may have a relation to the representation of Fanny Price. At one point in the novel, as Edmund expresses his own misperception, that Henry's failure to win Fanny stems merely from the exclusively active nature of his attempt, he adds: " 'I wish he had known you as well as I do, Fanny. Between us, I think we should have won you. My theoretical and his practical knowledge together, could not have failed.' "[48] What Edmund does not seem to know is that Fanny already loves him; what Henry's persistence indicates he could probably never know is that she will never love him. "Theoretical and practical knowledge" are equally inadequate in their understanding of experience, but Fanny, whose understanding is never deficient, is also never actively involved in experience. The pointedly *non*-dramatic persona of Fanny *is* the novel's representation of the "real life" of our experience: the life in which "practical" and

young friends finding their mutual consolation in each other for all that had occurred of disappointment to either; and the joyful consent which met Edmund's application, the high sense of having realised a great acquisition in the promise of Fanny for a daughter, formed just such a contrast with his early opinion on the subject when the poor little girl's coming had been first agitated, as time is for ever producing between the plans and decisions of mortals, for their own instruction, and their neighbours' entertainment.

"Fanny was indeed the daughter he wanted. His charitable kindness had been rearing a prime comfort for himself" (III:471–72).

[48] *Ibid.*, III:348.

"theoretical knowledge," contrary to Edmund's exclusively "theoretical" thinking, would at best supplant each other if they could ever be brought "together." All immediate engagement in practical action is bound up with "pleasure," or its opposite: what reader of Austen is not familiar with that peculiar narrative *topos* in her novels, of a mind overcome at once with "a thousand feelings of pleasure and pain," by which a character's reaction to an action in the plot is described as the usurpation of cognitive sense by sensation. Thus Fanny's story, the least pleasant of Austen's narratives, constantly refers to "pleasure" while narrating Fanny's removal from it: even the woods where she is confined to the fate of waiting and narrating, is named—as it well proves to be for others—the "pleasure-grounds" of the Rushworth estate.[49] For everyone in *Mansfield Park* is swayed by the experience of pleasure: both Bertram sisters are misled by the flattery of Henry Crawford, Maria discovering that her own pleasure had "destroyed her happiness"[50] forever; Edmund is moved to the last by Henry's thoroughly self-interested sister, and even Sir Thomas is explained in the opening sentence of the novel to have originally been "captivated" by the vain and indolent Lady Bertram, of whom at best it can be said that she pleases almost without meaning to, caring for no one and having no character at all. Only Fanny steers clear of acting on the "grounds" of "pleasure," but solely by remaining clear of the narrative's own action. She is most affected by Henry not when confronted with expressions of his personal desire but when listening to him "act" dramatically in reading from a book. Fanny, in other words, is the sacrifice of practical for theoretical knowledge, the "price" paid in sensory experience for an unfailing sense of judgment, paid here by the novelist in the narrative currencies in which she is most rich: force of dialogue, appealing character portraiture, subtlety of plot development, and comic wit. *Mansfield Park* is "real" without necessarily reflecting any given objects in reality as much as "Fanny Price" is what Austen as novelist pays, as we in life may objectively pay in other

[49] *Ibid.*, III:90.
[50] *Ibid.*, III:202.

ways, for the comprehension of a previous and unavoidable practical mistake.

Sense and Sensibility

The prior error I refer to is not the immediately appealing *Pride and Prejudice* but Austen's first novel, *Sense and Sensibility*, regarded generally as her least important work and her most limited success. Austen, on the other hand, expressed her own reservations about the more admired novel: the well-known observation in her correspondance that *Pride and Prejudice* is "rather too light, and bright, and sparkling" is followed by the suggestion that what it "wants . . . here and there" is "a long chapter of sense."[51] *Sense and Sensibility*, named in part for what *Pride and Prejudice* is said to lack, is indeed the more serious novel of the two, just as the general dichotomy implied in its title between reason and our sensory nature is more fundamentally encompassing than the coupling of the equally alliterative, but not necessarily opposed terms, "pride and prejudice." Similarly, mistakes based on the mere affections of "pride" and "prejudice" are at once more amusing and more easily remedied than those made on the basis of either "sensibility" or judgments of "sense." Thanks in part to the truly "sparkling" character and fate of Elizabeth Bennett, *Pride and Prejudice* is not only the most popular Austen novel, but that most praised critically for the excellence of its irony.[52] Indeed, the critical emphasis on the successful employment of irony in both *Pride and Prejudice* and Austen's other great comic novel, *Emma*, seems to indicate that the very meaning of "irony" may have become synonymous in Austen criticism with the welcome recognition of a particular Austen plot: that of an attractive, basically good-natured, if at first somewhat self-deluded, young woman, who, through the intervention of a more judicious, though nonetheless thoroughly enamoured,

[51] Letter to Cassandra of Feb. 4, 1813, in *Jane Austen's Letters (to her sister Cassandra and others)*, ed. R. W. Chapman (Clarendon: Oxford University Press, 1952), pp. 299–300.

[52] See, in particular, Brower, "Light, and Bright"; Mudrick, *Jane Austen*; Trilling, *The Opposing Self*; and Litz, *Jane Austen*.

man, comes ultimately to a more than moderately satisfying end. Whether such a plot resembles "real life" must of course remain an open question for each of us, and again, it is not the plot or "conduct" of Austen's novels but the individual "occurrences," the "motives and principles," they represent which had been described by Scott as recognizable in life. But to equate "successful" irony with a happy turn in already essentially happy events is perhaps to lack precisely what Austen suggested her own creation might "want," i.e., "sense."

There is no lack of "sense," however, in *Sense and Sensibility*, and indeed its own irony, usually found to be either failed in execution or poorly conceived,[53] may stem most fundamentally from that fact. Elinor, of the Dashwood sisters, is easily recognized as the novel's personification of "sense." Some critics have also perceptively proposed that the distinction between the two sisters, Elinor and Marianne, is perhaps not as mutually exclusive as the title which represents them: that Elinor has her own moments of sensibility, just as Marianne shares some of her sister's sense.[54] Yet the reason most critics of the novel are less apt to view it as ironic is that they begin by reading its title as a mutually exclusive opposition. The chief and immediate irony already inherent in *Sense and Sensibility*, however, is that, unlike the purely alliterative liaison existing between "pride" and "prejudice," the alliterative or sensory link between "sense" and "sensibility" is also a link of "sense." For both words share, to begin with, a single root of meaning—a fact that may only become apparent when we recall that "sensibility," cleared of its acquired meaning of an aestheticist proclivity, could be substituted for by the definite

---

[53] Cf. Mudrick, who generally reads Austen's "ironic" narratives at—ironically—the most directly referential level of meaning: "Irony, which has till now been Jane Austen's defense against feeling, is here reinforced and ultimately superseded by another defense . . . social conventions . . . convention is her defense as the genteel spinster when the artist is overcome, perhaps by some powerful social or domestic pressure" (*Jane Austen*, p. 91).

[54] Cf. Moler, *Jane Austen's Art*, pp. 61–73, on the limitations of "sense" represented in Elinor, including, most significantly, her failure to recognize Marianne's illness as more than a mere "romantic illusion" (p. 68); Wright, *Jane Austen's Novels*, p. 86; and Ian Watt, "On *Sense and Sensibility*," in *Jane Austen: A Collection of Critical Essays*, pp. 41–51 (p. 48).

plural of "sense." "Sense and the senses," as William Empson discovered in reading Wordsworth's *Prelude*,[55] are far more difficult to keep neatly separate once one admits that but for the additional distinction of the definite article—itself adding to the plural form a "sense" of the material—both terms have an equal claim to being the proper meaning of "sense."

What has disturbed most readers of *Sense and Sensibility*, however, is that the two terms appear not to have an equal claim to the Austen happy end. Sensible (in the contemporary "sense" of reasonable!) Elinor marries the man she has loved from the beginning of the novel, whereas Marianne marries a man for whom she has never felt an emotion more vital than indifference. The man Marianne does love, Willoughby, has married another woman for her wealth. After visiting the Dashwoods repeatedly, and leading Marianne, as well her sister and mother, to believe in the sincerity of his attentions, Willoughby leaves suddenly for London, ignores Marianne when she sees him there, and merely writes to announce his engagement without properly accounting for his behavior. The next (and last) we see of Willoughby is a scene whose own internal composition and further effects upon the novel's final development provide the focus of the present analysis of narrative representation in *Sense and Sensibility*. The conceptual issue which *has* divided the two sisters throughout the novel is whether the actions undertaken by Willoughby with Marianne need rest on the foundation of a formal, verbal engagement. Elinor objects to her mother, who sides with Marianne, that the failure of the two lovers to constate their mutual attachment formally makes their own active engagement with each other, while fully harmonious, highly improper. This opposition between word and action as media of cognition arises

[55] See Empson's excellent analysis, "Sense in the *Prelude*" in *The Study of Complex Words* (London: Chatto & Windus, 1951), which concludes that Wordsworth intended a "double meaning" for the term: "both the process of sensing," with its own immediate "actual horror," and "the eventual exultation" of "the supreme act of imagination." Empson, interestingly, also happens to mention *Sense and Sensibility* in this particular context, finding—probably uniquely in Austen's reception—that, like Wordsworth in his use of "sense," she is "perfectly at home with horror" (pp. 301–302).

most clearly in an interchange between Elinor and Mrs. Dashwood after Willoughby's abrupt departure for London:

> "I want no proof of their affection," said Elinor; "but of their engagement I do."
> "I am perfectly satisfied of both."
> "Yet not a syllable has been said to you on the subject, by either of them."
> "I have not wanted syllables where actions have spoken so plainly. . . . Have we not perfectly understood each other? Has not my consent been daily asked by his looks, his manner, his attentive and affectionate respect? My Elinor, is it possible to doubt their engagement? . . ."
> "I confess," replied Elinor, "that every circumstance except *one* is in favour of their engagement; but that *one* is the total silence of both on the subject, and with me it almost outweighs the other."[56]

Like her mother, Marianne prefers actions to words as the only truly meaningful, because immediate, form of "proof"; she condemns "commonplace phrases" whose effect is destroyed by time,[57] and considers expressive or descriptive language which has endured temporally to be reduced in meaning to "a mere jargon": " 'I detest jargon of every kind, and sometimes I have kept my feelings to myself, because I could find no language to describe them in but what was worn and hackneyed out of all sense and meaning.' "[58] Thus, when Elinor rebukes her for visiting Willoughby's residence in his presence alone, Marianne returns that any "real" moral transgression should make itself "sensible" in the very instant and act of doing "wrong." For were words to be valued instead of actions as the true "proof of impropriety in conduct," then all morality would merely be measured by the verbal estimations offered at "every moment": " 'if there had been any real impropriety in what I did, I should have been sensible of it at the time, for we always know when we are acting wrong, and with such a con-

[56] *Sense and Sensibility*, I:79–80.
[57] *Ibid.*, I:45.
[58] *Ibid.*, I:97.

viction I could have had no pleasure. . . . If the impertinent remarks of Mrs. Jennings are to be the proof of impropriety of
conduct, we are all offending every moment of all our
lives.' "[59] Marianne's emphatic belief in the integrity of action
and consequent disdain for the verbal judgments, or "remarks," of others, seem to make her as unlike Fanny of *Mansfield Park* as the latter appears to resemble Elinor. Yet on at
least one prior occasion Elinor had happened to overhear a
conversation between her sister and Willoughby, and her understanding of its content derives more from the "manner" of
Willoughby's actions in speaking than the specific significance
of the particular words she hears. Willoughby, having presented Marianne with a horse which Elinor has convinced her
she must refuse, offers "to keep it" at his own residence "only
till [Marianne] can claim it." Elinor's assumption of Willoughby's "meaning" here so nearly resembles what we imagine to
be her sister's that one must read the following passage twice
to realize that Elinor *is* the "Miss Dashwood" of which it
speaks:

> This was all overheard by Miss Dashwood; and in the
> whole of the sentence, in his manner of pronouncing it,
> and in his addressing her sister by her christian name
> alone, she instantly saw an intimacy so decided, a mean-
> ing so direct, as marked a perfect agreement between
> them. From that moment she doubted not of their being
> engaged to each other; and the belief of it created no other
> surprise, than that she, or any of their friends, should be
> left by tempers so frank, to discover it by accident.[60]

This last conversation remains, for the major part of the
novel, the only communication between Marianne and Willoughby to which Elinor is audience. What Elinor "instantly
saw" in its performance will prove deceptive; moreover, in
seeing "instantly," she has seen with her senses and not with
"sense." The final encounter with Willoughby in the novel
takes place between him and Elinor alone, and though she will

[59] *Ibid.*, I:68.
[60] *Ibid.*, I:59–60.

already be aware of that previous deception, Elinor's second experience of Willoughby will prove even more persuasive, more inducive of "belief." The factual evidence against Willoughby's character has mounted in the meantime: Colonel Brandon has named him as the seducer of his daughter, Elinor herself has both seen him shun her sister in person and read the contents of his cruelly dismissive letter; finally, his marriage to another woman is now widely known. Yet Elinor, for whom the value of formal "engagement" "almost outweighs every other," finds, in listening to Willoughby, that even the formal meaning of words, once they are spoken, cannot be separated from the *act* of their articulation; that while words must indeed be formally static if they are to provide the proper medium for an "agreement" of "sense," their very appearance as medium can result in an experience of action, and thus of a meaning more "direct." The scene referred to begins, in Chapter 8 of Volume III of the novel, with the memorable image of Elinor "staring back with a look of horror" at the unexpected sight of Willoughby: "her hand was already on the lock, when its action was suspended by his hastily advancing, and saying, in a voice rather of command than supplication, 'Miss Dashwood, for half an hour—for ten minutes—I entreat you to stay.' "[61] The censuring action of a lock is represented here as suspended by the action of present and appealing speech. While Elinor herself remains momentarily suspended—"she knew not what to do"—her inaction soon yields to Willoughby's wishes, for her "curiosity," the narrator relates, "no less than her honour was *engaged*."[62] When Willoughby explains he has come for "something like forgiveness," Elinor asks if that is indeed his "real reason." The narrative relates the words, and, more importantly, the effect caused by the manner, of his reponse: " 'Upon my soul it is,'—was his answer, with a warmth which brought all the former Willoughby to her remembrance, and in spite of herself made her think him sincere."[63] For the remainder of the chapter, Elinor hears and

[61] *Ibid.*, I:317.
[62] *Ibid.*; my emphasis.
[63] *Ibid.*, I:319.

is "softened" by Willoughby's story,[64] that of falling in love with Marianne without meaning to, and of having finally decided to "engage [his] faith" formally when the discovery of his involvement with Colonel Brandon's daughter called him away. Instead of trying to excuse the "scrupling" inaction which first prevented his proposal of engagement, he indicates the inadequacy of verbal reason itself to the force of "proof" provided only by "the event": " 'I will not reason here—nor will I stop for *you* to expatiate on the absurdity, and the worse than absurdity, of scrupling to engage my faith where my honour was already bound. The event has proved, that I was a cunning fool, providing with great circumspection for a possible opportunity of making myself contemptible and wretched for ever.' "[65] When Elinor objects to the content of what she had recognized to be his own letter, she learns further that words, by their power to formalize meaning, can continue to be read as meaningful even when reproduced in form alone. Willoughby admits that while he had physically written and signed the letter, the author of its "original" writing, or mental conception, was his present wife. Furthermore, the reason he gives for his agreement to this deceptive scheme is none other than that of his being "engaged": " 'I had only the credit of servilely copying such sentences as I was ashamed to put my name to. The original was all her own—her own happy thoughts and gentle diction. But what could I do?—we were engaged.' "[66] Formal engagement, the very commitment of immediate experience to conventional verbal expression which had been lacking between him and Marianne, here usurps Willoughby's ability to recognize the active and unmediated effect of "language" upon its reader: the meaning of the words he copies becomes, like the act of copying, secondary, in the knowledge that they are *only* being used formally, i.e., toward "one end": "after all, what did it signify to my character in the opinion of Marianne and her friends, in what language my answer was couched?—It must have been only to one end. My

[64] *Ibid.*, I:321, 325.
[65] *Ibid.*, I:321.
[66] *Ibid.*, I:328.

business was to declare myself a scoundrel, and whether I did it with a bow or a bluster was of little importance."[67] The "end" foreseen by the fact of Willoughby's formal engagement has, not coincidentally, prevented Elinor's own happiness from the novel's beginning. Edward Ferrars makes Elinor's acquaintance while secretly engaged to another woman. His engagement having long ceased to represent any meaning other than that of a word given, Edward defers its translation into actual experience long enough to have its insignificance, in Willoughby's words, "proven" by "the event": his fiancée's elopement with his own brother. Ultimately Willoughby, and not Edward, can be seen to suffer the consequences of taking the meaning of engagement too literally. For only because he is and remains "sincere" about the engagement of his own meaning—or as he calls it, "faith"—does Willoughby defer the verbal act, rather than actual consummation, of engagement too long, and, in announcing his purely formal "engagement," to another woman, to the woman he loves more than ever before, find that the specific words chosen to do so did not "signify." Edward, considered like Elinor to be the more reasonable of the two suitors, is in fact less "faithful" to his word than Willoughby in that he initiates his visits to Elinor, having already given his word to Lucy Steele: only the superficial circumstance of the secrecy of his engagement renders those visits, made in essentially bad "faith," possible. Edward, admired by Elinor for his modest and principled nature, may appear in retrospect to have "acted" with considerably more cleverness than Willoughby, in that by merely waiting—rather than acting—for the ambitious Lucy to lose interest, he wins Elinor, the woman he loves, merely by hedging his bets. Had Willoughby done the same, the narrator informs us at the close of the novel—and indeed it is almost more than we can stand to be told—both Marianne and the wealth he was accustomed to would have eventually been his: "Willoughby could not hear of [Marianne's] marriage without a pang; and his punishment was soon afterwards complete in the voluntary forgiveness of Mrs. Smith, who, by stating his marriage with a woman of character, as the source of her clemency, gave him reason for

[67] *Ibid.*

believing that had he behaved with honour towards Marianne, he might at once have been happy and rich."[68]

Willoughby had made his visit to the Dashwoods because he had heard that Marianne was dying; having learned she has recovered and explained his past actions, he leaves Elinor without attempting to persuade her further: " 'But I will not stay to rob myself of all your compassionate good-will, by shewing that where I have most injured I can least forgive. Goodbye,— God bless you!' And with these words, he almost ran out of the room."[69] His effect upon Elinor is narrated at the opening of Chapter 9, which follows immediately; surpassing even the change evidenced in Willoughby's actions toward Marianne, this passage describes a reversal in "character" which, in occurring internally, is by far the most forceful the novel represents:

> Elinor, for some time after he left her, for some time even after the sound of his carriage had died away, remained too much oppressed by a croud of ideas, widely differing in themselves, but of which sadness was the general result, to think even of her sister.
>
> Willoughby, he, whom only half an hour ago she had abhorred as the most worthless of men, Willoughby, in spite of all his faults, excited a degree of commiseration for the sufferings produced by them, which made her think of him as now separated for ever from her family with a tenderness, a regret, rather in proportion, as she soon acknowledged within herself—to his wishes than to his merits. She felt that his influence over her mind was heightened by circumstances which ought not in reason to have weight; by that person of uncommon attraction, that open, affectionate, and lively manner which it was no merit to possess; and by that still ardent love for Marianne, which it was not even innocent to indulge. But she felt that it was so, long, long before she could feel his influence less.[70]

[68] *Ibid.*, I:379.
[69] *Ibid.*, I:332.
[70] *Ibid.*, I:333.

The mistake made by Elinor is an error of "the senses," stemming not from an act of cognitive deception but rather from the fact of having seen and listened to Willoughby at all. In having assented to "curiosity," that unreasoning stimulus to "sense," Elinor has come under the "influence" of "circumstances which ought not in reason to have weight," and thus whose effect weighs instead upon reason, as her mind is "oppressed by a croud of ideas." Rather than deceive Elinor, Willoughby has engaged her sensibility, her "tenderness" and "regret," through virtues of his "person" which "it was no merit to possess." It is again Willoughby's "manner," the "uncommon attraction" of his presence, and the perceivable sincerity of his "still ardent love for Marianne" that perform his work of persuasion for him. Elinor, in other words, simply by experiencing them directly, has been made no less "sensible" than Marianne of Willoughby's charms. Those charms may not be moral "merits," but neither can they be condemned as moral flaws. For while they are inevitably persuasive, they cannot be said to persuade to an untruth; Willoughby's appeal through reason *to* the senses seems to embody a truth of its own. Indeed, as Austen has represented Willoughby's appearance before Elinor to us, the inevitable effect of the man, "whom only half an hour ago she had abhorred as the most worthless of men," is best described by Willoughby's own account of unintentionally falling in love with Marianne: " 'To have resisted such attractions, to have withstood such tenderness!—Is there a man on earth who could have done it! Yes, I found myself, by insensible degrees, sincerely fond of her. . . .' " If not Elinor then truly no woman would be capable of "resist[ing] such attractions" as Willoughby's, for even more than the qualities of his own "person" and "manner," Willoughby persuades, as Marianne persuaded him, because he too is "sincere" in his love. While the effect of this scene upon the narrative as a whole has been generally underestimated, Mudrick has gone so far in the opposite sense of the narrative to suggest that Elinor herself is "quite amorally in love" with Willoughby "after his disclosure."[71] Yet it seems less rather than more enlight-

[71] Mudrick, *Jane Austen*, p. 85.

ened than Elinor to accuse her of amoral behavior in Willoughby's place, and far less enlightened than the author of
this scene, to suggest that Austen, in the absence of the "defense" of "irony" here, "is herself revealed in a posture of
yearning for the impossible . . . the absolute lover."[72] Rather,
if it is difficult for the reader, after the relation of this encounter with Willoughby, to distinguish between the titular identi-
ties of the two sisters, this confusion of "sense and sensibility"
just previous to the marriages which end the novel must be no
less known to Austen than it is recognized by Elinor herself:

> Willoughby, "poor Willoughby," as she now allowed her-
> self to call him, was constantly in her thoughts; she would
> not but have heard his vindication for the world, and now
> blamed, now acquitted herself for having judged him so
> harshly before. But her promise of relating it to her sister
> was invariably painful. She dreaded the performance of it,
> dreaded what its effect on Marianne might be; doubted
> whether after such an explanation she could ever be
> happy with another; and for a moment wished Wil-
> loughby a widower. Then, remembering Colonel Bran-
> don, reproved herself, felt that to *his* sufferings and *his*
> constancy far more than to his rival's, the reward of her
> sister was due, and wished any thing rather than Mrs.
> Willoughby's death.[73]

In "wish[ing] Willoughby a widower," even if only "for a moment," Elinor experiences the underside of her excessively reasonable and self-effacing treatment of Edward's secret fiancée,
her own rival, Lucy Steele. When her mother informs her, soon
after this passage, that the same deserving Colonel Brandon
has revealed his love for Marianne, Elinor's "feeling" is "by
turns both pleased and pained."[74] Nor can she "quite agree"
with her mother in the latter's new-found conviction that
"Marianne would yet never have been so happy with *him*, as
she will be with Colonel Brandon."[75] In all good sense, the nar-

---

[72] *Ibid.*
[73] Austen, I:334–35.
[74] *Ibid.*, I:336.
[75] *Ibid.*, I:338.

rator relates, Elinor "wish[es] success to her friend," Colonel Brandon, but simultaneously—even "in wishing it"—she "feel[s] a pang for Willoughby."[76]

In the private confusion of her constant thoughts of Willoughby, Elinor seems to embody alone, and without need for external expression, the double meaning of the novel's title. Yet Austen does not end her narrative of "sense and sensibility" here. For the two kinds of "sense" seem capable of cohabitation only until Elinor herself is placed in the narrative position: that of effecting comprehension through the representation of "occurrences" connected causally within structured, cognitive limits. In the little noted coda to her experience of sensibility, Elinor relates to Marianne her meeting with Willoughby. Marianne has just admitted that the recent disability of her senses in sickness has led her to reflect upon the series of her own actions from the beginning: " 'My illness has made me think—It has given me leisure and calmness for serious recollection. Long before I was enough recovered to talk, I was perfectly able to reflect. I considered the past; I saw in my own behaviour since the beginning of our acquaintance with him last autumn, nothing but a series of imprudence towards myself, and want of kindness to others.' "[77] Yet Marianne adds to this speech, narrating her own conversion to reason, the single desire *for* knowledge upon which its realization depends: "She paused—and added in a lower voice, 'If I could but know *his* heart, everything would become easy.' "[78] As it happens, the granting of that knowledge, induced by this explanation of its expected result, produces, to the ignorance of both sisters, a highly sensible and contrary effect. Although Elinor already alters the content of her conversation with Willoughby so as to delete precisely the knowledge Marianne desired—that of "*his* heart"—her narrative still proves disarmingly significant for its listener:

> Elinor, who had now been for some time reflecting on the propriety or impropriety of speedily hazarding her

[76] *Ibid.*, I:339.
[77] *Ibid.*, I:345.
[78] *Ibid.*, I:347.

narration, without feeling at all nearer decision than at first, heard this; and perceiving that as reflection did nothing, resolution must do all, soon found herself leading to the fact.

She managed the recital, as she hoped, with address; prepared her anxious listener with caution; related simply and honestly the chief points on which Willoughby grounded his apology; did justice to his repentance, and softened only his protestations of present regard. Marianne said not a word.—She trembled, her eyes were fixed on the ground, and her lips became whiter than even sickness had left them. A thousand inquiries sprung up from her heart, but she dared not urge one. She caught every syllable with panting eagerness; her hand, unknowingly to herself, closely pressed her sister's, and tears covered her cheeks.[79]

"Softened" in the aspect which Marianne must feel most, Elinor's relation nonetheless affects her sister with an active, physical strength. When bid by Marianne to tell her story to their mother, Elinor is next left "with a mind anxiously pre-arranging its result."[80] Whatever additional "softening," or falsification, that "pre-arranging" will entail, most remarkable in its transformation is the narrative's own falsification of itself. For the narrative turns, apparently with Elinor, upon the very feelings of sympathy she has experienced and it has narrated. Willoughby's explanation, although represented, and unquestioned by Elinor, as undeceiving, is abruptly replaced with what the narrative now calls, speaking for Elinor, "the simple truth": Willoughby's speech retold specifically on the basis of such "merits" as the meeting with him had revealed to be irrelevant. Rather than the immediate, mentally disabling sense of their encounter, Elinor will now "lay open such facts as were really due to his character"—"facts," that is, constituting a hypothetical fiction which Willoughby's own narrative, in "sense" as well as "sensibility," directly contradicts. The narrative of the novel seems to become indistinguishable

[79] *Ibid.*, I:347–48.
[80] *Ibid.*, I:348.

from that of the mind it represents in justifying Elinor's act of discursive deception as a means of obviating its own reason: "the feelings" which Willoughby's own speech had "called forth in herself." In the narratively uncanny moment which follows, it is difficult to discern who is deceiving whom. For with immediately suspect—because for the first time evidently self-serving—self-effacement, the narrator states that Elinor, whose honest and simple "recital" had just been narrated to move her sister to tears, wishes now to tell "the simple truth" *instead* of "Willoughby's story," because she would in any case have been incapable of "rous[ing] such feelings in another":

> Had Mrs. Dashwood, like her daughter, heard Willoughby's story from himself—had she witnessed his distress, and been under the influence of his countenance and his manner, it is probable that her compassion would have been greater. But it was neither in Elinor's power, nor in her wish, to rouse such feelings in another, by her retailed explanation, as had at first been called forth in herself. Reflection had given calmness to her judgment, and sobered her own opinion of Willoughby's deserts; —she wished, therefore, to declare only the simple truth, and lay open such facts as were really due to his character, without any embellishment of tenderness to lead the fancy astray.[81]

[81] *Ibid.*, I:349. The significance of Elinor's encounter with Willoughby until this point in the narration has been the focus of a recent discussion by David Miller (*Narrative and Its Discontents*, pp. 66–76). Perhaps because Miller's reading of the incident stops here, the viewpoint developed in the present analysis seems directly opposed to his own with regard to the consequences of Elinor's version of the "simple truth," namely, that "what is lost in translation . . . is not something a reader has much cared about" (p. 76). Whatever a particular reader's concern for Willoughby might be, his significance for the novel lies in the fact that, by its own design, Willoughby represents the point at which sense and sensibility must collide. Furthermore, in dismissing Willoughby, Miller also necessarily fails to remember Marianne, and all that *is* "lost" in Elinor's "translation" of Willoughby to her. This omission of Marianne with respect to a narration that concerns her directly seems unconsciously to repeat her own highly conspicuous—and thus assumedly conscious—occlusion from the narrative. In overlooking the effect of Elinor's

When Marianne, who is present for this "retailed explanation," offers her own statement of resignation to her situation—" 'I wish for no change' "[82]—Elinor appears driven to
represent her certain misery *had* she married Willoughby. As
the tense of that auxiliary verb should indicate, the most noteworthy aspect of this entirely imagined narration is that it is
told, as it must be, in the conditional and past, or "contrary-
to-fact," subjunctive. While no grammatical mode of narration could be less reminiscent of Austen's own, this relation of
pure conjecture on Elinor's part, lasting several paragraphs
and succeeding the lengthy interview with Willoughby it dis-
figures, cannot be simply regarded either as a lapse in, or strategic "pre-arrangement" of, the larger narrative. If, on the
most superficial level of the story of the narrative, Austen,
much like Willoughby in copying his wife's letter, is preparing
Marianne, through whatever means of "language" necessary,
to meet the novel's own "end," she is also calling specific attention to that act. For Elinor's recitation of subjunctive hypotheses posing as reality creates a distinct cognitive effect
bordering more closely on self-inflating paranoia than the
measured sense of reality conveyed by Austen's own characteristic use of the indicative. Those hypotheses begin:

> "I dare say, you perceive, as well as myself, reason enough
> to be convinced that your marriage *must have* involved
> you in many certain troubles and disappointments, in
> which you *would have* been poorly supported by an affec-
> tion, on his side, much less certain. *Had* you married, you
> *must have* been always poor. . . . His demands and your
> inexperience together on a small, very small income, *must*

---

narration upon the character represented specifically to have "cared" most
about "what" it deletes and deforms, Miller finally ignores the resemblance
between Elinor's "simple truth" and the emphatically contrived quality of the
novel's remaining narrative resolution. With the all-important difference that
one pretends to a direct, though unavoidably hypothetical, knowledge of Marianne's life *had* she really married Willoughby, while the other makes evident
that it can only speak hypothetically about the reality of Marianne's given
marriage to Colonel Brandon, Elinor's projected conclusion and the novel's
own concluding narrative are strikingly similar falsifications.

[82] *Ibid.*, p. 307.

have brought on distresses which *would* not be the *less* grievous to you, from having been entirely unknown and unthought of before. *Your* sense of honour and honesty *would have* led you . . . to attempt all the economy that *would* appear to you possible; and perhaps, as long as your frugality retrenched only on your own comfort, you *might have* been suffered to practice it, but beyond that . . . *had* you endeavoured, however reasonably, to abridge *his* enjoyments, is it not to be feared, that instead of prevailing on feelings so selfish to consent to it, you *would have* lessened your own influence on his heart, and made him regret the connection which had involved him in such difficulties?"

Marianne's lips quivered, and she repeated the word "Selfish?" in a tone that implied—"do you really think him selfish?"

"The whole of his behaviour," replied Elinor, "from the beginning to the end of the affair, has been grounded on selfishness."[83]

Elinor narrates a grisly sequel which will never be to a story, explained "from the beginning to end," which never was. The knowledge of Willoughby's "character" she pretends to with great force of persuasion utterly misrepresents the direct experience of him which gave rise to this speech itself. Furthermore, the decidedly "*negative* capability" of Elinor's imagination is belied later by the narrator's own single conditional hypothesis, already mentioned above, that Willoughby, had he married Marianne, "might at once have been happy and rich" (see footnote 68). As in the exposition of a didactic allegory or recapitulation of a morality play, the plot of all preceding narration—"the whole of [Willoughby's] behaviour"—is exposed to be "grounded on" a single vice, "selfishness," whose worldly damages Elinor's narration seems merely faithfully to relay. Finally, as in any narrative of a fall from grace, Elinor goes on to name the "first" cause of Willoughby's present unhappy state: " '*One* observation may, I think, be fairly drawn from the whole of the story—that all Willoughby's difficulties

---

[83] *Ibid.*, I:350–51; all emphasis of verbal tenses my own.

have arisen from the first offence against virtue, in his behaviour to Eliza Williams. That crime has been the origin of every lesser one, and of all his present discontents.' "[84] In thus granting her own story the structural coherence of a narrative whole, Elinor neglects to mention that Willoughby himself not only admitted and regretted his crime, but also indicated that the virtue of its victim might have been less than beyond reproof.[85]

Edward, whose original offense would be more difficult to identify in that he has spoken little and done even less—neither broken his word nor acted upon it—is misapprehended by Elinor, soon after this scene, to be married. The narrator's description of her reaction to that knowledge speaks directly to the probable effect of her own cognitive fiction upon her sister: "Elinor now found the difference between the expectation of an unpleasant event, however certain the mind may be told to consider it, and certainty itself."[86] The false "certainty" Elinor provides Marianne of Willoughby's irreparable character is never shown in the narrative to be disproven; Willoughby does not appear again, and by his mere presence regain his good name. Yet Elinor's error with regard to Edward is dispelled immediately by his own surprise arrival, and the discovery that Lucy Steele is not "Mrs. *Edward*" but "Mrs. *Robert* Ferrars."[87] Elinor's momentary "certainty" of her loss owes to a simple error of mistaken identity based on a single sensory element, a shared name; it is quickly replaced, when Edward next proposes, by the certain knowledge of her gain. Edward himself, in further contrast to Willoughby's sincere anxiety in approaching Elinor, is reported to act *as if* fearing disapproval when he arrives: "he did not, upon the whole, expect a very cruel reception. It was his business, however, to say that he *did*,

[84] *Ibid.*, I:352.
[85] See *ibid.*, I:322: " 'Remember,' cried Willoughby, 'from whom you received the account. Could it be an impartial one? . . . I do not mean to justify myself, but at the same time cannot leave you to suppose . . . that because she was injured she was irreproachable, and because *I* was a libertine, *she* must be a saint.' "
[86] *Ibid.*, I:357.
[87] *Ibid.*, I:359–60.

and he said it very prettily."[88] The speech in which he explains his predicament is in fact a direct reversal of Willoughby's own: "He could only plead an ignorance of his own heart, and a mistaken confidence in the force of his engagement. 'I was simple enough to think, that because my *faith* was plighted to another, there could be no danger in my being with you; and that the consciousness of my engagement was to keep my heart as sage and sacred as my honour.' "[89] Whereas Willoughby had recognized "the more than absurdity of scrupling to engage . . . faith where . . . honour was already bound" (see footnote 65), Edward, having kept the faith he had plighted, without knowledge of its object, in word alone, believed his honor safe in "the consciousness of [his] engagement" and thus felt no scruples in otherwise engaging his heart.

Willoughby, we are told, in the light tone of mockery the novel abruptly assumes in closing, does not "die of a broken heart" but "always retained that decided regard which interested him in everything that befell [Marianne]."[90] Yet, beginning with her sister's "retailed" narration, there is nothing we know less about than what does "befall" Marianne. Her marriage to Colonel Brandon is described as the "wish" and "reward" prescribed him by all his friends: "They each felt his sorrows, and their own obligations, and Marianne, by general consent, was to be the reward of all."[91] Of Marianne's own "sensibility" we read no narration; of the remaining plot of the novel, described in mildly derisive but no less certain terms as a plot "against" her, we are told the following:

> With such a confederacy against her—with a knowledge so intimate of his goodness—with a conviction of his fond attachment to herself, which at last, though long after it was observable to everybody else—burst on her—what could she do?
>
> Marianne Dashwood was born to an extraordinary fate. She was born to discover the falsehood of her own

[88] *Ibid.*, I:366.
[89] *Ibid.*, I:368.
[90] *Ibid.*, I:379.
[91] *Ibid.*, I:378.

opinions and to counteract, by her conduct, her most fa-
vourite maxims. She was born to overcome an affection
formed so late in life as at seventeen, and with no sentiment superior to strong esteem and lively friendship, vol-
untarily to give her hand to another![92]

Marianne's "fate," as it is knowingly related, is singularly ordinary; what is "extraordinary" is the fact of its being related
in this too obviously "ironic," disturbingly flippant, manner at
all. Her own occluded feelings are ultimately referred to only
subsequent to Colonel Brandon's and strictly from the viewpoint of his friends. In the last words dedicated to Marianne,
the narrator seems to join ranks with the latter, thereby casting
doubt upon the credibility of those words themselves:

> Colonel Brandon was now as happy, as all those who
> best loved him, believed he deserved to be;—in Marianne
> he was consoled for every past affliction;—her regard and
> her society restored his mind to animation, and his spirits
> to cheerfulness; and that Marianne found her own hap-
> piness in forming his, was equally the persuasion and de-
> light of each observing friend. Marianne could never love
> by halves; and her whole heart became, in time, as much
> devoted to her husband, as it had once been to Wil-
> loughby.[93]

That time would produce the effect of a reasoned passion in
Marianne, substituting an erosion of feeling by force of pro-
longed estrangement for the true synthesis of sense and sensibility which the narrative itself does not achieve, was narrated
earlier as Elinor's own hope with regard to her sister.[94] The
positing of change not through narrated action but projected
temporal decay is the narrator's conclusion to a novel whose
own "pre-arranged result" is itself too evident, too "sincerely"
dishonest, to warrant, of any but the least sensible of readings,
self-righteous dismay. Clearly legible beneath the purposefully
thin veneer of happy resolution provided by the narrator is the

[92] *Ibid.*
[93] *Ibid.*, I:379.
[94] *Ibid.*, I:352.

author's own dismay at the recognition that no other *resolution* could have been possible. Had Marianne ever known the true "sense" of Willoughby's visit, her marriage to Colonel Brandon, rather than providing a hypothetical happiness "in time," would undoubtedly have undergone an infinite delay. That Austen's narrative makes the fictional nature of its ending apparent in the purposefully empty formality of its terms[95] is what makes its story represent our own comprehension of "real life." Happy endings that betray in words the nature of the characters to which they relate, as that nature can only become apparent, i.e., through the representation of those characters' actions,[96] may be the "real" and "observable" condition of the nonidentity between "sense and sensibility." To read in the narration of that condition a willed and malicious, or merely failed, "irony" on the part of the author is to lose sight of the irony upon which any "faithful" representation of reality depends—"faithful" precisely in the "sense" of words "plighted" either to stand commensurate with "sensibility" *or* to give the lie to the latter and the attempt at such commensuration. It all depends on where one's "honour" is "engaged."

Persuasion

The end of *Sense and Sensibility* has been described as Austen's "return to comedy,"[97] probably more with a view to *Pride and Prejudice*, which follows it directly, than a clear recollection either of the preceding action of the novel or its own indication, in Elinor's fictionalized "simple truth," that narrative never offers itself as a harmless endeavor. After *Pride and Prejudice*, it was suggested earlier, Austen turns entirely from the "sparkling" resolution of comedy to a narrative which maintains its own discursive integrity by pointedly removing "character" from action, thus preserving the "sense" of its meaning from the pleasure of "sensibility." After the rewriting of com-

[95] Cf. Litz, *Jane Austen*, p. 82, on Austen's "reversion to literary stereotypes in the final chapter."

[96] Cf. the observation in the *Farbenlehre* of the visible appearance of character in action (chap. 2, footnote 17, above).

[97] Mudrick, *Jane Austen*, p. 239.

edy in *Emma*, consisting, for the most part, in a focused en-
largement of the dangers of self-credited certainty represented
earlier in Elizabeth Bennett, Austen writes what is to become
her final novel. *Persuasion* (1818), as unique to Austen's narratives as *Mansfield Park*, with which it shares some primary
structural characteristics, presents a resolution of the original
dilemma of *Sense and Sensibility*[98] in another, perhaps more
radically, divergent form.[99] "Persuasion," which after "pleasure," may be the second most frequent noun representing an
action upon the senses in *Mansfield Park*, was used in the unsettling close of *Sense and Sensibility* to designate the conviction of Marianne's "observing friends" that what they observe
is what they desire (see footnote 93). What *Persuasion* demonstrates, stated in brief, is Austen's own recognition "in
time" that the story, "Sense and Sensibility," still remained to
be written. Elinor's hypothetical narrative, whose projected effect is ascribed with extraordinary banality to Marianne's "extraordinary fate," results from the sensible persuasion exercised by Willoughby's presence. The narrative of *Persuasion*
reverses the order and outcome of the earlier novel by including "in [the] time" *previous* to the narrative a meaningful absence effected as consequence of a dangerous "persuasion" to
"sense." Anne Elliot, who like Fanny Price personifies the
point of view of the narrator, is introduced as having been persuaded seven years earlier by her good friend, Lady Russell, to
reject the offer of marriage made to her by the man she loved.
When the novel opens she is twenty-seven, the exact age at
which Marianne Dashwood deemed " 'a woman . . . can never
hope to feel or inspire affection again.' "[100] While Anne's own
sensibility had clearly been affected by Frederick Wentworth,
her consideration of "prudence," rather than of feeling, is con-

[98] Cf. Robert Garis, "Learning Experience and Change," in *Critical Essays
on Jane Austen*, ed. B. C. Southam (London: Routledge & Kegan Paul, 1968),
pp. 60–82, for the further contention that *Persuasion* can only be "a conscious
rethinking of *Sense and Sensibility*" (p. 80).
[99] *Persuasion* has been variously viewed as the promise of a new direction in
Austen's fiction. Cf. Mudrick, *Jane Austen*, p. 240: "Certainly, it marks the
most abrupt turn in Jane Austen's work."
[100] Austen, I:8.

cluded from the beginning to have been her major delusion. Anne is related to have achieved in the past what Marianne cannot be said, without mock sincerity, to achieve in the future. Her situation, in the "time" intervening, is sharply distinguished, however, from that of Marianne, for Austen has specifically provided no one (the pun is unavoidable) to marry Anne:

> Lady Russell, whom she had always loved and relied on, could not, with such steadiness of opinion, and such tenderness of manner, be continually advising her in vain. She was persuaded to believe the engagement a wrong thing. . . . But it was not a merely selfish caution, under which she acted, in putting an end to it. Had she not imagined herself consulting his good, even more than her own, she could hardly have given him up.—The belief of being prudent, and self-denying principally for *his* advantage, was her chief consolation, under the misery of a parting— a final parting. . . . He left the country in consequence.
>
> A few months had seen the beginning and the end of their acquaintance; but, not with a few months ended Anne's share of suffering from it. Her attachment and regrets had, for a long time, clouded every enjoyment of youth; and an early loss of bloom and spirits had been their lasting effect.
>
> More than seven years were gone since this little history of sorrowful interest had reached its close; and time had softened down much, perhaps nearly all of peculiar attachment to him,—but she had been too dependent on time alone; no aid had been given in change of place. . . . No one had even come within the Kellynich circle, who could bear a comparison with Frederick Wentworth. . . . No second attachment, the only thoroughly natural, happy, and sufficient cure, at her time of life, had been possible . . . in the small limits of the society around them.[101]

In this retrospective narrative passage, almost every curative aspect of temporality foreseen at the end of *Sense and Sensi-*

---

[101] *Persuasion*, V:27–28.

bility is turned around. Anne is said to have acted—as we will learn, misguidedly—in the belief of her own self-denying motives; to have trusted mistakenly to "time alone" to dispel her regrets; to have suffered in appearance as well as in spirits, and found no "second attachment" which could "bear a comparison" with the first. At this point in the opening of the novel "the small limits" of her society are offered as the possible cause for Anne's sustained disinterest in other suitors: Austen appears to suggest the efficacy of an alternative prescription for plot development—second only to change over "time"—change in "place." The development of the novel will in fact implement the variable of "place" to the very purpose suggested here: the Elliots' move to Bath, precipitated by Sir Elliot's mismanagement of his estate, will place Anne in the social sphere of her fashionable cousin, William Elliot. Yet the same move also brings about the accident of her reencounter with Wentworth. Austen seems to include the reasonable means of change within *Persuasion* for no other reason than to prove that they will not—indeed, should not—work. Anne, like Austen, takes no pleasure in the affected society of Bath, and Mr. Elliot is revealed, in an unequivocally condemning narrative by Mrs. Smith, to be a man " 'without heart . . . totally beyond the reach of any sentiment of justice or compassion.' "[102] Indeed, the very introduction of Mr. Elliot, while providing a standard plot mechanism in arousing Wentworth's jealousy, seems most fundamentally to underscore the ongoing danger of Anne's original mistake. For Mrs. Smith only relates her story *after* Anne has made clear that she had not " 'the smallest intention of accepting' " Elliot; and Anne's reaction to that story includes her sudden understanding that in its absence Lady Russell's power of persuasion might again have held sway: "Anne could just acknowledge within herself such a possibility of having been induced to marry him, as made her shudder at the idea of the misery which must have followed. It was just possible that she might have been persuaded by Lady Russell! And under such a supposition, which

---

[102] *Ibid.*, V:199.

would have been more miserable, when time had disclosed all, too late?"[103]

But *Persuasion* is the novel in which Austen "plights" her "faith" to sensibility, giving Anne the power to discriminate against every illusion but that of sense. It is the novel in which Austen asserts, on the one hand, that it is never "too late" for happiness, while, on the other, that it is always too late for happiness the senses do not intend. The union between Anne Elliot and Frederick Wentworth is undoubtedly the most moving in Austen's fiction because it is essentially a reunion of past affections, rather than the discovery of past affection as mistake. That reunion requires only the chance proximity of the lovers to be enacted, since the constancy of their senses had undergone *no* significant dissuasion "in time."[104]

The narrator of *Persuasion* says of Anne Elliot what, in view of *Persuasion*, has been said of Austen's narratives: "She had been forced into prudence in her youth, she learned romance as she grew older—the natural sequel of an unnatural beginning."[105] This would imply that in giving up narrative "irony"—more profoundly understood by Scott, as well as Austen's reading public, to be the representation of "real life"—the author turned ultimately to the genre of narrative from which Scott observed she had departed. The universal praise that *Persuasion* has enjoyed—and indeed one would need be fully senseless *not* to enjoy this novel—suggests that Austen, at her untimely death, had finally left "irony" behind for the pleasures of "romance." But if "irony" is to be named in opposition to "romance," certainly *Sense and Sensibility* provides the *natural* "beginning," if also a less than natural "sequel," to romance in the truncated story of Marianne. If *Persuasion*, on the other hand, presents a romantic ending, it is one severed from its beginning. Austen's narratives do not narrate, as her own most "successfully" persuasive characters

[103] *Ibid.*, V:211.

[104] *Sense and Sensibility*, p. 379.

[105] *Persuasion*, V:30. Cf. Woolf, *The Common Reader*, p. 147: "We feel it to be true of herself when she says of Anne, 'She had been forced into prudence in her youth . . . ,' " echoed by Mudrick (*Jane Austen*, p. 225) and Mansell (*Novels of Jane Austen*, p. 220).

explicitly do, hypotheses figuring the "whole" of reality in the fictional form of a reasoned narration. Whether in the immediate admission of an appeal to the senses formerly censured by reason, or the contingency of a meeting between lovers foolish enough to have separated and remained apart, some sensible element of living, Austen implies, is necessarily at odds with the sense of its narration. If her last and first novels, in attempting to represent that element in particular, lack, perforce, the representation of a matching beginning or end, it is due neither to the visible presence of "irony," nor its recognizable absence, "romance." No more, that is, than both terms are first recognized and criticized as forms of the necessarily narrative persuasion of our understanding of "real life."

CHAPTER 5

LUCIEN AND JULIEN: POETRY AND THOUGHT IN THE FORM OF THE NOVEL

The word was given to man to hide his thought.
—STENDHAL, *Le Rouge et le noir*

Between Austen and Balzac lies little temporal but enormous representational difference; and if both Goethe and Austen, while writing in the nineteenth century, seem peculiarly eighteenth-century novelists, few novelists can be said to "represent" the nineteenth century, both as "real life" and in its forms of fiction, as thoroughly as Balzac. It is not difficult to identify, in theme and in diction, the presence of epistemological concerns in the narratives of Goethe and Austen: whether in the form of discursive figuration or of external, observable events, both authors relate narrative representation to experiences of cognition. But of all the experiences composing and crowding the world of Balzacian representation, none probably figures less prominently than that of cognition. Balzac is the author of narrative *appearances* in themselves: his most vital fictions live, so to speak, at the level of their own surfaces, just as Vautrin, the motivating character beneath the surface of Balzac's central novels, thrives on the visibility of the other lives he plots.[1] Vision, in the Vautrin cycle in

[1] For a discussion of the dual register of Vautrin's activities and of the levels

particular,[2] desires only what it sees rather than any unapparent significance. By the same token, appearances appear strangely "pure" in these novels not because they hide nothing—we know full well when the machinations of Vautrin, of his adversary, Corentin, or the sacrifices of David Séchard and Esther lie behind them—but because the novels never seek to disillusion us as to their own source of meaning. What one sees may not ultimately be what one gets in Balzac, but it is almost always what is wanted,[3] and very few second thoughts, indeed very little critical or reflective thinking at all, seem to come between the passion and the event. Instead, the extraordinary dynamism both of the narrative style and actions narrated in these novels[4] reflects desires put into practice without any speculative problems to speak of, and, most remarkably, with occasionally stunning success.

Language, however, is where speculation takes on its own

---

of surface and depth represented in Balzacian narrative in general, see Peter Brooks, "Balzac: Representation and Signification," in *The Melodramatic Imagination: Balzac, Henry James, Melodrama, and the Mode of Excess* (New Haven: Yale University Press, 1976), pp. 110–52.

[2] *Le Père Goriot* (1834–35), *Illusions perdues* (1837–43), and *Splendeurs et misères de courtisanes* (1844–47). A different understanding of vision, however, characterizes some of Balzac's most outstanding short narratives of the same period, such as *Le Chef-d'oeuvre inconnu* (1831), *Louis Lambert* (1832), *La Recherche de l'absolu* (1834), *Séraphita* (1835), *Facino Cane* (1836), and *Les Secrets de la princesse de Cadignan* (1839). Indeed, it can be argued that what makes these narratives "short," as compared to the lengthy individual novels and extended vision of the Vautrin cycle as a whole, is the centralization of their own narrative action upon a problem of cognition.

[3] On the operative power of desire in the formation of subjective representation in Balzac, see Frederic Jameson, "Realism and Desire: Balzac and the Problem of the Subject," in *The Political Unconscious* (Ithaca: Cornell University Press, 1981).

[4] Erich Auerbach, in an early formulation of the dimension of "realist" narration later identified by Roman Jakobson with metonymy (Jakobson, "Two Aspects of Language and Two Types of Aphasic Disturbances," *Fundamental of Language* [The Hague: Mouton & Co., 1956]), refers to the unrestingly active nature of Balzac's narrative descriptions as "demonic." See Auerbach's comparative analysis of the divergent forms of French "realism" (Balzac's "demonic" emphasis upon the physically contiguous versus Stendhal's representational symbolism of the "spirit," in "The Hôtel de la Mole," *Mimesis* (Princeton: Princeton University Press, 1953 [Berne, 1946]).

appearance, and while many words, both spoken and written, are exchanged between Balzac's characters, they serve for the most part either to express a personal desire or to produce a desired effect upon another agent of action. Thus it seems unlikely that the major character in Balzac's central novel, and the most extensively narrated participant in all *La Comédie humaine*, should be designated as someone who uses words explicitly for their own sake: "un poète." Lucien de Rubempré, né Chardon, the locus of perpetual motion within *Illusions perdues*, makes his way to and within Paris on the insubstantial grounds of being "a poet." The appraisal of a publisher, who at one point refuses to print his poems, may in fact be seen to represent the unsteady footing of Lucien within *Illusions perdues* as a whole: " 'Vous êtes aussi grand poète que vous êtes joli garçon, mon petit. . . . Vos Marguerites sont un beau livre, mais ce n'est pas une affaire, et je ne peux m'occuper que de vastes entreprises . . .' "[5] ["You are as great a poet as you are a handsome boy, my little one. . . . Your Marguerites are a beautiful book, but not a business matter and I can only get involved in vast enterprises . . ."]. While the status of his poetry will require further scrutiny, the description of Lucien himself as a "joli garçon" is confirmed repeatedly by narrator and characters alike. The fact of Lucien's beauty is referred to frequently in the novel as the primary condition upon which his continuing attempts at social advancement depend. The influence of Lucien's beautiful appearance may be viewed as a primarily erotic rather than aesthetic phenomenon, yet it is all the more remarkable in exhibiting no specific sexual affiliations in its effect. It is attributed with finding its first passionate admirer, before Lucien's mistress, Louise de Bargeton,

[5] Honoré de Balzac, *Illusions perdues* (Paris: Garnier, 1961), p. 399 (all translations my own). While the Garnier and Pléiade editions both rely on the 1843 Furne edition of all three parts of the novel corrected by Balzac, only the Garnier reproduces the division of the novel according to the chapter headings included in the first editions of the First and Second Parts (the former published by Werdet [1837] under the title "Illusions perdues" before being named "Les Deux poètes" in the Furne edition), and in the original serialized publication of the Third Part in *L'Etat* and *Le Parisien-Etat* (1843) under the title: "David Séchard ou les Souffrances d'un inventeur" (David Séchard or the Sufferings of an Inventor).

in his sister Eve's own suitor, David Séchard. In the opening of Part One of the novel, "Les Deux poètes," the narrator reveals the longstanding relation between the two men to stem from David's devotion to, and from Lucien's self-identification with, the "commanding" power of "physical beauty": "Dans cette amitié déjà vieille, l'un des deux aimait avec idolâtrie, et c'était David. Aussi Lucien commandait-il en femme qui se sait aimée. David obéissait avec plaisir. La beauté physique de son ami comportait une supériorité qu'il acceptait en se trouvant lourd et commun"[6] [In this already old friendship, one of the two loved with idolatry and it was David. Lucien also commanded like a woman who knows herself loved. David obeyed with pleasure. The physical beauty of his friend carried with it a superiority which he accepted in finding himself heavy and common].

The disproportion of affection which binds this friendship is understood as a direct function of Lucien's visible beauty. The various physical attributes of his appearance, described in detail previous to this passage, appear external, in an unexpectedly literal fashion, to the "character" called Lucien. "La beauté physique"—a pointedly superficial rather than spiritual aspect of the "poet"—is granted an autonomous "superiority" *over* character here. Furthermore, the power of Lucien's beauty, while decisive at each turn of the narrative, is narrated to function synchronically and unpredictably, that is, to disrupt the diachronic and causal nature of narrative itself. As the conspiring Petit-Claud discovers late in the novel, when Lucien's appearance, freshly refurbished, arises phoenixlike to conquer again,[7] a pleasing appearance keeps its own appointments, often obliterating the logical consequences of past events in the process. Similarly, Lucien's own character, rather than developing in depth through his narrated experience, acts

---

[6] *Ibid.*, p. 31.

[7] See "Revanche de Lucien a l'hôtel de Bargeton," in which the meeting between Louise de Bargeton, now Madame de Châtelet, and Lucien arranged by Petit-Claud produces the effect directly opposed to that Petit-Claud intended. Lucien not only succeeds in gaining the assistance of the woman he had previously spurned in Paris but wins the admiration of Petit-Claud's own pretended fiancée (*ibid.*, pp. 685–91).

according to the immediate persuasions of his appearance.[8] The title of the novel suggests that it is a story of education and enlightenment—that the central narrative of *La Comédie humaine* is also a major contribution to the generic conception of the novel as Bildungsroman—but it is never clear in the course of its events when and whether Lucien "loses" *his* illusions. For, beginning with the adoration of David Séchard and ending with that of Vautrin, Lucien's involvement in the narrative derives from illusions experienced by others: those which the given fact of his beauty effects. The poses Lucien adopts are

---

[8] Even Lucien's naive insistence upon receiving an *ordonnance* is directly linked in his own mind to the power of his appearance. The "restoration" he plans of the name "de Rubempré" is desired as a kind of cosmetic aid to "his beauty," itself already understood to serve as a supplement to "chance": "[Lucien] s'en tint à son unique désir: avoir son ordonnance, en comprenant que cette restauration lui vaudrait un beau mariage. Sa fortune ne dépendrait plus alors que d'un hasard auquel aidrait sa beauté." [(Lucien) held to his unique desire: to have his *ordonnance*, understanding that this restoration would be worth a "good" marriage. His fortune would then only depend upon chance aided by his beauty] (*ibid.*, p. 502).
Lucien's beliefs are in fact well founded on the basis of the novel itself, for his original introduction into the narrative had already been founded on "chance," and it is only due to David's "generous" response to his beauty that he retains the "fortune" of remaining a narratable character at all. For, rather than becoming more enlightened as the novel progresses, Lucien, we are told at the very beginning of the novel, had already contemplated the "extreme" act of suicide he will consider at the end: "L'ami de David Séchard était un jeune homme, alors âgé d'environ vingt et un ans, nommé Lucien Chardon, et fils d'un ancien chirurgien-major des armées républicaines mis hors de service par une blessure. La nature avait fait un chimiste ce monsieur Chardon le père, et *le hasard* l'avait établi pharmacien à Angoulême. . . . Quand *le hasard* fit rencontrer les deux camarades de collège, Lucien, fatigué de boire à la grossière coupe de la misère, était sur le point de prendre un de ces partis extrêmes auxquels on se décide à vingt ans. Quarante francs par mois que David donna généreusement à Lucien . . . sauva Lucien de son désespoir" [David Séchard's friend was a young man, then about twenty-one years old, named Lucien Chardon, son of an old surgeon-major of the republican armies who had been put out of service by injury. Nature had made this Mr. Chardon senior a chemist, and *chance* had established him pharmacist at Angoulême. . . . When *chance* made the two school friends meet, Lucien, tired of drinking misery by the gallon, was on the point of committing one of those extreme acts one decides upon at twenty. Forty francs a month given generously to Lucien by David . . . saved Lucien from his despair"] (*ibid.*, pp. 23–25 [my emphasis]).

those which serve his face and figure best; yet rather than posing any speculative problems in return, his pleasing appearances imply no sense of duplicity, precisely because appearance and not character acts as their source. Furthermore, the chronological time in which Lucien's actions are related to take place bears no resemblance either to temporal "reality" or to its allotment of actual narrative duration: a few days of Lucien's activities in Paris, requiring a few hundred pages of narration, might also resume more than a few lifelong careers. The temporal incongruity already prevalent in this "realist" fiction thus renders redundant any phenomenological claim to its understanding, i.e., that what might be called Lucien's consciousness cannot keep time with the pace of circumstance. For a self viewed in any traditional manner to be distinct from its presentation[9] seems instead superfluous to this densely eventful narrative. Balzac represents the actions, and oversteps the mind, of Lucien by basing them upon a single, and strictly speaking, unidentifiable mental attribute: the "mobility of [his] character."[10]

While moments of speculative reflection are not only absent from Lucien's characterization but made to appear appropriately so, the brilliance of his appearance is reflected in the narration down to the last "diamond button" he wears.[11] The

[9] The contemporary refutation of that view most closely resembling this nineteenth-century elision of intrinsic character in Lucien can be found in Erving Goffman's "sociology" of the "self," or analysis of the "self" as the stage for a series of self-presentational actions. See Goffman's seminal *Behavior in Public Places* (New York: The Free Press, 1963); *Strategic Interaction* (Philadelphia: University of Pennsylvania Press, 1969); and *The Presentation of Self in Everyday Life* (Woodstock, N.Y.: Overlook Press, 1973). Goffman's consideration of language itself, in *Forms of Talk* (Philadelphia: University of Pennsylvania Press, 1981), as another set of self-presenting gestures, ultimately distinguishes, however, his own highly literary analyses of language, in its immediate manifestation as speech, from the analysis of indirect and ambiguous language formalized in literature.

[10] See Balzac, *Illusions perdues*, pp. 158, 249 ("son esprit méridional"), and 279 ("cet esprit mobile").

[11] *Ibid.*, p. 450: "Lucien eut alors des cannes merveilleuses, une charmante lorgnette, des boutons de diamants, des anneaux pour ses cravates du matin, des bagues à la chevalière" [Lucien had at that time marvelous canes, a charming eyeglass, diamond buttons, rings for his morning ties, signet rings].

central personal subject of *Illusions perdues* is narrated repeatedly to dress successfully for whatever part he must play
in a drama he adeptly identifies but neither causes nor controls. For as Balzac added to the description of his relationship
with David Séchard, Lucien, too, must conform to the effects
of his beauty: "Lucien also commanded like a woman who
knows herself loved." The subordination of Lucien as character to his own appearance is, of course, made most visible at
the end of the novel when, deferred from suicide by a concern
wholly superficial in itself—the "spectacle" of his drowned
body resurfacing "deformed": the projection, the narrator explains, of an "amour propre posthume"[12] (posthumous self-
love)—Lucien is supplied a new appearance in *La Comédie humaine* by means of an embodiment of even greater externality.
Vautrin, otherwise known as "Trompe-la-Mort," has already
performed the role of his own death in order to survive, thus
condemned to live at the loss of all possible personal appearance, when he assumes command of the beauty of Lucien. The
double theme of Vautrin's "monomania" and multiple "rein-
carnations" serves most obviously to provide a relational link
between many of the individual narratives of *La Comédie humaine*. But the radical intentionality, and invisibility, of purpose characterized by Vautrin are required at the close of *Illusions perdues* because of the very "mobility of character"
placed at its center. The plot for his future that Vautrin describes to Lucien, thereby permitting the novel to end, can be
viewed critically as a dramatic caricature of theories of the
novel, in which the fundamental concepts of discursive purpose and sensual appearance are cast into separate character
parts.[13] The story of Lucien de Rubempré, however, includes

[12] *Ibid.*, pp. 701–702. Lucien considers drowning as one of many "means"
of committing suicide, for, the narrator explains, "le poète voulut finir poé-
tiquement." [The poet wanted to finish poetically.] "L'affreux spectacle de son
corps revenu sur l'eau, déformé" [the hideous spectacle of his body surfacing
upon the water deformed], proves, however, not to conform to this poet's notion of the "poetic." Thus the "poetic," the narrator implies at this closing moment, may well be identifiable in the novel with physical beauty itself.
[13] The dialogue between Vautrin and Lucien states the separation of those
functions best: "Mais avez-vous rapporté tous vos vouloirs, toutes vos actions
à une idée? . . .—Hélas! non, dit Lucien.—Vous avez été ce que les Anglais ap-

this caricature, like Lucien's foresight of his own corpse, within its narration. For Lucien is both the central character of the novel and the character least likely to invest his appearance constructively, i.e., in a consequential, temporally developed, narrative form. The illusion of "character" which appears manifest to the eye must derive its significance from the same source of vision: it cannot see, or know, itself. Thus Vautrin observes, in *both* senses of the verb, the brilliant ignorance of the "joli garçon" whose initial narration he concludes: "Le prêtre regarda Lucien en souriant et lui dit avec une grâce infinie et un sourire presque ironique:—'Le diamant ignore sa valeur' "[14] [The priest, smiling, observed Lucien and told him with an infinite grace and an almost ironic smile: "The diamond does not know its value"].

In the comment of the publisher cited earlier, however, the issue of Lucien's beauty is further complicated by serving as criterion for another, and necessarily nonexternal estimation. While Lucien is personally addressed in the diminutive, his appearance is compared to his greatness as a poet: " 'Vous êtes *aussi grand poète que* vous êtes joli garçon, *mon petit.*' " Whether or not one can tell a book by its cover, the judgment which esteems Lucien's poems "un beau livre" clearly rests on their equation with a pretty face. Dauriat's appreciation of the "Marguerites" is transparently superficial; the problem it presents with regard to our own understanding of Lucien as "poet" is that the poems themselves cannot be seen through it. Analogous to the eclipse of Lucien's character by his appearance, here the surface of an aesthetic stance, rather than deepened or probed, is itself more fully substantiated as a matter of surfaces. For the critical question of the "poetic" status of Lu-

---

pellent *inconsistent*, reprit le chanoine en souriant.—Qu'importe ce que j'ai été, si je ne puis plus rien être! répondit Lucien.—Qu'il se trouve derrière toutes vos belles qualités une force *semper virens* . . . et rien ne vous résistera dans le monde" ["But have you related all your wishes, all your actions to an idea?" . . . "Unfortunately no," said Lucien. "You have been what the English call 'inconsistent,' " reproved the canon smiling. "What does it matter what I have been if I can't be anything anymore!" responded Lucien. "Let a force *semper virens* find itself behind all your beautiful qualities and nothing will resist you in the world"] (*ibid.*, pp. 712–13).

[14] *Ibid.*, p. 705.

cien's writings is immediately displaced by material evidence
that they have remained unread: the seal set upon them previously by the journalist Lousteau[15] is noted to be unbroken.
This purely physical condition of the poems then gives rise to
a causal sequence in the narrative as Lousteau suggests that
Lucien's revenge, against a publisher who rejects writings he
has not read, would be most effective if committed to written
form. The question of what poetry *is* becomes one of what poetry *does* within the novel as writing is turned by the "mobility" of the "poet" into further grounds for narrative action.
The later characterization of the "poet" by Petit-Claud speaks
directly to the purely narrative function served by his poems:
" 'Ce n'est pas un poète, ce garçon-là, c'est un roman conti-
nuel' "[16] ["This is no poet, this young man, but a continual
novel"].

The ability in the art of poetry which first recommended Lucien to Louise de Bargeton and then, upon his arrival in Paris,
as "un grand homme de province," proves as persuasive in effect as his physical appearance. The poems presented verbatim
by Lucien in the novel[17] are in fact attributable to four different factual authors including Balzac himself.[18] Yet their inclusion as part of the narrative directly undermines their consideration as poetry. The reader of *Illusions perdues* inevitably
regards Lucien's poems in a manner similar to that of the dishonest publisher: we "read" them only in the course of reading
the narration, concerned less with their own composition than
with how their reception will figure within the novel, just as
Daurait is concerned solely with their reception in the world
the novel narrates. The responses offered in the novel by those
who hear Lucien recite his poems merely emphasize the performative aspect of his spoken readings. Lucien's first recita-

[15] *Ibid.*, p. 287.

[16] *Ibid.*, p. 735. Petit-Claud is responding here to the news, at the end of the
novel, that Lucien, having announced his intention to kill himself, has recently
been seen in motion again: he is in fact on his way back to Paris, in a "calèche
en poste," which he shares with Vautrin.

[17] *Ibid.*, pp. 98–99, 265–68.

[18] The others are: de Lassailly, Delphine de Girardin, and Théophile Gau-
tier. See Antoine Adam's notes and commentary, *ibid.*, pp. 265–68.

tion is universally interpreted as proof of his love for Louise de Bargeton.[19] Lousteau responds specifically to the sonoric effect of the poems, calling them "elegant nightingales," and, warning Lucien prophetically that their pages will remain "chastely uncut," counsels that his talent would be turned more profitably to "polemics."[20] Cynical in posture, Lousteau's comment is nonetheless apt, for the personal integrity of this "poet," like the internal integrity of his poems, appears strikingly irrelevant to the narrative of *Illusions perdues*. Finally, the logic of its narrative representation travels full circle as Lucien's discursive ability derives a practical purpose from the very fact that it has *not* been judged. Lousteau advises Lucien that in order to injure the publisher, he should criticize a novel by the established author Nathan which Dauriat plans to publish in a second edition. While Lucien had been angered by the publisher's pretended admiration for poems he had not read, he is uncomprehending of the proposal that he condemn a work he has read and, furthermore, found beautiful: " 'Mais que peut-on dire contre ce livre? Il est beau,' s'ecria Lucien"[21] ["But what can one say against this book? It is beautiful," cried Lucien]. The category of the "beautiful" is challenged for the first time in the novel, as Lousteau resolves to teach Lucien—referred to as "poet" throughout a narrative which never sees the publication of his poems[22]—the mode of writing characterizing the "métier" of thinking: the art, or "acrobatics," of criticism.[23] Lucien's article, disguised repayment for an insult itself based on a lie, should approach its own apparent subject matter, Lousteau advises, by an avenue no less oblique. Rather than discuss Nathan's novel directly, Lucien is told to incorporate it within the construction of a general critical theory.

[19] *Ibid.*, p. 100.

[20] *Ibid.*, pp. 269–72.

[21] *Ibid.*, p. 402.

[22] The only character who appears disturbed by or even aware of that fact is Lucien's sister Eve; she remarks with unique perspecuity when Lucien is received as Poet Laureate of Angoulême: "—Les *Marguerites* ne sont d'ailleurs pas encore publiées, comment peut-on le féliciter d'un succès à venir" ["Besides, the *Marguerites* have not yet been published, how can we celebrate a success to come"] (*ibid.*, p. 660).

[23] *Ibid.*, pp. 402–403.

The categories of analysis that constitute the theory would provide a critique of the novel as part of their own proof. I quote Lousteau's lesson at length because each critical step it prescribes is integral to its strategy. Directly relevant to the present analysis of narrative representation and discursive cognition, it is also a passage of considerable rarity in all of Balzac's narrative fictions. Serving marginally to advance the story of the novel, it offers a fully developed explication of fundamental critical distinctions drawn between literary forms:

> "Mon cher, un journaliste est un acrobate, il faut t'habituer aux inconvéniences de l'état. . . . Voici la manière de procéder en semblable occurrence. . . . Tu commenceras par trouver l'oeuvre *belle*, et tu peux t'amuser à écrire *ce que tu en penses*. Le public se dira: Ce critique est sans jalousie, il sera sans doute impartial. Dès lors le public tiendra sa critique pour consciencieuse. Après avoir conquis l'estime de ton lecteur, tu regretteras d'avoir à blâmer le système dans lequel des semblables livres vont faire entrer la littérature française. La France, diras-tu, ne gouverne-t-elle pas l'intelligence du monde entier? Jusqu'aujourd'hui, de siècle en siècle, les écrivains français maintenaient l'Europe dans la voie de l'analyse, de l'examen philosophique, par la puissance du style et par *la forme originale qu'ils donnaient aux idées*. Ici, tu places, pour le bourgeois, un éloge de Voltaire, de Rousseau, de Diderot, de Montesquieu, de Buffon. Tu expliquera combien en France la langue est impitoyable, tu prouveras qu'elle est *un vernis étendu sur la pensée*. Tu lâcheras des axiomes, comme: Un grand écrivain en France est toujours un grand homme, *il est tenu par la langue à toujours penser*, il n'en est pas ainsi dans les autres pays, etc. . . . Une fois sur ce terrain, tu lances un mot qui résume et explique aux niais le système de nos hommes de génie du dernier siècle, en appelant leur littérature une *littérature idéée*. . . . Tu expliques alors que de nos jours il se produit une nouvelle littérature où l'on abuse du dialogue (la plus facile des formes littéraires), et *des descriptions qui dispensent de penser*. Tu opposeras les romans de Voltaire,

de Diderot, de Sterne, de Lesage, si substantiels, si incisifs, au roman moderne *où tout se traduit par des images.* . . . Dans un pareil genre, il n'y a place que pour l'inventeur. Le roman à la Walter Scott est un genre funeste où *l'on delaye des idées,* où elles sont passées au laminoir, genre accessible à tous les esprits, genre que tu nommeras enfin la *littérature imagée.* Tu feras tomber cette argumentation sur Nathan, en démontrant qu'il est un imitateur et n'a que l'apparence du talent. Le grand style serré du dix-huitième siècle manque à son livre, tu prouveras que l'auteur y a substitué les événements aux sentiments. *Le mouvement n'est pas la vie, le tableau n'est pas l'idée!* Lâche de ces sentences-là, le public les répète . . . tu peux écraser Nathan dont l'ouvrage, quoique renfermant *des beautés supérieures,* donne en France droit de bourgeoisie à *une littérature sans idées.* Dès lors, il ne s'agit plus de Nathan ni de son livre, comprends-tu? mais de la gloire de la France."[24]

[24] ["My dear, a journalist is an acrobat, you must become accustomed to the inconveniences of the state. . . . Here is the manner to proceed in such occurrences. . . . You will begin by finding the work *beautiful,* and you can enjoy yourself by writing *what you think of it.* The public will say to itself: This critic is without jealousy, he will without doubt be impartial. From then on the public will hold his criticism for conscientious. After having conquered the esteem of your reader, you will regret to have to blame the system into which such books are making French literature enter. Does not France, you will say, govern the intelligence of the entire world? Up till today, from century to century, French writers have maintained Europe in the path of analysis, of philosophical examination, by the power of their style and by the *original form which they gave to ideas.* Here you place, for the *bourgeois,* a praise of Voltaire, of Rousseau, of Diderot, of Montesquieu, of Buffon. You will explain how language in France is pitiless, you will prove that it is *a varnish spread over thought.* You will let loose some axioms, like: A great writer in France is always a great man, *he is forced by language always to think,* it isn't so in other countries, etc. . . . Once on this ground, you throw out a catchword which resumes and explains to the fools the system of our men of genius of the last century, in calling their literature a *literature of ideas.* . . . You explain then that in our time a new literature is being produced in which one abuses dialogue (the easiest of the literary forms), and *descriptions which allow one not to think.* You will oppose the novels of Voltaire, of Diderot, of Sterne, of Lesage, so substantial, so incisive, to the modern novel *where everything is translated by images.* . . . In such a genre, there is only room for the inventor. The novel

Balzac's own "form" of fiction perhaps never better betrays its most conventional and unreflective characterization than in this extraordinary theoretical fiction of the history of a hegemonous national literature whose language is "pitiless" and "compels" its writers "always to think." For among the literary forms condemned by this theory are Balzac's own primary means of representation, "dialogue" and "description," criticized here for replacing thought by "image": "a new literature in which one abuses dialogue . . . and descriptions which allow one not to think." Unlike such a nonspeculative literature, and unlike the representation of Lucien we have been reading, the "manner of proceeding" practiced as it is espoused by Lousteau dazzles not with diamond buttons but with illuminating conceptual distinctions. Its elegant sophistry sets "beauty" against "ideas," "original forms" against "imitation," and "events" against "mind" and "sentiment": dichotomies wholly appropriate to a "philosophical examination" of *Illusions perdues* itself. Yet the division of literary forms according to the primary categories of "analysis" and "movement," while most obviously relevant to Lucien's own story, is also most clearly overcome by the very speech which proposes it: the tremendous mental acceleration displayed by Lousteau's analytic abilities successfully combines movement with the discrete moments of inspection. His lesson in discursive persuasion is itself as persuasive as Lucien's natural appearance, but Lousteau, like any *thinking* teacher of persuasion, knows the distinctions he draws to be as effective as they are false. Performative commands ranging widely in affect and action,

---

in the style of Walter Scott is a deadly genre where *one spins out ideas*, where they are passed to the rolling-mill, a genre which is accessible to all minds, a genre which you will finally name *imaged literature*. You will let fall this line of reasoning on Nathan, demonstrating that he is an imitator and only has the appearance of talent. The great concise style of the eighteenth century is lacking in his book, you will prove that the author has substituted events in it for sentiments. *Movement is not life, the tableau is not the idea!* Loose with such sentences as those, the public repeats them . . . you can crush Nathan whose work, while containing some *aspects of superior beauty*, gives *bourgeois* rights in France to a *literature without ideas*. From then on it is no longer a matter of Nathan or his book—do you understand?—but of the glory of France"], *ibid.*, pp. 402–403; my emphasis.

such as "you will begin," "you will regret," "you will prove," "you will let fall," "you can crush," are necessarily inserted at every turn of Lousteau's argument, thereby underscoring the artificial and programmatic nature of its development.[25] As Lucien will later itemize in a letter to Lousteau the exact attire he requires upon returning to Angoulême,[26] Lousteau indicates to the "poet" the precise discursive operations an effective critical polemic must make in a seemingly logical, while essentially manipulative, predetermined sequence. Manipulation here is in fact so sharply detailed that its defining intention, that of rhetorical deception, is obscured in significance: Lucien's revenge comes to appear less the purpose of, than the pretext for, Lousteau's plan of "action."

Finally, more disarming than the injustice to be done to the innocent novelist Nathan is the realization that the persuasiveness of Lousteau's proposal lies within the very concepts it uses as catchwords. For "littérature idéée" and "littérature imagée," pseudocategories of a self-consciously contrived polemic, can also be seen to represent the binary framework in which textual analysis continues to be most "successfully" carried out. Pairs of fundamental critical terms, such as "portrait" and "tableau," "form" and "movement," "thought" and "description," "analysis" and "invention," "system" and "genre," and "style" and "language," are all shown to belong to a series pertaining in structure to a convincing, if fictitious, idea/image opposition. Indeed, Lousteau's postulation of separate literary traditions can be directly likened to the contemporary "discovery" of an opposition between the organizing figures of metaphor and metonymy: a formal distinction serving primarily to distinguish the literatures of poetry and prose, and within them, at a historical metalevel most relevant to Bal-

---

[25] Other performatives in the passage indicate the crossover between motion and analysis, between disposition and exposition, directed by its verbal commands: "you will say," "you place," "you will explain," "you will let loose," "you release," "you will throw out," "you will oppose," "you will sink," "you will make apparent," "you can give yourself over to," "you will show."

[26] *Ibid.*, p. 672.

zac himself, a split between the literatures of romanticism and realism.

But the exposure of the intentional function of theoretical oppositions—or in the more radical case of Lousteau, the use of such an exposure *as* a means of persuasion—is not shown in *Illusions perdues* to conclude in their loss of efficacy. The review of Nathan's novel, written by Lucien as stipulated, proves to fulfill the purpose of its design. Yet even before its publication, Lousteau's argument is revealed to overstep its end: the character whose personal conflict provides its occasion is the first to be won over by its effect. Immediately after the close of Lousteau's speech, the narrator states unequivocally: "Lucien fut stupéfait en entendant parler Lousteau: à la parole du journaliste, il lui tombait des écailles des yeux, il découvrait des vérités littéraires qu'il n'avait même pas soupçonnées"[27] [Lucien was stupefied in hearing Lousteau speak: at the word of the journalist, the scales fell from his eyes, he discovered literary truths which he had not even suspected]. The full disclosure of its intention has only made Lousteau's deception appear more convincing, as "real" motivation is overtaken by spoken intent. Lucien's "reason" for criticizing Nathan has been eclipsed by the (false) reasoning of criticism, and in simply stating that conversion as fact—"the scales fell from his eyes, he discovered . . . truths he had not . . . suspected"—the narrator fails to comment on its own objective validity. Common devices of authorial indirection used to distance a specific occurrence from its perception (such as "comme si," "il a cru," "il lui apparaîssait" ["as if," "he believed," "it seemed to him"]), are also entirely absent here. Instead, like his beauty, Lucien's new-found conviction is treated as an external given granting motion to narration, as the original aim of the plot against Dauriat yields another opportunity for Lucien to exercise his "mobility."

The problem of enlightenment produced through persuasion becomes a cognitive one in the very course of the action to which it gives rise, as Lucien, having already succeeded in reproducing Lousteau's "literary truths," is subsequently in-

---

[27] *Ibid.*, pp. 405–406.

formed that for the sake of the novel he hopes to sell, he must write another article reversing his unfavorable review.[28] Objecting to this second suggestion as vehemently as he had to the first, Lucien has already completely forgotten that he had ever held a favorable opinion of Nathan's work. Assuming that he believes himself hindered by the mere printed appearance of personal duplicity—the ascription of opposing opinions on a single subject to a single name—the other journalists are quick to explain that names themselves need not maintain their identity: his own may remain anonymous or be published in various ways. But Lucien's continued refusal implies that the "change of mind" induced by Lousteau has occurred in more than name alone: " 'Les signatures ne m'inquiètent pas,' dit Lucien; 'mais je ne vois rien à dire en faveur du livre' " ["Signatures don't worry me," said Lucien; "but I see nothing to say in favor of this book"]. At this point the troubling coincidence of persuasive and cognitive discourse becomes clear, as Lousteau's original suggestion, "tu peux t'amuser alors à écrire ce que tu en penses" [you can enjoy yourself by writing what you think of it], is repeated by another journalist in the interrogative form: " 'Tu pensais donc ce que tu as écrit?' dit Hector à Lucien 'Oui' "[29] ["Then you thought what you wrote?" said Hector to Lucien. "Yes"]. The verb "to think" here appears transformed in meaning as soon as it becomes narrational, i.e., when it refers to an action already committed in the past. By the time what Lucien "*thinks*" ("en pens[e]") is "written" to be what he "*thought*" ("pensais"), the relation between thinking and writing has changed from one of personal opinion to the personal affirmation of truth. The visible appearance of "thinking" in words, whether or not intended to deceive, seems itself to be structured by its own diachronic dimension as duplicity.

While the recognition of what he *has* "thought" seems momentarily to halt the "mobility" of the "poet," Lucien's "char-

---

[28] *Ibid.*, p. 421. Balzac's wryly descriptive title for this chapter speaks directly to the nonsensical equality of meanings that such a "reversal" of opinion would involve: "Etude sur l'art de chanter la palinodie" ["Study in the art of singing palinodes"] (p. 418).

[29] *Ibid.*, p. 421.

acter" remains unencumbered by conventional notions of internal consistency. A forceful recombination of the same critical terms by Lousteau convinces Lucien to write the second review which, like the first, having appeared groundless when suggested, proves to be no less elevating in effect. Indeed, the narrator goes on to relate, "beauty," "new" reflections, and Lucien's own "poetic" identity are all born of a "contradiction" now "balanced" by the same critical theory by which it was posed:

> Sous sa plume se rencontrèrent les beautés que fait naître la contradiction. Il fut spirituel et moqueur, il s'éleva même à des considérations neuves sur le sentiment, sur l'idée et l'image en littérature. . . . De sanglant et âpre critique, de moqueur comique, il devint poète en quelques phrases finales qui se balancèrent majestueusement comme un encensoir chargé de parfums vers l'autel.[30]

> Beneath his pen met the beauties which are born of contradiction. He was spiritual and mocking, he even raised himself to new considerations on the subject of sentiments, of ideas and of images in literature. . . . From cutting and bitter critic, from comic mocker, he became a poet in a few final phrases which swung majesterially like a censer bearing perfume to the altar.

Lucien's critical acrobatics do not end even with the redoubtable feat of complete reversal, a full backward flip. His "mobility," having been supplied with a formal means of presentation, can now invoke at will the discursive formulas it has learned: in the professional parlance of contemporary criticism, it would probably be said with complacency that Lucien's "mobility" had successfully assimilated the right critical "moves." The persuasive skills of the "poet" in his metamorphosis[31] as critic are called into service once again

---

[30] *Ibid.*, p. 427.

[31] Interestingly, David Séchard, the second of the "deux poètes" named in the First Part of the novel, is stated to have begun the study of metamorphosis as the narrative ends: "Après avoir dit adieu sans retour à la gloire, il s'est bravement rangé dans la classe des rêveurs et des collectionneurs; il s'adonne

when Lucien discovers that the negative review he had written of a drama has appeared transformed in print. He returns to Nathan's novel and writes yet another review in which all previous claims—"the expressed opinions"—are gathered to consolidate and "establish" his own critical "power": "Pour établir définitivement sa puissance, il écrivait l'article où il résumait et balançait toutes les opinions émises à propos du livre de Nathan pour la Revue de Dauriat et de Finot"[32] [In order to establish his power definitively, he wrote the article in which he summed up and balanced all expressed opinions with regard to Nathan's book for the Review of Daurait and of Finot]. The words composing persuasive argumentation finally appear no more than technical tools held firmly in his grasp when Lucien learns from Lousteau that the theater he

---

à l'entomologie, et recherche les transformations jusqu'à présent si secrètes des insectes que la science ne connaît que dans leur dernier état" [After having said goodbye without return to glory, he bravely entered the ranks of the class of dreamers and collectors; he devotes himself to entomology and researches the transformations, so secret up till now, of insects that science only knows in their last state] (*ibid.*, p. 752).

The possibility that David may indeed be viewed by Balzac as the only "poet" of the novel, in the sense that he is its only true "inventor"—not of poetry or persuasive arguments but of the material paper on which they are written—is supported by a simile in the "Préface de la Deuxième Partie," in which the life of insects is compared to those of books: "N'est-ce pas beaucoup pour un livre, aujourd'hui que les livres naissent, vivent et meurent comme ces insectes de l'Hypanis, dont les moeurs ont fourni peut-être le premier de tous les articles de journaux à je ne sais quel Grec" ["Isn't that a lot for a book, today when books are born, live, and die like those insects of the Hypanis whose habits furnished perhaps the first of all newspaper articles to I don't know what Greek"] (*ibid.*, p. 763).

Natural rather than discursive morphology may be Balzac's own view (related, of course, to the envisioned social morphology of *La Comédie humaine*) of the only real "poetry" remaining, i.e., that which remains true to the integrity of its own conceptual forms, when literary forms, like the paper they are written on, are "invented," sold, and consumed at a price. Balzac's morphological conception of his own writing is represented most explicitly in the well-known "Avant-Propos" (1842) to *La Comédie humaine* (see *ibid.*, I:7–20).

On the distinctly literary link proposed by Balzac between typical natural *and* conceptual forms, see, in particular, Peter Demetz, "Balzac and the Zoologists: A Concept of Type," in *The Disciplines of Criticism*, pp. 397–418 (pp. 407–10 esp.).

[32] *Ibid.*, p. 432.

has attacked, for no other reason than that it had not reserved him a seat, pays the newspaper which employs him generously for its favor. What might well be considered the most "poetic" moment of *Illusions perdues* occurs as Lucien expresses his dismay without understanding the significance of the very words he uses. In speaking, he inadvertently epitomizes the entire chain of narrated events which precede his response: " '*Je comprends que je ne suis pas libre d'écrire ce que je pense*' "[33] ["I understand that I am not free to write what I think"]. An illusion is most certainly, if self-servingly, lost here.[34] But that loss is founded upon a series of illusory conceptions whose own sequential movement could be patterned with no greater precision than the simple syntax composing Lucien's sentence. For Lucien recognizes here, with regard to the activity of writing as it is represented in *Illusions perdues*, what he is about to learn, albeit abortively, at the end of the novel, and must learn at the close of the novel's sequel, *Splendeurs et misères des courtisanes*, at the cost of his own life. Lucien learns through learning the "art" of writing what the effects of his own beauty had always concealed: that the "mobility" which makes him the perfect participant in the game of musical positions played throughout Balzac's fiction, also makes it wholly impossible for him to take any internally consistent—or conversely, externally "free"—cognitive position. Lucien's "understanding" that while an ostensible subject of understanding (" '*Je* comprends . . . *je* ne suis pas . . . *je* pense"), he is "not free to write what [he] think[s]," is predicated upon the more formidable illusion that in writing he has ever thought at all. For in employing writing as a means of persuasion toward his own (narrative) advancement, he has never been "free" of the pure appearances governing his narration. Thus in recognizing that forms of persuasion, like the forms of physical beauty, are as

[33] *Ibid.*, p. 433; my emphasis.

[34] Of note with regard to the implied significance of the novel's title, i.e., that human knowledge increases with the loss of illusions, is Balzac's own statement of ambivalence, in the "Préface de la Deuxième Partie," as to the novel's desired effect: "Cette oeuvre, *conservera-t-elle quelques illusions* à des gens heureux? l'auteur en doute" [This work, will it conserve some illusions for happy people? The author doubts it] (*ibid.*, p. 763; my emphasis).

binding upon their agent as upon those they affect, Lucien *does* think and *is* for a single moment freed from the course of narration. At the same time, since that very recognition consists in thinking for the first time that he is *not* "free," his state of illusionment is never more acute.

The representation of a disjuncture between persuasive appearances and thought—between critical polemics and "free" cognition, or the beauty and extraneous integrity of Lucien—is not confined in Balzac's writings to the person of the "poet," nor to representational fictions of character alone. Contemporary to the composition of *Illusions perdues*, Balzac formulated a critical theory of distinct literary systems in his own review of another novelist, Stendhal. "Etudes sur M. Beyle" (*Revue Parisienne*, Sept. 25, 1840) offers, for the most part, praise of *La Chartreuse de Parme* and displays Balzac's awareness of being among the first to recognize its author's "worth": "Après le courage de la critique vient le courage de l'éloge. Certes, il est temps de rendre justice au mérite de M. Beyle. Notre époque lui doit beaucoup . . ."[35] [After the courage of criticism comes the courage of praise. Certainly it is time to do justice to the merit of Mr. Beyle. Our epoch owes him much . . .]. Balzac prefaces his critical estimation of Stendhal by positioning the novelist within a constellation of theoretical figures—"trois formes, faces ou systèmes"—"*la Littérature des Images*," "*la Littérature des Idées*," and "*l'Eclectisme littéraire*."[36] The third, "eclectic" "system" of literature, true to its name, is described to combine "ideas" and "images" in whatever manner best suits its purpose: "une representation du monde comme il est: les images et les idées, l'idée dans l'image ou l'image dans l'idée . . ."[37] [a representation of the world as it is: images in ideas, the idea in the image or the image in the idea]. Balzac states his own affiliation with this additional literary "school"—itself absent from Lousteau's recitation of binary oppositions—based on motives first described as mimetic

---

[35] Honoré de Balzac, *Oeuvres complètes*, ed. La Société des Etudes Balzaciennes (Paris: Guy le Prat, 1963), 28 vols., XXVIII:236.

[36] *Ibid.*, pp. 197–98.

[37] *Ibid.*.

208 | CHAPTER 5

and historical in premise, but which give way to a reflection upon the self-exhaustion inherent in nonrepresentational formalism:

> Quant à moi, je me range sous la bannière de l'Eclectisme littéraire par la raison que voici: je ne crois pas la peinture de la société moderne possible par le procédé sévère de la littérature du XVIIème siècle. L'introduction de l'élément dramatique, de l'image, du tableau, de la description, du dialogue me paraît indispensable dans la littérature moderne. Avouons-le franchement, *Gil Blas* est fatigant comme forme: l'entassement des événements et des idées a je ne sais quoi de sterile. L'Idée, devenue Personnage, est d'une plus belle intelligence. Platon dialoguait sa morale psychlogique.[38]

> In as far as I am concerned, I rank myself under the banner of literary eclecticism for the following reason: I do not believe the painting of modern society possible by the severe process of the literature of the seventeenth century. The introduction of the dramatic element, of the image, of the *tableau*, of description, of dialogue seems to me indispensable in modern literature. Let us admit it frankly, *Gil Blas* is tiring as form: the accumulation of events and of ideas has an I don't know what kind of sterility. The Idea, become a Personage, is of a more beautiful intelligence. Plato dialogued his psychological morals.

In defending the "introduction" of new literary forms into fiction—"the dramatic element . . . the image . . . the *tableau* . . . description . . . dialogue"—Balzac defends his own novels as a historical necessity. Yet the narrative modes he enumerates as "indispensable" to "modern" writing will only succeed in replacing previous fictions in as far as they further complicate their interest. The "severity" of seventeenth century fiction may derive from a sparsity of representational images, but "the painting," or specifically mimetic representation of

---

[38] *Ibid.*, p. 198.

"modern society"[39] will necessarily reorganize, rather than obviate, the relation in language of thought to image. The unsettling "mobility of character" central to *Illusions perdues*, which stands, like Lucien himself, for the extraordinary representational range of *La Comédie humaine*, can be viewed as part of a literary-historical process aimed at producing "une plus belle intelligence." Yet, as the vehicles of that transformative development, Balzac's characters cannot themselves be shown to have achieved the status—in the definitive sense indicated here—of *Personnages*. Indeed, if the narratives of human fortune comprising *La Comédie humaine* can be said to share a single structural characteristic, it is the turn they take from appearing any less fortuitous in essence. Whether by circumstance, accident, or the chance persuasions of pleasure, the "ideas" held within these stories are narrated over and over again to be misguided by practice. Similarly, no theory of literature could be less "platonic" in perspective than that of an "intelligence" made "more beautiful" by the fact of its representation, as if the addition of its personal, imaged appearance would provide an improvement upon *l'Idée*.

Assuming that the motives Balzac offers for his own "literary eclecticism" are, like his outspoken political views, exceeded by the literature they are meant to explain, the example

---

[39] Whether or not Balzac, in employing the commonplace, while wholly metaphorical, conception of *discursive* representation as "painting," proves himself, by his own words, to be a primarily mimetic or "realist" author appears a moot question in view of his fully unorthodox vision *of* the act of painting. See, for example, his ascription of a *double* temporality to literary painting by which "the painter" must make an effort to keep pace with the rate of "living" of the painted. He compares the historical *tableau* of *Illusions perdues* to the self-consuming history of the Empire itself: "Au lieu d'une face de la vie individuelle, il s'agît d'une des faces les plus curieuses de ce siècle, d'une face prête à s'user, comme s'est usé l'Empire; *aussi faut-il se hâter de la peindre pour ce que qui est vivant ne devienne pas un cadavre sous les yeux même du peintre*" [In place of the face of individual life, one has to do here with one of the most curious faces of this century, a face ready to use itself up, as the Empire used itself up; *one must also hurry to paint it so that what is living does not become a corpse beneath the very eyes of the painter*] ("Préface de la Première partie," *Illusions perdues*, p. 758; my emphasis). See also Chap. 6, footnote 16, of this book, for Proust's description of the specifically conceptual nature of Balzac's *peinture*.

of another "face" inscribed in his theory may prove more critical with regard to the problem of cognition and representation. Balzac names Stendhal as a "master" of "the literature of
ideas," a discursive system characterized by "an abundance of
facts, a sobriety of images . . . and by a manner of narrating
possessed by the eighteenth century."[40] Furthermore, in Stendhal's writing in particular these qualities of form are given
"content" by a vital "feeling for the comic": "surtout M. Beyle
et M. Merimée, malgré leur profonds sérieux, ont je ne sais
quoi d'ironique et de narquois dans la manière avec laquelle ils
posent les faits. Chez eux, le comique est contenu"[41] [above all
Mr. Beyle and Mr. Merimée, in spite of their profound seriousness, have I don't know what kind of irony and banter in the
way in which they pose the facts. In their work the comic is
content]. "In spite of [its] profound seriousness," the "literature of ideas" is seen by Balzac to possess a peculiar sense of
comedy in its "manner of posing the facts." The simultaneous
presence of comedy and seriousness result in a "*je ne sais quoi*
of irony." "Irony" reminiscent of the eighteenth century may
seem preferable to seventeenth-century "sterility," yet both
irony and comedy appear irrelevant to another aspect of Stendhal's fiction described later in the review to be of exclusively
serious significance. Balzac rarely reveals himself as humorless
as when, following an enthusiastic summary of the plot of *La
Chartreuse de Parme*, he criticizes what he calls its "weak
side," its "style." This sudden negative turn in Balzac's review
recalls the strategy, and in fact shares many of the phrases, of
the lesson in review-writing given to Lucien by Lousteau. Instead of an emphasis on representational images, however,
here a prominence of "thought" is held to be "dangerous" to
the ("French") literary tradition. The criticism of a specific
"system" of literature, referred in this case to an actual author
and work, is supported by Balzac upon strictly technical, textual observations:

[40] *Ibid.*, p. 199: "par l'abondance des faits, par sa sobriété d'images, par la
concision, par la netteté, par la petite phrase de Voltaire, par une façon de con-
ter qu'a eue la XVIIIème siècle."
[41] *Ibid.*

Le côté faible de cette oeuvre est le style, *tant qu'arrangement de mots, car la pensée, éminemment française, soutient la phrase.* Les fautes que commet M. Beyle sont purement *grammaticales:* il est négligé, incorrect à la manière des écrivains du XVIIème siècle. . . . Tantôt un désaccord de temps dans les verbes, quelquefois l'absence du verbe; tantôt des "c'est," des "ce que," des "que," qui fatiguent le lecteur, et font à l'esprit l'effet d'un voyage dans une voiture mal suspendue, sur une route de France. Ces fautes assez grossières annoncent un défaut de travail. Mais, *si le français est un vernis sur la pensée,* on doit être aussi indulgent pour ceux chez lesquels ils courvrent des beaux tableaux que l'on est sévère pour ceux qui n'ont que le vernis. Si, chez M. Beyle, ce vernis est ici quelque peu jaune . . . *il laisse voir du moins une suite de pensées qui se déduisent d'après les lois de la logique.* Sa phrase longue est mal construite, sa phrase courte est sans rondeur. Il écrit à peu près dans le genre de Diderot, qui n'était pas écrivain; mais la conception est grande et forte; mais *la pensée est originale,* et souvent bien rendue. *Ce système n'est pas à imiter. Il serait trop dangereux de laisser les auteurs se croire de profonds penseurs.*[42]

The weak side of this work is the style *as arrangement of words, for the thought, eminently French, sustains the phrase.* The mistakes that Mr. Beyle commits are purely *grammatical:* he is negligent, incorrect, in the manner of the writers of the seventeenth century. . . . Sometimes a disagreement of tenses in the verbs, sometimes the absence of the verb; sometimes [the use of] an "it is" a "that which," a "that," which tire the reader, and bring to mind the effect of a voyage in a badly hung wagon, on a road in France. These unpolished mistakes announce a lack of work. But, *if French is a varnish over thought,* one must be as indulgent with those in whose works it covers beautiful *tableaux* as one is severe with those who only have the varnish. If, in the works of Mr. Beyle, this varnish is here

---

[42] *Ibid.,* pp. 234–35; my emphasis.

and there a little yellow . . . *at least it lets one see a chain of thoughts which are deduced following the laws of logic.* His long sentence is badly constructed, his short sentence is without roundness. He writes somewhat in the genre of Diderot, who was not a writer; but the conception is large and strong; but *the thought is original,* and often well rendered. *This system is not to be imitated. It would be too dangerous to let authors believe themselves profound thinkers.*

The problem with literature perceived to be outstanding for its "thoughts" is that thought itself does damage to the appearance of literature. The area of injury indicated is no less encompassing than the grammar of the language in which Stendhal writes, the abuse of which displays, if not an unimaginable ignorance, at least a condemnable lack of polish or "varnish" on the author's part: "These unpolished mistakes announce a lack of work." Mistakes in the temporal concordance of verbs, predicative structures from which verbs themselves are deleted, and an excessive reliance upon pronominal relations—errors excused at first as "purely grammatical"— threaten to break the surface of discursive understanding in Stendhal. As a means of transportation ("une voiture") along roads known not to be smooth in a linguistic landscape known as one's own ("sur une route de France"), the stylistic vehicle of Stendhal's "grand conception" "tires" comprehension: the construction of its sentences is "badly hung." Thoughts following the "laws of logic" in their sequential deduction are made visible ("il laisse voir") in their transgression of grammatical conventions. Coherent linguistic meaning is sacrificed to "original thinking," as thought is composed at the expense of the rules of its expression. Thus Balzac's final warning against "thinking" authors is both wholly justified and without reason. For the "belief" ("se croire") that thinking and writing can take a single self-identical and comprehensible discursive form belies the significant understanding of either: the literary "system" which "is not to be imitated," cannot be, since it disrupts the systematization of language itself.

Thinking, so conceived, would seem most destructive of the

forms of narrative fiction. Yet, in accordance with Balzac's description of his narrative prose, the characters in Stendhal's novels are distinguished more for their mental faculties than their physical appearance. Stendhal's disturbingly "logical" "style" of narration posits human figures who appear most compelling for their thoughts. In *Le Rouge et le noir* (1830), the Stendhal novel whose basic plot is followed most closely by the later *Illusions perdues*, the movements of Julien Sorel are told to turn primarily on the power of his mind. As described early in the novel, when surrounded by an indistinguishable mass of *seminaristes*, Julien stands out from his narrative surroundings by the very "look of thought about him": "Julien avait," the narrator states, "l'air de *penser*."[43] This appearance of thinking, however, is specified throughout the novel to stem from a mental ability dependent upon an essential absence of thought. Julien acquires and plays the roles of student, tutor, seminarian, secretary, political envoy, and lover due to a skill which is neither logical nor conceptual, nor in any way discursive in itself, but more precisely that of commending the pure forms of discourse to memory. Lucien de Rubempré learns to use the forms of persuasion effectively by confusing their own distinctions between imitation and invention, critical polemic and critical thinking. Julien, however, learns the words of persuasion themselves by heart, regardless of whether the form they take happens to be designated the New Testament or newsprint. The accuracy of Julien's memory bears no relation to the content it records; its exercise derives neither from personal comprehension nor received opinion. Instead, just as he learns orthography in order to remain in the service of the Marquis de la Mole,[44] and sends Mme de Fervaques a se-

---

[43] Stendhal, *Romans et Nouvelles* (Paris: Bibliothèque de la Pléiade, 1952), 2 vols., I:388; emphasis in text.

[44] Julien spells the word *cela cella*, demonstrating, in the Marquis's words, that he is not " 'un homme sûr.' " The significant function of that particular pronoun (spelled correctly, of course) is indicated by the narrative in a preceding paragraph describing Julien's first visit to the library of the Marquis: "Pour n'être pas surpris dans son émotion, il alla se cacher dans un petit coin sombre; de là il contemplait avec ravissement le dos brillant des livres: Je pourrai lire tout cela, se disait-il" [In order not to be surprised in his emotion, he went to hide himself in a little dark corner; from there he contemplated with ravish-

quence of love letters ordered by number and copied from a master form in order to attract the attentions of Mathilde,[45] Julien employs his power to memorize throughout the novel for the same reason one always unconsciously resorts to memory: to provide information for a future moment, which at the instant of its memorization, is meaningless. The narrative first refers to his "astonishing memory" as a capacity "often united with idiocy," in its inherent inability to discriminate meaningfully, at a moment when Julien begins explicitly to look to his "future":

> Avec une âme de feu, Julien avait une de ces mémoires étonnantes si souvent unies à la sottise. Pour gagner le vieux curé Chélan, duquel il voyait bien que dépendait *son sort à venir*, il avait appris par coeur tout le Nouveau Testament en latin, il savait aussi le livre du *Pape* de M. de Maistre et croyait à l'un aussi peu qu'à l'autre.[46]

> With a soul of fire, Julien had one of those astonishing memories so often united with idiocy. In order to win over the old curate Chélan, upon whom he saw clearly *his future fate* depended, he had learned by heart all of the New Testament in Latin, he also knew the book *On the Pope* of M. de Maistre and believed in one as little as in the other.

The independence of memorization from any but a formal attachment to its material ("he believed in one as little as in the other"), and of memory itself from a governing judgment of its use ("united with idiocy"), are given as general assumptions here. The operation of Julien's memory appears less arbitrary, however, as the significance of the circumstances in which it is exercised increases. As the plot of the novel develops, the specific nature of the discursive items memorized stands in closer

---

ment the brilliant back of the books: I could read all that, he said to himself] (*ibid.*, I:448).

[45] "Ce qu'il copiait lui semblait si absurde, qu'il en vint à transcrire ligne par ligne, sans songer au sens" [That which he copied seemed to him so absurd that he proceeded to transcribe it line by line without thinking of the meaning] (*ibid.*, I:605).

[46] *Ibid.*, I:235; my emphasis.

causal relation to the narrative action. Random selections from the New Testament are followed, for example, by sections from *La Nouvelle Héloïse* recited during scenes of seduction,[47] passages of scriptural doctrine used to win Pirard,[48] excerpts from Horace, Martial, and Tacitus, performed for their scholarly effect,[49] a *procès-verbal* aimed at reinstating the monarchy (recited for several pages in the novel following a claim of protest by the narrator),[50] and a "monologue" of

[47] *Ibid.*, I:372: "Sa mémoire le servit bien; depuis dix minutes il récitait *la Nouvelle Héloïse* à mademoiselle Amanda ravie" [His memory served him well; for ten minutes now he recited *La Nouvelle Héloïse* to a ravished Mlle Amanda]; I:541: "Il eut recours à sa mémoire, comme jadis à Besançon auprès d'Amanda Binet, et récita plusieurs des plus belles phrases de *la Nouvelle Héloïse*" [He had recourse to his memory, as then at Besançon in the company of Amanda Binet, and recited several of the most beautiful phrases from *La Nouvelle Héloïse*].

[48] *Ibid.*, I:379.

[49] *Ibid.*, pp. 405, 411, 452. This last recitation follows Julien's first sensation of attraction to Mathilde, itself based on his confusion, based in turn on his memory, of the "fire" that "shone in" her eyes with the "fire of passion" that had shone in Mme de Rênal's: "Julien n'avait pas assez d'usage pour distinguer que c'était du feu de la saillie que brillaient de temps en temps les yeux de Mlle Mathilde, c'est ainsi qu'il l'entendit nommer. Quand les yeux de Mme de Rênal s'animaient, c'était du feu des passions, ou par l'effet d'une indignation généreuse au récit de quelque action méchante" [Julien didn't have enough practice to distinguish that it was the fire of wit that shone from time to time in the eyes of Mlle Mathilde, it was thus that he heard her named. When the eyes of Mme de Rênal became animated, it was the fire of passions, or by the effect of a generous indignation at the narration of some evil action] (*ibid.*, I:450). This is also the only occasion in which Julien is said to speak *and* think: "Julien répondait en inventant ses idées" [Julien responded in inventing his ideas] (I:451). His cognitive inventions are attributed soon after, however, to his recollection of material previously memorized for a verbal examination at the seminary. Thus, Julien's success at this moment with Mathilde owes to a power of memory that remains operative even without his own knowledge: the "new ideas" (I:451) he expresses are memorized phrases whose memorization he does not recall. His power of memory thereby prevents Julien from articulating *presently* creative speech, the simultaneous experience of cognition *and* verbal utterance referred to in one of Stendhal's most striking epigraphs as a fate to be lamented: "Malheur à qui invente en parlant" [Misfortune to who invents while speaking] (p. 467).

[50] In a parenthetical dialogue between "l'auteur" and "l'éditeur," the former offers a now famous metaphor for political realism in literature: "la politique au milieu des intérêts d'imagination, c'est un coup de pistolet au milieu

"picturesque and sentimental phrases" addressed to Mme de Fervaques with the purpose of provoking Mathilde.[51] The purely functional status of Julien's memory is overshadowed as its reproduction of intelligible forms involves him in a chain of narrative events. Yet truer to the appearance of thought in *Le Rouge et le noir* is the consideration that there could be no novel, *Le Rouge et le noir*, if "l'air de *penser*" by which it identifies its hero took no causal form within it. The empty character of thought appears replaced by significant events because in the act of appearing *as* memory—a form perhaps most adequately defined as the pure anticipation of its future—thought provides the condition for those events, and thus also for its own replacement. Beginning with Julien's desire to "gain" the favor of the curate Chélan,[52] the possibility of a narrative plot is gained by the particular appearance of thought in this novel: the exercise of a mechanical mental faculty motivated, like the plots of novels themselves, upon the premise of looking ahead.

In addition, while thoughts which conform to logic and trespass the laws of grammar are viewed as inappropriate to literature by Balzac (writing as critic), thought as it appears in *Le Rouge et le noir* can be equated with the literary basis of language. For, unmindful of the rules of either logic or grammar, Julien's memory is shown to maintain both these means of ordering understanding[53] by repeating words strictly according

---

d'un concert" [Politics in the midst of the interests of imagination, it is a pistol shot in the midst of a concert]. "L'éditeur" responds with a reminder of the novel's most well-known epigraph—perhaps the most pervasive metaphor for the representational novel itself, and the least critically analyzed. "Un roman: c'est un miroir qu'on promène le long d'un chemin" [The novel: it is a mirror one walks along the length of a road] (*ibid.*, I:288). "L'éditeur": "Si vos personnages ne parlent pas politique . . . ce ne sont plus Français de 1830, et votre livre n'est plus un miroir, comme vous en avez la prétention. . . ." [If your personages don't talk politics . . . they are no longer Frenchmen of 1830, and your book is no longer a mirror, as you pretended it was. . . ."] (I:575–76).

[51] *Ibid.*, I:606.

[52] *Ibid.*, I:235.

[53] See, in particular, the remarkable passage in which Julien's purely memorized "responses" are commended for their "clarity," "precision," and "logic" by the seminary director who is soon to become his protector, the Jansenist Pirard: "Ce fut en vain que [l'abbé Picard] interrogea Julien pour tâcher de deviner s'il croyait sérieusement à la doctrine de M. de Maistre. *Le jeune*

to the sequence in which they have already been written and read. No discursive act could be more assured of its own comprehension than the statement of "thoughts" previously formulated, whose memorization, undertaken for the sake of expediency alone, excludes any consideration of the referents or patterns of meaning of which they are composed. The function of Julien's memory, always causal in its appearance,[54] guarantees the generation of coherent, diachronic narration: an inevitability no less "étonnante" than the ability of total recall itself. As the latter produces a surface of discourse which is perfectly impenetrable in principle, the fiction of exhaustive causality offered in the form of narration can offer, by definition of that "fiction," no "real" alternatives to its represented course of events.

Narrative fiction characterized not by the representation of

---

homme ne répondait qu'avec sa mémoire. De ce moment, Julien fut réellement très bien, il sentait qu'il était maître de soi. Après un examen fort long, il lui sembla que la sévérité de M. Picard envers lui n'était plus qu'affectée. En effet . . . le directeur du séminaire eût embrassé Julien *au nom de la logique, tant il trouvait de clarté, de précision et de netteté dans ses réponses*" [It was in vain that (the Abbot Picard) interrogated Julien to try to find out if he seriously believed in the doctrine of M. de Maistre. *The young man only responded with his memory*. From that moment on, Julien was really very well, he felt he was master of himself. After a very long examination, it seemed to him that the severity of M. Picard toward him was only affected. In effect . . . the director of the seminary had to embrace Julien *in the name of logic, so much clarity, precision and distinctness had he found in his responses*] (*ibid.*, I:380; my emphasis).

[54] The narrator, in fact, indicates that Julien's own story might have ended differently had his memory been applied to the reading of other kinds of writings, specifically, "novels": "On voit que Julien n'avait aucune expérience de la vie, il n'avait pas même lu des romans; s'il eût été un peu moins gauche et qu'il eût dit avec quelque sang-froid à cette jeune fille, par lui si adorée et qui lui faisait des confidences si étranges: Convenez . . . c'est pourtant moi que vous aimez . . ." [One sees that Julien had had no experience of life, he hadn't even read novels; if he has been a little less *gauche*, he would have said with some composure to the young girl, so adored by him and who shared such strange confidences with him: Admit it . . . it is however me whom you love. . . .] (*ibid.*, I:551); "Il voulut inventer, il demandait quelque chose de nouveau à une imagination tout occupée ailleurs. Il fallait avoir recours à la mémoire, la sienne était, il faut l'avouer, peu riche en ressources de ce genre . . ." [He wanted to invent, he demanded something new of an imagination wholly occupied elsewhere. He had to have recourse to memory, his was, it must be admitted, little rich in resources of this kind. . . .] (*ibid.*, I:564).

thinking but by its own representational "eclecticism" is threatened, with respect to its diachronic coherency, by the immediately effective forms of beauty and chance. As discussed above, the encounter between Lucien and David which provides the basis for *Illusions perdues* is told by the narrator to occur by accident: "When chance made the two friends meet . . ." (see footnote 8). Conversely, in keeping with the exclusively diachronic function of his memory, Julien is first referred to in *Le Rouge et le noir* as a means of *preventing* accidents from taking place. In the second chapter of the novel, M. and Mme de Rênal engage in conversation while walking along the path of a buttressing "wall of support": the "immense *mur de soutènement*" of Verrières.[55] The significance of the wall as a symbol of delineation is clearly conveyed in the narrator's description of its regulatory protective and aesthetic functions: in shielding the hillside public promenade from the threat of natural elements, the wall also guards "one of the most picturesque views in France" while "immortalizing [the] administration" of its builder, M. de Rênal.[56] The other, ongoing backdrop of this scene is the extraordinarily difficult, because almost entirely *un*delineated, beginning of the novel itself. While the opening pages of the novel directly challenge their comprehension by moving immediately between the story presently being told and a retelling of its own narrative precedents, M. de Rênal is posed a question he cannot answer by his wife. The question in fact refers the reader and the narrative to a knowledge of its background not as fiction but as history.

[55] *Ibid.*, I:222; emphasis in text.
[56] *Ibid.*, I:222–23. The sense of a borderline between representation and reality communicated by this setting is emphasized in the narrator's rare reference to and representation of himself: he recalls being "supported" by the wall while looking down into the underlying valley and "dreaming" of scenes—such as Julien will later see (Book II, Chap. 9: "Le Bal," I:493–501)—which he has already "abandoned" in Paris: "Combien de fois, songeant aux bals de Paris abandonnés la veille, et la poitrine appuyée contre ces grands blocs de pierre d'un beau gris tirant sur le bleu, mes regards ont plongé dans la vallé du Doubst" [How many times, dreaming of the balls of Paris abandoned at eve, with my chest supported against the large blocks of stone of a beautiful grey bordering on blue, have my eyes plunged into the valley of the Doubst] (I:223).

Mme de Rênal's query concerns "M. Appert," a figure identical in name with the real political activist who attempted to save the life of Antoine Berthet, the young man executed for attempted murder in 1828, whose bizarre and celebrated history provided Stendhal's model for the story of Julien.[57] Through a rapid series of chronological dislocations, M. Appert's visit to the prison at Verrières, its assistance by Chélan and opposition by Rênal and Valenod are narrated in fragments alternating closely with those of the conversation about them. The narrator reflects upon the inevitable confusion—literally reproduced verbally within the narrative at this moment—between "facts" as "such" and their temporal extension into service as discursive referents: "Tels sont les faits qui, commentés, exagérés de vingt façons différentes, agitaient depuis deux jours toutes les passions haineuses de la petite ville de Verrières. *Dans ce moment, ils servaient de texte à la petite discussion* que M. de Rênal avait avec sa femme"[58] [Such are the facts that, commented upon, exaggerated in twenty different ways, had been exciting the hateful passions of the little town of Verrières for two days. *At this moment they served as text for the little discussion* that M. de Rênal had with his wife]. The specific purpose of Appert's visit remains unreported in the novel, as indeed it must. For, in accordance with the codetermination of fiction and history enforced discursively at the narrative's beginning, "Appert" would have to be visiting Antoine Berthet in the fictive persona of Lucien; yet the latter, according to the sequence of the narrative, will of course not be emprisoned until the novel's end. While "the [historical] facts" of Appert's visit are thus structurally excluded from the text, "the brief discussion" for which they "serve *as* text" is directly recorded as follows. M. de Rênal, when asked by his wife what harm Appert could do, responds that the Parisian will "tip" or "incline" (*déverser*) "the blame" by publishing "articles in liberal newspapers." Mme de Rênal finds her hus-

---

[57] For a recapitulation of "le procès Berthet," see the Préface to the novel by Henri Martineau (*ibid.*, pp. 199–201); on Appert and his intervention on Berthet's behalf, see p. 225n.

[58] *Ibid.*, p. 227; my emphasis.

band's answer additionally perplexing for a reason she states openly:

> "Vous ne les lisez jamais, mon ami."
> "Mais on nous parle de ces articles jacobins; tout cela nous distrait et *nous êmpeche de faire le bien.** Quant à moi, je ne pardonnerai jamais au curé."[59]

> "You never read them, my friend."
> "But one speaks to us of these Jacobin articles; all that distracts us and *impedes us from doing the good.** As far as I am concerned, I will never pardon the curate."

In the midst of this exchange the specific nature of the general "good" from which Rênal fears "distraction" is indicated by the narrator by way of an asterisk distracting the reader from the text. The narrative points outside itself to a single word in the space of its bottom margin: *Historique* (emphasis in text). The actual divergence of the novel from an interest in "the [Historical] good"—a *telos* already made to appear questionable in being attributed to the self-interested Rênal—is demonstrated by the persistence of Mme de Rênal's curiosity and an occurrence attributable solely to the narrative context in which it is expressed.[60] As Mme de Rênal, in innocent disregard for "the good done" in the name of "History," rephrases her question by asking what "bad" Appert could "do" to the prisoners themselves, her husband, disconcerted by his own lack of an explanation, is saved by a "small event." The direct effect of that event upon M. and Mme de Rênal is stated to be a change in the course of their conversation. Its effect upon the novel is to replace, without trace, the historical text serving their discussion with the represented text of the novel itself:

[59] *Ibid.*, p. 225; emphasis in text.

[60] A 1923 edition of Stendhal's complete works refers the note "Historique" to its occurrence in the novel, *M. le Prefet*, by Lamothe Langnon, "whose documentary value Stendhal had praised." (Stendhal, *Oeuvres complètes*, ed. Jules Marsan [Paris: Librairie Champion, 1923], VIII:393.) Since *Le Rouge et le noir* is perhaps least of all a "documentary" novel, it would seem Stendhal's "note" of the "Historical" serves instead to emphasize the discrepancy between history and story in his text.

M. de Rênal vivait fort bien avec sa femme; mais ne sa-chant que répondre à cette idée, qu'elle lui répétait timide-ment: "Quel mal ce monsieur de Paris peut-il faire aux prisonniers?" il était sur le point de se facher tout à fait quand elle jeta un cri. Le second de ses fils venait de mon-ter sur le parapet du mur de la terrasse, et y courait, quoique ce mur fût élévé de plus de vingt pieds sur la vigne qui est de l'autre côté. La crainte d'effrayer son fils et de le faire tomber empêchait Mme de Rênal de lui addresser la parole. Enfin l'enfant qui riait de sa prouesse, ayant enfin regardé sa mère, vit sa pâleur, sauta sur la promenade et accourut à elle. Il fut bien grondé.

Ce petit événement changea le cours de la conversation.

—Je veux absolument prendre chez moi Sorel, le fils du scieur de planches, dit M. de Rênal; il surveillera les en-fants qui commencent à devenir trop diables pour nous. C'est un jeune prêtre, ou autant vaut, bon latiniste. . . .[61]

M. de Rênal lived very well with his wife; but not knowing what to respond to this idea, which she repeated to him timidly: "What harm can this *monsieur* from Paris do to the prisoners?" he was about to become completely enraged when all at once she screamed. The second of his sons had just gotten up on the parapet of the wall of the terrace, and was running there, although this wall was raised more than twenty feet above the vineyard that was on the other side. The fear of frightening her son and mak-ing him fall stopped Mme de Rênal from addressing him. Finally, the child, who laughed at his prowess, having fi-nally looked at his mother, saw her pallor, jumped on the promenade and ran to her. He was well scolded.

This small event changed the course of the conversa-tion.

"I want absolutely to take in Sorel, the son of the lum-berman," said M. de Rênal; "he will look after the chil-dren who are beginning to become too devilish for us. He is a young priest, or what's the same, a good latinist. . . ."

[61] Stendhal, *Romans*, I:227–28.

M. and Mme Rênal, having "well scolded" their son for a fall which never takes place, proceed to take steps whose pitfalls they cannot see and from which they will never regain their equilibrium. This "little event," more properly a non-event, proves to "change" the narrative "course" of the novel: free of disjunctive elipses between history and fiction from this point on, the text of the novel will in fact proceed far more smoothly. In representing an occurrence interpreted upon sight, the narrative founds itself as an integral series of events independent of a historical referent. Mme de Rênal's fear, the significant cause of the fiction, substitutes for the question of the significance of "History" to which the narrative, like M. de Rênal, does not know "what to respond." The desire to prevent further random occurrences turns the attention of M. de Rênal to Julien, and the novel to the constitution of a coherent narrative plot. Similarly, the stipulated function of Julien—recommended by his memory as "a young priest, or what's the same, a good latinist"—will be to ensure, by *surveillance*, the future safekeeping of the Rênal sons.

Yet the event upon which the introduction of Julien is predicated is not shown to necessitate that predication as its result. Clearly, M. de Rênal may only express the "wish" to employ Julien in order to avoid renewing the subject of Appert's visit. Not equally clear, however, is whether Mme de Rênal's real terror corresponded to an equally real external cause. The laughing child at play upon the parapet is able to jump, without injury, from the upper rim of the wall to the promenade it guards below. Unconscious of the potential danger of his position, he in fact moves with full agility, only jumping upon recognizing his mother's discomfort: "[he] saw her pallor." Furthermore, Mme de Rênal's instantaneous awareness that her own speech might cause her son's fall indicates that her fear owes less to the action she sees than to the fact, itself an accident, that she sees it. Yet her vision is no less terrifying, nor less binding, for that consideration. Followed by the reference to Julien, it gives rise to the novel's consecutive narration as its ground. The "mur de soutènement" represents the novel's own support: the margin between any historical moment and the present of writing, between writing as representation of reality and as pure fiction. The freedom of motion enjoyed atop this borderline endures only until its own status is conceived as highly precarious and that conception itself can be "seen." For the child runs to his mother not because he knows himself to have been in peril, but because her perceivable appearance—"a small event" with regard to his own vision—causes him to "change" "course" as well.[62]

Such appearances of meaning which lack a direct relation to substantial reality are hereafter provided by the active memory of Julien. The separation between his power to recollect and the referential significance of the discursive forms he remembers is both the "support" upon which Julien is perceived in the story and its own representation of a purely mental correspondence between fact and perception. The scattered references to Julien's "imagination" within the novel have contributed to a critical appreciation of the poetic quality of his character,[63] and even to his direct identification as poet.[64] In a rare instance when Julien's memory receives more than passing critical attention, it is considered to be an ironic device serving to underscore his "spontaneity" and contributing to the overall poetic of the work.[65] But "imagination" is a term given no specific definition in the novel: it is associated in one

[62] If there is an antecedent cause to the original movement of the child, it must continually recede from a narrative distracted, like the Rênals at this moment, by its own concern with "history" and which that movement will thus always take by surprise. A possible motive for such motion, and for the general attraction of heights represented throughout Stendhal's novels, is suggested, however, by the narrator of *Illusions perdues*. With reference to Lucien's own motion in the upper spheres of society, the narrator states simply in the "Préface de la Deuxième Partie": "Les abîmes ont leur magnetisme" [Abysses have their magnetic attraction] (*Illusions perdues*, p. 763). The true attraction of heights of action, the narrator thus implies, may lie in their effective creation of an otherwise absent sense of depth.

[63] Cf. Auerbach, *Mimesis*, pp. 481–82.

[64] Cf. F.W.J. Hemmings, *Stendhal: A Study of His Novels* (Oxford: Clarendon Press, 1964), p. 121.

[65] See Victor Brombert, *Stendhal et la voie oblique* (Presses Universitaires de France, 1954), pp. 46, 164–66. Brombert's study of the dynamic structure of indirection in Stendhal's narratives remains the most individually insightful work on the novelist to date.

instance with a "lack of thought,"[66] is linked with "illusion" in another,[67] and is used to describe the "errors" imposed upon "judgment" by sensual desire.[68] Applied to characters other than Julien, it serves to explain the capricious behavior of Mathilde,[69] as well as the admirable dignity of the Marquis.[70] The narrator also invokes the term with purposeful naiveté to defend his own representations from charges of inverisimilitude.[71]

While "imagination" refers to a variety of mental activities in the novel, the qualifying term "poetic," related to the exclusively narrative function of Lucien's appearance and poems in *Illusions perdues*, refers to a single and necessarily unique moment in the narrative of *Le Rouge et le noir*. The appearance of the "poetic" in a narrative plot dependent explicitly upon the mechanism of memory can only occur at the instant that mechanism breaks down: when the character whose memory is represented as the "appearance of thinking" thinks the one thought which can never be memorized, lacking the very time it would take to appear. At that moment the otherwise indefinite extension of a narrative whose only "bien," or common good, is "l'air de penser" of its own vehicle, must come to an end. If, returning to Balzac's terms, the vehicle of Stendhal's writing is "suspended" upon "the appearance of thought," the narrative of Julien, once deprived of that appearance, cannot maintain its suspense. The one objective indication of the "po-

---

[66] Stendhal, *Romans*, I:498.

[67] *Ibid.*, I:488.

[68] *Ibid.*, I:558.

[69] *Ibid.*, I:592.

[70] *Ibid.*, I:636.

[71] Of his morally objectionable characterization of Mathilde, the narrator states: "Ce personnage est tout à fait d'imagination, et même imaginé bien en dehors des habitudes sociales. . . . Maintenant qu'il est bien convenue que le caractère de Mathilde est impossible dans notre siècle, non moins prudent que vertueux, je crains moins d'irriter en continuant le récit des folies de cette aimable fille" [This personage is completely made from imagination, and even imagined well outside of social customs. . . . Now that it is well agreed upon that the character of Mathilde is impossible in our century, no less prudent than it is virtuous, I fear less that I will irritate in continuing the narration of the madnesses of this likable girl] (*ibid.*, I:556–57).

etic" in the novel refers to a mind which can no longer appear to think by having already thought ahead:[72]

> Jamais cette tête n'avait été aussi poétique qu'au moment où elle allait tomber. Les plus doux moments qu'il avait trouvés jadis dans les bois de Vergy revenaient en foule à sa pensée et avec une extrême énergie.
>
> Tout se passa simplement, convenablement, et de sa part sans aucune affectation.[73]

> This head had never been as poetic as at the moment it was going to fall. The sweetest moments which he had found at another time in the forests of Vergy returned to his thought in a crowd and with extreme energy.
>
> Everything went simply, fittingly, and without any affectation on his part.

As if to prove that the "poetic" can only appear in narration "at the moment" which "simply, fittingly," and in its entirety ("tout"), has "passed," the narrative itself continues briefly. In a return to the temporal disjunctures of the opening of the novel, Julien's speculations upon an afterlife are reported posthumously. The physical place of memory, now severed from the fiction whose narration it has served, is celebrated in an orchestrated historical ritual by Mathilde. For its "part," however, the novel has cut itself off from its own source of narrative generation, calling that literal fact of discursive representation "poetic," without claiming to appear to be poetry or confusing the appearance of the poetic with beauty: that is, in its own words, "sans aucune affectation."

The "real" heroes of *Le Rouge et le noir* and *Illusions perdues* are, in the directly relevant terms provided by Kant, "mere appearances": the "appearance of thought" granted by the

---

[72] Cf. Peter Brooks's suggestion that Julien is guillotined as punishment for "the fact of having had a plot" (*Reading for the Plot*, p. 85). The activity of plotting, of course, relates directly to the fact of Julien's prodigious memory: both are "based," as Brooks states of Stendhal's novels in general, on "desire in and for the future" (p. 77).

[73] Stendhal, I:697.

power of memorization and the appearance of the "poetic" in the visible phenomenon of physical beauty represent to us the central characters of these narrations. Ultimately severed from all narrative action and made into a historical prop in one case, and serving in the other to keep the future of further narrative action alive, "mere appearances" are responsible in both these novels for keeping the narrative moving ahead in time. If the surface qualities of beauty and purely repetitive memory are linked to more essential qualities of "character" in Lucien and Julien, such qualities are excluded from representation by the very narratives they effect. From the point of view of their narrated "appearances"—the single point of view the narratives allow—these characters "in themselves" can only be considered, in the remarkable words of Lucien's "suicide" letter, to be "zeros."[74] In the terms posed by Kant with regard to the possibility of a critical epistemology, the narratives of *Illusions perdues* and *Le Rouge et le noir* force us to question whether, with regard to the "appearances" represented in the novel, "there *is* something that there appears."[75] Balzac and Stendhal employ the media of image and idea in character personifications of beauty and thinking—a separation of kinds of discur-

[74] Once removed (although, as it will turn out, only temporarily) from engagement in action, Lucien appears capable of real perception. In announcing his intended suicide to his sister he observes: "Certains êtres sont comme des zéros, il leur faut un chiffre qui les précède, et leur néant acquiert alors une valeur décuplé. Je ne puis acquérir de valeur que par un mariage avec une volonté forte, impitoyable" [Certain beings are like zeros, they need a figure which precedes them, and their nothingness acquires then a tenfold value. I cannot acquire value except through a marriage with a strong, pitiless will]. The external source of "will" Lucien regrets not having married here is Louise de Bargeton: "j'ai manqué ma vie" he continues, "en n'abandonnant pas Coralie pour elle" [I missed my life in not abandoning Coralie for her] (*Illusions perdues*, pp. 698–99). Thus, Lucien's correct perception of his own (lack of) character overlooks the factor of the immediate mutability of his narrative situation, for the far more powerful external force of *Trompe-la-mort* will momentarily return to, and conduct for, him the "life" he "failed" to lead. Vautrin, incidentally, will confirm Lucien's image of "a zero" in declaring the grounds for his own attraction to this now *suicide manqué*: "Savez-vous ce qui me plaît en vous? . . . Vous avez fait en vous-même table rase" (p. 713) ["Do you know what I like about you? . . . You have made in yourself *tabula rasa*"].

[75] See Chapter 1, footnote 96.

sive "appearances" reflected in the general conceptual distinction between poetry and philosophy—but they employ them *as* media, they represent them *as* representations, thus separating the "appearances" motivating and composing narrative from any independent reason of, or for, narration. Both authors seem to demonstrate that Lucien's individual predicament, glimpsed and articulated in an instant, is universally pervasive: all writers of narrative, in that they are authors of "appearances," are—as Kant concluded from the very definition of "appearances"—"not *free* to write what they think."

In the case of Herman Melville's *Pierre, Or the Ambiguities*, the reason for the very "appearance" of narrative form is criticized, as an author of novels seems to ask—and answer—the question of whether he is in fact "free" to narrate. The status of the representational medium of novels is probed in *Pierre* . . . : while the story it tells is purposefully overdetermined, the original representation from which it stems is conceived, crucially, to be "ambiguous," thus prompting overdetermination to take place. Rather than presented, as Kant proposes and the novels of Balzac and Stendhal effect, as the necessary, *a priori* given of cognition, the representations which compose narration are interrogated as to their own basis of meaning—whether verbal or visual, mimetic or allegorical in origin—and narrative literature is questioned as to its own necessity.

CHAPTER 6

THE DETERMINATION OF
PIERRE, OR THE AMBIGUITIES

In the story of Herman Melville's career as a writer, no work plays as central or determining a role as his *Pierre, Or the Ambiguities*. Written during the winter following the publication of *Moby Dick* in 1851, *Pierre* . . . is the single work Melville made known he hoped would turn his failing critical and financial fortunes around.[1] Vigorously and unilaterally denounced when published, it has since become best known for the forty year "silence" which succeeded it. For the appearance of *Pierre* . . . did effectively transform its author's fortunes— from the precarious condition of artistic promise to one of certain, or at least publically celebrated, failure. The reception of *Pierre* . . . , both in America and England, varied only in the kind and degree of abuse the novel drew. The prose style of the work was parodied to serve as the mouthpiece of its own attack, Melville's personal morality—as well as his mental sanity—were directly questioned, and his pen severely com-

---

[1] See Melville's letter of April 16, 1852, to his English publisher, cited in *The Writings of Herman Melville* (Evanston & Chicago: Northwestern University Press and the Newberry Library, 1971), VII:367. Melville takes objection to the financial terms which have been offered him, based on his previous sales record, for the publication of *Pierre* . . . : "I [am] impelled to decline those overtures upon the ground that my new book . . . [is] very much more calculated for popularity than anything you have yet published of mine—being a regular romance, with a mysterious plot to it, & stirring passions at work, and withall, representing a new & elevated aspect of American life. . . ." (Melville eventually broke with the same publisher when the latter demanded the right to alter *Pierre* . . . to better suit an English "audience" [VII:379].)

mended to an early grave.[2] With six published works behind him, the thirty-three-year-old Melville was himself turned, by the appearance of *Pierre* . . . , from a precocious into a passé literary phenomenon. From 1852 to his death in 1891, he wrote a small number of short narratives, including *Bartleby the Scrivener* (1853), *Benito Cereno* (1855), and the posthumously published *Billy Budd* (1924), as well as the overtly satirical and allegorical *Confidence Man* (1856). He also published by private means the poetic works *Battle-Pieces* (1866) and *Clarel* (1876) which, while currently read with interest,[3] have been generally recognized as falling far short of his fiction. As Melville's first novel to treat of "landed" subject matter, to make use, in the novelist's own words, of a popular narrative genre, "romance" (see footnote 1), as well as the traditional form of third-person narration, *Pierre* . . . represented for Melville in many ways a new narrative beginning: it was also essentially his last long narrative fiction. Melville, the former sailor who had written *Moby Dick*, the longest American work of its time, in less than two years, spent the last twenty years of his life employed neither at writing nor at sea

[2] See, reprinted in *Melville: The Critical Heritage*, ed. Watson G. Branch (London and Boston: Routledge & Kegan Paul, 1974), the review in *Godey's* (Oct. 1852), for an "off-hand imitation" of *Pierre* . . . , (p. 312) and, among others, those in *The American Whig Review* (Nov. 1852), *Literary World* (Aug. 1852), *Southern Literary Messenger* (Sept. 1852), *Albion* (Aug. 1852), *Graham's Magazine* (Oct. 1852), and *The Boston Post* (Aug. 1852), for such descriptive phrases as, "repulsive," "of no ordinary depravity," "outrages on the moral sense," "the most immoral *moral* of the story," "the diseased brain of a romancer," "mental malady," and "affectation & insanity . . . the craziest fiction extant," respectively (pp. 312, 314–22, 300–302, 304–307, 298–99, 313, and 294–96). See also the *Day Book* review (Sept. 1852), entitled, "Herman Melville Crazy" (cited in the Newberry Edition [VII:380–81]), which suggests that as "treatment" for his "derangement" the author be "secluded stringently from pen & ink."

[3] See in particular Robert Penn Warren's edition of the *Selected Poems of Herman Melville* (New York: Random House, 1967), including detailed textual analyses in his "Introduction" and "Notes"; William H. Shurr's chronological study, *The Mystery of Iniquity: Melville as Poet, 1857–1891* (Lexington: University of Kentucky Press, 1972); Vincent Kerny, *Herman Melville's Clarel* (Hamden, Conn.: Archon Books, 1973); and Edward H. Rosenberry, *Melville* (London: Routledge & Kegan Paul, 1979), pp. 131–54.

but, by a twist of personal history itself bordering on the literary, as a customs inspector for the city of New York. By one of the most infamous coincidences of literature and history, the author of *Pierre* . . . lived on after *Pierre* . . . to fulfill its critics' worst predictions.

The Melville "revival," roughly coincident with the centenary in 1919 of his birth, demonstrated, with rare exceptions,[4] as much confirmed disappointment with *Pierre* . . . as newly discovered enthusiasm for *Moby Dick*. Frank Jewett Mather's centenary *Review*, a milestone in the reevaluation of Melville, suggested that, "*Moby Dick* exhausted Melville's vein," the novelist "last[ing] just as long as his incomparable sea material, and no longer." *Pierre* . . . , written after "Melville had written himself out," was mentioned by Mather merely as a "literary curiosity worth reading."[5] Cesar Pavese, in the first major European assessment of Melville's work, compared the "miracle of *Moby Dick*" to the "dramatic failure of *Pierre*," explaining that while Melville's other flawed works may be viewed sympathetically as the necessary prefaces to *Moby Dick*, "there is no such excuse . . . for *Pierre*." Concerned to prove the premise that "even moral perfection cannot lead to good," and composed in a "convulsive . . . epileptic style," "the book really looks," Pavese memorably concludes, as "though it had been written by Ahab."[6] In his Introduction to the canonizing Norton Edition of Melville in 1938, Willard Thorp linked the "insecurity" of "style" pervading *Pierre* with our own inability "to apprehend the intended tone" of "any particular passage." He nevertheless recommended *Pierre* as "a foreshadowing book," but on grounds which directly con-

---

[4] See Arnold Bennett's singular praise of *Pierre* . . . in 1928: "I recommend it exclusively to the adventurous and the fearless. These, if the book does not defeat them, will rise up after recovering from their exhaustion, and thank me" (*The Recognition of Herman Melville: Selected Criticism Since 1846*, ed. Herschel Parker [Ann Arbor: University of Michigan Press, 1967], p. 187); and Charles Feidelson's more recent critical contention that, "Defective as it is, *Pierre*, not *Moby-Dick*, is the best vantage point for a general view of Melville's work (*Symbolism and American Literature* [Chicago: University of Chicago Press, 1953], p. 186).

[5] Reprinted in *The Recognition of Herman Melville*, pp. 164–65.

[6] *Ibid.*, pp. 200–201.

tradict both the novel's own hyperdevelopment of plot and Melville's subsequent, arrested development as writer: "It possesses the vigor and promise of greater things to come which any primitive displays."[7]

Dissatisfaction with *Pierre* . . . based on stylistic considerations has given way over the past few decades to its critical acceptance on moral terms. The theme of incest which immediately outraged Melville's contemporaries has come, ironically, in our own era to be viewed as the novel's major strength. Thus, Melville's description of the novel as a "romance" has been replaced by the appreciation of its "psychological realism."[8] Difficulties inhering in the novel's compositional style have been subordinated to the issue of its psychological probity, as if the psyche were itself somehow both faithfully representable in narrative fiction and incompatible with the demand for a consistent representational style. The most insightful departure from this critical retreat before the text of *Pierre* . . . into the amorphous territory of primal psychologism can be found in R. P. Blackmur's excellent "technical" consideration of the work as a *novel*, and of Melville in general as novelist: "The Craft of Herman Melville: A Putative Statement."[9] Blackmur's contention that Melville's writing was in fact never suited to the form of the novel, is most interesting not for its own negative thrust but for the important distinction he draws between the novel as "dramatic" form and the more properly "putative" form of narration, the form of abstract rather than

---

[7] *Ibid.* p. 217.

[8] Cf. William Emery Sedgewick, *Herman Melville: The Tragedy of Mind* (Cambridge, Mass.: Harvard University Press, 1944), pp. 138, 144–45; Lawrance Thompson, *Melville's Quarrel with God* (Princeton, N.J.: Princeton University Press, 1952), pp. 250ff.; Harry Levin, *The Power of Blackness: Hawthorne, Poe, Melville* (New York: Alfred A. Knopf, 1970), p. 184; Richard Brodhead, *Hawthorne, Melville, and the Novel* (Chicago: Chicago University Press, 1976), p. 171; Brian Higgens and Herschel Parker, "The Flawed Grandeur of *Pierre*," in *New Perspectives on Melville*, ed. Faith Pullin (Edinburgh: The University Press, 1978), pp. 171ff.; and Rosenberry, *Melville*, pp. 93ff.

[9] Reprinted in *Melville: A Collection of Critical Essays*, ed. Richard Chase (Englewood Cliffs, N.J.: Prentice-Hall, 1962), pp. 75–90 (p. 76).

representational thinking, allegory.[10] Asserting that Melville "added nothing to the novel as a form . . . left nothing . . . unlike most great writers of fiction . . . to those that followed him . . . ," Blackmur states of *Pierre* . . . , as compared to *Moby Dick*: "Melville had never predominantly relied upon the means of the novelist, had never attempted to use more than the overt form of the novel, until he attempted to compose *Pierre*."[11] Melville, Blackmur argues, was "condemned," in writing as a novelist, to "employ conventions of character and form in which he obviously and almost avowedly did not believe . . . conventions he used for dramatic purposes not only as if they were unreal but also as if they were artificial."[12] As opposed to representational, plot-intensive narrative, Blackmur continues, "Melville . . . preferred the nondramatic mode . . . he did not write of characters in action; he employed the shells of stock characters, heightened or resounding only by the eloquence of the author's voice, to witness, illustrate, decorate, and often as it happened to impede and stultify an idea in motion. This is, if you like, the mode of allegory—the highest form of the putative imagination, in which things are *said* but need not be *shown* to be other than they seem, and thus hardly require to *be* much of anything." Because neither Melville, nor "anyone in nineteenth century America or since," was "equipped" with the "complete and stable body of beliefs" upon which "successful allegory" depends, his "allegorical devices and patterns had to act *as if* they were agents in a novel," thereby "compelling" us "to judge Melville at his most allegorical yet formally as a novelist."[13]

The "putative imagination," following Blackmur, expresses itself in "the mode of allegory," for in allegory, imagination is subordinated to thought, just as objective vision of being is subordinated to a conceptualization of objects in language: "things are *said* but need not be *shown* to be other than they seem." Melville must be regarded as a necessarily failed, or in-

---

[10] *Ibid.*, p. 75.
[11] *Ibid.*, pp. 75–76.
[12] *Ibid.*, pp. 78–79.
[13] *Ibid.*, p. 80.

effective, novelist in as much as he was a successful allegorist, for in novels, most especially, there can be almost no "saying" without a being "shown." Representational, as opposed to allegorical, fiction demands that we "see" what is "said," and through *both* modes of cognition know equally what "things are" and what "they seem." Thus *Pierre . . .* "fails" as a novel because, while it is Melville's most novelistic endeavor, it is also, as Blackmur writes, Melville "at his most allegorical," which is to say, his least representational.

Yet the precise significance of the allegory *Pierre . . .* tells remains unclear.[14] What does the novel "say" that it does not "show"? What does the novel *mean* to say as an allegory that makes what it "shows" us, as a story, "seem" so flawed? A closer "look" at the composition of *Pierre . . .* may indicate why the allegory we "see" represented must indeed make for rather bizarre reading as a story, while comprising at the same time the most novellike of Melville's works. For, it can be argued, the "allegory" of *Pierre . . .* , rather than abstractly imaging a pure, putative "idea," is precisely the allegory of the necessity of the novel: the nonallegorical. *Pierre . . .* is not an allegory which also happens "technically" to take the form of a novel; it is a novel which tells the story of why there are novels: the story of the necessity of a literary form which would allow us to "see" what is "said," to know not ideally but discursively *and* by being "shown."

Pierre Glendinning, the last male descendant of a pure American "pedigree," grandson of heroes in the War for Independence, and sole heir to the considerable Glendinning estate, loves his fiancée, the neighboring Lucy Tartar, and is the "noble" apple of his mother's eye.[15] Pierre's "perfect father," the absent idol of both mother and son, died when Pierre was

[14] Blackmur, while stressing the novel's allegorical nature, never states the nature of its allegorical meaning, asserting instead that "the real weight of the book—what it was really about: tragedy by unconsidered virtue—was left for the author's digressions and soliloquies to carry as it could . . ." (p. 83).

[15] *The Writings of Herman Melville*, VII:11–12, 19. All quotations following are from that edition.

twelve; as the novel opens he is nineteen.[16] Lucy, the "beautiful" and "docile" daughter of a friend of his father's, enjoys
the full approval of Pierre's unnaturally youthful mother, who
in turn enjoys the "courteous lover-like adoration of Pierre."[17]
Mary Glendinning calls her son, "brother"; Pierre addresses
his mother as "sister Mary":[18] the two carry out together a
mentally and phsycially flirtatious "courtship" perpetuated by
its own conscious, inconsummate character. The play of love
between "sister" and "brother" can be enjoyed repeatedly and
without reflection, since, the narrator explains, it is "not to be
limited in duration by that climax which is so fatal to ordinary
love." Thus it may seem, the narrator suggests, "to realize"
representations painted to us on earth of the infinite passion
enjoyed in heaven:

> This softened spell which still wheeled the mother and son
> in one orbit of joy, seemed a glimpse of the glorious pos-
> sibility that the divinest of those emotions, which are in-
> cident to the sweetest season of love, is capable of an in-
> definite translation into many of the less signal relations
> of our many chequered life. In a detached and individual
> way, it seemed almost to realize here below the sweet
> dreams of those religious enthusiasts, who paint to us a
> Paradise to come, when etherealized from all drosses and
> stains, the holiest passion of man shall unite all kindreds
> and climes in one circle of pure and unimpairable de-
> light.[19]

The overdeterminantly incestuous potential of this mother-son
relation is made to take on the "painted," or allegorical, significance of "pure," because totally *in*determinate, paradisal
"delight." As long as they remain acted out rather than acted
upon, the "emotions" which maintain the "spell" of incestuous attraction pose the "glorious possibility" of their own
"indefinite translation." An endless incestuous "courtship"
would be like love without a proper object and thus also with-

[16] *Ibid.*, VII:19, 68–69.
[17] *Ibid.*, VII:20, 16.
[18] *Ibid.*, VII:17–18.
[19] *Ibid.*, VII:16.

out the objective status of impropriety. Yet if incest appears "capable of indefinite translation" into any number and kind of human "relations," why do Pierre and his mother first translate themselves into "sister" and "brother"? Earlier in the novel, as the narrator had begun to describe Pierre, he stated openly, as if merely restating a truism, the fundamentally incestuous nature of all "fraternal love": that "delicious . . . feeling" experienced by every brother for his sister:

> So perfect to Pierre had long seemed the illuminated scroll of his life thus far, that only one hiatus was discoverable by him in that sweetly-writ manuscript. A sister had been omitted from the text. He mourned that so delicious a feeling as fraternal love had been denied him. Nor could the fictitious title, which he so often lavished upon his mother, at all supply the absent reality. This emotion was most natural; and the full cause and reason of it even Pierre did not at that time entirely appreciate. For surely a gentle sister is the second best gift to a man; and it is first in point of occurrence; for the wife comes after. He who is sisterless, is as a bachelor before his time. For much that goes to make up the deliciousness of a wife, already lies in the sister.[20]

In stating Pierre's desire to complete the "text" of his life with a sister, and in defining a brother's love for his sister as the model for any later marital relation—so that the advent of sexual consummation in marriage will itself seem like a belated enactment of incest—the narrator both predetermines the course of his own text and describes that text to be determined by certain universal truths of life. A man without a sister is "a bachelor before his time"; thus Pierre, in wishing himself a sister, essentially experiences the desire to marry. A man with a sister will marry for the most part "what already lies in the sister"; thus Pierre, in that he is not "already" married, could not cease to be a "bachelor" merely by taking a wife. Pierre will only make up for the "hiatus" in his life's "manuscript" by marrying the very textual model for marrying he misses: the

[20] *Ibid.*, VII:7.

"second best gift" noted however to take temporal precedence over the first, just as a copy must be preceded by an earlier "point of occurrence," the form of its original. What the narrator states as a general truth is that marriages are made not providentially in heaven, but merely to fulfill their own prior determination as incest. Or, the "heaven" in which they are made is, according to the narrator of *Pierre* . . . , precisely the "Paradise" described to be "realized" by inconsummate incest itself. While the determination of marriage as an imitation of incest is presented as a general rule holding no less for Pierre, the objective means of fulfilling that determination have been "omitted" from Pierre's "text." Thus the text of *Pierre* . . . , if it is to proceed with the story "of his life," must present the single plot by which his premature bachelorhood could come to an end. Following the narrator's own reflections on the matter, the only marriage permitted Pierre must also be the most taboo. *In order to* marry at all, Pierre must marry not only the copy of the "feeling . . . denied him," but its "omitted" original. He must at once marry *and* commit incest by marrying his sister.

This is, admittedly, a rather large dose of overdetermination for any literary context, let alone the opening of a novel whose subsequent narrative development will rely largely upon the principles of dramatic confrontation and suspense. What is most astonishing, however, is that this determination is itself admitted: proceeding deductively from statements given to hold universally to their specific application to the particular, the narrator spells out in advance, and with wholly coherent, logical consistency, the perversity which is both unmistakable in, and indispensable to, his plot. That mother and son should name each other "sister" and "brother" seems, in light of the narrator's universalizing observations, a kind of superstructural detail no more decisively significant than the accoutrements of Mrs. Glendinning's "toilette," or the contents of the breakfast for which she is dressing when the two are first reported to exchange those names.[21] The overt flirtations of mother and son, their incestuously charged appellations ap-

[21] *Ibid.*, VII:14.

pear, after the narrator's admission of the determining condition of incestuous "feeling," like flashy window dressing for a proposition upon which we have all, inevitably, already been sold. An interpretation of Pierre's story in Freudian terms is thus, of course, rendered no less superfluous, for the narrator not only foresees the Freudian categories for understanding narration but embraces and exploits their aspect as forms of determinism, starting, so to speak, with the "interpretation" and then proceeding to weave the "dream." Furthermore, like the Freudian analyst responsibly resigned to the effective limitations of the therapeutic, or hermeneutic, session, the narrative forewarns against the very desire it indicates to be determining: what "Pierre did not then know," the narrator continues, is "that if there be any thing a man might well pray against, that thing is the responsive gratification of some of the devoutest prayers of his youth."[22] The precision and severity of this statement on the part of the narrator convey the import, and fatalistic flavor, of many of Freud's own darkest conclusions, for the prayers of youth best prayed against, according to the dicta of pyschoanalysis, are the specifically incestuous ambitions for which we are never too young. It denies itself any possible psychoanalytic function, however, in that rather than marking the hard-earned terminus of an analytic process, it is offered at the very opening of the novel and thus makes the endeavor to analyze Pierre's, or any other psyche, seem gratuitous. Ignorance itself, what "Pierre did not then know," is here concluded by the narrator to be yet another predetermined dimension of the very determinism he is just beginning, in the representation of Pierre's particular story, to describe.

The plot of *Pierre* . . . thus presents, from its inception, a kind of determinism as universal and unavoidable as the arbitrary biological fact of "having" or not "having" siblings, not to speak of the desire to transform that accident of "having" through the action metaphorically referred to as the state of "physical possession," or the belief of being possessed oneself by the confines of Freud's own four-sided metaphor, "the family romance." The plot of *Pierre* . . . , like incest itself, it might

---

[22] *Ibid.*, VII:7.

be suggested, seems no more than a dramatized metaphor for the very desire for overdetermination. Yet the *title* of *Pierre* . . . is not "Pierre," but *Pierre, Or the Ambiguities*, and perhaps no title of a modern fiction has figured less determinately in the considerations of its critics. While the word "ambiguity" appears in some grammatical form—nominal, adjectival, or adverbial—more than a dozen times in the first "half" of the novel alone (the first thirteen of the twenty-six subdivided chapters entitled "Books"), it is a concept granted no special significance, when mentioned at all, in virtually the entire corpus of the novel's criticism.[23] Interpretations of *Pierre* . . . have not neglected but more simply not even noted "the Ambiguities" named in apposition to "Pierre" for reasons which themselves are not in the least ambiguous. No elusive, enormous whale and accompanying speculations upon its definedly enig-

---

[23] Cf. Mather, in *The Recognition of Herman Melville*, p. 164; Matthieson's brief mention of "ambiguities" in relation to the incest theme in *Hamlet*, in *American Renaissance* (New York: Oxford University Press, 1941), p. 477; Feidelson's emphasis upon "dualism" rather than ambiguousness with regard to what he takes to be "the central action" of *Pierre* . . . , "the effort to realize the world . . . epitomized in the effort to write a novel" (p. 191). The "ambiguous" portrait, upon which the present argument focuses, and which is closer, both physically and conceptually, to the "center" of the novel, is unusually mentioned by Feidelson (p. 193), but only insofar as it relates directly to the issue of Pierre's authorship, itself arising comparatively late in the novel. Edgar A. Dryden, in *Melville's Thematics of Form* (Baltimore: The Johns Hopkins University Press, 1968), departs slightly from Feidelson in seeing *Pierre* . . . as "a satiric appraisal of Melville's own career as a writer, of the American literary scene in general, and finally, of the nature of fiction" (p. 129); while the concept of ambiguity figures prominently in Dryden's insightful analyses of Melville's other major works, it is most strangely missing from his discussion of the single work named for it. John Seelye, in "*Pierre*: The Structure of Ambiguity," in his *Melville: The Ironic Diagram* (Evanston, Ill.: Northwestern University Press, 1970), pp. 74–89, incorrectly equates the term "antithesis"—central to his mappings of polar oppositions throughout Melville—with "ambiguity," substituting it for the latter in his study of "oppositional structure" in the novel and making no mention of the "ambiguities" named in the novel itself. No reference to "ambiguities" in any form is made by Sedgewick, *Herman Melville*; Thompson, *Melville's Quarrel*; Martin Stern, *The Fine Hammered Steel of Herman Melville* (Urbana: University of Illnois Press, 1968); Rowland A. Sherrill, *The Prophetic Melville* (Athens: University of Georgia Press, 1979), among others.

matic "whiteness"; no hired scrivener who coolly states enragingly that he "would prefer not to" write meaningfully; no beautiful embodiment of unadulterated honesty crucified by an embodiment not of evil but of justice; no expressly cryptical host of characters cast, like a medieval ship of fools, upon the protean waters of false "confidence"; in short, none of the clearly thematized, and critically canonized, "ambiguities" characterizing Melville's most celebrated works are in evidence in his critically disputed *Pierre, Or the Ambiguities*. Instead, *Pierre* . . . presents the immediate inconvenience of being named in part for the concept of "ambiguities" itself. The self-determining story of the desire for a sister, further overdetermined by the narrator's intrusive reflections upon the universality of that desire, and the apparently real, historically determining effect of writing *Pierre* . . . upon Melville as an author, are all, of course, suggestive of anything but the ambiguous. In fact, *Pierre, Or the Ambiguities* lends itself so readily to its understanding in terms of unambiguous determinism that it is no wonder its readers automatically enact the choice presented in its titular "Or" by interpreting a work they refer to solely, and with unintended accuracy, as "Pierre." Whether in the name of his troubled psyche, the turbulent style of its representation, or his own equally disturbed attempts to write professionally, "Pierre" has been preferred by far, as topic of interpretation, over "the Ambiguities."

While the meaning of the word speaks against our asking exactly "what" these unscrutinized "ambiguities" are, the frequent inclusion of the term within the work leads us, if only by force of the repetition encountered in reading, at least to note "where" they are. Of the twenty odd times it appears in some form in the text, "ambiguity" is used in a few instances to describe the status of an unsettled or undetermined relationship.[24] In no instance does the term occur in reference to any

---

[24] A surprise encounter between Lucy, her brothers, and the visiting Pierre, randomly resulting in the formal announcment of their engagement, is said to have "accelerated a before ambiguous and highly incommendable state of affairs between the now affianced lovers" (VII:29); when Pierre, "chancing to encounter Lucy," tells her of the mysterious "face" he has seen, his fiancée is said to be kept awake that night by "wild, Beethoven sounds of distant, waltz-

of the actions of dubious *moral* status in the plot, including not
only incest, but possible incestuous polygamy, religious blas-
phemy, artistic profiteering, philosphical sophistry, murder,
and finally, double suicide. More than half of the instances in
which the word appears refer not to plot-related action, nor to
any personal relation at all, but instead to a single, visual image. What is principally named "ambiguous" in this heavily
melodramatic, stylistically and eventfully tortured tale, is, of
all unlikely images, a "smile": a facial expression which does
not take part in the dramatic "action" of the story, in that it
itself is not represented as living, but *said* by the narrator to be
visible in a nondiscursive image, a picture. The picture is a portrait of Pierre's deceased father; the "smile" is what "looked"
at Pierre "frankly and cheerfully . . . and yet again, a little ambiguously," whenever Pierre became "speculative" about the
meaning of that expression, "thinking, and thinking, and
thinking, and thinking. . . ."[25] The portrait was painted before
Pierre was born,[26] at a time when, according to Pierre's aunt—
who, after his father's death, made him a secret present of the
portrait—his "father was always in motion," and "it was hard
to get him to stand still."[27] For at that time, Pierre's father frequently visited a beautiful emigrant from France. So frequent
were his visits that his friends suspected he courted and was
tempted to marry the girl—an idea from which they soon
"eandeavoured to dissuade him," since, most unlike the Glendinnings, aristocrats of the American democracy by unblem-
ished tradition, "no one . . . certainly knew her history." While
rumoured to be of "noblest birth," she remained fundamentally "a foreigner" not only to America but, universally, to the
harmony of history and countryside represented in particular

---

ing melodies, as of ambiguous fairies dancing on the heath" (VII:54); when
Pierre's cousin, Glendinning Stanly, with whom he formerly exchanged letters
of "boy-love" ("which only comes short, by one degree, of the sweetest sentiment entertained between the sexes"), sends him gifts of sweets at the event of
his "betrothment . . . to Lucy," Pierre, "in certain little roguish ambiguities
begged leave, on the ground of cloying, to return him inclosed by far the
greater portion of his present . . ." (VII:216, 220).
[25] *Writings of Melville*, VII:80.
[26] *Ibid.*, VII:74.
[27] *Ibid.*, VII:75.

by the pastoral Glendinnings. As a refugee from her own nation's revolution, her lineage did not lie in the American, nor
any longer in any other, landscape like an unsoiled yet naturally rooted, open and organic book. Thus, when Pierre's father later "discontinued his visits" and the young lady disappeared, it was generally agreed she "would not have made so
suitable and excellent a match . . . as [Pierre's] mother after-
ward did."[28]

The portrait was painted, however, when Pierre's father had
just returned from one of "his daily visits"; the painter, a
cousin of Pierre's father, had wished to "catch some sort of
corresponding expression" on canvas of the state of mind
those visits induced.[29] He asked Pierre's father to tell him
"something of the emigrants" in order to "get [his] thoughts
running that supposed wooing way." Thus, as Pierre's aunt explained to him, "by many little cunning shifts and contriv-
ances, cousin Ralph kept your father there sitting, and sitting
in the chair, rattling and rattling away, and so self-forgetful
too, that he never heeded that all the while sly cousin Ralph
was painting and painting just as fast as ever he could; and
only making believe to laugh at your father's wit; in short,
cousin Ralph was stealing his portrait."[30]

Pierre's father is painted "sitting and sitting" while "rattling
and rattling": unconsciously, physically still rather than in
motion. What is "moving" instead is his mind, expressing itself verbally: a mind at once "*self*-forgetful" as it is occupied
by its own wit. A self which, in speaking, forgets itself, is thus
the "stolen" subject of the portrait being painted, and the appearance it takes, as a "still," visual image, is one which combines statis *with* motion, external physical determinacy with
the internal "running" of "thoughts," the visible with the ver-

[28] *Ibid.*, VII:75–76.
[29] *Ibid.*, VII:77.
[30] When Pierre immediately takes objection to the term, "stealing," his Aunt
responds that cousin Ralph instead "slyly picked" his father's "portrait"—a
modification in fact as additionally objectionable as it is precise, for it indicates, as was indeed the case with Pierre's father, a subject of theft who acts as
unwitting accomplice to his own deception (VII:77).

bal: an "ambiguous smile."[31] The "corresponding expression" of a self which speaks while oblivious of how it looks will correspond neither positively to the familiar, physical appearance of that self nor negatively—as a nonrepresentational, allegorical image—to the content of thoughts being verbally expressed. A pictorial image which portrays neither the mimetic nor the allegorical exclusively, in that it represents both the visual and the conceptual, can only strike the mind *as* it strikes the naked eye, that is, as "ambiguous."

Pierre's father, whose own eye could never be naked of mental preconceptions in viewing this particular representation, guesses instinctively at its existence without ever seeing it; indeed, he "never knew for certain, whether there was such a painting in the world." Nevertheless, he orders his cousin "to destroy it," or at least to "keep it out of sight."[32] As the subject in which thought and physical appearance were allowed by its own "self-forgetting" to intersect, Pierre's father has no desire to look that forgotten "self" in the face. Having forgotten himself for a moment, just long enough to be "stolen" in the form of a static image, he now imagines that self to be universally externalized: anyone who looks at the portrait will not only know him but know, *like* him, its undisguised and specific meaning.

Yet the meaning of the portrait (for which *Pierre* . . . is named)[33] is specifically not specific but "ambiguous." Or at least it appears "ambiguous" to the eye of a beholder who had already idealized a certain image of its subject, Pierre. When Pierre stares in private at the "strange" painting, comparing it in his mind with the "larger and more expansive portrait" of his father prominently displayed in the Glendinnings' "great drawing-room"—a portrait painted for public viewing "at the particular desire" of Pierre's mother, who alone "could never abide" the earlier work—it "seems" to him, the narrator relates, that its "ambiguous" expression expresses itself by

[31] *Ibid.*, VII:83.

[32] *Ibid.*, VII:78.

[33] "Pierre" and *Pierre* . . . , for the son here is also the father's "namesake" (VII:73).

speaking directly to him.[34] The central conceptual articulation of "the ambiguities" in the novel occurs as Pierre *sees* what the portrait "seems to say." In a remarkable reversal of conventional poetic apostrophe, the inanimate picture addresses its living viewer, "as [Pierre] look[s] on," by name:

—Pierre, believe not the drawing-room painting; that is not thy father; or, at least, is not *all* thy father. Consider in thy mind, Pierre, whether we two paintings may not make only one. Faithful wives are ever over-fond of a certain imaginary image of their husbands; and faithful widows are ever over-reverential to a certain imagined ghost of that same imagined image, Pierre. Look again, I am thy father as he more truly was. In mature life, the world overlays and varnishes us, Pierre; the thousand proprieties and polished finenesses and grimaces intervene, Pierre; then, we, as it were, abdicate ourselves, and take unto us another self, Pierre; in youth we *are*, Pierre, but in age we *seem*. Look again. I am thy real father, so much the more truly, as thou thinkest thou recognizest me not, Pierre. . . . Consider this strange, ambiguous smile, Pierre; more narrowly regard this mouth. Behold, what is this too ardent and, as it were, unchastened light in these eyes, Pierre? I am thy father, boy. There was once a certain, oh, but too lovely young Frenchwoman, Pierre. Youth is hot, and temptation strong, Pierre; and in the minutest moment momentous things are irrevocably done, Pierre; and Time sweeps on, and the thing is not always carried down by its stream, but may be left stranded on its bank. . . . Look again. Doth thy mother dislike me for naught? . . . Consider. Is there no little mystery here? Probe a little, Pierre! . . . Look, do I not smile?—yes, and with an unchangeable smile; and thus I have unchangeably smiled for many long years gone by, Pierre. Oh it is a permanent smile! . . . even thus, in thy father's later life, when his body may have been in grief, still—hidden away in Aunt Dorothea's secretary—I thus smiled as before; and just so I'd smile were I now hung up in the deepest dungeon of

[34] *Ibid.*, VII:82–83.

the Spanish Inquisition, Pierre; though suspended in outer darkness, still would I smile with this smile, though then not a soul should be near. Consider; *for a smile is the chosen vehicle of all ambiguities*, Pierre. When we would deceive, we smile; when we are hatching any nice little artifice, Pierre; only just a little gratifying our own sweet little appetites, Pierre; then watch us, and out comes the odd little smile. . . . Oh, a strange sort of story, that, thy dear old Aunt Dorothea once told thee, Pierre. . . . Probe, probe a little—see—there seems one little crack there, Pierre—a wedge, a wedge. Something ever comes of all persistent inquiry; we are not so continually curious for nothing, Pierre; not for nothing, do we so intrigue and become wily diplomatists, and glozers with our own minds, Pierre. . . .[35]

The "ambiguous smile" which repeatedly bids Pierre, "look again," is itself "permanent"; this grinning appearance of "the chosen vehicle of all ambiguities" bears as little relationship to the frustrated attempts at its interpretation as it does to the temporal limitations within which those attempts are made. The painted portrait has smiled in the past, when the particular "body" it represents "may have been in grief," continues to smile in the present, although that "body," Pierre's father, exists no longer, and so will go on smiling when there are no extant bodies to view it, when neither Pierre nor any other "soul should be near." Indeed the "ambiguous smile" seems to outlive Pierre even as it outstares him, repeatedly providing the object upon which Pierre's consciousness fixes until, by force of concentration, it loses consciousness of itself, "thinking, and thinking, and thinking, and thinking, till by-and-by all thoughts were blurred, and at last there were no thoughts at all."[36] While itself a static visual image, the smile "seems to say" that it is the physical vehicle for representing a discrete and fleeting, ambiguous moment in the mind. It is also, however, the vehicle chosen over and over by Pierre for the recurrent, nonprogressive process of mentally considering "all am-

[35] *Ibid.*, VII:83–84; my emphasis.
[36] *Ibid.*, VII:80.

biguities": a process which exhausts and doubles back upon itself rather than developing linearly through time. That process can be noted—as it is here by the narrator—analyzed and described, but could not in itself be more antithetical to its immediate, written context: the causal and diachronic narrative form of the novel. Nor does it provide an opening, through the reflex of self-consciousness, for a satiric or metacritical, parodic or "antinovel," novel; there is nothing on the order of intellectual amusement, enlightenment, or experiment about Pierre's repeated encounters with "the ambiguities." The narrator relates their recurrence not in terms of an intellectual development of any kind, but, on the contrary, by way of reference to the independent temporal cycle of the changing seasons—seasons, furthermore, made to seem essentially *un*-changed in changing by virtue of an exclusively visual, physical likeness between them:[37] "Thus sometimes . . . either when the hushed mansion was banked round by the thick-fallen December snows, or banked round by the immovable white August moonlight . . . thus sometimes stood Pierre before the portrait of his father."[38] The alternation of consciousness and unconsciousness in Pierre's mind is further described as being itself as void of consciousness as the precipitations and clearings occurring suddenly in nature:

> Thus sometimes stood Pierre . . . unconsciously throwing himself open to all those ineffable hints and ambiguities, and undefined half-suggestions, which now and then peo-

[37] Melville, an avid reader of Goethe, seems to offer his own version of "Dauer im Wechsel" here: his description of the seasons most strikingly resembles the "seeming appearance" of nonprogressive time represented by Goethe in the *Wahlverwandtschaften*. Melville's narrator temporally relates events devoid of temporal development on the basis of a single, purely superficial, or graphic, characteristic they share. By the same figural device Goethe's narrator "pardons" the "madness" of perceiving events in precisely that light, i.e., as if unmediated and unaffected by intervening time (see Chap. 2, footnote 52). The one narrative, an allegory of novels, in which novels themselves will later be overtly condemned, includes within it a figural description that seems to eliminate the essential diachronic dimension of the novel; the other, self-consciously called a "Roman," uses such a description to explain the atemporal "delusion" of relations experienced nondiachronically, i.e., non-novelistically.

[38] *Ibid.*, VII:84.

ple the soul's atmosphere, as thickly as in a soft, steady snow-storm, the snow-flakes people the air. Yet as often starting from these reveries and trances, Pierre would regain the assured element of consciously bidden and self-propelled thought; and then in a moment the air is cleared, not a snow-flake descended. ... Nor did the streams of these reveries seem to leave any conscious sediment in his mind; they were so light and so rapid, that they rolled their own alluvial along; and seemed to leave all Pierre's thought-channels as clean and dry as though never any alluvial stream had rolled there at all.[39]

Like the disappearance of the last snowflake in a storm, or the last drop of water from a channel already dry, the precise moment at which Pierre's "mind" turns from unconscious back to "consciously bidden . . . thought" cannot be identified. Its very occurrence can at best be hypothesized in retrospect, since no telling trace of the preceding storm or stream remains. The moment of a change in mind, itself symbolic of the constitutive conception of time as the necessary condition and universal vehicle defining all change, is narrated to be necessarily occluded here. In the meantime, however, the "ambiguous smile" itself remains "unchangeable," and as long as it does—which is indeed longer than it may ever be seen to by any mortal eye—it will continue to provide its viewer, as it continually "seems to say," with the vehicle both for being "continually curious" and for concluding provisionally and repeatedly, or in the absence of reaching a conclusion, that one *is* "continually curious for nothing."

"Nothing" is, however, specifically not the conclusion to which a particular perusal—that which occasioned this narration of Pierre's habitual perusals—of the portrait leads. "The ambiguities" were introduced not as a phenomenon in and of themselves but in order to explain a moment in which Pierre does *not* return from "unconsciously throwing himself open to all those . . . ambiguities" to the "assured element of consciously bidden and self-propelled thought." That moment, singled out from all other recurrent encounters with the

[39] *Ibid.*, VII:84–85.

painting's temporally unlimited smile, is called by the narrator, still speaking in the past tense of narration, "*now!*"[40] "*Now!*" is a moment defined by an addition to Pierre's vision of the portrait: specifically, in terms of the novel's story, the receipt of Isabel's letter claiming him as her brother; generally, in terms of the novel's allegory, the addition of the verbal to the visual. A visual representation which, while it always remains itself "seemed" not itself—a mute visible image—but instead to speak, seems "now" to Pierre to be spoken for by the verbal proper. The appearance—itself a succinct definition of the ambiguous—of speaking in being seen, and of speaking not, per Lessing's classic distinction between the plastic and verbal arts, of a transformative dramatic climax to come, but, perpetually and permanently, of a mobility which itself will never change, is an "ambiguity" apparently resolved for Pierre by a single instance of revealing speech. Again, in terms of the story of the novel, Isabel's letter completes the "text" of Pierre's life by filling in the "omitted" words, *and* promising to provide the "absent reality," of "a sister." In terms of the allegory of the novel, however, it completes the visual by effectively separating from it its own representation of the verbal. Understood by Pierre to explain the speaking appearance of "ambiguities," Isabel's letter removes "those ineffable hints . . . and undefined half-suggestions" from his father's smile. It renders the painted representation for the first time purely visual by externally articulating and taking the place of its unarticulated verbal meaning. The addition of the verbal here serves, in other words, to *deverbalize* the visual. The letter provides the hitherto ambiguously speaking painting with a single, determined, or unambiguous meaning. The narrator explains:

> But now, *now!* —Isabel's letter read: swift as the first light that slides from the sun, Pierre saw all preceding ambiguities, all mysteries ripped open as if with a keen sword. . . . Now his remotest infantile reminiscences . . . , the mystical midnight suggestions of the portrait itself; and, above all, his mother's intuitive aversion, all, all overwhelmed him with reciprocal testimonies.

[40] *Ibid.*, VII:85.

And now, by irresistible intuitions, all that had been inexplicably mysterious to him in the portrait, all that had been inexplicably familiar in the face, most magically these now coincided; the merriness of the one not inharmonious with the mournfulness of the other, but by some ineffable correlativeness, they reciprocally identified each other, and, as it were, melted into each other, and thus interpenetratingly uniting, presented lineaments of an added supernaturalness.

On all sides, the physical world of solid objects now slidingly displaced itself from around him and he floated into an ether of visions; and, starting to his feet with clenched hands and outstaring eyes at the transfixed face in the air, he ejaculated that wonderful verse from Dante, descriptive of the two mutually absorbing shapes in the Inferno:

> "Ah! how dost thou change,
> Agnello! See! thou art not double now,
> Nor only one!"[41]

As "all preceding ambiguities" are seen to be "ripped open," the "mysterious" and "familiar," to coincide and "reciprocally identify each other," the identity of habitually unambiguous surroundings becomes unclear. In this moment of verbal illumination, "swift as the first light that slides from the sun," "the physical world of solid objects" is not brought into sharper focus but "slidingly displaced." Able "now" to outstare the smiling painting, Pierre's ability to see the external world is dissolved in "an ether of visions." His father's previously mobile, speaking face appears transfixed by the external, verbal determination of its meaning. The determinate vision of external objects is, at the same time, replaced by a new tendency on the part of the viewer toward verbalism. What is immediately born of "ambiguities . . . ripped open" is not empirical or epistemological certainty but a part of a recognizable, complete, and historically determined, "text." The first words "ejaculated" by the newly enlightened Pierre—and the last words of this centrally enlightening Book of *Pierre* . . .—are lines di-

---

[41] *Ibid.*

rectly taken from a familiar work of literature. Pierre is said to quote "that wonderful verse" from the twenty-fifth Canto of the *Inferno* in which two condemned sinners are described to undergo, physically and visibly, what language alone can conceptually effect: the transformation of their separate forms into a single, unnatural figure.[42] These lines from Dante constitute the first directly quoted literary passage in the novel; later reproductions of original "text" within *Pierre* . . . serve primarily to cast doubt on the serious significance of texts themselves: the scrap, found by Pierre, of Plinlimmon's fanciful pamphlet on time, and the "title page" designed by a pair of ex-clothiers for a commerical volume of Pierre's scant and spurious verse. Subsequent to these quoted lines, whose subject matter is a verbally effected, bodily transformation, the text of *Pierre* . . . is transformed into a corpus of literary allusions. In Book V, "Misgivings and Preparatives," beginning immediately after this quotation, Pierre "reverses the picture on the wall": "for him the fair structure of the world must, in some then unknown way, be entirely rebuilded again." Finally, the portrait he had secretly studied for so long is removed from the wall by Pierre in the attempt "to banish the least trace of his altered father"—the image of his father now appearing to him visibly changed by its attribution with a distinct, discursive meaning.[43] Once the portrait is spoken for and thus itself reduced of speech, the question it had formerly asked, of *what* it represents, is replaced by that of *how* to actively respond to its meaning: "To a less enthusiastic heart than Pierre's the foremost question in respect to Isabel which would have presented itself, would have been, *What* must I do? . . . such a question never presented itself to Pierre. . . . But if the object was plain, not so the path to it. *How* must I do it? was a problem for which at first there seemed no chance of solution."[44] Pierre is to find "the surest solution of perplexities" not through discursive speculation but in "subservience," the narrator states,

---

[42] See Canto XXV, ll.68–69: "Omè, Agnel, come ti muti! / Vedi che già non se' né due né uno" (Dante, *Inferno*, trans. and intro. Allen Mandelbaum [New York: Bantam, 1980], p. 228).

[43] *Writings of Melville*, VII:87.

[44] *Ibid.*, VII:87–88.

to a controlling notion of verbal *plot*: "the god-like dictation of events themselves"; he trusts "the coming interview with Isabel" to "unerringly inspire him."[45] But "how," we may ask on the other hand, will the discourse of the novel respond to its own determination of plot? We already know, from the overdetermined origins of his story, "how" Pierre will do "what" he "must." How the novel will proceed, in the absence of its central ambiguous image, is "inspired" instead by literature itself. For Pierre's "misgivings and preparatives" of mind are narrated in what is perhaps the most densely allusive, "poetic" language to be found in any work of nineteenth-century American fiction. Poetic allusion begins most unmistakably with a prose rendering of the major romantic, universalizing metaphor for sublime revelation: the "flashes" of "Visionary power" and "Imagination" in Wordsworth's *Prelude* (published just before *Pierre . . .* in 1850), closely followed by further images and formulations of vision from that poem, including "the blasted tree" Wordsworth associates with his own father's death (Bk XII), and the notion of a "sustaining," unreverting state of imaginative enlightenment upon which it concludes (Bk XIV):

> If it be the sacred province and—by the wisest, deemed—the inestimable compensation of the heavier woes, that they both purge the soul of gay-hearted errors and replenish it with a saddened truth; that holy office is not so much accomplished by any covertly inductive reasoning process, whose original motive is received from the particular affliction; as it is the magical effect of the admission into man's inmost spirit of a before unexperienced and wholly inexplicable element, which like electricity suddenly received into any sultry atmosphere of the dark, in all directions splits itself into nimble lances of purifying light . . . so that objects which before, in the uncertainty of the dark, assumed shadowy and romantic outlines, now are lighted up in their substantial realities; so that in these flashing revelations of grief's wonderful fire, we see all things as they are; and though, when the electric

[45] *Ibid.*, VII:88.

element is gone, the shadows once more descend, and the false outlines of objects again return; yet not with their former power to deceive. . . .

Thus with Pierre. In the joyous times, ere his great grief came upon him, all the objects which surrounded him were concealingly deceptive. Not only was the long-cherished image of his father now transfigured before him from a green foliaged tree into a blasted trunk, but every other image in his mind attested the universality of that electral light which had darted into his soul.[46]

"Imagination . . . when the light of sense / Goes out, but with a flash that has revealed / The invisible world" (*Prelude* Bk VI, ll. 592–602), and the "Visionary power" through which "forms and substances . . . / Present themselves as objects recognized, / In flashes, and with a glory not their own" (Bk V, ll. 595–605), are referred by Wordsworth not to the visible objects given in nature but to the "mystery of words": in the one instance, words relating a demystifying fact of nature (*"we had crossed the Alps"* [Bk V, l. 591]), in the other "the great Nature that exists in works / Of mighty Poets" (Bk V, ll. 594–96). The relation of Pierre's thoughts which follows this application of the "universality" of enlightenment to the particular ("Thus with Pierre"), is in fact riddled with "the work of mighty Poets." The Shakespearean echoes in the prose of *Pierre* . . . have often been noted,[47] and *Richard III, Macbeth*, and, of

---

[46] *Ibid.* While no specific notice of this direct paraphrase of Wordsworth has been taken, the comparison between the novel as a whole and "*The Prelude*, its great Romantic prototype," has been made generally by Werner Berthoff, in *The Example of Melville* (New York: Norton, 1962), p. 49.

[47] See, for example, Matthieson, "The Troubled Mind: An American Hamlet," pp. 467–87; Sedgewick, *Herman Melville*, pp. 164ff.; Dryden, *Melville's Thematics of Form*, p. 136; and the "Historical Note," by Leon Howard and Herschel Parker, to the Newberry Edition: "The influence of Shakespeare, which had been so strong in *Moby-Dick*, became increasingly dominant in the latter part of *Pierre*. It had existed from the beginning, of course, for Pierre was obviously imagined as a Romeo and there are a number of Shakespearean allusions in the first eight Books. But in the second portion the characters become almost parodies of Shakespearean counterparts. Pierre became a Hamlet . . . , Lucy was an Ophelia . . . Mrs. Glendinning became a vengeful Lady Macbeth or Volumnia who went insane and died. Glen Stanly played Tybalt

course, *Hamlet* are conspicuously legible in the narration of Pierre's deliberations.[48] Equally present, however, are Keats, Shelley, Blake, Coleridge, and Wordsworth: Pierre's mind, in the sequel to its sudden illumination, reads like an anthology of the images, themes, and phrasings which articulate "the great Nature that exists" principally "in" English Romantic poetry. "The Triumph of Life" and "Ode to the West Wind"; "Ode on a Grecian Urn," "On Sitting Down to Read King Lear Once Again," "Ode to a Nightingale," "Ode on Melancholy," and "Sleep and Poetry"; "Lamia," "Christabel," and "Frost at Midnight"; "Songs of Experience"—and doubtless others other readers would recall—all leave their signatures in the following pages. The reading of Isabel's letter results in an outbreak of recognizable "poetic" passages within the novel: in "see[ing] all things as they are," Pierre sees not "things" but a verbal world without visible counterparts, Wordsworth's "invisible world" of "Imagination." What Pierre sees is neither physically visible nor ambiguous in meaning: when transferred to the visible world it will transform the novel into a general attack upon that world, as well as upon the "novels" which attempt to represent it, and our own attempts at reading them. Indeed, the overdeterminacy of the novel's plot from this point on, combined with the pronounced intellectual cynicism which overtakes it as soon as Pierre arrives in New York, transform the further reading of *Pierre . . .* into a struggle between its own and the reader's determination. As the plot born of "ambiguities ripped open" continues, Pierre will recognize

---

to what was left of Pierre's Romeo, and Charlie Millthorpe was a Shakespearean clown. Pierre's Lear-like wanderings in the storm and Melville's references to his Timonism and to a jealousy like Othello's all bear witness to the conscious Shakespearean quality in the author's later imagination" (p. 373).

[48] "She loveth me, ay;—but why? Had I been cast in a cripple's mold, how then?" (VII:90); "Well may this head hang on my breast,—it holds too much; well may my heart knock at my ribs" (VII:91); "She, who in her less splendid but finer and more spiritual part, had ever seemed to Pierre not only as a beautiful saint before whom to offer up his daily orisons, but also as a gentle lady-counsellor and confessor, and her revered chamber as a soft satin-hung cabinet and confessional;—his mother was no longer this all-alluring thing; no more, he too keenly felt, could he go to his mother . . ." (VII:89); "Favorable Goddess, that didst clothe this form with all the beauty of a man, that so thou mightest hide from me all this truth of a man" (VII:89), *et passim*.

in Isabel a face already fixed in his mind from a previous, non-verbal encounter,[49] listen to her recitation of the (Wordsworth-ian) "spots" of time she can recall individually but cannot narratively relate,[50] and decide that the only way to ensure the "vital realness" of their love would be to disregard "empty nominalness" and exchange the name of brother for that of husband.[51] That "realness" takes the immediate form of an unnamed act of incest once Pierre reveals his plan of marriage: "Then they changed; they coiled together, and entangledly stood mute."[52] The previously phlegmatic Pierre plots their escape to New York with yet another disowned woman, the unwed mother, Delly Dulver. Once in New York, Pierre plots his own career as author, welcomes yet a third woman, his refugee fiancée Lucy (who arrives complete with her painter's "easel") into his incestuous *mènage*, responds to a written accusation that he is "a liar"[53] with pistol shots, is joined in jail by both his fiancée and his sister-wife, brings about Lucy's death in being named as Isabel's brother, and dies with Isabel by "a death-milk" she carries hidden in her bosom: "a secret vial" of poison of which they both partake.[54] The extreme hyperplottedness of the novel following the removal of the visual and turn to the verbal seems an overcompensation on Pierre's part for the "unraveled plot" of Isabel's life, a thought which

---

[49] See Book III, "The Presentment and the Verification": "The face . . . had been visibly beheld by Pierre . . . without one word of speech . . . some weeks previous . . ." (VII:43).

[50] *Ibid.*, VII:119.

[51] Again, rather than discursively speculating, or speaking his "own" mind, Pierre effectively quotes to Isabel (additionally claiming to speak both for her and in the name of a father he has already rejected) the very premise of fundamentally incestuous "fraternal love" stated earlier as fact by the narrator: " 'But without gratuitous dishonor to a memory which—for right cause or wrong—is ever sacred and inviolate to me, I can not be an open brother to thee, Isabel. But thou wantest not the openness; for thou dost not pine for empty nominalness, but for vital realness; what thou wantest, is not the occasional openness of my brotherly love; but its continual domestic confidence. Do I not speak thine own hidden heart to thee? say, Isabel? Well, then, still listen to me' " (VII:192).

[52] *Ibid.*

[53] *Ibid.*, VII:357.

[54] *Ibid.*, VII:360.

links his meeting with his sister to a new-found contempt for the "novel" form:

> In her life there was an unraveled plot; and he felt that unraveled it would eternally remain to him. . . . Like all youths, Pierre had conned his novel lessons; had read more novels than most persons of his years; but their false, inverted attempts at systematizing eternally unsystemizable elements; their audacious, intermeddling impotency, in trying to unravel, and spread out, and classify, the more thing than gossamer threads which make up the complex web of life; these things over Pierre had no power now. Straight through their helpless miserableness he pierced; the one sensational truth in him transfixed like beetles all the speculative lies in them . . . he saw . . . that while the countless tribes of common novels laboriously spin vails of mystery, only to complacently clear them up at last; and while the countless tribe of common dramas do but repeat the same; yet the profounder emanations of the human mind . . . these never unravel their own intricacies, and have no proper endings; but in imperfect, unanticipated, and disappointing sequels (as mutilated stumps), hurry to abrupt intermergings with the eternal tides of time and fate.
>
> So Pierre renounced all thought of ever having Isabel's dark-lantern illuminated to him. Her light was lidded, and the lid was locked.[55]

It may be argued that Pierre's discontentment with "novels" which "laboriously spin vails of mystery" is all too well reflected in the preponderent dissatisfaction felt, on the part of its readers, with *Pierre*. . . . Yet whether Pierre, or the second half of *Pierre* . . . , speaks for the author Herman Melville on the subject of the form of the novel, or to Melville's own "inability" to write a novel properly, are anything but unambiguous truths. Such "flashes" of insight occurring to readers of *Pierre* . . . merely take part in the overdeterminism it plots. For Pierre's dismissal of novels occurs after he has already dis-

[55] *Ibid.*, VII:141.

missed, from sight and from mind, "the ambiguities." With the addition of text to visual image, Pierre no longer questions the appearance of meaning: he "sees" what he reads and proceeds to act as if all action were ascribable to a legible "god-like dictation." As a result, the single novel, *Pierre* . . . , which before the reading of Isabel's letter, read like a self-consciously insipid, pastoral "romance," reads thereafter, if read at all,[56] like a strenuous exercise in polymorphous perversity. What makes *Pierre* . . . barely legible *as* a novel, from the moment Pierre reads Isabel's letter allegorically, is that it tells a story in which novels, itself included, are no longer read. The "ambiguous" relation between the visual and verbal modes of meaning which distinguishes the representational nature of the novel is destroyed by a conceptual, or allegorical, correlation of a visual image with its verbal determination. The "regular romance" which preceded the identification of the visual and the verbal gives way to a highly irregular romance in which both forms of meaning appear individually, and repeatedly, debased. *Pierre* . . . is a novel predetermined, like a romance, as to its plot; yet in order to complete the "text" of that plot, it must "banish the least trace" of its basis as a novel: the "ambiguity" of representations which "seem to say" they are not what they seem. In rejecting "novels," Pierre only carries out verbally the rejection of the "ambiguous smile"—the representation of all representations of ambiguous status—which he had previously "removed" from vision. At the same time, he becomes guilty of the very crime of "novels" he protests against, for in verbally determining the meaning of an ambiguously speaking image, he serves to "clear up" "vails of mystery," and "unravel . . . intricacies." In so doing, Pierre not only "removes" "the ambiguities" physically from a wall but, figuratively and effectively, from the novel itself. *Pierre* . . .

---

[56] When, in an edition of the *New York Times Book Review* (June 2, 1984), a selection of currently prominent authors was asked to name the literary classic they could never manage to finish, one respondent frankly replied that, while an avid admirer of Melville, he could never seem to get past "p. 112" of *Pierre* . . .—roughly the point, in the major paperback edition of *Pierre* . . . , at which Pierre's distinctly literary "revelations" take the place of "the ambiguities."

reads with such difficulty because there is, admittedly, "too much" to read in *Pierre* . . . : too much action and too much speculation all related in too many words for the purpose of representation, just as there are always—even in the narrow confines of a jail cell—too many women too busily relating to Pierre. But the story of *Pierre* . . . includes "too much" to read because, after the removal of the portrait, it means too little. All that is left when *the Ambiguities* are taken from *Pierre* . . . lacks the single, insistent voice "seen" in the ambiguous image, and the many versions of ambiguity which follow the portrait's banishment—the contrived conceit of Plinlimmon's "horlogical and chronological time,"[57] the empty speculative pretensions of the new "Apostles" who make a living barking shares in philosophy ("Stump the State on the Kantian Philosophy! A dollar a head . . ."),[58] Pierre's own fancied career as a "writer-Apostle" (" 'I will gospelize the world anew, and show them deeper secrets than the Apocalypse!—I will write it, I will write it!' "),[59] and the "pervading ambiguity" of his "peculiar relationship" with his cousin *Glendinning* Stanly,[60]—all entail superficial verbal complications of an original complexity they cannot replace.

The portrait he "removes" is later destroyed by Pierre. After identifying the face he had seen to be Isabel's and joining his sister in incestuous embrace, Pierre sees a "certain lurking lineament" in the "noiseless, ever-nameless, and ambiguous, unchanging smile"; a line also "visible in the countenance of Isabel," it renders the portrait "now somehow detestable."[61] Watching the portrait he set afire as it "disappeared forever," Pierre sees himself positioned between a past he has just eradicated and a "Future . . . blank to all . . . therefore free to do his own self-will and present fancy to whatever ends."[62] The particular portrait is indeed destroyed, but the image it represents has not "disappeared forever." A second portrait appears

[57] *Writings of Melville*, VII:210–15.
[58] *Ibid.*, VII:281.
[59] *Ibid.*, VII:273.
[60] *Ibid.*, VII:224.
[61] *Ibid.*, VII:196.
[62] *Ibid.*, VII:198–99.

toward the close of *Pierre* . . . which not only re-represents but reinstates the original "ambiguities." In the last Book of the novel, Pierre, Isabel, and Lucy read an announcement posted in the street for an exhibition of paintings soon to be sold by auction. They come upon the exhibition by chance: it is an "encounter . . . entirely unforeseen" by the plot-conscious Pierre, who suggests, on a "sudden impulse," that they see the paintings "at once."[63] In keeping with the parodic, public, and discreditable character of all artistic and speculative undertakings in the second half of the novel, the paintings openly displayed are weak attempts at representational grandeur, falsely attributed to famous European masters: "empty and impotent . . . grandly outlined, but miserably filled," the paintings are listed in the exhibition catalogue under "the loftiest names known to Art."[64] In the by now familiar atmosphere of determinate verbal meanings made meaningless by their divorce from any meaningful visual image (names such as "Rubens, Raphael . . . Da Vinci" made to refer to paintings which do not represent them: allegory itself thus debased here to the status of petty fraud), Pierre and Isabel find a painting named instead for its visual and verbal anonymity: *"No. 99 A stranger's head, by an unknown hand."*[65] Hanging across from this painting and seeming to talk "in secret" with it, is a second version of a known painting of a named and familiar allegorical figure: a "copy" of the "Cenci of Guido," easily recognizable, the narrator reminds us, for its own determined meanings of "incest and parricide."[66] For the first time the would-be *un*-ambiguous themes of the novel are named. Yet, rather than the known, and clearly significant, allegorical painting, it is the unidentified "head" which attracts the attention of Isabel and Pierre, as the narrator describes the "smiling" reappearance of the ambiguous:

> With the aspect of the Cenci every one is familiar. "The Stranger" was a dark, comely, youthful man's head, por-

---

[63] *Ibid.*, VII:349.
[64] *Ibid.*, VII:350.
[65] *Ibid.*, VII:349.
[66] *Ibid.*, VII:351.

tentously looking out of a dark, shaded ground, and ambiguously smiling. There was no discoverable drapery;
the dark head, with its crisp, curly, jetty hair, seemed just
disentangling itself from out of curtains and clouds. But to
Isabel, in the eye and on the brow, were certain shadowy
traces of her own unmistakable likeness; while to Pierre,
this face was in part as the resurrection of the one he had
burnt at the Inn. Not that the separate features were the
same; but the pervading look of it, the subtler interior
keeping of the entirety, was almost identical; still, for all
this, there was an unequivocal aspect of foreignness, of
Europeanism about both the face itself and the general
painting.[67]

What is unequivocal about this face is not only its foreignness, but the fact that it is recognized to resemble two distinct,
original images: to Isabel, "her own . . . likeness"; to Pierre,
the face "he had burnt at the Inn." A single object at a single
moment is narrated to correspond "to entirely different con-
templations. . . . Pierre was thinking of the chair-portrait: Isabel, of the living face," and this duplicity of vision is explicitly
stated to be masked by the verbal mode of its identification:
"Yet Isabel's fervid exclamations having reference to the living
face, were now, as it were, mechanically responded to by
Pierre, in syllables having reference to the chair-portrait."[68]
The problem with this mechanical or unconscious "contradiction" in "reference,"[69] the narrator goes on to explain, is that
it at once proves and disproves the identity of Isabel as Pierre's
"real," rather than "nominal," sister. For the second time in
the novel, Pierre undergoes "the most displacing and revolu-
tionizing thoughts," yet for the first time they regard his own
"reference to Isabel."[70] The question Pierre's study of the first
portrait automatically precluded is now posed by this *un*plotted, or "unforeseen" vision of a second. Again, Pierre is said to
be "hardly conscious" of his own thoughts as they now ask not

[67] *Ibid.*
[68] *Ibid.*, VII:352.
[69] *Ibid.*
[70] *Ibid.*, VII:353.

"how" he should act but if his actions had proceeded from *knowledge*: whether to identify the visual with the verbal allegorically is in any way to "know":

> How did he know that Isabel was his sister? . . . how did he *know*. . . . Nothing that he saw in her face could he remember as having seen in his father's. The chair-portrait, *that* was the entire sum and substance of all possible, rakable, downright presumptive evidence, which peculiarly appealed to his own separate self. Yet here was another portrait of a complete stranger—a European; a portrait imported from across the seas, and to be sold at public auction, which was just as strong an evidence as the other. Then, the original of this second portrait was as much the father of Isabel as the original of the chair-portrait. But perhaps there was no original at all to this second portrait; it might have been a pure fancy-piece; to which conceit, indeed, the uncharacterizing style of the filling-up seemed to furnish no small testimony.[71]

Isabel's father may have been his own, "the original of the chair-portrait," or "the original of this second portrait" which offered "just as strong an evidence as the other." Or at the same time, Pierre considers, the second smiling portrait may be "a pure fancy-piece," lacking an "original at all." The earlier enlightened and determined Pierre is now struck by the possibility that ambiguity itself may be original and thus preclude any referential solution. The noncoincidence of the visual and verbal represented in the ambiguity of this and all "novels" is in turn narrated by a representation of the purely physically, or metonymically, visible, and the stated omission of the verbal from the text: "With such bewildering meditations as these in him . . . and with both Isabel and Lucy bodily touching his sides as he walked; the feelings of Pierre were entirely untranslatable into any words that can be used."[72] The "smile" which is foreign and does not refer necessarily to *any* father, or for that matter, any specific meaning, at all, is not "removed"

---

[71] *Ibid.*; emphasis in text.
[72] *Ibid.*

either physically by Pierre or verbally and figuratively by the sublimity of "poetic" vision. That "smile," the resurfacing, allegorical image of mimetic representation in any novel, survives its verbal determination and visible destruction, just as *Pierre* . . . survives its destruction as a novel by the overdetermined action and language of its plot.

Not one of the main characters of the novel, however, does survive that plot. The orgy of death which terminates the novel returns it, almost gratuitously, to the mode of overplotted melodrama. The novel, in returning to ambiguous representation immediately previous to that end, leaves the reader with the determination, and consequent death, of "Pierre"—"Or, the Ambiguities." For the "ambiguities" themselves, as they seemed to say in the presence of Pierre, will continue in his absence, "unchangeably," to smile. The public and visible "silence" which succeeded them may have been that of Melville, the *novelist*, seeing them speak.

Representations are represented in *Pierre* . . . as *a priori* "ambiguities," and just as that representation denies all grounds for certain knowledge in presenting the object of "thinking and thinking and thinking," it provides no grounds for causal narration. The recurrence of the mental experience of "ambiguities" in the novel distinguishes the peculiar status of narrative representation from the merely functional meaning accorded representation by narrative form, plot. For plots, *Pierre* . . . suggests, are (over)determined either visually or verbally, conceived by way of pictoral allegory or verbal designation: unlike *verbal representations* they cannot be seen and heard at once. Proust's *A la recherche du temps perdu* is a novel which effectively denies the representational status of representation itself. The *Recherche* is the narrative to which any analysis of narrative representation must finally turn because, more than any other, it identifies its own structure with that of narration. What exists of the *Recherche*—an existence only delimited by its author's death—is equated by its narrator with the very extension of the life he narrates. That life is said to be given narrative form by way of memory, but the personal memory described by the first-person narrator in Proust could hardly be less similar to the mechanical faculty of Julien Sorel. Memory for the narrator of the *Recherche* is not only not the memory of prior forms of discourse: according to that narrator it occurs by means of no discursive form. The memory which produces narration is unrelated, the narrator explains, to representation: it tastes, it feels, it smells the past in the present but in no way does it *represent* the past in order to know it as narration. The concept of "involuntary memory," whose specifically nonintellectual, indeed pointedly nonconceptual, nature has both attracted great numbers of readers to the *Recherche* and remained all that many have remembered of it, states that narrative is contained, in its diachronic entirety, in the synchronous experience of sensation. Literature, it implies, is a spontaneous creation, having as little to do with formal knowledge of experience as the taste of a pastry to an untrained palate depends upon a previous awareness of the recipe used to make it. A potential *Recherche* can be found in every sensory experience, the narrator suggests, and will write itself as soon as we cease wishing to know how to, just as the memory triggered by the sensation must be one we first forget. Sensation absent of any formalization is said in the *Recherche* to give birth to narration. Yet another story of memory, ascribed to a third person, is told in the novel. The distinction of Swann's memory from both the involuntary and voluntary experiences narrated by the narrator, and the way in which it is "remembered" by a narrator who can have had no immediate experience of it, are the forms of narrative representation turned to in conclusion.

CHAPTER 7

REMEMBERING SWANN

We feel in one world, we think, we name in another; we can
establish a concordance between the two but never fill up the
interval.
—MARCEL PROUST, *Le côté de Guermantes*

The senses do not judge at all.
—IMMANUEL KANT, *Logic*

Not even that culinary extravagance attributed to a chef in
Napoleon's employ which was fated, by the mistranslation of
its name, to serve the further fame of its maker's master, is
likely to have more greatly contributed to the international
recognition afforded French pastries than the formative reference made to one of the latter in the narrative undertaking of
Marcel Proust. Moreover, while the intricate style of description which has prompted the critical comparison of Proustian
composition with the spatially superimposed form of the
palimpseste[1] may, by coincidence, be seen to be most suggestive of the many-layered artifice of the *mille-feuille* itself, the

---

[1] See Gérard Genette's attempt at a metaphoric substantiation of Proust's
"style" in "Proust palimpseste," *Figures* (Paris: Editions de Seuil, 1966), pp.
39–67. A grammatical and syntactic analysis of the accumulative character of
Proustian composition is offered by Yvette Louria in *La convergence stylistique chez Proust* (Paris: Nizet, 1971).

particular edible commemorated by Proust's own endless compilation of discrete surfaces is most notable, if at all, for its thoroughly homogeneous content and distinctively simple, representational form. One need not have read widely in the history of Proust criticism,[2] nor further in *A la recherche du*

[2] Regardless of the particular interpretative viewpoint involved, faithful observance of the "miracle" of the madeleine reappears throughout the criticism of the *Recherche* with the insistence of a ritual performed as prerequisite to the act of commentary. Among the many, otherwise heterogeneous moments highlighting and defining this critical tradition, the following references may serve in summary to represent its scope: Ramon Fernandez, *Proust* (Paris: Editions de la Nouvelle Revue Critique, 1943), p. 55; Erich Auerbach, *Mimesis* (Princeton: Princeton University Press, 1953 [Berne: A. Francke, 1946]), p. 541; Robert Vigneron, "Structure de *Swann*: Combray ou le cercle parfait," *Modern Philology* 45 (1948), p. 186; Louis Martin-Chauffier, "Proust and the Double 'I' of Two Characters," *Partisan Review* 10 (1949), p. 1025; Germaine Brée, *Marcel Proust and the Deliverance from Time*, trans. C. J. Richards and A. D. Truitt (New Brunswick, N.J.: Rutgers University Press, 1955 [orig.: *Du Temps perdu au temps retrouvé* (Paris: Les Belles Lettres, 1950)]), p. 21; Léon Guichard, *Introduction à la lecture de Proust* (Paris: Nizet, 1956), p. 41; Samuel Beckett, *Proust* (New York: Grove Press, 1957), p. 21; Georges Poulet, *L'Espace proustien* (Paris: Gallimard), p. 90 (although Poulet specifies that in the wake of involuntary memory, "Everything remains to be done," it is the *Recherche*'s own description of involuntary memory that Poulet's conception of a distinctly spatial memory does little more than repeat, that is "memory of the entire work" [see pp. 133–34]); Harry Levin, *The Gates of Horn* (New York: Oxford University Press, 1963), pp. 390, 436; Gilles Deleuze, *Proust et les signes* (Paris: Presses Universitaires de France, 1964), pp. 70–79; Wallace Fowlie, *A Reading of Proust* (New York: Doubleday, 1964), p. 57; Elizabeth R. Jackson, *L'Evolution de la mémoire involontaire dans l'oeuvre de Marcel Proust* (Paris: Nizet, 1966), pp. 15–16 esp.; Gérard Genette, "Proust et le langage indirect," *Figures II* (Paris: Editions de Seuil, 1969), pp. 193–94; idem, "Métonymie chez Proust," *Figures III* (Paris: Editions de Seuil, 1972), pp. 57–58; and Jean-Pierre Richard, *Proust et le monde sensible* (Paris: Editions de Seuil, 1974), p. 11 esp.

Studies which, dealing with the structural dynamics of the *Recherche*, question the importance of the madeleine for their understanding are Leo Bersani's *Marcel Proust: The Fictions of Life and of Art* (New York: Oxford University Press, 1965), pp. 214–15 esp., and B. G. Rogers's *Proust's Narrative Techniques* (Geneve: Libraire Droz, 1965), p. 201. The greatest verbal mileage, outside the *Recherche* itself, gained in reference to the madeleine is Serge Doubrovsky's extraordinary rhapsody, based exclusively on psychoanalytic correlations, of sexual perversities for which the eating of the madeleine, like

temps perdu itself than the concluding pages of "Combray (I)"—i.e., Section One, Part One of the first volume, *Du côté de chez Swann*—to have become acquainted with the complex recollective power ascribed by its narrator to the taste of a tea-soaked "Petite Madeleine":[3] that miniature shell-shaped confection whose momentary state of dissolution is turned discursively, by undoubtedly the most well-known of Proust's typically oxymoronic constructions, into the single bearer and support of "l'édifice immense du souvenir."[4] In fact, knowledge of the singularly important position Proust grants the madeleine requires no prior knowledge of his narrative at all. For

any other literary "fantasm," is said to stand (*La place de la madeleine: écriture et fantasme chez Proust* [Mercure de France, 1974]). Maurice Blanchot considers Proust's entire work antithetically as the "deforming," while "fruitful," "abuse" he makes of his "revelation" by memory ("L'Expérience de Proust," in *Faux Pas* [Paris: Gallimard, 1943], pp. 57–58), while Walter Benjamin proposes, most provocatively and critically, that "Proust's *mémoire involontaire* stands much closer to forgetting than that which is usually called memory" ("Zum Bilde Prousts" in *Illuminationen* [Frankfurt: Suhrkamp, 1955], p. 356). Hans Robert Jauss clearly restates the synthesizing role of the madeleine episode for both narrator and reader: "in the madeleine-experience the remembering I becomes the remembered I and the remembered I ('Marcel') begins its way through the same time that the remembering I had lost, till it is refound 'in a cup of tea'. . . . In the madeleine-episode the time of remembering transforms itself for the reader into remembered (= refound) time." Jauss's illuminating technical analysis of the *non*synthetic nature of the typical three-clause Proustian sentence is then referred back by him, for its unity, to the "remembering I." (H. R. Jauss, *Zeit und Erinnerung in Marcel Prousts A la recherche du temps perdue: Ein Beitrag zur Theorie des Romans* [diss. Heidelberg, 1952; Frankfurt: Suhrkamp, 1986], pp. 108–109, 153–66.)

Concentrating not on the narrator's explicit account of the genesis of his story, but on the complications involved in the formulation and understanding of any story that are borne out by his text, Roland Barthes and Paul de Man—analyzing the mythic and demystifying dimensions of the language of the *Recherche* respectively—go so far as to make no direct mention of the madeleine at all. (See Barthes, "Proust et les noms," in *Nouveaux essais critiques* [Paris: Editions de Seuil, 1953], and De Man, "Proust et l'allégorie de la lecture" in *Mouvements premiers: Etudes critiques offertes à Georges Poulet* [Paris: Librairie José Corti, 1972]).

[3] Marcel Proust, *A la recherche du temps perdu*, 3 vols. (Paris: Bibliothèque de la Pléiade, 1954), I:45. All quotations are from that edition; all translations are my own.

[4] *Ibid.*, I:47.

a trip made to the extant Proust home in "Illiers/Combray" (as that town, this author can attest, is actually designated by its traffic signs) may still reveal, as if transposed from the narrative text to Marcel's erstwhile bedside, the spectacle of the timeless, if also lifeless, encounter between an empty, authentically Proustian teacup and a glue-afixed, apparently papier-mâché, Petite Madeleine.

The preceding comments, while purposefully mundane, are no more intended to dismiss the significance of Proust's most famous referent than they are meant to disparage either the deserved status of French pastry-making in general, or the particular desire to preserve for visitation the former Proust household in Illiers, as has been carried out, in full spirit of the fictional matter at hand, by that literary-historical society calling itself, Des Amis de Marcel Proust et des Amis de Combray. Least of all should these introductory remarks be considered to question the propriety or efficacy, within a first-person narrative whose enormity of autobiographical design might well be subtitled, per Wordsworth's *Prelude*, "Growth of a Novelist's Mind," of that narrative's insistence upon the real referential being of the object by which its own self-referentiality appears to be ensured. For the madeleine is described as the vehicle by which the presently dead—including the narrator's own, temporally static perceptions of the past in "Combray (I)"[5]—are

[5] "C'est ainsi que, pendant longtemps, quand, réveillé la nuit, je me ressouvenais de Combray, je n'en revis jamais que cette sorte de pan lumineux, découpé au milieu d'indistinctes ténèbres . . . en un mot, toujours vu à la même heure, isolé de tout ce qu'il pouvait y avoir autour, se détachant seul sur l'obscurité . . . comme si Combray n'avait consisté qu'en deux étages reliés par un mince escalier et comme s'il n'y avait jamais été que sept heures du soir. A vrai dire, j'aurais pu répondre à qui m'eût interrogé que Combray comprenait encore autre chose et existait à d'autres heures. Mais . . . je n'aurais jamais eu envie de songer à ce reste de Combray. Tout cela était en réalité mort pour moi" [So it is that, for a long time, when, awake in the night, I remembered Combray, I always only saw of it a kind of luminous section, cut out at the middle from indistinct darknesses . . . in a word, seen always at the same hour, isolated from all that there could be around it, detaching itself alone upon the obscurity . . . as if Combray had only consisted of two floors linked by a narrow staircase and as if it had only ever been seven in the evening. In truth, I would have been able to respond to someone who would have interrogated me that Combray included something else and existed at other hours. But . . . I

transported to their first coherent, temporally sequential representation in "Combray (II)," and it is the necessary banality of that vehicle which these opening observations are meant to stress. That is to say, the external source indicated by the narrator for his extraordinary ability to remember had better indeed belong to the realm of daily, familiar elements, its status as a discursive object, be as referentially demonstrable,[6] and as little mythological, as discourse will allow, if paradoxically, it is to act as the novel's own mythic Charon, carrying "temps perdu" to the afterlife of its narration. For it is upon the identity,[7] over time, of the purely sensory experience brought on by the madeleine's ingestion that the narrator's own identity over time, substantiated by no more than the repetition of that experience, is said to depend.

Hence, while the objective origin given for the narration of the *Recherche* cannot be, the language used to describe that origin must be of a highly imaginative, mythologizing effect. The episode of the madeleine, exemplary for the execution of any history relying upon representation, and thus perforce of any autobiographically descriptive text, is purposed to persuade us of an immediate perceptual link between the actual experience of the real and its eventual recovery as fiction.[8] As indispensa-

---

would never have felt like thinking of this rest of Combray. All that was in reality dead for me] (I:43–44).

[6] The bakeries of Illiers, in fact, seem to have intuitively understood—insofar as it affects their own living—the indicative power of that proposition. Their windows display large transparent bags of this otherwise unremarkable little cake and, in at least one enterprising instance, a sign beneath them which says: "C'était ici que Marcel Proust a acheté ses madeleines" [It was here that Marcel Proust bought his Madeleines].

[7] "Arrivera-t-il jusqu'à la surface de ma claire conscience, ce souvenir, l'instant ancien que l'attraction d'un instant identique est venue de si loin solliciter, émouvoir, soulever tout au fond de moi?" [Will it reach the surface of my clear consciousness, this memory, the past instant that the attraction of an identical instant has come from so far to solicit, to move, to raise in the depths of me?] (I:46).

[8] Testimonials to the achievement of that precise persuasive purpose are offered by Brée, *Marcel Proust*, p. 5; Beckett, *Proust*, pp. 55–56; and Karl Holz, *Das Thema der Erinnerung bei Marcel Proust* (München: Wilhelm Fink Verlag, 1972), pp. 56, 207–208. A similar view is presented in Leo Spitzer's extensive analysis of Proust's compositional style, "Zum Stil Marcel Prousts"

ble, therefore, as the mundanity of the madeleine itself is the brilliance of the rhetoric by which its influence upon the narrator is evoked: a rhetoric which, whether "successful" or not when viewed as a discrete act of persuasion, can, as a structure of narrative presentation, only succeed. For the claims made for eating the madeleine may seem at once openly disproportionate to any single sensory experience, or sensory experience itself may seem an implausible cause of such extensive narrative effects. Yet skepticism in this case on the part of the reader toward an apparent flight into poetry on the part of the narrator will merely serve to underscore the major objective of that narrative flight: that of recounting the narrative's own founding event as one whose cause it cannot identify,[9] and whose occurrence, since inexplicable, is thus all the more indisputable in effect. In the mythology the narrator offers of his own coming into authorship, the sudden, synchronic experience of taste, unexpected and innocent of artifice, is told to bear what will prove to be among the richest of this, or any other century's narrative fruit. As we read at its beginning and are made to remember at its circularly structured end, *A la re-*

(*Stilstudien* v.II [München: Max Hueber Verlag, 1961]): "[Proust's] sentence structure is nothing other than the linguistic derivative of this swelling up of experience" (p. 376). The notion of a "derivative" relation of linguistic articulation to inner experience is complicated by Spitzer slightly further on, however, as the direction of that derivation is presented in reverse. Referring to the narrator's early experiences of Gilberte in Paris, Spitzer specifies that the effective cause of their intensity was not Gilberte herself, "who simply appears nearby, dependent upon the *morceau de l'après midi* [*piece of the afternoon*]," but the mental perception of her "name": "it is 'important' that the child hears the name Gilberte with all the fullness of its experience—what importance, compared to that, could the playing Gilberte herself . . . could all of external life have, when the inner life pulses with such heat and effervescence. The hero of this sentence structure is the *Name* Gilberte, with the impression that it calls forth . . . we feel, that something grand, something that is determining must have occurred, when such verbal splendor unfolds before us: such sentences give notice of the majesty of an experience, no matter how pointless it may seem to the average man: the naming of a name" (pp. 378–79).

[9] "Il y a beaucoup de hasard en tout ceci, et un second hasard, celui de notre mort, souvent ne nous permet pas d'attendre longtemps les faveurs du premier" [There is a lot of chance in all this, and a second chance, that of our death, often does not permit us to wait long for the favors of the first] (I:44).

cherche du temps perdu derives as a diachronic, representational narrative[10] from the near magic of visual and verbalizable memory springing, without the aid of any additional mental image, from the undesigning depths of a "tasse de thé."[11]

In a literary work, however, whose own critical or epistemological impetus consists in questioning the sensual *and* intellectual events it remembers, recognizing them "plus tard," to have been experienced by mistake, the narrator's own account of how memory is made to appear would seem to deserve at least as much retrospective scrutiny in return. Indeed, another mode of understanding the advent of memory—itself the paradigmatic means of all reference to experience—is offered at the opening of the *Recherche*. But unlike the enlight-

[10] "ainsi . . . je restais souvent jusqu'au matin à songer au temps de Combray, à mes tristes soirées sans sommeil, à *tant de jours aussi dont l'image* m'avait été plus récemment rendue par la saveur . . . d'une tasse de thé" [so . . . I often remained until morning thinking of the time of Combray, of my sad evenings without sleep, of *so many days too whose image* had been more recently rendered me by the taste . . . of a cup of tea] (I:186); "Or ce moyen qui me paraissait le seul, qu'était-ce autre chose que faire une oeuvre d'art? . . . car qu'il s'agît de réminiscences dans le genre du bruit de la fourchette ou du goût de la madeleine, ou de ces vérités écrites à l'aide de figures dont j'essayais de chercher le sens dans ma tête . . . justement la façon fortuite, inévitable, dont la sensation avait été rencontrée, *contrôlait la vérité du passé* qu'elle ressuscitait, des *images* qu'elle déclenchait. . . . Elle est le contrôle aussi de la vérité de *tout le tableau*" [Now the means which seemed to be the only one to me, what was it but making a work of art? . . . for it had to do with reminiscences of the kind of the noise of the fork or the taste of the madeleine, or of the kind of truths written with the aid of figures whose sense I tried to find in my head . . . precisely the fortuitous, inevitable manner in which the sensation had been met *controlled the truth of the past* which it resuscitated, of the *images* which it unleashed. . . . It is also the control of the truth of the whole *tableau*] (III:879); "trouvant seulement cette impression de beauté quand, une sensation actuelle, si insignifiante fût-elle, étant donnée par le hasard, une sensation semblable, renaissant spontanément en moi, venait étendre la première sur *plusieurs époques à la fois*" [only finding that impression of beauty when an actual sensation, no matter how insignificant, being given by chance, a similar sensation, being reborn spontaneously in me, proceeded to extend the first over *several epochs at the same time*] (III:918), my emphasis. [Note that the category of "truths written with the aid of figures" is also subordinated, in the second passage, under the experience of "sensation."]

[11] I:48.

ened perspective said to be gained by the narrator at a "later" date (i.e., at the time culminating in his decision to write the narrative of perceptual mistakes which he has written and which we read), this alternative version of memory, while succeeding the Madeleine episode in narrative sequence, recounts events whose occurrence so far precedes that incident as to lie outside the narrative's own temporal scope. I refer to the part of the first volume entitled, "Un amour de Swann": the section of the *Recherche* distinguished on the one hand for the easier legibility afforded by its third-person viewpoint, and on the other, for the difficulties involved in accounting for its appearance in the narrative at all. For not only does the story of "Un amour de Swann" predate, without overlap, the narrator's own,[12] but its technique of narration seems to belong to a literary aesthetic and era which the *Recherche* in particular is famed for having left behind: the style, predominant in the nineteenth century, of "realistic" or "omniscient" narrative, supposedly transformed by the advance of such modern "subjectivists" as Proust into an irretrievable, if still entertaining or admirable, primitive art.[13] The thought that "Un amour de Swann" is in fact Proust's own swan song to "simpler" narra-

[12] See Gérard Genette, "Discours du récit," *Figures III*, p. 125, for the difficulties involved in constructing even a hypothetical date of occurrence for the events, predating the narrator's birth, of "Un amour de Swann."

[13] On the "subjective" turn in narrative taken by the *Recherche*, see Fernandez, *Proust*, p. 139; Martin-Chauffier, "Proust and the Double 'I,' " p. 1026; Rogers, *Proust's Narrative Techniques*, pp. 81–93, 141; René de Chantal, *Marcel Proust: Critique littéraire* (Montréal: Les Presses de l'Université de Montréal, 1967), V.II, p. 497; and Brée's assertion (p. 21) that "it is not [the narrator's] life which changes; it is the narrator's own evaluation of it which is so dramatically altered. This is necessarily a subjective experience which could not be effectively recounted by a third person." In discussing "Un amour de Swann" in particular, however, Brée finds that Swann fails as a lover due to his inability to recognize Odette as a "real person," concluding: "In this sense *Du côté de chez Swann* is a penetrating critique of that perennial source of error in love—subjectivity" (pp. 150–51). If the significance of "Un amour de Swann" is to be limited to such a reading, it should also be noted that its "unrealistic" "subjective experience" is, contrary to Brée's previous assertion, very "effectively recounted by a third person."

For the dissenting view of Proust as "realist," see Chap. 7, "Proust," in Levin's *The Gates of Horn*, pp. 372–444.

tive forms has probably occurred to not a few readers of the *Recherche*, and on not altogether gratuitous grounds. For among the important points of departure for the composition of the novel were the seminarrative appreciations of Balzac which Proust was to include in his unfinished criticism of Sainte-Beuve.[14] Yet while Proust's observations on his leading nineteenth-century predecessor moved quickly into the form of short metafictions, in which the observations of such figures as M. de Guermantes and the Marquise de Villeparisis were represented in turn,[15] the analytical approach he posed against

[14] See "Sainte-Beuve et Balzac," *Contre Sainte-Beuve* (Paris: Bilbliothéque de la Pléiade, 1971), pp. 263–98.

Whether one's interpretative categories are those of literary history, stylistics, or the study of influence, relations between Balzacian narrative and the *Recherche* are anything but easily accommodated to schematization. The variety of current critical assessments ranges from Jean-Yves Tadié's statement that the Balzac material collected in *Contre Sainte-Beuve* represents "a last goodbye to the Balzacian temptation over which Proust triumphed" (*Proust et le roman* [Paris: Gallimard, 1971], p. 87) and Chantal's contention, in a similar vein, that Proust's defense of Balzac against Sainte-Beuve was also a plea "against the best part of himself" (a notion used by Chantal to support his thesis that, rather than "against," Proust was in fact a *confrère* of, Sainte-Beuve [II:477–500; I:123]), to Walter A. Strauss's discussion, in *Proust and Literature: The Novelist as Critic* (Cambridge, Mass.: Harvard University Press, 1957), of Balzac's guiding "Virgilian" role in Proust's development (see pp. 8–11 esp.). Hans Robert Jauss signals both Proust's debt to Balzac's conception of the epic cycle and his modern transformation of that conception through the introduction of the integrating dimension of psychological time (*Zeit und Erinnerung*, pp. 88–95). To my knowledge, John Porter Houston is the only critic of Proust to have identified his technical organization of temporality specifically with that of Balzac. (See "Les structures temporelles dans la *Recherche*," in *Recherche de Proust*, ed. G. Genette and T. Todorov [Paris: Editions de Seuil, 1980].) By way of comparative grammatical analyses Houston arrives at the conclusion that the *Recherche*, famed for its own proclaimed revolution in the conception of time itself, could only be written in accordance with a mode of temporal construction which had already been discarded not only by Proust's contemporaries but by his direct literary predecessors, most notably Flaubert and the "naturalistes" (see pp. 90, 104 esp.). On the thematic influence of Balzac on Proust in general, see Harry Levin, "Balzac and Proust," in *Hommage à Balzac* (Paris: Mercure de France, 1950).

[15] See *Le Balzac de Monsieur de Guermantes* (Neuchatel, Paris: Ides et Calendes, 1950), published from Proust's *cahiers* and included in "Sainte-Beuve et Balzac," pp. 279–85.

the purely referential "method" of Sainte-Beuve stressed the concept of "an idea," rather than of mimetic, narrational "painting," as the critical means most relevant to an understanding of Balzac's art.[16] Thus the narrative form which "Un amour de Swann" may seem to recall consciously from a past largely delimited by the *Recherche* itself is viewed by Proust to have already been misrepresented, historically, as realism.

Furthermore, such a stylistically divided reading of *Du côté de chez Swann* cannot aid us in understanding why Swann's story arises in the narrative at the particularly peculiar moment that it does. "Un amour de Swann" is introduced in the novel when, following the confusion of spatial relations ending with the madeleine scene in "Combray (I)," the *Recherche* had begun to pursue, similar to the separate ways of Swann and Guermantes, the distinctly chronological path of its narration in "Combray (II)." Thus, even if one prefers the "nineteenth-century" style of "Un amour de Swann" to the "modernist" style of "Combray," the question its appearance raises for any reader of the *Recherche* must be roughly the same.

---

[16] "C'est l'idée de génie de Balzac que Sainte-Beuve méconnaît. . . . Or, Balzac ne s'est pas proposé cette simple peinture, au moins dans le simple sens de peintre de portraits fidèles. Ses livres résultaient de belles idées, d'idées de belles peintures si l'on veut, car il concevait souvent un art dans la forme d'un autre, mais alors d'un bel effet de peinture, d'une grande idée de peinture. Comme il voyait dans un effet de peinture une belle idée, de même il pouvait voir dans une idée de livre un bel effet. . . . Amateur passionné de peinture, il avait parfois joie à penser que lui aussi avait une belle idée de tableau, d'un tableau dont on raffolerait. Mais toujours c'était une idée, une idée dominante, et non une peinture non préconçue comme le croit Sainte-Beuve. A ce point de vue Flaubert même avait moins cette idée préconçue que lui" [It is the idea of Balzac's genius that Sainte-Beuve fails to recognize. . . . Now, Balzac did not propose for himself this simple painting, at least in the simple sense of a painter of faithful portraits. His books resulted from beautiful ideas, beautiful paintings if you want, for he often conceived one art in the form of another, but then from the beautiful effect of painting, from a grand idea of painting. As he saw a beautiful idea in an effect of painting, just so he could see in an idea of a book a beautiful effect. . . . An impassioned amateur of painting, he took joy sometimes in thinking that he too had a beautiful idea of a tableau, of a tableau one would be mad about. But it was always an idea, a dominant idea, and not an unpreconceived painting as Sainte-Beuve believes. From this point of view even Flaubert had this preconceived idea less than he] ("Sainte-Beuve et Balzac," pp. 274–76).

That is why, once the narrator's story of time regained in Combray has been gotten smoothly underway, should we start to read another story of how a third person named Swann wastes his own time in Paris pursuing a woman whose "style" he realizes does not "please" him at all?[17] Considered as an example of the narrative subgenre, the love story, "Un amour de Swann" is itself not especially appealing. It takes us abruptly from the lush gardens and family rituals of Combray to the vacuous gatherings of the Verdurin clan and Odette's insipid flirtations and deceits. Indeed, very much like the figure of Odette herself, Swann's love, as love, is neither attractive nor convincing:[18] the "reality" of its full sensory experience is said to be doubted even by Swann himself.[19] But by a turn of logic most nearly reminiscent of the Cartesian disproof of epistemological skepticism—a mental resemblance which philosopher and lover alike would have been the last to desire or to intend[20]—Swann's doubts, rather than serving to destroy the

[17] Proust, I:382.

[18] See Ortega y Gasset's highly relevant observation of the "form" or "figure" of love in "Un amour de Swann" ("Le temps, la distance et la forme chez Proust," *Nouvelle Revue Française* 20: Hommage à Proust [1923]): "Proust . . . describes to us a love of Swann's which has nothing of the form of love. In it there is everything . . . a single thing is lacking in it: love. Love here is the result, as in a tapestry the figure results from the intersection of threads of which none has the form of the figure" (p. 274).

[19] "Et cette volupté d'être amoureux, de ne vivre que d'amour, de la réalité de laquelle il doutait parfois, le prix dont en somme il la payait, en dilettante de sensations immatérielles, lui en augmentait la valeur—comme on voit des gens incertains si le spectacle de la mer et le bruit de ses vagues sont délicieux, s'en convaincre ainsi que de la rare qualité de leurs goûts désintéressés, en louant cent francs par jour la chambre d'hôtel qui leur permet de les goûter" [And this voluptuousness of being in love, of living only from love, the reality of which he doubted sometimes, the price which he payed for it in sum, as a dilettante of immaterial sensations, added to its value for him—as one sees people who are uncertain whether the spectacle of the sea and the noise of its waves are delicious, convince themselves of the rare quality of their disinterested taste by renting for one hundred francs a day a hotel room which allows them to appreciate them] (I:267).

[20] More surprising than the suggestion of this comparison in relation to the fictional context of Swann is the fact that it has been made on several occasions with respect to the actual intentionality of, and "method" employed by, Proust. See Marcel Muller, *De Descartes à Marcel Proust: essais sur la théorie*

premise of his love, are found ultimately to define the modus of its existence. Like Descartes's realization that all certainty of knowledge depends upon an unrelenting distrust of sensory experience, Swann discovers that his doubts with regard to his lover must prove no less hyperbolical than his love: not, however, in order to match the genius of a willfully imagined evil

des essences, le positivisme et les méthodes dialectique et réflexive (Neuchatel: Editions de la Baconnière, 1947), who offers a classically Cartesian description of the function and telos of doubt in Proust: "Proust puts the reality of the world in doubt in order to find the essential again in himself. . . . And it is enough that this absolute is discovered in us for it not to be in vain, for us to refuse to declare it without value" (pp. 71–72). A similar view of the definitive "value" sought by Proust—such as could *not* be applied, significantly, to the story of Swann—is also presented in distinctly Cartesian terms by Blanchot: "On the one hand [Proust] admits without examination that these interior states . . . can be utilized by knowledge united with art and have a meaning beyond the conditions in which they are produced. He intends to seize through them something of definitive value . . ." (p. 37). Poulet defines the novel as "a *method*, in the Cartesian sense of the term, that is to say, an ensemble of reasoned steps for approximating of reality" (*L'Espace proustien*, p. 105); Fernandez describes as Cartesian "the desire for clarification" made manifest in Proust's "style" (*Proust*, p. 30); and M. Suzuki ("Le 'Je' Proustien," *Bulletin de la Société des Amis de Marcel Proust et des Amis de Combray* 9 [1959]) identifies Proust as "the most direct descendent of the philosopher of *The Discourse on Method*" (p. 82). By the same token, Martin Turnell's criticism of Proust compares the "weaknesses" of his "sensibility" to the "absolute spiritual neutrality" of Descartes (*The Novel in France* [New York: New Directions, 1951], p. 404).

Finally, the comparison has been made, most surprisingly, by Proust himself. However, rather than focusing on the rigor of Descartes's "method," or on any "value" it reveals, Proust's comment refers to an ambiguously natural understanding, on the part of the philosopher, of "good sense." In a footnote to the well-known analogy he draws in opening his review of Flaubert, between the renewal of "our vision of things" effected by Flaubert's grammatical innovations and that effected by "Kant, with his Catégories, the theories of Knowledge and of the Reality of the external world*," he adds: "*I know well that Descartes had begun with his 'good sense' which is nothing other than rational principles. One used to learn that in class. How can M. Reinach . . . believe that Descartes displays a 'delicious irony' in saying that good sense is the most shared thing in the world? This means in Descartes that the stupidest man uses the principle of causality in spite of himself, etc. But the French seventeenth century had a very simple way of saying profound things. When I try in my novels to put myself in its school, the philosophers reproach me for employing the word 'intelligence' in its current sense, etc." ("A propos du 'style' de Flaubert," *Nouvelle Revue Française* 14 [1920], p. 72).

deceiver, but rather to be merely commensurate with the real
lack of skill with which Odette lies.[21] For Odette not only fails
each test of truth Swann conceives; she demonstrates that each
test was too modest in its conception, that Swann's doubts, at
their very worst, were always too naive. Without a touch of genius in her, Odette inadvertently unsettles every form of certainty which Swann meticulously recalls, every sensory indi-
cator he has inspected and preserved, down to the first fallen
catleya set aright at a moment of apparently happy, metonymic circumstance, when Forcheville, as Swann learns later,
was only slightly less close by. Finally, the series of deceptions
and investigations constituting "Un amour de Swann"[22] leads
Swann, by a deductive route diverging sharply from that of his
philosophical forerunner, to a conclusion most nearly opposite
the Cartesian affirmation of a subject of deduction whose
being is essentially independent, or severed, from his senses.
For the more perceivable reason Swann is given to doubt
Odette, the more exhaustively he understands his dependence
upon her to be exclusive; the more she lies, the more he desires
to know the truth from her alone:[23] a desire he does not will,

[21] "Certes quand Odette venait de faire quelque chose qu'elle ne voulait pas
révéler, elle le cachait bien au fond d'elle-même. Mais dès qu'elle se trouvait en
présence de celui à qui elle voulait mentir, un trouble la prenait, toutes ses idées
s'effondraient, ses facultés d'invention et de raisonnement étaient paralysées,
elle ne trouvait plus dans sa tête que le vide . . ." [Of course when Odette had
just done something she did not want to reveal, she hid it well in the depths of
herself. But as soon as she found herself in the presence of the one to whom she
wanted to lie, a disorder took her, all her ideas collapsed, her faculties of invention and of reason were paralyzed, she found nothing more in her head
than a void . . .] (I:278); "Mais c'est en vain que Swann lui exposait ainsi
toutes les raison qu'elles avait de ne pas mentir; elles auraient pu ruiner chez
Odette un système général du mensonge; mais Odette n'en possédait pas . . ."
[But it was in vain that Swann exposed to her thus all the reasons she had not
to lie; they could have ruined a general system of lying in Odette; but Odette
did not have one . . ."] (I:291).

[22] "La vie de l'amour de Swann, la fidélité de sa jalousie, étaient faites de la
mort, de l'infidélité d'innombrables désirs, d'innombrables doutes, qui avaient
tous Odette pour objet" [The life of the love of Swann, the fidelity of his jealousy, were made of the death, of the infidelity of innumerable desires, of innumerable doubts, all of which had Odette for their object] (I:372).

[23] "c'était une autre faculté de sa studieuse jeunesse que sa jalousie ranimait,
la passion de la vérité, mais d'une vérité, elle aussi interposée entre lui et sa

and without which he would probably no longer suffer, but which he can no more avoid than the recognition that Odette, divorced from that desire, would probably bore him to death.

This description of "Un amour de Swann" may seem directly at odds with the meaning of "Un amour de Swann," i.e., that of a love *of* Swann's, one which belongs to him or which he possesses. That meaning will be offset later in the *Recherche*, as the reader discovers that by the time Swann does possess Odette—when her name has been changed to Madame Swann—he has long since ceased to love her.[24] But it is also contradicted at least once during the narrative of Swann's love, within a context whose immediate subject matter is the derivation of meaning itself: the appearance and employment of the phrase, *faire catleya*, in the private language of Swann and Odette. In the course of tracing the lexical evolution of this metaphor for the act of love, used first in the presence and then the absence of the object to which it refers, and eventually in the absence of any thought of that referent, of any thought at

---

maîtresse, ne recevant sa lumière que d'elle, vérité tout individuelle qui avait pour objet unique, d'un prix infini et presque d'une beauté désinteressée, les actions d'Odette, ses relations, ses projets, son passé" [it was another faculty of his studious youth which his jealousy revived, the passion for truth, but for a truth also interposed between himself and his mistress, receiving its light only from her, a wholly individual truth which had for its unique object, of an infinite price and an almost disinterested beauty, the actions of Odette, her relations, her projects, her past] (I:273–74).

[24] Referring to the unlikely alliance between Odette and the Duchesse de Guermantes desired by Swann during his life, which, according to the strange "work of causality," would only take place after his death, the narrator considers: "Swann ne le savait-il pas par sa propre expérience, et n'était-ce pas déjà, dans sa vie—comme une préfiguration de ce qui devait arriver après sa mort—un bonheur après décès que ce mariage avec cette Odette qu'il avait passionnément aimée—si elle ne lui avait pas plu au premier abord—et qu'il avait épousée quand il ne l'aimait plus, quand l'être qui, en Swann, avait tant souhaité et tant désespéré de vivre toute sa vie avec Odette, quand cet être-là était mort?" [Didn't Swann know from his own experience, wasn't it already in his life—like a prefiguration of that which must arrive after his death—a happiness after decease, this marriage with this Odette whom he had passionately loved—if she hadn't pleased him at first—and whom he had married when he no longer loved her, when the being who, in Swann, had so desired and despaired to live all his life with Odette, when that being was dead?] (*A l'ombre de jeunes filles en fleurs*, I:471).

all, the narrator interjects an additional remark on the act of possession it has come to signify. He defines that act in passing as having nothing as its object. Thus the development of "faire catleya" into an intentionally figural denotation is coterminus with the repetition in practice of the unrealizable intention to possess which it names. The narrator outlines the double progress of that repetition and its correspondant linguistic function *chez* Swann:

> Mais il était si timide avec elle, qu'ayant fini par la posséder ce soir-là, en commençant par arranger ses catleyas, soit crainte de la froisser, soit peur de paraître rétrospectivement avoir menti, soit manque d'audace pour formuler une exigence plus grande que celle-là (qu'il pouvait renouveler puisqu'elle n'avait pas fâché Odette la première fois), les jours suivants il usa du même prétexte. Si elle avait des catleyas à son corsage, il disait: "C'est malheureux, ce soir, les catleyas n'ont pas besoin d'être arrangés, ils n'ont pas été déplacés comme l'autre soir; il me semble pourtant que celui-ci n'est pas très droit. Je peux voir s'ils ne sentent pas plus que les autres?" Ou bien, si elle n'en avait pas: "Oh! pas de catleyas ce soir, pas moyen de me livrer à mes petits arrangements." De sorte que, pendant quelque temps, ne fut pas changé l'ordre qu'il avait suivi le premier soir, en débutant par des attouchements de doigts et de lèvres sur la gorge d'Odette, et que ce fut par eux encore que commençaient chaque fois ses caresses; et bien plus tard, quand l'arrangement (ou le simulacre rituel d'arrangement) des catleyas fut depuis longtemps tombé en désuétude, la métaphore "faire catleya," devenue un simple vocable qu'ils employaient sans y penser quand ils voulaient signifier l'acte de la possession physique—où d'ailleurs l'on ne possède rien,—survécut dans leur langage, où elle le commémorait, à cet usage oublié.[25]

But he was so timid with her, that having finished by possessing her that evening, in beginning by arranging her

---

[25] *Ibid.*, I:233–34.

catleyas, whether for fear of offending her or of appearing retrospectively to have lied, or for lack of audacity in formulating a greater demand than that one (which he could renew since it hadn't angered Odette the first time), he used the same pretext the following days. If she had catleyas in her corsage he said: "It's sad, tonight, the catleyas don't need to be arranged, they haven't been displaced like the other evening; it seems to me however that this one is not exactly straight. I can see if they don't smell more than the others?" Or, if she didn't have any: "Oh! no catleyas this evening, no way for me to indulge in my little arrangements." So that for some time the order he had followed the first evening was not changed, in beginning by touches of fingers and lips on Odette's throat, and it was still through them that his caresses began each time; and much later, when the arrangement (or the ritual simulacrum of arrangement) of the catleyas had long since fallen into disuse, the metaphor, *faire catleya*, having become a simple vocable which they employed without thinking about it when they wanted to signify the act of physical possession—where, moreover, one possesses nothing,—survived in their language, where it commemorated that act by this forgotten usage.

Just as to say the act of love in this narrative is to say a quoted phrase which does not refer to what it means, nor could, since the direct object of that act is "nothing," "rien,"[26]

---

[26] The concept of "nothing" is distinguished here most strongly from any conception of the unconscious, such as is put forward in the place of "nothing" by Doubrovsky in, "Faire Catleya" (*Proust et le texte produceur*, ed. John D. Erickson and Irene Pages [Guelph, Ontario: University of Guelph, 1980]), and in psychoanalytic criticism in general. Rewriting "the *metaphor*, 'faire catleya,' " as Swann's own fantasmic *sensory* object, or madeleine, Doubrovsky states: "There where the erotic fantasm of the Narrator is to masturbate on the dead mother, that of Swann is to *faire catleya* with her. . . . With his customary sureness, Proust intimately links art and sexual perversion here . . ." (p. 13). Regardless of how one feels about dead mothers (or what one imagines the unconscious would do with one if it could) Doubrovsky's re-"inscription" (p. 20) of "faire catleya" as the name for possessing *something* (identified metaphorically *as* the "dead mother," one fantasmic object among others) is a critical step backwards from Proust's "simple vocable" *and* "act

to say that the love narrated is "Swann's," "de Swann," may only provide meaning if understood within quotation marks, i.e., as meaning other than what it says. These indications of a rather bizarre relation between the articulations, in "Un amour de Swann," of verbal form and referential meaning do not, of course, answer the question of what the story of that relation is doing in the narrator's autobiographical text. They do, however, provide an important structural link between "Un amour de Swann" and the narrator's most extensive personal interaction with, and description of, Swann in "Combray." Most readers of the *Recherche* clearly remember Swann as the figure whose nocturnal arrivals at the narrator's home in Combray signified for him, as their immediate consequence, the agonizing experience of his mother's absence. For Swann is presented in "Combray" as the principal *metteur en scène* of what the narrator himself calls "le théâtre et le drame de mon coucher":[27] an event whose highly ceremonial quality of representation, that which allows it to be returned to and restaged repeatedly throughout the first section of "Combray," also renders Swann's attributed role in it so visibly memorable. But less likely to be remembered is another apsect of Swann which made his appearance a particularly annoying presence for the narrator. Perhaps less memorable in the course of narration because it is in fact invisible, that second aspect is the peculiar way in which Swann spoke: Swann's habit, noted by the narrator, of refusing to say what he means. Indeed, since this particular characteristic of Swann is purely verbal in nature, the narrator, in order to represent it objectively, and thus to narrate it at all, must first supply the reader with the means of its visualization: means which Swann's speech itself specifically does not present. Not the content of what Swann says, but his own attitude relative to the act of speaking must be repre-

---

. . . where, moreover one possesses *nothing*." (Ironically, in the course of generating his own series of metaphoric substitutions for "the metaphor" named in the text, Doubrovsky refers the emptiness of meaning of "faire catleya" to the narrative reference to "nothing": "The semantic void refers back here to the very void of the act it designates: '. . . where . . . one possesses nothing . . .' " [p. 19].)

[27] *Proust*, I:44.

sented by the narrator as an observable, and ultimately, legible phenomenon. The necessarily nonreferential condition of that "representation" is made prominent by the narrator's use, in the place of properly descriptive terms, of signs of demarcation applicable by definition to the reading of texts alone. In seeming to say other than what they mean, Swann's words are said *and* written by the narrator to be spoken *entre guillemets*. Swann himself is said to speak as if quoting the speech of others; to disavow the significance of what he says in the same instance of saying it. Thus while Swann, as a character of narration, is dramatized as being directly culpable for the narrator's pains in Combray, Swann, as a linguistic subject—as a narrator in his own right—is best characterized by his questioning of that right: by his effective and repetitive dedramatization of himself. In being articulated "between quotation marks," his words appear at once to have been articulated twice. Consequently, his speech, while intelligibly referential in its bearing, presents its speaker as no reliable source of reference for what he says. The unsettling quality of this verbal tendency on Swann's part is further enforced by the narrator's equally displeasing perception that Swann, in choosing the human referents of his speech, self-consciously declines to talk about those he actually knows. The distance between Swann and the narrator that these peculiarities of utterance are made to represent is itself perfectly represented in the narrative by the occasion taken by the narrator for their description. When Swann, for the sake of the narrator's interest in Bergotte, takes the exceptional stance of speaking of the latter as his friend, the narrator, ironically, can only respond by asking Swann who the author's favorite actor is. Their short dialogue on that pointedly irrelevant detail is followed by the narrator's observation of the anamolous use of speech which seems to imply something fundamentally "contradictory" about Swann. The gradual, reflective development of this largely undiscussed passage requires its quotation at length:

"Est-ce que vous pourriez me dire quel est l'acteur qu'il préfère?"

"L'acteur, je ne sais pas. Mais je sais qu'il n'égale aucun

artiste homme à la Berma qu'il met au-dessus de tout.
L'avez-vous entendue?"

"Non Monsieur, mes parents ne me permettent pas
d'aller au théâtre."

"C'est malheureux. Vous devriez leur demander. La
Berma dans *Phédre*, dans *le Cid*, ce n'est qu'une actrice si
vous voulez, mais vous savez, je ne crois pas beaucoup à
la '*hiérarchie!*' des arts"; (et je remarquai, comme cela
m'avait souvent frappé dans ses conversations avec les
soeurs de ma grand'mère, que quand il parlait de choses
sérieuses, quand il employait une expression qui semblait
impliquer une opinion sur un sujet important, il avait soin
de l'isoler dans une intonations spéciale, machinale et
ironique, comme s'il l'avait mise entre guillemets, sem-
blant ne pas vouloir la prendre à son compte, et dire: "la
hiérarchie, vous savez, comme disent les gens ridicules."
Mais alors, si c'était un ridicule, pourquoi disait-il la hiérarchie?). Un instant après il ajouta: "Cela vous donnera
une vision aussi noble que n'importe quel chef-d'oeuvre,
je ne sais pas moi . . . que—et il se mit à rire—'les Reines
de Chartres!' " Jusque-là cette horreur d'exprimer sérieusement son opinion m'avait paru quelque chose qui
devait être élégant et parisien et qui s'opposait au dog-
matisme provincial des soeurs de ma grand'mère; et je
soupçonnais aussi que c'était une des formes de l'esprit
dans la coterie où vivait Swann et où, par réaction sur le
lyrisme des générations antérieures, on réhabilitait à
l'excès les petits faits précis, réputés vulgaires autrefois, et
on proscrivait les "phrases." Mais maintenant je trouvais
quelque chose de choquant dans cette attitude de Swann
en face des choses. Il avait l'air de ne pas oser avoir une
opinion et de n'être tranquille que quand il pouvait don-
ner méticuleusement des renseignements précis. Mais il ne
se rendait donc pas compte que c'était professor l'opinion, postuler que l'exactitude de ces détails avait de l'importance. Je repensai alors à ce dîner où j'étais si triste
parce que maman ne devait pas monter dans ma chambre
et où il avait dit que les bals chez la princesse de Léon
n'avaient aucune importance. Mais c'était pourtant à ce

genre de plaisirs qu'il employait sa vie. Je trouvais tout cela contradictoire. Pour quelle autre vie réservait-il de dire enfin sérieusement ce qu'il pensait des choses, de formuler des jugements qu'il pût ne pas mettre entre guillemets, et de ne plus se livrer avec une politesse pointilleuse à des occupations dont il professait en même temps qu'elles sont ridicules?[28]

What the narrator tells us he finds "shocking" for the first time at this moment about Swann is that which he calls the lat-

---

[28] "Could you tell me which is the actor he prefers?"

"The actor, I don't know. But I know that he equates no male artist with la Berma, whom he puts above all. Have you heard her?"

"No sir, my parents don't permit me to go to the theater."

"That's unfortunate. You should ask them. La Berma in *Phedre*, in *Le Cid*, she's only an actress if you will, but you know, I don't believe much in the '*hierarchy!*' of the arts"; (and I noticed, as it had often struck me in his conversations with the sisters of my grandmother, that when he spoke of serious things, when he employed an expression which seemed to imply an opinion on an important subject, he took care to isolate it in a special, mechanical and ironic intonation, as if he had put it between quotation marks, seeming not to want to take responsibility for it, and to say: "the *hierarchy*, you know, as ridiculous people say." But then, if it was ridiculous, why did he say hierarchy?). An instant later he added: "That will give you a vision as noble as any masterpiece, I don't know ... as—and he began to laugh—'the Queens of Chartres!' " Up until then this horror of expressing his opinion seriously had seemed to me something which must be elegant and Parisian and which opposed itself to the provincial dogmatism of the sisters of my grandmother; and I suspected also that it was one of the forms of spirit in the circles in which Swann lived and where, by reaction against the lyricism of the preceding generations, one rehabilitated to excess small precise facts, reputed to be vulgar earlier, and one proscribed "phrases." But now I found something shocking in this attitude of Swann's in face of things. He appeared not to dare to have an opinion and to only be tranquil when he could meticulously give precise pieces of information. But he didn't realize that postulating that the exactitude of these details had importance was to profess an opinion. I thought again then of the dinner when I was so sad because maman was not going to come up to my room and when he had said that the balls at the Princesse de Léon had no importance. But it was, however, to this kind of pleasures that he employed his life. I found all that contradictory. For what other life did he reserve finally saying seriously what he thought of things, formulating judgments which he could not put between quotation marks, and not indulging himself with a punctilious politeness in occupations which he professed at the same time to be ridiculous?" (I:97–98).

ter's "attitude . . . en face des choses." What the reader may find somewhat shocking, on the part of this painstakingly precise and denominatively sensitive narrator, is his own mistaking here, and misnaming, of the acutal object of Swann's "ironic" attitude, words, for "things." It is not "the arts" themselves but the abstract *word* "hierarchy" used to modify them which Swann "isolates" in the "special intonation" of "ironic" quotations, speaking as if citing the vocabulary of "gens ridicules." The false identification of things with our names for them will provide a major theme of narrative irony in the final part of *Du côté de chez Swann*, as the narrator, in apparent oblivion of having interrupted himself at some length with the preceding story of Swann, returns directly to the autobiographical story begun in "Combray." As the very graphics of its title, "Noms de pays: le nom," spells out clearly for the eye, the narrator of the final section of *Du côté de chez Swann* is well aware of the unmitigable distinction to be made between words and the general localities they are used to designate.[29] But the immediate mistake made by the narrator in judging the focus of Swann's irresolute stance in "Combray," the unconscious confusion of things with words which he will go on to reveal as a fundamental error of experience in "Noms de pays: le nom," is narrated to take place within "Un amour de Swann" in a form which no degree of irony can either remedy or dissuade. Before directly investigating the different status of "things" in the course of Swann's love, or relating the description cited above of Swann in Combray[30] to the larger

[29] See the famous discussion of the effect of place-names upon the imagination (I:387ff.), and the narrator's expansion of this theme from "l'univers physique" to "l'univers social" in *Le côté de Guermantes* ([II:11], II:10–15, 209, and 438). Critical discussions of the narrator's nominalist "experiences," conceived of as "a Cratylian consciousness of signs" and, from a directly opposing perspective, as bordering upon "Word-aestheticism," are presented by Barthes ("Proust et les noms" p. 134) and Spitzer ("Zum Stil Marcel Prousts" [p. 435], pp. 423–47) respectively.

[30] The only other mention I have seen made of this description of Swann as speaker arises, not surprisingly, in Spitzer's scrupulously attentive stylistic study. In the section of "On the Style of Marcel Proust" entitled "The Relationship to Language," Spitzer briefly refers to Swann's "citational tone" as a "fleeing from responsibility . . . which obviously posed a problem for Proust

narrative of "Un amour de Swann," we would do best to turn first to the passage *in* "Un amour de Swann" in which that description in fact appears repeated. The larger context of that passage within the linear development of "Un amour de Swann" is the first visit paid by Swann to the Verdurin salon. Its immediate context, however, is a narration of the event of memorization: Swann's initial "transcription," as the activity of memory in this case is called, of the *petite phrase* of the Vinteuil sonata. At this instance in the sequence of the story's events, Swann is about to hear, by Odette's side, the "petite phrase" he has heard before but which he "had finished by forgetting," having been unable to discover the name of its author, and thereby, "procure" a copy of it for himself. For, having maintained the "forms" of the phrase "before his eyes," as the narrator continues some lines later to explain, Swann found himself unable to reproduce its sense to the ear: to sing it so that it might be recognized by others and identified. Suddenly, within the context of this description of an actively formalizing representational power of memory, itself placed within a narrative context which represents a scene of recognition by memory, the narrator steps out of the narrative moment at hand and into a diachronic description of Swann *before* he had first heard the "petite phrase de sonate." The trait which we are told *had* characterized Swann until he heard the phrase was, as stated in "Combray," the "ironic tone" with which he stated opinions, or could be said to speak his mind.

---

himself" ("Zum Stil Marcel Prousts," p. 427). That is, Proust as author is viewed by Spitzer to have recognized and struggled with this "equivalent of nihilistic evasion in face of decisions" found to be condemnable in the character Swann (p. 428). Yet this move from textual to moral and pragmatic interpretation on Spitzer's part is followed by an observation implying that Proust's personal battle with quotation was more nearly a no-contest defeat, accounting for the major portion of representation in the *Recherche*: "One can say that all human representation in Proust is a quoting, a reproducing of 'speech tonality,' a creating of 'pastiches' " (p. 429). The difference, then, in Spitzer's terms, between Swann's and Proust's own use of quotation would be that which makes a "nihilistic evasion" into a work of endlessly engaging representations: the wholesale assimilation and reemission, rather than suspicion, of quoted speech (see pp. 423–31).

Aside from a few additionally illustrative details, the passage seems to be making the same point about Swann:

> Même cet amour pour une phrase musicale sembla un instant devoir amorcer chez Swann la possibilité d'une sorte de rajeunissement. Depuis si longtemps il avait renoncé à appliquer sa vie à un but idéal et la bornait à la poursuite de satisfactions quotidiennes, qu'il croyait, sans jamais se le dire formellement, que cela ne changerait plus jusqu'à sa mort; bien plus, ne se sentant plus d'idées élevées dans l'esprit, il avait cessé de croire à leur réalité, sans pouvoir non plus la nier tout à fait. Aussi avait-il pris l'habitude de se réfugier dans des pensées sans importance qui lui permettaient de laisser de côté le fond des choses . . . dans sa conversation il s'efforçait de ne jamais exprimer avec coeur une opinion intime sur les choses, mais de fournir des détails matériels qui valaient en quelque sorte par eux-mêmes et lui permettaient de ne pas donner sa mesure. Il était extrêmement précis pour une recette de cuisine, pour la date de la naissance ou de la mort d'un peintre, pour la nomenclature de ses oeuvres. Parfois, malgré tout, il se laissait aller à émettre un jugement sur une oeuvre, sur une manière de comprendre la vie, mais il donnait alors à ses paroles un ton ironique comme s'il n'adhérait pas tout entier à ce qu'il disait. Or . . . Swann trouvait, en lui, dans le souvenir de la phrase qu'il avait entendue, dans certaines sonates qu'il s'était fait jouer, pour voir s'il ne l'y découvrirait pas, la présence d'une de ces réalités invisibles auxquelles il avait cessé de croire et auxquelles, comme si la musique avait eu sur la sécheresse morale dont il souffrait une sorte d'influence élective, il se sentait de nouveau le désir et presque la force de consacrer sa vie. Mais n'étant pas arrivé à savoir de qui était l'oeuvre qu'il avait entendue, il n'avait pu se la procurer et avait fini par l'oublier.[31]

Even this love for a musical phrase seemed for an instant to have to initiate in Swann the possibility of a sort

---

[31] Proust, I:210–11.

of rejuvenation. For so long he had renounced applying his life to an ideal goal and limited it to the pursuit of quotidian satisfactions, which he believed, without ever saying it to himself formally, would not change further until his death; moreover, no longer feeling elevated ideas in his spirit, he had ceased to believe in their reality, while equally unable to deny that reality altogether. Also he had taken the habit of finding refuge in thoughts without importance which allowed him to leave aside the depth of things . . . in his conversation he forced himself never to express with heart an intimate opinion about things, but to furnish material details that had some value in themselves and which permitted him never to give his measure. He was extremely precise about a cooking recipe, the date of the birth or death of a painter, the nomenclature of his works. Sometimes, in spite of everything, he let himself emit a judgment about a work, about a way of understanding life, but then he gave his words an ironic tone as if he did not entirely adhere to what he said. Now . . . Swann found, in himself, in the memory of the phrase which he had heard, in certain sonatas which he had played for him, to see if he would not discover it in them, the presence of one of these invisible realities in which he had ceased to believe and to which, as if the music had a sort of elective influence upon the moral aridity from which he suffered, he felt again the desire and almost the force to consecrate his life. But not having arrived at knowing whose work it was that he had heard, he hadn't been able to procure it for himself and had finished by forgetting it.

If the treatment of Swann's speech in this departure from the narrative sequence proper of "Un amour de Swann" seems to reproduce, with some redundance, its treatment in "Combray," one significant alteration should immediately be seen in reading: the "quotation marks" which were written and reported to characterize that speech have been removed. In the place of quoted dialogue, and in the place of the graphic representation of an "ironic tone," we are given the narrator's explanation of why Swann "*used* to give his words" that tone, and of why Swann's past is about to change into his future: because "now," in the Verdurin salon, he will hear the phrase *and* discover its name. In short, instead of the description of a synchronic occurrence which can only be represented within quotation marks, since evoking a sense of contradiction in its narrator, we read a formally authorial narrative which tells the story, over time, of why Swann had spoken the way he did, and why he will no longer. We read Swann the speaker explicated as a character, his quotation marks removed, a diachronic narrative put in their place. What we read, in effect, is the "other life" of Swann that the narrator of "Combray" postulated must exist—the "other life" for which Swann reserved serious, definitive speech. The story of that life is the story of "un amour de Swann," in which the hero leaves a life in society he has always recognized as absurd, to pursue a life of passion in the most mediocre of milieus: a milieu in which, compared to all other speakers, he is unquestionably the most sincere. Swann, the self-effacing frequenter of a circle "where one proscribed '*les phrases*,' " in love with a phrase instead; Swann, so faithful and well-intentioned in his speech as to be misunderstood and condemned by those who hear it; so loyal to his "phrase" as to be ousted from the petty salon in which it is played. Swann, the unswerving and pathetic lover, wise enough to doubt whether he loves at all, true to an "other life" which he cannot help but take seriously, "to express *avec coeur*," and thus foolish enough to be true to those who abuse him. Swann—until the very end of "Un amour de Swann"—*en dehors de guillemets*: out of quotation marks. Or is he?

For, turning again to the relation between "Un amour de Swann" and "Combray," this narrative of an "other life" lived in "face of things" does not follow the narrative in which it is hypothesized without first being mediated by some narrative in between. Included in the last pages of "Combray" is a brief introduction to "Un amour de Swann." Posed between the movement back from the second subsection of "Combray" to the first, as the narrator reflects upon the new and truly sensational developments of his memory, the passage to "Un amour de Swann" is easy to overlook. Indeed, the introduction of the throwback to third-person reporting represented by "Un amour de Swann" within a narrative viewed to be its own autobiography, the history of its own first-person narration, has gone virtually unnoticed in critical discussions of the novel's development. While charged with effecting a major formal and thematic narrative transition, this particular passage offers no explicitly theoretical or aesthetic explanation for its presence, and thus may well appear a textual phenomenon of far lesser critical significance than the pure "signs of art,"[32] the literary importance of the psychic fantasy,[33] or the artless good fortune of having a "mémoire involontaire." The unusual interpretative instances referring directly to this transition in the text seem to do so merely in order to excuse it as a technical necessity of narration or to replace its own word on the problem it raises with a more referentially credible explanation.[34] Once

[32] Cf. the aesthetic-essentialist tenet shared by such evidently divergent critics as F. C. Green (*The Mind of Proust* [Cambridge: Cambridge University Press, 1949]) and Gilles Deleuze (*Proust et les signes*, chap. 4, esp.).

[33] Cf. Bersani's central thesis of art and life defining each other along the lines of their mutual medium, "a world of fantasy" (*Marcel Proust*, p. 246; see also pp. 17–18 *et passim*) and Doubrovsky's formulation of the specifically *psycho*analytical aim of his *Place de la madeleine* (p. 62 *et passim*).

[34] Rogers treats the passage as an exclusively expeditious fictive device intended to compensate for the "mistake," committed in *Jean Santeuil*, of knowledge presented in excess of all possible *vraisemblance* (p. 102; see also pp. 111–12). Fowlie substitutes the concept of a "flashback" for the narrator's explanation, thus fostering the more familiar but highly misleading impression of Swann's story as the extensive recovery of a personal experience on the part of its subject (*A Reading of Proust*, p. 51). Levin similarly calls the story a "flashback, which could stand by itself" (*The Gates of Horn*, p. 391), yet contradicts that notion by hypothetically locating its content in "gossip, hearsay and the occasional confidences of [the narrator's] third-person protagonist" (p. 392). Genette calls "Un amour de Swann" a narrative "*ab ovo*" ("Discour du récit," p. 88), and dismisses its introduction as an "excuse," more "maladroite" than convincing, for the narrator's "so precise knowledge" of Swann's love. In place of the passage itself Genette presents his own "hypothesis," which, based on no instance of evidence in the text, also demonstrates a more serious misunderstanding of the story's own rejection of verisimilitude as a basis for composing any narrative, including its own: "the only hypothesis capable of accounting for the focalization on Swann of the narrative within the narrative: that is, whatever would be the possible relays, the first source can only be Swann himself" (p. 221).

that passage is taken at its word, however, the distinctions between first- and third-person narratives, between technical and experiential plausibilities, begin to appear less clear. For the narrator states, in the concluding pages of "Combray," that the past he remembers is associated *by* memory with what he had been told, or had learned by report, about a love of Swann's:

> C'est ainsi que je restais souvent jusqu'au matin à songer au temps du Combray, à mes triste soirées sans sommeil . . . et, par association de souvenirs, à ce que, bien des années après avoir quitté cette petite ville, j'avais appris au sujet d'un amour que Swann avait eu avant ma naissance, avec cette précision dans les détails plus facile à obtenir quelquefois pour la vie de personnes mortes il y a des siècles que pour celle de nos meilleurs amis, et qui semble impossible comme semblait impossible de causer d'une ville à une autre—tant qu'on ignore le biais par lequel cette impossibilité a été tournée.[35]

> It is thus that I often stayed thinking until morning of the time at Combray, of my sad evenings without sleep . . . and, by association of memories, of that which, many years after having left that little town, I had learned about a love that Swann had had before my birth, with that precision in details easier to obtain sometimes for the life of persons dead for centuries than for that of our best friends, and which seems impossible as it seemed impossible to talk from one town to another—so much does one ignore [or, so little does one know] the contrivance by which this impossibility has been circumvented [or turned around].

The reference offered by the narrator for his relation of "Un amour de Swann," in a gesture of self-disclaimer so unique to the whole of the *Recherche* as either not to be noticed or to be disclaimed itself, is a specifically nondemonstrable, textual event. For the narrator informs us, before "Un amour de Swann" begins, that the problem posed him in his youth by

[35] I:186.

single words spoken in quotation is about to be solved by their replacement with an entire narrative told in quotation, having already been told or reported to him. The story of "un amour de Swann"—the solution of the contradiction in meaning presented by Swann's speech—is described here to be structured like that contradiction. Within the passage cited from "Un amour de Swann" that discusses Swann's speech, the narrator's original sense of the contradictory is completely deleted.[36] Just as it removes the quotation marks from what Swann says, the story told of his "other life" excludes, like any good solution, all trace of the dilemma it had been meant to resolve.

But how was that solution arrived at; how is that story told? How does any narrator come to know the details of the life of the dead with a precision exceeding his knowledge of the living he knows best? Finally, what is this unidentified "biais" to which the narrator refers:[37] an unusual term translated into English as "contrivance" in both the standard and revised Moncrieff editions, used later in another context in the novel in apposition to the word, "detour,"[38] and otherwise translatable as "slant," "angle," or "expedient"; as an oblique means of proceeding, a "movement aside" or "askew"? The narrator states that it remains unknown or ignored until after it has "circumvented an impossibility," reversed or turned it around. What contrivance, then, what particular slant on the matter or detour, would permit the narrator to tell a story simultane-

---

[36] Interestingly enough, the sentence "Je trouvai tout cela contradictoire" (I:210–11) is entirely deleted from the standard Moncrieff translation of "Combray." (See *Swann's Way* [New York: Random House, 1970], p. 75.) It is restored to the text by the Terence Kilmartin revision (*Remembrance of Things Past*, 3 vols., trans. Moncrieff and Kilmartin [New York: Random House and Chatto & Windus, 1981], I:106).

[37] F. C. Green dubs it "hearsay" (*The Mind of Proust*, p. 45); Tadié, who notes the exclusion from the definitive text of this passage of the specific informational sources—"a cousin," "an uncle"—included in earlier drafts, concludes that, "the secret [of the 'biais'] . . . we will never know it—it is of the domain of art more than of life, it stems from a verisimilitude superior to that of the quotidian" (*Proust et le roman*, pp. 56–57).

[38] Moncrieff, *Swann's Way*, p. 143; Moncrieff and Kilmartin, *Remembrance of Things Past*, I:203. Proust, I:391.

ously in and out of quotation marks: a story which he could not have referentially known, since it takes place before his own birth; a tale about a dead man which no one, not even Swann, could have told with such precision, which no one, who *was* its subject, could have lived to tell.

As stated at the opening of this chapter, the "contrivance" which forms the larger narrative of the *Recherche* is given to be the immediate sensory experience of the taste of a madeleine dipped in tea: a soggy pastry from which the solid edifice of the narrator's personal story is said to arise. A very different version of the slant of memory is brought to fore within the story of Swann. Unlike the division into separate "before" and "after" parts by which the appearance of diachronic memory organizes the narrative sequence of "Combray," memory in Swann is first presented, as referred to earlier, when the single, linear narration of "Un amour de Swann" is already fully underway: as Swann, on the point of hearing the "petite phrase de sonate" in the Verdurin salon, is about to become a different Swann, he who for the first time will find Odette *délicieuse*.[39] In order to explain at this moment the change in Swann to come, the narrator must first explain that the "petite phrase" is not entirely new to him, that what he will hear for the first time with Odette he has heard before without her, and can recall. Thus the narrator's explanation of an incipient transformation—one which will prove to be no less than the major peripety in the story of Swann—is rendered identical with his description of the internal event of memory. That is, memory here, rather than described as recalling previous events to mind in a mysteriously seamless, narrative shape, is referred to as the sole effective cause for the present occurrence of events themselves. As dissimilar as the function ascribed to memory in Swann is the rhetorical device by which its distinctly causal role is brought to light. With an undisguised force radically foreign to the manner of narration characterizing the *Recherche* up to this point, the narrator begins his explanation by announcing that it *is* one, stating directly and

[39] Proust, I:212.

abruptly, "Voici pourquoi:"[40] [This is why:], before starting,
in a new paragraph, his narration of Swann's past: "The preceding year. . . ."[41] Included in what follows is the passage on
Swann's "ironic tone" and the narration of the transformation
it will undergo when he recognizes and discovers the name of
the sonata. But what follows first is the description of how that
recognition had been made possible: the prior moment of
memorization initiated by Swann's having "suddenly seen," in
the musical work whose "material quality" alone he had until
then "enjoyed . . . [with] great pleasure," the indistinct but
perceivable appearance of an expressive form: "the multiform
undivided mass of the piano part trying to elevate itself in a liquid tide."[42] The narrator goes on to relate the result of this visualization:

> Et cette impression continuerait à envelopper de sa liqui-
> dité et de son "fondu" les motifs qui par instant en émer-
> gent, à peine discernables, pour plonger aussitôt et dispa-
> raître, connus seulement par le plaisir particulier qu'ils
> donnent, impossibles à décrire, à se rappeler, à nommer,
> ineffables—si la mémoire, comme un ouvrier qui travaille
> à établir des fondations durables au milieu des flots, en fa-
> briquant pour nous des fac-similés de ces phrases fugi-

[40] This derailing demonstration of verbal authority, immediately alien in
Proust, should, however, be easily recognizable to readers of Balzac. Or, as
Proust himself writes in the Sainte-Beuve criticism: "And when there is an explanation to give, Balzac does not mince words; he writes: 'This is why'; a
chapter follows" (*Contre Sainte-Beuve*, p. 271). Genette makes unique mention of this Balzacien moment in the narrative but offers no commentary on its
possible motivation ("*Discour du récit*," p. 103). In keeping with the employment of third-person narrative as the vehicle for telling "Un amour de Swann,"
the usage of a Balzacien topos to introduce the central subtext of Swann's
story might be most significantly viewed as a consciously artificial marking
serving to further sever its implications from the surrounding autobiographical story.

[41] Proust, I:208

[42] "D'abord, il n'avait goûté que la qualité matérielle des sons sécrétés par
les instruments. Et ç'avait déjà été un grand plaisir quand, au-dessous de la petite ligne du violin, mince, résistante, dense et directrice, il avait vu tout d'un
coup chercher à s'élever en un clapotement liquide, la masse de la partie du
piano, multiforme, indivise . . ." (I:208).

tives, ne nous permettait de les comparer à celles qui leur succèdent et de les différencier. Ainsi, à peine la sensation délicieuse que Swann avait ressentie était-elle expirée, que sa mémoire lui en avait fourni séance tenante une transcription sommaire et provisoire, mais sur laquelle il avait jeté les yeux tandis que le morceau continuait, si bien que, quand la même impression était tout d'un coup revenue, elle n'était déjà plus insaisissable. Il s'en *représentait* l'étendue, les groupements symétriques, la graphie, la valeur expressive; *il avait devant lui cette chose qui n'est plus de la musique pure*, qui est du dessin, de l'architecture, de la pensée, *et qui permet de se rappeler la musique*. Cette fois il avait distingué nettement une phrase s'élevant pendant quelques instants au-dessus des ondes sonores.[43]

And this impression would continue to envelop in its liquidity and its "fondu" the motifs which emerge for an instant, hardly discernible, to plunge immediately and disappear, known only by the particular pleasure they give, impossible to describe, to remember, to name, ineffable— if memory, like a laborer who works to establish durable foundations in the middle of tides, in fabricating for us facsimiles of these fugitive phrases, didn't permit us to compare them to those which succeeded them and to differentiate them. Thus, hardly had the delicious sensation which Swann had felt expired, when his memory had furnished him on the spot with a transcription, summary and provisional, but upon which he had thrown his eyes while the piece continued, so much that the same impression returning all of a sudden was no longer unseizable. He *represented* to himself its extension, symmetrical groupings, graphics, expressive value; *he had before him that thing which is no longer pure music*, which is drawing, architecture, thought *and which permits us to recall music*. This time he had neatly distinguished a phrase rising for some instants above the sonorous waves.

[43] *Ibid.*, I:209; my emphasis.

The work of the "ouvrier," memory, described here[44] is not predicated as being either voluntary or involuntary. It does not summon up past personal experiences through their association with a bodily sensation. Instead, it graphs or "represents" in a repeatable form the pure sensation of sound, free of associations. The facsimile it transcribes, complete with symmetrical design and "expressive value," can be seen in the mind almost simultaneously with the sound upon which it works. The moment that "summary and provisional" transcription is made it is not a sensation but a "thing" of the mind—no longer "pure music," but that which permits us to "recall music." The "thing" which Swann distinguishes clearly the next time he hears, or more precisely, *sees* it, is the phrase which becomes the anthem of his love: that "thing," in other words, in "face of" which his irony is rendered mute. No more identifiable with things themselves than with the words called as such by the narrator in "Combray," the phrase which Swann remembers thus occupies a position of significance which neither the articulations of speech nor objectivity of things can attain, since it is articulated, and objectified as thing, in the mind of Swann alone.

The separation of Swann's mental representation from the sensory experience to which it refers, the formal divergence of the mind from its own senses of perception, is told as another moment within the narrative as Swann's image of the phrase is further defined. Through his ritual attendance of its performance, Swann has already arrived at a numerical analysis of the phrase's composition when he recognizes that the foundations laid by his memory have indeed been laid on a certain slant: that what he recalls in the form of a phrase is itself not even "the phrase itself":

> Il s'était rendu compte que c'était au faible écart entre les cinq notes qui la composaient et au rappel constant de deux d'entre elles qu'était due cette impression de dou-

<hr>

[44] Cf. the narrator's reference, in "Noms de pays: le nom," to the "unknown" and "invisible *ouvrière*," whose manipulations, independent of his "love," make his uninterpretable experience of Gilberte take on "sense" (I:411, 412).

ceur rétractée et frileuse; mais en réalité il savait qu'il rai-
sonnait ainsi non sur la phrase elle-même, mais sur de
simples valeurs, substituées pour la commodité de son
intelligence à la mystérieuse entité qu'il avait perçue,
avant de connaître les Verdurin, à cette soirée où il avait
entendu pour la première fois la sonate. Il savait que le
souvenir même du piano faussait encore le plan dans le-
quel il voyait les choses de la musique.[45]

He had realized that this impression of retracted and chilly
sweetness was due to the weak divergence between the
five notes that composed it and to the constant repetition
of two of them; but in reality he knew that he reasoned
thus not about the phrase itself, but about simple values
substituted, for the convenience of his intelligence, for the
mysterious entity which he had perceived, before meeting
the Verdurins, at that soiree where he had heard the sonata for the first time. He knew that even the memory of
the piano falsified still more the plan in which he saw the
things of the music.

The "things" of Swann's memory falsify the "things of the music": memory itself is revealed here to be incapable of reproducing "in reality" the precise crossing-over of formal intelligence and sensory experience by which such "things" as those
of music may most accurately be said to be "seen." Aware of
that falsification, Swann is, however, as unable to undo its effects as he is to prevent his passion for the otherwise unalluring
woman in whose presence the maneuvers of his memory are
first purposefully employed. Swann's pursuit of the "truth"
from Odette, concurrent with the attempt of his memory to
perfect his knowledge of "the phrase itself," must also suffer
with it an inherently dissatisfying fate. For the developments of
both can only serve to distance him further from the embodiment of his own ignorance to which he originally was drawn:
"the mysterious entity which he had perceived, *before* meeting
the Verdurins," or before having had the occasion to remember it at all.

[45] *Ibid.*, I:349.

The description of memory in "Un amour de Swann" thus opposes that given by the narrator of "Combray" not only in the origin and means of its enactment but in the ultimate consequences represented by its effects. In reading *Du côté de chez Swann* we may feel free to choose, between the sensations occasioned by a pastry and the articulations of a representational phrase, the form of memory, much like the style of narrative, which suits our own tastes, or representations, best. But there is at least one encompassing indication in reading the rest of the *Recherche* that its narrator enjoyed no such choice in the matter: that he could not choose the "contrivance" he used, in as much as, "in reality," it remains for him a thing unknown ("tant qu'on ignore le biais" [see footnote 35]). At the end of the *Recherche* the narrator states openly that he owes the work he will write to Swann. The reasons he gives form an outline of the causal continuum of his narrated experiences, including that of his decision *to* narrate them in a book:

> En somme, si j'y réfléchissais, la matière de mon expérience, laquelle serait la matière de mon livre, me venait de Swann, non pas seulement par tout ce qui le concernait lui-même et Gilberte; mais c'était lui qui m'avait dès Combray donné le désir d'aller à Balbec, où sans cela mes parents n'eussent jamais eu l'idée de m'envoyer, et sans quoi je n'aurais pas connu Albertine, mais même les Guermantes, puisque ma grand'mère n'eût pas retrouvé Mme de Villeparisis, moi fait la connaissance de Saint-Loup et de M. de Charlus, ce qui m'avait fait connaître la duchesse de Guermantes et par elle sa cousine, de sorte que ma présence même en ce moment chez le prince de Guermantes, où venait de me venir brusquement l'idée de mon oeuvre (ce qui faisait que je devais à Swann non seulement la matière mais la décision), me venait aussi de Swann.[46]

In short, if I reflected on it, the matter of my experience, that which would be the matter of my book, came to me from Swann, not only through all that which concerned himself and Gilberte; but it was he who since Combray

---

[46] *Ibid.*, III:915.

had given me the desire to go to Balbec, where my parents would never have had the idea of sending me otherwise, and without which I would not have met Albertine, not even the Guermantes, since my grandmother wouldn't have refound Mme de Villeparisis, I, made the acquaintance of Saint-Loup and M. de Charlus, who introduced me to the Duchesse de Guermantes and through her, her cousin, so that even my presence this very moment at the Prince de Guermantes' home, where the idea of my work had just come to me brusquely (which meant that I owed to Swann not only the matter but the decision), also came to me from Swann.

It is to Swann that the narrator owes his visits to Balbec, thus his acquaintance with Albertine and the "côté de Guermantes," and so on along the chain of the story's events up to the moment in the Guermantes' library, just previously narrated, when the idea of writing a book of his life first became apparent to him. Slightly less obvious than this causal delineation of the narrator's history, and mentioned in analogies and asides throughout the *Recherche* (including the opening of *Du côté de chez Swann*)[47] is that "Un amour de Swann"—the love story attributed to Swann—sets the pattern for every experience of love the narrator will attribute to himself. The parallels in the work between Odette and Albertine, Swann and the narrator, Charlus and Saint-Loup, while never perfectly symmetrical, are strikingly clear. Thus another debt to Swann, to the story within and without quotation marks of "un amour de Swann," would be, in terms internal to the causality of the narrator's plot, the dynamics of passion and doubt, of imprisonment and flight, which structure each event and each character in that plot.[48]

[47] See *ibid.*, I:30: "L'angoisse que je venais d'éprouver, je pensais que Swann s'en serait bien moqué . . . or, au contraire, comme je l'ai appris plus tard, une angoisse semblable fut le torment de longues années de sa vie, et personne aussi bien que lui peut-être n'aurait pu me comprendre . . ." [The anguish that I had just felt, I thought that Swann would have made fun of it . . . now, on the contrary, as I learned later, a similar anguish was the torment of long years of his life, and no one perhaps would have been able to understand me as well as he . . .].

[48] Cf. Becket (*Proust*, p. 21) who, while stating that "the whole of Proust's

Yet the greater debt to Swann, as he is narrated in "Un amour de Swann," but one which the narrator does not name nor his own story imply, is Swann's simulation by memory of the "phrase de sonate": his construction of the intelligible ground upon which further recollections, and a narrative connecting those recollections, can occur.[49] Like the narrator's designation of the object of the act of love, "rien," the "transcriptive" work of Swann's memory has as its object no given script: the "things" it sees in music are "nothing" it can actively possess or compose. This act of representation within the mind of "things" which are nothing outside the mind,

---

world comes out of a teacup," adds, echoing the narrator, that "to Swann may be related every element of the Proustian experience . . . Swann is the cornerstone of the entire structure." The present analysis underscores that view of Swann's significance yet adds: the *story* of Swann is a cornerstone as ungrounded *within* the structure of the *Recherche* (which *it* must ground) as Kant's key- or cornerstone concept, "freedom," is within the structure of his *Critique*.

The narrator's own speculations on this issue, in *Sodome et Gomorrhe*, restate, more specifically, the fundamentally discursive nature of the model he reenacts: "Au fond, si je veux y penser, l'hypothèse qui me fit peu à peu construire tout le caractère d'Albertine et interpréter douleureusement chaque moment d'une vie que je ne pouvais pas contrôler toute entière, ce fut le souvenir, l'idée fixe du caractère de Mme Swann, *tel qu'on m'avait raconté qu'il était. Ces récits* contribuèrent à faire que, dans l'avenir, mon imagination faisait le jeu de supposer qu'Albertine aurait pu, au lieu d'être la bonne jeune fille qu'elle était, avoir la même immoralité, la même faculté de tromperie qu'une ancienne grue, et je pensais à toutes les souffrances qui m'auraient attendu dans ce cas si j'avait dû l'aimer" [At bottom, if I want to think of it, the hypothesis which made me construct the entire character of Albertine little by little and painfully interpret each moment of a life which I could not control in its entirety, this was the memory, the fixed idea of the character of Mme. Swann, *such as one had recounted to me that it was. These narratives* contributed to the fact that, in the future, my imagination played the game of supposing that Albertine, instead of being the good young girl she was, could have had the same immorality, the same faculty for betrayal as an old prostitute, and I thought of all the suffering which would have awaited me in the case that I should love her] (II:804, my emphasis; see also II:1115).

[49] In pointing to what the narrator does not point to, the present argument questions neither the intentionality nor the narrational strategy of the narrator's author. Perhaps it would be most appropriate to say instead that the narrator's memory, in appearing divided between its voluntary and involuntary exercise, presents as an opposition that which it cannot represent: itself. The single narrative detail that the *Recherche* cannot remember is how it remembers.

memory as described and applied not to the narrator's own experience but to the reported story of Swann, can be seen in turn in the largest structural terms made available by this self-enclosing narration to have laid the ground for what is told to occur within it. Within a narrative whose apparently effortless relational fluidity places its reader in a position most similar to that of the celebrated, diacritically explicated, jars in the Vivonne—that of "containing" and "being contained" by a story in whose otherwise uninterrupted flow he is suspended[50]—the articulations of Swann's memory, while first referred to at the center of *Du côté de chez Swann*, may be recognized as the narrative's own external marks of punctuation. For the activity of memory referred to Swann imposes upon the pure sensations of past experience a shape or form which, excluding what it itself renders "immaterial" to those experiences,[51] thus indicates in them, as their medium of reference "plus tard," the internal content by which sensation is conceived to embody sense.

Returning for a final time to "Combray," it may be recalled that Swann is first mentioned as the sole name the narrator knows to be signified when a certain bell, "la clochette pour les étrangers," is rung unexpectedly at his home in Combray. The narrator states of those evenings doomed to be spent alone in his bedroom:

> Mais ces soir-là, où maman en somme restait si peu de temps dans ma chambre, étaient doux encore en comparaison de ceux où il y avait du monde à dîner et où, à cause de cela, elle ne montait pas me dire bonsoir. Le monde se bornait habituellement à M. Swann.... Les soirs où, assis devant la maison sous le grand marronier, autour de la table de fer, nous entendions au bout du jardin, non pas le grelot profus et criard qui arrosait, qui étourdiassait au

---

[50] *Ibid.*, I:168. On the text of the "carafes," see Genette, "Métonymie," pp. 53–54; Richard, *Proust et le monde sensible*, p. 21; Philippe Lejeune, "Les carafes de la Vivonne," *Poétique* 31 (1977); and Randolph Splitter, *Proust's Recherche: A Psychoanalytic Interpretation* (London and Boston: Routledge & Kegan Paul, 1981), p. 128.

[51] Cf. the narrator's discussion of the "impression . . . pour ainsi dire *sine materia*" (impression . . . let us say, *sine matena*) left by the "phrase" itself before it is articulated and recognized as such by Swann (I:209).

passage de son bruit ferrugineux, intarissable et glacé, toute personne de la maison qui le déclenchait en entrant "sans sonner," mais le double tintement timide, ovale et doré de la clochette pour les étrangers, tout le monde aussitôt se demandait: "Une visite, qui cela peut-il être?" mais on savait bien que cela ne pouvait être que M. Swann.[52]

But those evenings when maman stayed so little time in my room were sweet in comparison with those when there were guests for dinner and when, because of that, she did not come up to tell me goodnight. Guests were limited usually to M. Swann. . . . The evenings when, seated before the house under the large chestnut tree, around the iron table, we heard at the end of the garden not the profuse and shrill small bell which poured upon, which stunned, in the passage of its rusty, inexhaustible and frozen noise, everyone in the house who unleashed it in entering "without ringing," but the double, timid, round, and golden tinkling of the bell for strangers, everyone immediately asked themselves: "A visit, who can that be?" but we knew well that it could only be M. Swann.

In being equated, by being repeated, with the arrival of Swann, the sound of the "clochette" tells the narrator that his mother will not "tell him goodnight": "me dire bonsoir" here itself a metaphor, similar to "faire catleya," for an awaited embrace. If the sound of the "clochette" thus signifies the sharp pain of uncertainty for the narrator, in that not having been told "goodnight" he will confuse night with day, lying awake in wait for his mother when he should be sleeping, then Swann, whose name is identified as the cause of that particular sound, can also be identified as the personal source of the narrator's distress. The narrator himself does so, when he refers to Swann slightly later on, as "the unconscious author of my sorrows."[53] Following this line of reasoning, we can go on to say that the narrator turns the tables on the disturbing "M. Swann" by be-

[52] *Ibid.*, I:13–14; see also p. 23.
[53] *Ibid.*, I:43.

coming the self-disclaimed, if not "unconscious," author of Swann's sorrows in "Un amour de Swann," thereby making out of Swann's unsettling name both a coherent story which his own first-person narrative will repeat and one of the returning characters within that narrative. Indeed, "Un amour de Swann," described as belonging both inside and outside quotation marks, and serving as the diachronic model for the narrative to come, seems to provide precisely that narrative continuity which Swann's arrival—the double peal of the "clochette"—disrupted in a way which could never be adequately repaired at the time it was heard. For, even when that sound renders the narrator more than he feared to lose—when, considerably more than a "goodnight," he is granted an entire night in his mother's presence at the pleasure of an inexplicably motivated father—his anxiety proves only to be increased, not appeased.[54] The particular "contrivance" which yields the narrative of Swann in Paris could thus be interpreted as the narrator's fantasized revenge for a repeated event he still remembers from Combray: the removal, by Swann, of the object of his youthful desire—the physical assurance of external certainty given him by his mother at night. The realm of the senses, that of the taste of the madeleine, would still be, merely manifested differently, that which prevails.[55]

But the bell with whose sound the name of Swann is originally associated returns alone at the very end of the novel, and in a manner given to be decisive for the composition of the narrative as a whole. It is referred to by the narrator in the final few pages of the *Recherche* as the single key—therein displacing the madeleine and kindred experiences of involuntary memory—to the necessary internal unity of the story he tells: the proof of the coherence of his own self over time. The sound

[54] *Ibid.*, I:36–38.
[55] The predominance of the senses would be no less central to a Lacanian, rather than traditionally Freudian, reading of Proust. See Samuel M. Weber, "The Madrepore," *MLN* 87 (1972), which translates the manifestation of desire narrated in the text into the text's own "desire" as a signifying system to do away with "the return of the body of the signifier. . . . It is the mortal materiality of the signifier that the Proustian discourse—its theory of art and its vouloir-dire—seeks to reduce and to master . . ." (p. 960).

of the bell at Combray, having never ceased in the narrator's memory, serves as the final sensory element which ties the narrative together, one now said in closing to demonstrate the unbroken continuity of the life in which it occurred and is recalled. After having recognized that the subject of his authorship for which he had long since ceased to search would be his own embodiment of past time itself; that, "c'était cette notion du temps incorporé, des années passées non séparées de nous, que j'avais maintenant l'intention de mettre si fort en relief"[56] [it was this notion of time incorporated, of the past years unseparated from us, which I now had the intention of putting so strongly in relief], the narrator names, as the specific referent of that recognition, his steady perception of the sound of a single, self-identical bell:

> Quand elle avait tinté, j'existais déjà, et depuis, pour que j'entendisse encore ce tintement, il fallait qu'il n'y eût pas eu discontinuité, que je n'eusse pas un instant cessé d'exister, de penser, d'avoir conscience de moi, puisque cet instant ancien tenait encore à moi, que je pouvais encore retourner jusqu'à lui, rien qu'en descendant plus profondément en moi.[57]

> When it had rung, I already existed, and since, so that I could still hear this ringing, there had to have been no discontinuity, I had to have not ceased existing, thinking, being conscious of myself for an instant, for that past instant still held to me, I could return again to it in doing nothing but descending more deeply in myself.

The formula for temporal indestructibility given here, the proof of subjective permanence by which the projected narrative of a subject capable of "incorporating" time will be put into effect, is an equation of the enduring integrity of the self with its ability to internalize its own sensory perceptions. The same bell producing the same sound may only be heard internally by the same narrator, with no "instant" of discontinuity or nonidentity between them.

[56] *Proust*, III:1046.
[57] *Ibid.*, III:1047.

But is it the same bell? The subject pronoun, "elle," in the passage just cited does indeed stand for a "bell" mentioned some lines before. Yet rather than the bell, called "clochette," of Combray, the direct referent of "elle," or "it"—of that thing which sounds at the end of *Le temps retrouvé*—is called, by the narrator, "la petite sonnette." It is the descriptive phrase, "la petite sonnette," which sounds, and sounds quite differently, upon being recalled. For not only is a different word for "bell" being employed by the narrator in this instance, but the action brought to mind by that word is diametrically opposed to that which it is said to recollect. The reference now understood by the narrator to be signified by the sound of the "bell" he "still hears" is the departure, rather than arrival, of "M. Swann": "ce tintement ... de la petite sonnette qui m'annonçait qu'enfin M. Swann était parti et que maman allait monter. ..."[58] [this ringing ... of the little bell which announced that finally M. Swann had gone and maman was going to come up ...]. Like the salutory internal discovery of the "habitually invisible" "form" of "Time" itself[59]—a form which, once brought into being by the act of writing to which it alone belongs, would relieve the very being of life from its own formal limitation in death[60]—the sound of the bell granting that discovery is seen to denote an earlier, yet heretofore *un*narrated, recognition that sufferings thought blindly to be interminable were at an end.

Between the arrival and departure of Swann, the span of a lifetime appears to be gained in the recollection of a single sensory perception. What is shown to be lost in that recollection is the identity of its object: the identity of a sound, once rep-

[58] *Ibid.*, III:1046.

[59] *Ibid.*, III:1045.

[60] "Moi je dis que la loi cruelle de l'art est que les êtres meurent et que nous-mêmes mourions en épuisant toutes les souffrances, pour que pousse l'herbe non de l'oubli mais de la vie éternelle, l'herbe drue des oeuvres fécondes, sur laquelle les générations viendront faire gaîment, sans souci de ceux qui dorment en dessous, leur 'déjeuner sur l'herbe'" [Me, I say that the cruel law of art is that beings die and that we ourselves die, exhausting all suffering, so that the grass not of oblivion but of eternal life will grow, the dense grass of fecund works, upon which generations will come gaily, without care for those who sleep below, to make their "*déjeuner sur l'herbe*"] (III:1038).

resented in language, with itself; of a "clochette" with a re-membered "sonnette" which replaces it. The narration of Swann's memorization of the "petite phrase de sonate" states that memory recalls by representation, not by sensation, and that the more precisely detailed the representation, the further removed it is from the pure sensation which no representation recalls. The comforting recollection of a "petite sonnette"—the narrator's own "petite phrase de sonate"—is anything but the disconcerting sound of the "clochette" which rang, when the narrative began, at Combray.

If the resemblance between "sonate" and "sonette" (or, al-ternatively, the sensory resemblance of the *word*, rather than object, "clochette," transformed by "sonate," with the word "sonnette") appears too remote to be significant by the end of the narrative, perhaps too remote even for its narrator, the reader can refer to the direct crossing of the two words pro-vided within the story of "un amour de Swann." During one of Swann's visits to the Verdurin salon, Forcheville, a frequent re-placement, chez Odette, for the sensory presence of Swann himself, substitutes the word "sonate" for "sonnette" in a pun. This instance of nonsensical wordplay, a rare occurrence in the narrative of the *Recherche*, which, by contrast, repeatedly seeks to carefully explain the *calembours* of its characters (as in the case of the *derniers mots* of the Duchesse) as well as to reveal the sense in sensory linguistic slips, such as those which for the most part compose the practical vocabulary of Fran-çoise, is narrated to stump one of its listeners, the literal-minded Doctor Cottard. The Doctor, as is his custom, does not get the joke, if there is one to get, and corrects Forcheville rather excitedly:

"Je vais jouer la phrase de la Sonate pour M. Swann," dit le pianiste.

"Ah! bigre! ce n'est pas au moins le 'Serpent à So-nates'?" demanda M. de Forcheville pour faire de l'effet.

Mais le docteur Cottard, qui n'avait jamais entendu ce calembour, ne le comprit pas et crut à une erreur de M. de Forcheville. Il s'approcha vivement pour la rectifier:

"Mais non, ce n'est pas serpent à sonates qu'on dit,

c'est serpent à sonnettes," dit-il d'un ton zélé, impatient et triomphal.

Forcheville lui expliqua le calembour. Le docteur rougit.

"Avouez qu'il est drôle, Docteur?"

"Oh! je le connais depuis si longtemps," répondit Cottard.[61]

"I'm gong to play the phrase of the Sonata for M. Swann," said the pianist.

"Ah, the devil! it's not at least the 'Serpent à Sonates' " asked M. de Forcheville to make an effect.

But Doctor Cottard, who had never heard this pun, didn't understand and believed it an error of M. de Forcheville. He approached quickly to rectify it:

"But no, it isn't serpent à sonates that one says, it is serpent à sonnettes [rattlesnake]," he said with a zealous, impatient and triumphant tone.

Forcheville explained the pun to him. The Doctor blushed.

"Admit that it's a funny one, Doctor?"

"Oh! I've known it for so long," responded Cottard.

Although Cottard, the unfailing diagnostician, is an unbearable conversationalist who would probably prove an even worse novelist, there is something more truthful in his distress at this confusion of meaning through sound than in the narrator's affirmation of his own self-identity based on a sound which his narrative cannot name the same way twice. More important for an understanding of the Recherche, however, is the fact that, like the description of Swann's recollection of the "petite phrase de sonate," the placement of this particular pun within "Un amour de Swann" implies an ignorance on the part of the narrator, writing as autobiographer, which the narrator of Swann's story does not share. It is thus, by logical extension, with the nonautobiographical narrator—the narrator imparting that knowledge which he as third-person narrator cannot apply to himself—that Marcel Proust, understood as the om-

---

[61] Ibid., I:263–64.

niscient author of the *Recherche*, would have to be most properly identified. If, as the sole controlling source of both the first- and third-person stories, a single identity is to be ascribed to Proust himself, it can only then be located in the strict division his novel draws between experience, as the subject of narration, and the actual narrative of its recognition. For it is to the singular inability—shared by Proust with any *literary* narrator—to tell subject and story in one voice and at the same time, that the double-edged brilliance, reflecting both knowledge and ignorance, of his narration owes.[62]

The narrator of the last volume of the *Recherche*, having already traversed the course of his life, restates the creative superiority of sensory memory, wonders whether its "extratemporal joy" was not promised to Swann by the sonata, and finally decides that Swann could not in any case have known or used its "truth," since he never was the writer the narrator is about to become.[63] As for Swann himself, the increasing clarity of his graphic memory in "Un amour de Swann" affords him neither the joy, nor the saving "fourth dimension," of extratemporality. Toward the close of "Un amour de Swann" he hears the sonata again while Odette is not present. During this final narration of his perception of the sonata, Swann distinguishes for the first time a perfectly complementary dialogue being played out between the piano and violin. The sonata can finally be seen to have the precise shape and meaning of the love it has stood exclusively for:

---

[62] This analysis of the partitioning of knowledge in the narrative obviously runs contrary to the notion of a narrator and narrative "hero" united in the climactic experience of "revelation" in which the novel ends. Leaving aside the concrete circumstance, overshadowed by the powerful claims of that conclusion itself, that no further text in fact follows it (nor had ever been planned to follow it by Proust, who is known to have written his conclusion first, expanding the *Recherche* later from the inside out), the concept of "revelation," or of the elimination of the discursive dynamic of memory, is undermined, as it has been the burden of this analysis to suggest, by the textual relations involving Swann's story within the narrator's own.

[63] *Ibid.*, III:877–78. Cf. Fernandez, *Proust*, p. 129, and Turnell, *The Novel in France*, p. 342, on Swann, as opposed to the narrator, lost vocationless in "temps perdu."

D'abord le piano solitaire se plaignait, comme un oiseau abandonné de sa compagne; le violin l'entendit, lui répondit comme d'un arbre voisin. C'était comme au commencement du monde, comme s'il n'y avait encore eu qu'eux deux sur la terre, ou plutôt dans ce monde fermé à tout le reste, construit par la logique d'un créateur et où ils ne seraient jamais que tous les deux: cette sonate.[64]

At first the solitary piano complained, like a bird abandoned by its companion; the violin heard him, responded to him like a neighboring tree. It was like at the beginning of the world, as if there still were only they two on the earth, or rather in this world closed to all the rest, constructed by the logic of a creator and where they would never be but two together: this sonata.

The truth which Swann does realize at that moment—or rather, in accordance with the narrative form of its comprehension, shortly thereafter—is that like the effect of his memory upon the pure sound it transcribes, the dialogue now rendered visible to him in the music will never be born again in life: "A partir de cette soirée, Swann comprit que le sentiment qu'Odette avait eu pour lui ne renaîtrait jamais, que ses espérances de bonheur ne se réaliseraient plus"[65] [From that evening on Swann understood that the feeling Odette had had for him would never be reborn, that his hopes of happiness would no longer be realized]. By the end of the *Recherche*, Proust's narrator has, circumventing an "impossibility" he cannot imagine by means he cannot know until it is "turned around," transcribed the sound of a "clochette" associated with the name of Swann, along the line of a story of a love of Swann, into the recollected shape of a "petite sonnette." His transcription has rendered visible, in unforgettably vivid detail, the long phrase of a life whose continuity he identifies with the memory of the senses: senses, however, whose identity has been no less visibly lost to memory, like the life which, exhausted, as it is embodied, in narration, will never, by any other means, be born again.

[64] *Ibid.*, I:351–52.
[65] *Ibid.*, I:353.

CODA

The *Recherche* provides a fitting conclusion to the analysis of narrative presented in this work in that it takes the reader back to the beginning. Both Proust's novel and Kant's schematic epistemology indicate that all knowledge of experience takes representational narrative form. Kant proposes that since the "forms" of experience are given *a priori*, experience itself is simultaneously its representation. Proust narrates an autobiographical story whose major theme is the proposition that we first see cognitively when we look back at experience: that we can only *know* reality when we no longer experience, but rather represent it to ourselves over time. Yet both epistemologist and novelist, writing *critically* with regard to the representational systems they project, recognize that the representational capacity of the mind cannot be equated with an exclusively narrative competence. The ability to represent perception in an *a priori* narrative form is related by Kant to the noncausal, nonnarrative concept of "freedom." In Proust such an immediate and nonrepresentational source of narrative form is named "involuntary memory." "Freedom," Kant argues, must be knowable, but cannot be deduced from the critical premises which limit "pure" or purely speculative reason. In the course of the deduction of "freedom," a hypothetical *narrative* replaces formal argument as its proof. That narrative claims to afford knowledge of the only "real" object of knowledge through direct reference to empirical phenomena, and thus, according to the cognitive theory it is intended to ground, cannot be related to knowledge at all. Proust's narrator, about to tell his own story of narrative gained through involuntary memory, tells another story of specifically representational memory which falsifies the experience it represents. As Kant's narrative proof of "freedom" cannot be one its narrator "knows," the narrator of the *Recherche*, as he states, "ignores" the detour by which he tells a story he did not experience, appearing incognizant of the description of memory he gives within that story while in the course of telling his own. When Kant and Proust point to a basis for narration which itself would not be narrative in nature, they begin instead to represent narration. Thus their writings represent the most encompassing demonstrations of the paradoxical cognitive necessity of narration.

The other texts analyzed depart from the premise of an *a priori* relation between knowledge and representation. As Stendhal's graphic reference to the "Historical" most explicitly displays, they exclude, *as* representational narratives, any nonnarrative grounding outside themselves. Yet the stories told within these narratives prove directly critical of an equation of narration with knowledge. Through a structural emphasis upon primary forms of narration—the representation of characters and the relations between them, of actions related causally as plot, and of the relation of discursive representation to narrative form itself—these novels narrate that narrative will become a form of discursive ignorance whenever employed to exhaustive cognitive ends. At the same time, in representing, like Kant and Proust, their own criticism of the forms they necessarily employ, these narratives can never be "known" to be exhausted themselves.

BIBLIOGRAPHY

Primary Texts

Austen, Jane. *Jane Austen's Letters (to her sister Cassandra and others)*. Ed. R. W. Chapman. Clarendon: Oxford University Press, 1952.

————. *The Novels of Jane Austen*. Ed. R. W. Chapman. 5 vols. London: Oxford University Press, 1966.

Balzac, Honoré de. *Illusions perdues*. Paris: Garnier, 1961.

————. *Oeuvres complètes*. Ed. La Société des Études Balzaciennes. Paris: Guy le Prat, 1963.

Goethe, Johann Wolfgang von. *Briefe*. IV Bde. Hamburg: Christian Wegner Verlag, 1967.

————. *Conversations with Eckermann*. New York: Dunne, 1901.

————. *Werke*. XIV Bde. Hamburg: Christian Wegner Verlag, 1955.

Husserl, Edmund. *Cartesianische Meditationen*. The Hague: Martinus Nijhoff, 1950.

Kant, Immanuel. *Werkausgabe*. Ed. Wilhelm Weischedel. XII Bde. Frankfurt: Suhrkamp, 1977.

Kleist, Heinrich von. *Sämtliche Werke und Briefe*. Ed. Helmut Sembdner. II Bde. München: Carl Hanser Verlag, 1961.

Leibniz, G. W. *Hauptschriften zur Grundlegung der Philosophie*. Hrsg. Ernst Cassirer. Hamburg: Felix Meiner Verlag, 1966.

McKeon, Richard, ed. *The Basic Works of Aristotle*. New York: Random House, 1941.

Melville, Herman. *The Writings of Herman Melville*. Evanston and Chicago: Northwestern University Press and the Newberry Library, 1971—.

Pascal, Blaise. *Oeuvres*. Ed. Léon Brunschvicg et al. 14 vols. Paris: Librairie Hachette, 1914.

Pascal, Blaise. *Pensées et opuscules*. Ed. Léon Brunschvicg. Paris: Librairie Hachette, 1909.

Proust, Marcel. *A la recherche du temps perdu*. 3 vols. Paris: Bibliothèque de la Pléiade, 1954.

———. "A propos du 'style' de Flaubert." *Nouvelle Revue Française* 14 (1920).

———. *Le Balzac de Monsieur de Guermantes*. Neuchatel, Paris: Ides et Calendes, 1950.

———. "Dans un roman de Balzac" and "L'Affaire Lemoine par Gustave Flaubert." *Pastiches et mélanges*. Paris: Bibliothèque de la Pléiade, 1971.

———. "Sainte-Beuve et Balzac." *Contre Sainte-Beuve*. Paris: Bibliothèque de la Pléiade, 1971.

Scott, Walter. Review of *Emma* (unsigned). *Quarterly Review* (1816).

Stendhal. *Romans*. 2 vols. Paris: Bibliothèque de la Pléiade, 1952.

SECONDARY LITERATURE

Aarsleff, Hans. "Wordsworth, Language and Romanticism." *Essays in Criticism* 30 (1980).

Abraham, Pierre. *Proust: recherche sur la création intellectuelle*. Paris: Editions Rider, 1930.

Abrams, M. H. "English Romanticism: The Spirit of the Age." In *Romanticism Reconsidered*, ed. Northrop Frye. New York: Columbia University Press, 1963.

Adams, Robert M. *Stendhal: Notes on a Novelist*. New York: Minerva Press, 1968.

Althusser, Louis. *Politics and Theory*. London: NLB, 1972.

——— and Etienne Balibar. *Reading Capital*. London: NLB, 1970. [Paris: Maspero, 1968].

Aquila, Richard E. *Representational Mind: A Study of Kant's Theory of Knowledge*. Bloomington: Indiana University Press, 1983.

Aschenberg, Reinhold. *Sprachanalyse und Transzendentalphilosophie*. Stuttgart: Klett Cotta, 1982.

Atherton, John. *Stendhal*. London: Bowes and Bowes, 1965.

Auerbach, Erich. *Mimesis.* Princeton: Princeton University Press, 1953 [Berne: A. Francke, 1946].

Austin, J. L. *How to Do Things with Words.* Cambridge, Mass.: Harvard University Press, 1962.

Bakhtin, Mikhail. *The Dialogic Imagination.* Ed. Michael Holquist. Austin: University of Texas Press, 1981.

——. *Problems of Dostoevsky's Poetics.* Ann Arbor, Mich.: Ardis, 1973.

Barbéris, Pierre. *Balzac et le mal du siècle: contribution à une physiologie du monde moderne.* 2 vols. Paris: Gallimard, 1970.

Barnes, H. G. *Goethe's Die Wahlverwandtschaften.* London: Oxford University Press, 1967.

Barthes, Roland. *Critique et vérité.* Paris: Editions de Seuil, 1966.

——. *Le degré zéro de l'écriture.* Paris: Editions de Seuil, 1953.

——. *Eléments de sémiologie.* Paris: Editions de Seuil, 1964.

——. *Essais critiques.* Paris: Editions de Seuil, 1964.

——. "Introduction à l'analyse structurale des récits." *Communications* 8 (1966).

——. *Mythologies.* Paris: Editions de Seuil, 1957.

——. *Nouveaux essais critiques.* Paris: Editions de Seuil, 1953.

——. *L'obvie et l'obtus.* Paris: Editions de Seuil, 1982.

——. *Le plaisir du texte.* Paris: Editions de Seuil, 1973.

——. *S/Z.* Paris: Editions de Seuil, 1964.

Beck, Lewis White. "Kant's Theory of Definitions." *Philosophical Review* 65 (1956).

——. *Studies in the Philosophy of Kant.* New York: Bobbs-Merrill, 1965.

Beckett, Samuel. *Proust* New York: Grove Press, 1957.

Béguin, Albert. *Balzac lu et relu.* Paris: Editions de Seuil, 1965.

Behler, Ernst. "The Origin of the Romantic Literary Theory." *Colloquia Germanica* 1 (1968).

——. "Die Theorie der romantischen Ironie im Lichte der handschriftlichen Fragmente Friedrich Schlegels." *Zeitschrift für deutsche Philologie* 88 (1969).

Bellemin-Noel, Jean. "Psychanalyser le rêve de Swann?" *Poétique* 8 (1971).

Benjamin, Walter. *Der Begriff der Kunstkritik in der deutschen Romantik*. Diss. Bern, 1919. In *Walter Benjamin: Gesammelte Schriften*, ed. Tiedemann and Schweppenhäuser. Bd. I.1. Frankfurt: Suhrkamp, 1974.

——. "Goethes *Wahlverwandtschaften*." In *Walter Benjamin. Gesammelte Schriften*, ed. Tiedemann and Schweppenhäuser. Bd. I.1. Frankfurt: Suhrkamp, 1974.

——. "Zum Bilde Prousts." In *Illuminationen*. Frankfurt: Suhrkamp, 1955.

Bersani, Leo. *Marcel Proust: The Fictions of Life and of Art*. New York: Oxford University Press, 1965.

Berthier, Phillipe. "Balzac et *La Chartreuse de Parme* roman corrégien." In *Stendhal et Balzac: Actes du VIIème Congrès International Stendhalien*, ed. V. Del Litto. Aran: Editions du Grand Chêne, 1972.

Berthoff, Werner. *The Example of Melville*. New York: Norton, 1962.

Biemal, Walter. *Die Bedeutung von Kants Begründung der Ästhetik für die Philosphie der Kunst*. Köln: Kölner Universitäts-Verlag, 1959.

Blackall, Eric A. *Goethe and the Novel*. Ithaca: Cornell University Press, 1976.

Blackmur, Richard P. "The Craft of Herman Melville." *Virginia Quarterly Review* 14 (1938).

Blanchot, Maurice. "L'Expérience de Proust." In *Faux Pas*. Paris: Gallimard, 1943.

Blin, Georges. *Stendhal et les problèmes du roman*. Paris: Librairie José Corti, 1954.

Böckerstelte, Heinrich. *Aporien der Freiheit und ihre Aufklärung durch Kant*. Stuttgart: Frommann Verlag, 1982.

Booth, Wayne C. *The Rhetoric of Fiction*. Chicago: University of Chicago Press, 1961.

Böversen, Fritz. *Die Idee der Freiheit in der Philosophie Kants*. Diss. Heidelberg, 1962.

Bradley, A. C. "Jane Austen." In *Essays and Studies by Members of the English Association* II (1912).

Branch, Watson G., ed. *Melville: The Critical Heritage.* London: Routledge & Kegan Paul, 1974.

Brée, Germaine. *Marcel Proust and the Deliverance from Time.* New Brunswick, N.J.: Rutgers University Press, 1955 [Paris: Les Belles Lettres, 1950].

Bremond, Claude. *La logique de récit.* Paris: Editions de Seuil, 1973.

――――. "The Logic of Narrative Possibilities." *NLH* 11 (1980).

Brodhead, Richard. *Hawthorne, Melville, and the Novel.* Chicago: University of Chicago Press, 1976.

Brombert, Victor. *Stendhal et la voie oblique.* Presses Universitaires de France, 1954.

――――. *Stendhal: Fiction and the Themes of Freedom.* New York: Random House, 1968.

――――. "Stendhal: The Happy Prison." In *The Romantic Prison.* Princeton: Princeton University Press, 1978.

Brooks, Peter. *The Melodramatic Imagination: Balzac, Henry James, Melodrama, and the Mode of Excess.* New Haven: Yale University Press, 1976.

――――. *The Novel of Worldliness: Crébillon, Marivaux, Laclos, Stendhal.* Princeton: Princeton University Press, 1969.

――――. *Reading for the Plot.* New York: Knopf, 1984.

Brower, Reuben. "Light, and Bright, and Sparkling: Irony and Fiction in *Pride and Prejudice.*" In *The Fields of Light.* New York: Oxford University Press, 1951.

Brown, Lloyd W. *Bits of Ivory: Narrative Technique in Jane Austen's Fiction.* Baton Rouge: Louisiana State University Press, 1973.

Burke, Kenneth. *A Grammar of Motives.* Berkeley: University of California Press, 1945.

――――. *Language as Symbolic Action.* Berkeley: University of California Press, 1966.

Butler, Marilyn. *Jane Austen and the War of Ideas.* London: Oxford University Press, 1975.

Cassirer, Ernst. *The Philosophy of Symbolic Forms.* 3 vols. New Haven: Yale University Press, 1953 [Berlin: Bruno Cassirer, 1923–29].

Cassirer, Ernst. *Rousseau, Kant, Goethe.* Princeton: Princeton University Press, 1945.

Chantal, René de. *Marcel Proust: Critique littéraire.* Montréal: Les Presses de l'Université de Montréal, 1967.

Chase, Richard, ed. *Melville: A Collection of Critical Essays.* Englewood Cliffs, N. J.: Prentice-Hall, 1962.

Chomsky, Noam. *Aspects of the Theory of Syntax.* Cambridge, Mass.: MIT Press, 1965.

———. *Cartesian Linguistics.* New York: Harper & Row, 1966.

———. *Language and Mind.* New York: Harcourt Brace Jovanovich, 1968.

———. "Remarks on Nominalization." In *Readings in English Transformational Grammar,* ed. Roderick Jacobs and Peter Rosenbaum. Waltham, Mass.: Ginn and Co. 1970.

———. *Rules and Representations.* New York: Columbia University Press, 1980.

———. *Syntactic Structures.* The Hague: Mouton, 1957.

Cohen, Hermann. *Kants Theorie der Erfahrung.* Berlin: Dümmler, 1871.

Colletti, Lucio. "A Political and Philosphical Interview." In *Western Marxism,* ed. *New Left Review.* London: Verso, 1978.

Cook, Charles H., Jr. "Ahab's 'Intolerable Allegory.' " *Boston University Studies in English* 1 (1955).

Crossman, Inge. *Metaphoric Narration: The Structure and Function of Metaphors in A la recherche du temps perdu.* Chapel Hill: University of North Carolina Press, 1978.

Crouzet, Michel. "Stendhal et les signes." *Romantisme* 1–2 (1971).

Curtius, Ernst Robert. "Wiederbegegnung mit Balzac." In *Kritische Essays zur europäischen Literatur.* Berne: A. Francke, 1950.

Daiches, David. "Jane Austen, Karl Marx, and the Aristocratic Dance." *American Scholar* XVII (1942).

———. "Literature and Social Mobility." In *Apsects of History and Class Consciousness,* ed. Istvan Mèszaros. London: Routledge & Kegan Paul, 1971.

Dante, *The Divine Comedy*. Trans. and intro. Allen Mandelbaum. New York: Bantam, 1980.

Deleuze, Gilles. *Proust et les signes*. Paris: Presses Universitaires de France, 1964.

De Man, Paul. *Allegories of Reading*. New Haven: Yale University Press, 1979.

———. *Blindness and Insight*. New York: Oxford University Press, 1971.

———. "Pascal's Allegory of Persuasion." In *Allegory and Representation*, ed. Stephen J. Greenblatt. Baltimore: The Johns Hopkins University Press, 1981.

———. "Proust et l'allégorie de la lecture." In *Mouvements premiers: Etudes critiques offertes à Georges Poulet*. Paris: Librairie José Corti, 1972.

———. *The Rhetoric of Romanticism*. New York: Columbia University Press, 1984.

Demetz, Peter. "Balzac and the Zoologists: A Concept of Type." In *The Disciplines of Criticism*, ed. Peter Demetz et al. New Haven: Yale University Press, 1968.

Derrida, Jacques. *De la grammatologie*. Paris: Minuit, 1967.

———. *Marges de la philosophie*. Paris: Minuit, 1972.

———. "La Mythologie blanche." *Poétique* 5 (1971).

———. *Positions*. Paris: Minuit, 1972.

———. *La Vérité en peinture*. Paris: Flammarion, 1978.

———. *La Voix et le phénomène*. Paris: Presses Universitaires de France, 1967.

Dieckmann, Herbert. "Goethe and Diderot." *Deutsche Vierteljahrsschrift* 10 (1932).

Dryden, Edgar A. *Melville's Thematics of Form*. Baltimore: The Johns Hopkins University Press, 1968.

Dubrovsky, Serge. *La place de la madeleine: écriture et fantasme chez Proust*. Paris: Mercure de France, 1974.

Dürr, Volker. "Wilhelm Meisters Lehrjahre: Hypotaxis, Abstraction and the Realistic Symbol." In *Versuche zu Goethe: Festschrift für Erich Heller*, ed. Volker Dürr and Géza V. Molnar. Heidelberg: Lothar Stiehm Verlag, 1976.

Eco, Umberto. *A Theory of Semiotics*. Bloomington: Indiana University Press, 1970.

Ehrlich, Victor. *Russian Formalism*. New Haven: Yale University Press, 1955.

Eldridge, Herbert G. " 'Careful Disorder': The Structure of *Moby Dick*." *American Literature* 39 (1967–68).

Empson, William. "Sense in the Prelude." In *The Structure of Complex Words*. London: Chatto and Windus, 1951.

Enskat, Rainer. *Kants Theorie des geometrischen Gegenstandes*. Berlin: Walter de Gruyter, 1978.

Feidelson, Charles. *Symbolism and American Literature*. Chicago: University of Chicago Press, 1953.

Fergus, Jan. *Jane Austen: The Didactic Novel*. Totawa, N.J.: Barnes and Noble Books, 1983.

Fernandez, Ramon. *Proust*. Paris: Editions de la Nouvelle Revue Critique, 1943.

Fogel, Richard Harter. "*Billy Budd*: The Order of the Fall." *Nineteenth Century Fiction* 15 (1960).

Fowlie, Wallace. *A Reading of Proust*. New York: Doubleday, 1964.

Freedman, Ralph. "The Possibility of a Theory of the Novel." In *The Disciplines of Criticism*, ed. Peter Demetz et al. New Haven: Yale University Press, 1968.

Fries, Thomas. *Die Wirklichkeit der Literatur*. Tübingen: Max Niemeyer Verlag, 1975.

Funke, Gerhard. "Kants Satz: die praktische Freiheit kann durch Erfahrung bewiesen werden." *Revue internationale de philosophie* 136–137 (1981).

Garis, Robert. "Learning, Experience and Change." In *Critical Essays on Jane Austen*, ed. B. C. Southam. London: Routledge & Kegan Paul, 1968.

Gelley, Andrew. "Metonymy, Schematism and the Space of Literature." *NLH* 3 (1980).

Genette, Gérard. *Figures*. Paris: Editions de Seuil, 1966.

———. *Figures II*. Paris: Editions de Seuil, 1969.

———. *Figures III*. Paris: Editions de Seuil, 1972.

Gleim, William S. "A Theory of *Moby Dick*." *The New England Quarterly* 2 (1929).

Goffman, Erving. *Behavior in Public Places*. New York: The Free Press, 1963.

————. *Forms of Talk*. Philadelphia: University of Pennsylvania Press, 1981.

————. *The Presentation of Self in Everyday Life*. Woodstock, N.Y.: Overlook Press, 1973.

————. *Strategic Interaction*. Philadelphia: University of Pennsylvania Press, 1969.

Graham, Victor E. *The Imagery of Proust*. New York: Barnes and Noble Books, 1966.

Green, F. C. *The Mind of Proust*. Cambridge: Cambridge University Press, 1949.

Greimas, A. J. *Du sens*. Paris: Editions de Seuil, 1970.

————. *Maupassant. La sémiotique de texte: exercises pratiques*. Paris: Editions de Seuil, 1976.

————. *Sémantique structurale*. Paris: Larousse, 1966.

Guichard, Léon. *Introduction à la lecture de Proust*. Paris: Nizet, 1956.

Halle, Morris, and Claude Lévi-Strauss. " 'Les Chats' de Charles Baudelaire." *L'Homme* 2 (1962).

Hamlin, Cyrus. "Strategies of Reversal in Literary Narrative." In *Interpretation of Narrative*, ed. Mario Valdés and Owen Miller. Toronto: University of Toronto Press, 1978.

Harmsel, Henrietta ten. *Jane Austen: A Study in Fictional Conventions*. The Hague: Mouton, 1963.

Hartman, Geoffrey H. "The Sublime and the Hermeneutic." In *Mouvements premiers: Études critiques offertes à Georges Poulet*. Paris: Librairie José Corti, 1972.

————. "Wordsworth and Goethe in Literary History." In *The Fate of Reading*. Chicago: University of Chicago Press, 1975.

Heidegger, Martin. *Kant und das Problem der Metaphysik*. Frankfurt: Klostermann, 1951.

Heimrich, Bernhard. *Fiktion und Fiktionsironie in Theorie und Dichtung der deutschen Romantik*. Tübingen: Max Niemeyer Verlag, 1968.

Hemmings, F.W.J. "Balzac's *Les Chouans* and Stendhal's *De l'Amour*." In *Balzac and the Nineteenth Century*, ed. D. G. Charlton et al. Edinburgh: Leicester University Press, 1972.

Hemmings, F.W.J. *Stendhal: A Study of His Novels*. Oxford: Clarendon Press, 1964.

Higgens, Brian, and Herschel Parker. "The Flawed Grandeur of *Pierre*." In *New Perspectives on Melville*, ed. Faith Pullin. Edinburgh: The University Press, 1978.

Högemann, Brigitte. *Die Idee der Freiheit und das Subjekt*. Köningstein: Verlag Anton Hain Meisenheim, 1980.

Holz, Karl. *Das Thema der Erinnerung bei Marcel Proust*. München: Wilhelm Fink Verlag, 1972.

Hopkins, James. "Visual Geometry." In *Kant on Pure Reason*, ed. Ralph C. S. Walker. London: Oxford University Press, 1982.

Horkheimer, Max. *Zur Kritik der instrumentellen Vernunft*. Frankfurt: S. Fischer Verlag, 1967.

———— and Theodor W. Adorno. *The Dialectic of Enlightenment*. New York: Seabury Press, 1977.

Houston, John Porter. "Les Structures temporelles dans la *Recherche*." In *Recherche de Proust*, ed. G. Genette and T. Todorov. Paris: Editions de Seuil, 1980.

Jackson, Elizabeth R. *L'Evolution de la mémoire involontaire dans l'oeuvre de Marcel Proust*. Paris: Nizet, 1966.

Jakobson, Roman. "Two Aspects of Language and Two Types of Aphasic Disturbances." In *Fundamentals of Language*. The Hague: Mouton, 1956.

James, Henry. *The Lesson of Balzac*. Cambridge: Riverside Press, 1905.

Jameson, Frederic. "*La Cousine Bette* and Allegorical Realism." *PMLA* 86 (1971).

————. "Criticism in History." In *Weapons of Criticism*. Palo Alto, Calif.: Ramparts Press, 1976.

————. "Of Islands and Trenches: Neutralization and the Production of Utopian Discourse." *Diacritics* (Summer 1977).

————. *Marxism and Form*. Princeton: Princeton University Press, 1971.

————. *The Prisonhouse of Language*. Princeton: Princeton University Press, 1972.

————. "Realism and Desire: Balzac and the Problems of the

Subject." In *The Political Unconscious*. Ithaca: Cornell University Press, 1981.

Jauss, Hans Robert. *Zeit und Erinnerung in Marcel Prousts A la recherche du temps perdu: Ein Beitrag zur Theorie des Romans*. Frankfurt: Suhrkamp, 1986.

Johnson, Barbara. "Melville's Fist: The Execution of *Billy Budd*." *Studies in Romanticism* 18 (1979).

Jones, W. T. *Morality and Freedom in the Philosophy of Immanuel Kant*. London: Oxford University Press, 1940.

Kellog, Robert, and Robert Scholes. *The Nature of Narrative*. New York: Oxford University Press, 1966.

Kern, Iso. *Husserl und Kant*. The Hague: Martinus Nijhoff, 1964.

Kerny, Vincent. *Herman Melville's Clarel*. Hamden, Conn.: Archon Books, 1973.

Kilmartin, Terence and Scott Moncrieff, trans. *Remembrance of Things Past*. 3 vols. New York: Random House and Chatto & Windus, 1981.

Klein, Zivia. *La Notion de dignité humaine dans la pensée de Kant et de Pascal*. Paris: Librairie Philosophique J. Vrin, 1968.

Kogan, Vivian. "Signs and Signals in *La Chartreuse de Parme*." *Nineteenth-Century French Studies* 2 (1973–74).

Körner, Josef. *Romantiker und Klassiker*. Berlin: Askanischen Verlag, 1924.

Körner, Stephan. "Kant's Conception of Freedom." *Proceedings of the British Academy* 53 (1967).

Kristeva, Julia. *Desire in Language: A Semiotic Approach to Literature and Art*. Ed. Leon S. Roudiez. Oxford: Basil Blackwell, 1980.

Kroeber, Karl. *Styles in Fictional Structure*. Princeton: Princeton University Press, 1971.

Lacoue-Labarthe, Philippe. "L'imprésentable." *Poétique* 21 (1975).

Lascelles, Mary, *Jane Austen and Her Art*. London: Oxford University Press, 1939.

Lejeune, Philippe. "Les carafes de la Vivonne." *Poétique* 31 (1977).

Levin, Harry. "Balzac and Proust." In *Hommage à Balzac*. Paris: Mercure de France, 1950.

―――. *The Gates of Horn*. New York: Oxford University Press, 1963.

―――. *The Power of Blackness: Hawthorne, Poe, Melville*. New York: Knopf, 1970.

Lévi-Strauss, Claude. *Introduction to a Science of Mythology*. 3 vols. New York: Harper & Row, 1969–74. [Paris: Plon, 1964–68].

―――. *The Savage Mind*. Chicago: University of Chicago Press, 1966 [Paris: Plon, 1964].

―――. *Structural Anthropology*. New York: Harper & Row: 1963 [Paris: Plon, 1958].

Liddell, Robert. *The Novels of Jane Austen*. London: Longmans, 1963.

Litz, A. Walton. *Jane Austen: A Study in her Artistic Development*. New York: Oxford University Press, 1965.

Lock, Peter W. "Point of View in Balzac's Short Stories." In *Balzac and the Nineteenth Century*, ed. D. G. Charlton et al. Edinburgh: Leicester University Press, 1972.

Louria, Yvette. *La convergence stylistique chez Proust*. Paris: Nizet, 1971.

Lukács, Georg. *Balzac et le réalisme français*. Paris: François Maspero, 1979.

―――. *Goethe und seine Zeit*. Bern: A. Francke Verlag, 1947.

―――. *The Historical Novel*. London: Merlin Press, 1962.

―――. "Narrate or Describe?" In *Writer and Critic*, ed. Arthur D. Kahn. New York: Grosset and Dunlap, 1971.

―――. *Probleme des Realismus*. Berlin: Aufbau Verlag, 1955.

―――. *The Theory of the Novel*. Cambridge, Mass.: MIT Press, 1971 [Berlin: B. Cassirer, 1920].

Mansell, Darrel. *The Novels of Jane Austen*. Bristol: Macmillan, 1973.

Martin-Chauffier, Louis. "Proust and the Double 'I' of Two Characters." *Partisan Review* 10 (1949).

Marx, Leo. "Melville's Parable of the Walls." *Sewanee Review* 61 (1953).

Mathiesson, F. O. *American Renaissance*. New York: Oxford University Press, 1941.

Matthaei, Rupprecht, ed. *Goethes Farbenlehre*. Ravensburg: Otto Maier Verlag, 1971.

May, Georges. *Le Dilemme du roman au XXIIIème siècle*. Paris: Presses Universitaires de France, 1963.

Miller, David I. *Narrative and its Discontents*. Princeton: Princeton University Press, 1981.

Miller, E. Morris. *The Basis of Freedom: A Study of Kant's Theory*. Sydney: Australasian Association of Psychology and Philosophy, 1924.

Miller, J. Hillis. "Ariadne's Thread: Repetition and the Narrative Line." In *Interpretation of Narrative*, ed. Mario Valdés and Owen Miller. Toronto: University of Toronto Press, 1978.

Miller, R. D. *Schiller and the Ideal of Freedom*. London: Oxford University Press, 1970.

Mitchell, John. *Stendhal: Le Rouge et le noir*. London: Edward Arnold Ltd., 1973.

Moler, Kenneth L. *Jane Austen's Art of Illusion*. Lincoln: University of Nebraska Press, 1968.

Moncrieff, Scott, trans. *Swann's Way*. New York: Random House, 1970.

Monk, Samuel. *The Sublime*. Ann Arbor: The University of Michigan Press, 1960.

Mudrick, Marvin. *Jane Austen: Irony as Defense and Discovery*. Princeton: Princeton University Press, 1952.

Muller, Marcel. *De Descartres à Marcel Proust: essais sur la théorie des essences, le positivisme et les méthodes dialectique et réflexive*. Neuchatel: Editions de la Baconnière, 1947.

Mylne, Vivienne. *The Eighteenth Century French Novel: Techniques of Illusion*. Manchester: The University Press, 1965.

Nancy, Jean-Luc. "*Logodaedalus* (Kant écrivain)." *Poétique* 21 (1975).

Odmark, John. *An Understanding of Jane Austen's Novels*. Oxford: Basil Blackwell, 1981.

Ortega y Gasset, José. "Le temps, la distance et la forme chez

Proust." *Nouvelle Revue Française: Hommage à Proust* 20 (1923).

Parker, Herschel, ed. *The Recognition of Herman Melville: Selected Criticism Since 1846*. Ann Arbor: The University of Michigan Press, 1967.

Poulet, Georges. "Balzac." In *Les Métapmorphoses du cercle*. Paris: Plon, 1961.

———. *L'Espace proustien*. Paris: Gallimard, 1963.

———. "Proust." In *Etudes sur le temps humain*. Paris: Plon, 1950.

Price, Martin. "Manners, Morals, and Jane Austen." *Nineteenth Century Fiction* 30 (1975).

Prince, Gerald. "Introduction à l'étude du narrataire." *Poétique* 14 (1973).

Propp, Vladamir. *The Morphology of the Folktale*. Austin: University of Texas Press, 1977. [orig. pub. 1928].

Reinert, Otto. "Bartleby the Inscrutable: Notes on a Melville Motif." In *Herman Melville*, ed. P. Buchloh and H. Drüger. Darmstadt: Wissenschaftliche Buchgesellschaft, 1974.

Reiss, Hans. "Introduction." In *Die Wahlverwandtschaften*. Oxford: Basil Blackwell, 1971.

———. *Goethe's Novels*. London: Macmillan, 1969.

Ress, Garret. "Baudelaire and Balzac." In *Balzac and the Nineteenth Century*, ed. D. G. Charlton et al. Edinburgh: Leicester University Press, 1972.

Richard, Jean-Pierre. *Proust et le monde sensible*. Paris: Editions de Seuil, 1974.

Riffaterre, Michael. *Semiotics of Poetry*. Bloomington: Indiana University Press, 1978.

———. "The Reader's Perception of Narrative: Balzac's *Paix de ménage*." In *Interpretation of Narrative*, ed. Valdés and Owen Miller. Toronto: University of Toronto Press, 1978.

Rogers, B. G. *Proust's Narrative Techniques*. Genève: Librairie Droz, 1965.

Rosenberry, Edward H. *Melville*. London: Routledge & Kegan Paul, 1979.

Rousset, Jean. "Proust: *A la recherche du temps perdu.*" In *Forme et Signification.* Paris: Librairie José Corti, 1962.

Ruge, Arnold. *Die Deduktion der praktischen und der moralischen Freiheit aus den Prinzipien der kantischen Morallehre.* Tübingen: H. Laupp, 1910.

Sartre, Jean Paul. *L'Idiot de la famille.* 3 vols. Paris: Gallimard, 1976.

Saussure, Ferdinand de. *Cours de linguistique générale.* Paris: Payot, 1978 [Genève, 1915].

Schlechta, Karl. *Goethes Wilhelm Meister.* Frankfurt: Klostermann, 1953.

Schmidt-Sauerhöfer, Paul. *Wahrhaftigkeit und Handeln aus Freiheit: zum Theorie-Praxis Problem der Ethik Immanuel Kants.* Bonn: Bouvier Verlag, 1978.

Sedgewick, William Emery. *Herman Melville: The Tragedy of Mind.* Cambridge, Mass.: Harvard University Press, 1944.

Seelye, John. *Melville: The Ironic Diagram.* Evanston, Ill.: Northwestern University Press, 1970.

Seidel, Fritz. *Goethe gegen Kant.* Berlin: Altberliner Verlag, 1949.

Sherrill, Rowland A. *The Prophetic Melville.* Athens: University of Georgia Press, 1979.

Short, Raymond W. "Melville as Symbolist." *The University of Kansas Review* 15 (1948).

Shurr, William H. *The Mystery of Iniquity: Melville as a Poet, 1857–1891.* Lexington: University of Kentucky Press, 1972.

Solomon, Pearl Chesler. *Dickens and Melville in Their Time.* New York: Columbia University Press, 1975.

Spitzer, Leo. "Zum Stil Marcel Prousts." In *Stilstudien.* II Bde. München: Max Hueber Verlag, 1961.

Splitter, Randolph. *Proust's Recherche: A Psychoanalytic Interpretation.* London and Boston: Routledge & Kegan Paul, 1981.

Starobinski, Jean. *La transparance et l'obstacle.* Paris: Gallimard, 1971.

———. *L'Oeil vivant.* Paris: Gallimard, 1961.

Stern, Martin. *The Fine Hammered Steel of Herman Melville.* Urbana: University of Illinois Press, 1968.

Stöcklein, Paul. "Einführung in die *Wahlverwandtschaften.*" In *Goethes Werke, Gedenk-Ausgabe.* Zürich: Artemis Verlag, 1949.

————. "Stil und Sinn der *Wahlverwandtschaften.*" In *Wege zum späten Goethe.* Hamburg: Schröder, 1960.

Strauss, Walter A. *Proust and Literature: The Novelist as Critic.* Cambridge, Mass.: Harvard University Press, 1957.

Striedter, Jurij, et al., ed. *Texte der russischen Formalisten.* München: Wilhelm Fink Verlag, 1969.

Stuhlmann-Laejsz, Rainer. *Kants Logik.* Berlin: Walter de Gruyter, 1976.

Suzuki, M. "Le 'Je' Proustien." *Bulletin de la Société des Amis de Marcel Proust et des Amis de Combray* 9 (1959).

Tadié, Jean-Yves. *Proust et le roman.* Paris: Gallimard, 1971.

Tanner, Tony. "Introduction." In *Mansfield Park.* Penguin Books, 1966.

Thompson, Lawrance. *Melville's Quarrel with God.* Princeton: Princeton University Press, 1952.

Todorov, Tzvetan. *Grammaire du Décaméron.* The Hague: Mouton, 1969.

————. *The Poetics of Prose.* Ithaca: Cornell University Press, 1977 [Paris: Editions de Seuil, 1971].

Trilling, Lionel. "*Mansfield Park.*" In *The Opposing Self.* New York: Viking Press, 1955.

Turnell, Martin. *The Novel in France.* New York: New Directions, 1951.

Vaihinger, Hans. *Die Philosophie des Als Ob. System der theoretischen, praktischen und religiösen Fiktionen der Menschheit auf Grund eines idealistischen Positivismus.* Leipzig: Felix Meiner Verlag, 1911.

Vigneron, Robert. "Structure de *Swann*: Combray ou le cercle parfait." *Modern Philology* 45 (1948).

Wahr, F. *Emerson and Goethe.* Ann Arbor, Mich.: George Wahr, 1915.

Warren, Robert Penn. *Selected Poems of Herman Melville.* New York: Random House, 1967.

Watt, Ian. *The Rise of the Novel.* Berkeley: University of California Press, 1957.

Weber, Samuel M. "The Madrepore." *MLN* 67 (1972).

———. *Unwrapping Balzac: A Reading of La Peau de Chagrin.* Toronto: University of Toronto Press, 1979.

Weinstein, Arnold. *Fictions of the Self: 1550–1800.* Princeton: Princeton University Press, 1981.

Williams, Ioan. *The Idea of the Novel in Europe, 1600–1800.* London: Macmillan, 1979.

———. *Novel and Romance: 1700–1800.* London: Routledge & Kegan Paul, 1970.

Wittgenstein, Ludwig. *Remarks on Colour.* Ed. G.E.M. Anscombe. Berkeley: University of California Press, 1978.

Woolf, Virginia. *The Common Reader.* New York: Harcourt Brace and World, 1925.

Wright, Andrews. *Jane Austen's Novels: A Study in Structure.* London: Chatto & Windus, 1964.

Library of Congress Cataloging-in-Publication Data

Brodsky, Claudia J., 1955–
The imposition of form.

Bibliography: p.   Includes index.
   1. Narration (Rhetoric) 2. Knowledge, Theory of.
3. Fiction—Technique. 4. Fiction—History and
criticism. I. Title.
PN212.B76 1987   801'.953   87–45512
ISBN 0–691–06717–1 (alk. paper)